AMERICA'S 100 MOST WANTED BIRDS

Finding the rarest regularly occurring

birds in the Lower 48 states

Steven G. Mlodinow
Michael O'Brien

FALCON®
Helena, Montana

AMERICA'S 100 MOST WANTED BIRDS
By Steven G. Mlodinow and Michael O'Brien

Falcon® is continually expanding its list of books. You can order additional copies of this book and get information and prices for other Falcon books by writing Falcon, P.O. Box 1718, Helena, MT 59624 or calling 1-800-582-2665. Please ask for a free copy of our current catalog listing all Falcon® books. To contact us by e-mail, visit our website at http:\\www.falconguide.com

Illustrations by Todd Telander
Front cover photos:
        Hook-Billed Kite ©Kevin T. Karlson
        Ruff ©R.J. Chandler/Vireo
        Lucifer Hummingbird ©D. True/Vireo
        Red-billed Tropicbird ©Jason Dewey/Vireo

Spine photo: Northern Hawk Owl ©Kevin T. Karlson
Back cover photo: Ross' Gull ©T. Vezo/Vireo

Printed in the United States of America.

ISBN 1-56044-492-4

Library of Congress Cataloging-in-Publication Data

Mlodinow, Steven.
    America's 100 most wanted birds : finding the lower 48's rarest
species / Steven G. Mlodinow and Michael O'Brien.
        p. cm.
    Includes bibliographical references.
    ISBN 1-56044-492-4
    1. Rare birds—United States—Identification. 2. Birding sites—
United States.   I. O'Brien, Michael, 1965– . II. Title.
QL676.55.M58 1996
598' .0723473—dc20   96-9547
                                          CIP

♻ Text pages printed on recycled paper.

Contents

Acknowledgments

Without the help of numerous people, this book would have been impossible. Many provided records from their state's rarities committees while others reviewed portions of earlier drafts of this text. Still others provided very useful bits of vital information. We would like to thank them all. Those who donated many hours of time or were otherwise crucial to our work and deserve extra-special thanks include Bruce Anderson, Wes Biggs, Greg Lasley, Paul Lehman, Guy McCaskie, Michael Patten, Don Roberson, Gary Rosenberg, David Stejskal, and Terry Wahl.

Others who provided much-needed help include Paul Baicich, Maurice Barnhill, H. Thomas Bartlett, Casey Beachell, Giff Beaton, Rick Blom, Ned Brinkley, Philip Chu, Charles Collins, James Cressman, Marian Cressman, Bob Curry, Phil Davis, Bruce Deuel, Vince Elia, Shawneen Finnegan, Jim Frank, Kimball Garrett, W. Grigg, Joseph Grzybowski, George Hall, Gene Hess, Wayne Hoffman, Lori Hunter, Teta Kain, Kevin Karlson, Kenn Kaufman, Thomas Kent, Rick Knight, Ted Koundakjian, Howard Langridge, Harry LeGrand, Jim Lowe, Harold Mayfield, Harry Nehls, Bob O'Brien, Paul O'Brien, Max Parker, Brian Patteson, Wayne Petersen, Galen Pittman, Bill Powell, Peter Pyle, Russell Rogers, Will Russell, David Sibley, P. William Smith, Chuck Sontag, Ella Sorenson, David Swanson, Mark Szantyr, Rick Taylor, Chuck Trost, Bill Tweit, Joan Walsh, Noel Wamer, Sherri Williamson, David Wingate, and Louise Zemaitis.

We would also like to thank the following institutions, which provided valuable resources: Cape May Bird Observatory, University of Washington libraries, and Mukilteo Coffee Shop.

Finally, Mel White helped write a number of species accounts. You'll see his handiwork in the sections on Greater Flamingo, Masked Booby, Brown Booby, Muscovy Duck, Northern Jacana, Black Noddy, Northern Hawk Owl, Ferruginous Pygmy-Owl, Great Gray Owl, Clay-colored Robin, Blue Bunting, and White-collared Seedeater.

Introduction

Bird watchers hoist their binoculars to their eyes for a wide variety of reasons. There's the brilliance of a Vermilion Flycatcher, the grace of a Swallow-tailed Kite, and the power of a Peregrine Falcon. Still, there are few birders whose heart does not quicken at the sight of a rarity—those out-of-place or hard-to-find birds that occasionally grace our view. It is indeed a rare birder who would remain placid on encountering an Eared Trogon or Ross' Gull in the United States. Such is the spice of birding, such is the glory.

America's 100 Most Wanted Birds is a study of many of these delectable species. It is your guide to seeing and finding the rarest regularly occurring birds in the Lower 48 states (i.e., contiguous United States). This book, however, is much more than just a collection of simple site guides. *America's 100 Most Wanted Birds* will also help your understanding of the status and distribution of these special birds and will provide identification tips not found in standard field guides. Using this book, you can plan trips to maximize your chances of seeing certain rarities and judge how the rarity you've seen fits in with existing patterns.

Birds were selected to be in this guide if they were rare in the Lower 48 states but regular enough to provide a pattern of occurrence. Some exceptions were made, most notably Slaty-backed and Ross' Gulls, because recent trends suggest that they will be seen on an annual or nearly annual basis. Some birds included here are considered subspecies—they generally fit this book's criteria but are not recognized as separate species. Each, however, has a fair potential to be "split" into a full species. Finally, some readers are going to ask why we haven't included certain birds, especially Black and Yellow Rails. Some of our selections are, to be honest, based on our own tastes. The two rails, however, are actually more numerous and widespread than most other species in *America's 100 Most Wanted Birds*. Also, their habitat tends to be rather fragile, and we had some concern about giving directions to places that might then be heavily visited and thus disturbed.

How To Use This Guide

Status and Distribution

The first portion of most species accounts covers status and distribution. Here we discuss patterns of occurrence in both place and time. Important points are normally illustrated by bar graphs or histograms. In most of the histograms, each bar indicates the number of records or individuals recorded during roughly a ten-day time period (e.g., early March, mid-March, late March). The bar graphs show relative abundance (e.g., uncommon) through the year. Preferred habitat is usually described, and unusual records are briefly reviewed. For some species, you will find that well-defined patterns exist. You can use this information to put yourself in the right place and time to see such a rarity. For instance, if Bananaquit is your heart's desire, then you may want to visit Florida in March rather than October. If you most want a Ruddy Ground-Dove and your vacation is in January, then you'd be better off in southeastern Arizona than southern California. Of course for certain birds (e.g., Green Violet-ear), records are so scattered that little pattern exists. Even for these species, however, "Status and Distribution" lends perspective to any given sighting.

Best Bets

"Best Bets" fine-tunes the information given earlier in the species account. The favored locales are quickly listed, and any handy tips (e.g., Ruddy Ground-Doves most often associate with Inca Doves) are provided. If the bird's habitat was not fully covered previously, it's discussed here.

For most species, the spots mentioned as best bets are discussed in more detail in the Site Guide section of this book. Sometimes, however, the top spot to see a given bird is only notable (in terms of *America's 100 Most Wanted Birds*) for that species. In these cases, full site guide details are provided in the best bets section.

Identification

If you can't identify a rarity, you'll never be certain you've seen it. Fortunately, popular field guides cover most of *America's 100 Most Wanted Birds*. However, not all important identification points are included in these guides, and often other sources must be consulted.

"Identification" supplements and critiques major field guides by reviewing important field marks, correcting misleading information, and listing other references. Using this section, you should be able to add to your identification repertoire and avoid some potential identification mishaps.

Sightings Lists/Tables

This section is meant to provide some of the raw data upon which the rest of the species account is based. For many species (e.g., Berylline Hummingbird, Ross' Gull) all records are listed; for other birds, though, the total is too great for all sightings to be included. In these cases, a variety of approaches is taken. Sometimes, only out-of-range records are provided (e.g., inland records of Yellow-billed Loon); in other instances, the last 10 or 20 years of records are given (e.g., White-eared Hummingbird). Often a hybrid approach is taken.

Records for this section and for this book come mostly from *American Birds* (and its various incarnations), state bird records committees, and state status-and-distribution guides. For some species, preexisting summaries exist, and if this is the case, they are used as well.

All state bird records committees extant in 1994 were contacted by mail. We requested a list of all accepted, rejected, or unsubmitted records from each committee. States that provided full information on accepted and rejected records include California, Oregon, Colorado, Texas, Michigan, Tennessee, Vermont, New York, and Maryland. States that gave data on accepted records only include Massachusetts, Delaware, Virginia, North Carolina, Minnesota, Wisconsin, Iowa, Indiana, Arkansas, South

Dakota, Kansas, Idaho, Wyoming, Utah, Arizona, and Nevada.

At times discrepancies arise, especially between published sightings and records accepted by state committees. In these cases, published sightings that we know have been rejected by rarities committees are usually listed under *Rejected by State BRC* at the end of the given table (or section thereof). If all states had responded, these reports might have been eliminated entirely. Unfortunately, few state records committees responded in full. Complete removal of rejected sightings from just those states might bias the record toward states that replied less completely or not at all. Additionally, the reader can tell that a given record was reviewed and rejected rather than just overlooked by the authors.

Records reviewed in this section are through November 1994, though a few significant sightings from December 1994 and thereafter have been included.

The tables vary in format. Some are by year, whereas others are by month and/or day; some are by state whereas others are not. The method chosen was based upon which approach gave the information in the clearest, most useful, and easiest way. Often the information in these tables is from 1972 on, 1977 on, 1982 on, and so on. This is because work for this tome began in 1992.

Site Guide

The "Site Guide" provides detailed information on top spots for the birds in this book. This guide will do more than just get you there: it furnishes tips on how to find your bird and usually makes recommendations on places to stay, eat, and—where it may be of concern—even find gasoline. It also refers you to more comprehensive local guides so that you can get full birding pleasure out of your visit.

Miscellany

Maps:

To get the most out of our guide in the field, having proper maps is essential. The maps in this book will be of use, of course, but they are not intended to be your entire armamentarium. For starters, the DeLorme state atlases are quite useful. These are currently available for Washington,

Oregon, California, Minnesota, Michigan, Delaware/Maryland, North Carolina, and Florida (among the states with sites mentioned in our guide). DeLorme atlases can be purchased from ABA sales (1-800-634-7736) or from DeLorme Mapping (207-865-4171). A similar style atlas is available for Texas. It's called the Roads of Texas and is published by Shearer Publishing (800-458-3808).

Most national parks, national wildlife refuges, national monuments, and the like have maps at their headquarters or can often be requested by phone. For other locations, the maps listed below may be of use.

- Ocean Shores, Washington: use Morse (1994)
- Skagit Flats, Washington: use the Skagit County map from King of the Road Map Service (206-774-7112).
- San Juan Island, Washington: use the San Juan Islands map from Pacific Horizons Publications, P.O. Box 2055, Olympia, WA 98507.
- California county maps: the American Automobile Association, California State chapter, puts out wonderful maps. Some California counties also have excellent maps made by Compass Maps (209-529-5017).
- Salton Sea, California: the Brawley/El Centro/Yuma/Imperial county map is very useful (published by Rockwell Enterprises, Inc., Road Map Division, 255 W. Torrance Blvd., Carson, CA 90745).
- Brownsville/McAllen, Texas: you may find the Rand McNally maps to Brownsville and McAllen helpful.
- Florida Keys: Rand McNally makes an excellent map for the Florida Keys.

Abbreviations

We have tried to limit abbreviations in *America's 100 Most Wanted Birds*. Some, however, have proved useful. Abbreviations have been used mostly in tables.

BRC—bird records committee (preceded by state's two letter postal abbreviation)

AB—*American Birds*

ABA—American Birding Association

AFN—*Audubon Field Notes*

a.k.a.—also known as

AOU—American Ornithologists' Union

CBC—Christmas Bird Count

FN—*Field Notes*

L.I.—Long Island

max—maximum

mi—miles

MGB—*Master Guide to Birding*

NARBA—North American Rare Bird Alert

NGS guide—National Geographic Society *Field Guide to the Birds of North America*

NWR—National Wildlife Refuge

pers comm—personal commentary

SGA—State Game Area

WMA—Wildlife Management Area

WB— *Western Birds* (journal of the Western Field Ornithologists)

Yellow-billed Loon

Gavia adamsii

Status and Distribution

The Yellow-billed Loon breeds on the Arctic tundra from central Canada west through Alaska and Siberia. In the Lower 48, it has long been considered a specialty of the Pacific Northwest, but to some degree this is changing. As recently as the 1970s, a dozen Yellow-bills per year in Washington and Oregon was the norm. During the 1980s and 1990s, however, this number has declined, so that roughly 6 birds per winter is now typical. While the coastal decline has been occurring, a simultaneous boom is happening inland. Prior to 1980, an inland Yellow-billed Loon would have caused gasps of awe, but between 1982 and 1987, 10 were seen, and between 1988 and 1994, there were 29. Inland records have come from Idaho, Montana, Colorado, Utah, Wyoming, Nevada, New Mexico, Arizona, Texas, Missouri, Oklahoma, Arkansas, Illinois, Minnesota, and Michigan. This species has also been seen in the interior of Washington, Oregon, and California and on the Atlantic Coast (eastern Long Island, NY, early 1930).

Pacific Coast records are most numerous in Washington and decline in frequency to the south. Yellow-bills are still regular as far south as northern California, but become accidental south of Monterey Bay. Of the 50-plus California records, only five are from southern California. In coastal areas, Yellow-billed Loons prefer sheltered saltwater such as bays, lagoons, harbors, and deltas. Inland sightings are usually from large lakes and reservoirs.

Yellow-billed Loons have been seen in the Lower 48 each month of the year, but they are distinctly rarer in summer. Fall migrants are expected as early as mid-September, and spring migrants are occasionally seen as late as early May. Peak numbers are seen from mid-December to early March.

Best Bets

Probably the best area for these birds is the almost endless collection of bays and coves in Puget Sound (including Point Roberts and the San Juan Islands—see below). Farther south, Yaquina and Tillamook bays are the best spots in Oregon, and Monterey Bay is tops in California.

Unfortunately, no Puget Sound locale is especially favored by Yellow-billed Loons. Instead, it is a large region with abundant habitat and few Yellow-bills. If you were to search for this species, some of the following approaches might bring success:

Search Point Roberts. This area, just south of Vancouver (British Columbia), is probably the best spot in the Lower 48. To get to this detached piece of Washington, you must first enter Canada. See Wahl and Paulson (1991) for details.

Ride the Puget Sound area ferries, especially the ferry from Anacortes to San Juan Island or the shorter ferry from Keystone (Whidbey Island) to Port Townsend (Olympic Peninsula). Call (800) 542-0810 for rate and schedule information.

Explore the San Juan Islands themselves (and see the Eurasian Skylark in the process). Lewis and Sharpe (1987) has thorough information on birding the San Juans. Also see the "Site Guide" on page 425.

Check the waterfront, wherever possible, between Point No Point (Kitsap Peninsula, near Kingston) and Port Angeles (Olympic Peninsula). Be sure to stop at Salisbury County Park just northeast of the Hood Canal Bridge. See Wahl and Paulson (1991) for more details.

Yellow-billed Loons are present in each of the above areas during most years, but for only a brief time. Finding one on any given day requires considerable luck. Yellow-bills often are nomadic, so birds on the hotline tend not to stick around.

Identification

Identification of Yellow-billed Loons in all plumages relies critically on bill pattern. In basic plumage, the Common Loon bill can be fairly pale, but the entire culmen and the distal cutting edges are dark. In the Yellow-billed Loon, the distal half of the culmen and distal cutting edges are both pale. Also, the bill is typically straw colored, usually noticeably different from the sometimes pale gray bill of the Common Loon. In breeding plumage, Common Loons have entirely black bills whereas Yellow-billed Loons have strikingly pale yellow to whitish bills. Yellow-billed Loons also tend to swim with their bills pointed up; Commons tend to hold their bills level. Furthermore, the Yellow-bill is even thicker necked than the Common. This makes the caliber of the Yellow-bill's neck similar to that of the head whereas the Common Loon's head is obviously larger around than the neck.

In basic and immature plumages, Yellow-billed Loons show paler sides of the head and neck with less contrast between the darker and lighter areas. Many Yellow-bills also show a dark auricular spot that is not present in Common Loons. For more details, see the exceptionally detailed account (under White-billed Diver) in Jonsson (1992) or Appleby, et al. (1986). Also, see Kaufman (1990). **(See color photo on page 457.)**

Yellow-billed Loon—*inland records since 1981*

LOCATION	NUMBERS SEEN	DATES SEEN
California		
Lake Perris	1	12/20/83 to 5/4/84
Lake Havasu (also in AZ)	1	12/24/89 to 3/14/90
Whiskeytown Reservoir	1	12/30/91 to 2/17/92
Oregon		
Timothy Lake	1	5/15 to 6/4/88
Fern Ridge Reservoir	1	12/31/89
Washington		
Priest Rapids	1	1/15 to 1/21/93
Priest Rapids (same bird)	1	3/14/93
Lake Wenatchee	1	mid-12/93
Idaho		
Lake Pend Oreille		4/26/86
near Sunnyside	1	11/15/86
American Falls Dam	1	11/19/91

LOCATION	NUMBERS SEEN	DATES SEEN
Idaho (cont.)		
Lake Coeur d'Alene	1	12/28/91 to 1/1/92
Lake Pend Oreille	1	12/18/93
Coeur d'Alene Lake	(2 on 1/29)	1/29 to 3/13/94
Lake Pend Oreille	1	5/94
Montana		
Great Falls	1	1/5 to 1/6/87
Fort Peck	1	11/11 to 11/25/94
Wyoming		
Sundance	2	11/4/86
Wheatland	1	11/22/88
near Sundance	1	11/19 to 12/2/89
Colorado		
Chatfield Reservoir	2	12/18 to 12/20/82
Denver	1	12/13 to 12/22/86
Pueblo	1	12/14 to 12/16/86
Pueblo (same as above?)	1	2/1 to 2/14/87
near Wellington	1	11/5/88 to 1/18/89
Cherry Creek Reservoir	1	11/20 to 11/21/89
Chatfield Reservoir	1	12/1/89 to 1/7/90
Hamilton Reservoir	1	12/5/90 to 6/9/91
Red Lion Wildlife Refuge	1	6/4/91
Union Reservoir	1	11/9 to 11/19/91
Chatfield Reservoir	1	12/2 to 12/6/91
Pueblo	1	11/26 to 11/29/92
Utah		
Fish Springs NWR	1	11/16/91
Lake Powell	1	2/10/94
Nevada		
Lake Mead	1	12/22/91 to 5/9/92
Lake Mead	1	10/17/92
Arizona		
Painted Rock Dam	1	1/15 to 2/11/84
Lake Havasu (also in CA)	1	12/24/89 to 3/14/90
New Mexico		
Navajo Lake	1	1/22 to 3/14/92
Navajo Lake	1	2/4 to 3/7/93
Storrie Lake	1	11/14 to 11/27/93
Texas		
Lake of the Pines	1	1/12 to 1/14/92
Lake Balmorrhea	1	11/25 to 12/10/93
Oklahoma		
Lake Yahola	1	12/11 to 12/20/88
Grand Lake Dam	1	1/11/92

LOCATION	NUMBERS SEEN	DATES SEEN
Arkansas		
Beaver Lake	1	11/17 to 11/31/91
Missouri		
Table Rock Lake	1	2/14 to 5/9/90
Table Rock Lake	1	12/27/90 to 4/1/91
Illinois		
Springfield	1	11/14 to 11/18/76
Rock Falls	1	12/14 to 12/29/86
Michigan		
Whitefish Point	1	5/13/87

Yellow-billed Loon—*summer records since 1981*

LOCATION	DATES SEEN
Humboldt Bay, CA	from 8/26/82 on
Yaquina Bay, OR	7/20 to 8/15/85
Yaquina Bay, OR	6/87 to early 7/87
Timothy Lake, OR	until 6/4/88
Bullard's Beach, OR	6/4/89
Hamilton Reservoir, CO	to 6/9/89
Red Lion Wildlife Refuge, CO	6/4/91

inland records since 1981

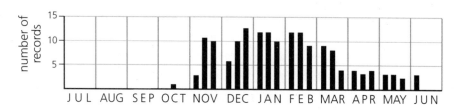

Laysan Albatross

Diomedea immutabilis

Status and Distribution

To many, albatrosses are the quintessential pelagic birds. A sighting of any species, even the fairly common Black-footed, often elicits shouts of excitement and cries of joy. The Laysan Albatross, being rare in our waters, creates an even greater ruckus.

The Laysan Albatross breeds mainly on the Hawaiian Islands, where it is commonly called a gooney bird. This species seems to be undergoing a range expansion; during the past few years, Laysans have been found breeding in small numbers on several islands off northwestern Mexico, including Guadelupe Island off northern Baja California (Howell and Webb 1992). This expansion seems to have been reflected in the Lower 48. From 1991 through 1993, there were at least 48 records involving 200-plus birds. Most sightings have been from northern and central California, but this is undoubtedly partly due to the relatively intense pelagic coverage there. In reality, Laysans are probably just as numerous off Washington and Oregon.

Important habitat features for finding Laysan Albatrosses in Lower 48 waters are water depth and temperature. Laysans are found most reliably in deep water at or beyond the edge of the continental shelf. For instance, the deepwater Sausalito trips have found Laysans on 8 of 16 voyages. Record high counts have all come from such deep seas: 59, up to 100 miles southwest of Point Reyes (12/14/91); 50, 60 to 90 miles southwest of Point Reyes (11/16/91); 45, 140 miles southwest of Point Arena to 74 miles southwest of Point Gorda (12/8/88). Laysan Albatrosses also like cool temperatures, preferring waters that are between 40° and 65°F (Fisher and Fisher 1972, Shuntov 1974) and air that is between 28° and 69°F (Shuntov 1974).

Despite the Laysan's preference for deep water, it is sometimes found in remarkably shallow water. For instance, there are several early spring (February to early April) records from San Francisco Bay (note: these may be birds that were following ships). An even odder phenomenon, however, is the nine May to July records from the southern California and Arizona deserts (see table). Presumably these birds had wandered up from the northern end of the Gulf of California. Where they went next, and if they survived, has been a matter of much speculation. Some feel that after passing north from the Salton Sea, these misguided albatrosses headed west through the San Gorgonio Pass and then out to the ocean. The truth may never be known. Another remarkable inland record comes from Whiskeytown Reservoir, Shasta County, California, where one was seen on March 15, 1991.

Records of Laysan Albatrosses span the calendar. There is, however, a distinct nadir from early June through late August. In Washington and Oregon, published records are distributed evenly from September through May. There is, however, a dearth of midwinter Pacific Northwest pelagic trips. The success of the few trips from this season suggests that winter (November through February) may indeed be best.

In northern California, published records are evenly distributed from mid-October through late April. The massive numbers recorded far offshore during November and December implies that these months may be the peak time over deep water. In southern California, records are far scarcer. There are only about 20 from nonresearch vessels, mostly between late January and mid-May.

Best Bets

Your best bet for seeing this species is to take a Sausalito pelagic trip, especially during November or December. If you don't want to go 100 miles out to sea, try one of the Westport trips, especially from November through February.

Identification

Separation from the Black-footed Albatross, even older faded individuals, is simple and well described in the major guides. However, Black-footeds and Laysans have been known to hybridize (Fisher 1948, Fisher 1978, Ely and Clapp 1973). Such individuals should have brown on the body, a feature that is absent in all Laysans.

Other species pose more of a problem. The Short-tailed Albatross, once down to only 300 or so individuals, is making a comeback and can be expected to occur increasingly in our area. The Short-tailed Albatross is a huge bird, much larger than the Laysan. In plumages where the Short-tail is white bodied, it also has white on the back and upperwings. Laysans always have dark backs and upperwings.

In the southern Pacific, there are five species of white-bodied/dark-mantled albatrosses that offer potential confusion with the Laysan: White-capped (or Shy), Black-browed, Gray-headed, Yellow-nosed, and Buller's. All have the potential for wandering north to the western Lower 48, and at least one, White-capped, already has (39 miles west of Quillayute River mouth, Grays Harbor County, WA, September 1, 1951). Two others from this list, the Black-browed and Yellow-nosed, have been seen off the East Coast. All five of these species can be distinguished from each other, and from Laysan Albatross, by paying careful attention to head and neck pattern, bill color and size, and underwing pattern. For a full discussion, see Harrison (1983) or Harrison (1987). **(See color photo on page 457.)**

Laysan Albatross—*desert records*

LOCATION	NUMBERS SEEN	DATES SEEN
near Desert Hot Springs, CA	1	5/5/76
Yuma, AZ	1	5/14/81
Anza-Borrego Desert State Park, CA	1	5/28/82
north end of Salton Sea, CA	1	5/21 to 6/20/84
north end of Salton Sea, CA	1	6/9 to 29/84
San Gorgonio Pass, CA	1	5/6/85
near Yuma, AZ	1	7/18/88
south end of Salton Sea, CA	1	5/9/91
north end of Salton Sea, CA	1	5/2/93

Black-capped Petrel

Pterodroma hasitata

Status and Distribution

This typical pterodroma is a joy to watch in flight. As soon as a good breeze kicks up, Black-caps launch themselves into the speedy, high arcing, roller-coaster flight for which gadfly petrels are well known. On a clear day, Black-caps can be detected at distances of over a mile as they arc 40 feet or more into the air.

The Black-capped Petrel is a tropical species that breeds in the highlands of Hispaniola and Cuba (Haney 1987). Its haunts at sea include the Caribbean and waters off the southeastern United States and Brazil. As recently as the early 1970s, this species was thought to occur in North America only as a casual storm-blown waif and little was known about its at-sea distribution. But since the mid-1970s, increased pelagic effort off the Carolinas, Georgia, and Florida has proven the Black-cap to be regular, even fairly common, year-round in the Gulf Stream. In fact, this area is believed to be the species' principal nonbreeding range (Haney 1987). Occurrence outside the Gulf Stream is still quite rare.

Best Bets

There is no better place to see a Black-capped Petrel than off North Carolina, where the Gulf Stream is easily reached in a day's trip. Any season will do, but organized trips are numerous from May to September and counts are highest in these months. Getting into the Gulf Stream is the key—a few of these trips may concentrate on the edge of the stream, where Black-caps are less common. Check with the trip organizer before you sign up.

Identification

The Black-capped Petrel is typically quite distinctive. The huge white patch on the rump and base of the tail is usually conspicuous even from a distance. The Greater Shearwater is similar, but look for the Black-cap's larger white rump patch; shorter, thicker bill; white forehead; and pure white belly (smudged with gray on the Greater Shearwater). The Black-capped Petrel is also smaller than the Greater Shearwater and usually flies with slightly crooked wings (wings held straight out from the body in the Greater).

A much more serious identification problem is distinguishing between a small, obscurely marked Black-cap and a Bermuda Petrel (*Pterodroma cahow*). The Bermuda Petrel has been reported several times off the southern Atlantic Coast, so even though extremely rare (currently about 50 pairs, plus nonbreeders, see D. Wingate), it should be considered a possibility. Proving the identification of a Bermuda Petrel would be very difficult and at the very least would require a prolonged view and superb photographs. Characters to look for on a potential Bermuda Petrel include small size, small bill, small gray-and-white rump patch (confined to the uppertail coverts), and a dark hood including cap, ear coverts, hind neck, and breast sides. Be aware, however, that none of these characters rules out a Black-capped Petrel.

Black-capped Petrel—*selected high counts*

LOCATION	NUMBERS SEEN	DATES SEEN
up to 180 mi off Georgia	97	5/1 to 5/7/83
off Ponce Inlet, FL	38	5/3/79
off Oregon Inlet, NC	82	5/15/93
off Hatteras, NC	114	5/18/93
off Oregon Inlet, NC	110	5/20/93
off Hatteras, NC	109	5/20/95
off Oregon Inlet, NC	150	5/21/93
off Oregon Inlet, NC	120	5/22/93
off Hatteras, NC	110	5/28/94
off Oregon Inlet, NC	133	6/3/94
off Oregon Inlet, NC	177	6/5/93
off Oregon Inlet, NC	138	6/7/93
off South Carolina	50	6/13/85
70-80 mi off Georgia	81	6/16 to 6/20/83
off Georgia	112	7/10/94

LOCATION	NUMBERS SEEN	DATES SEEN
off Oregon Inlet, NC	134	7/17/93
off Oregon Inlet, NC	116	NC 7/25/87
off Oregon Inlet, NC	134	7/25/92
off Oregon Inlet, NC	212	7/31/93
off Hatteras, NC	192	8/6/95
off Oregon Inlet, NC	104	8/7/93
off Oregon Inlet, NC	161	8/14/93
off Oregon Inlet, NC	165	8/20/94
off Oregon Inlet, NC	145	8/24/91
off Hatteras, NC	108	8/29/93
off Hatteras, NC	62	9/25/94
off Hatteras, NC	161	10/07/80
off Hatteras, NC	40+	10/08/78
off Oregon Inlet, NC	55	10/08/94
off Hatteras, NC	50	10/09/82
off North Carolina	115	12/28/82

Black-capped Petrel—*all Lower 48 records north of the Carolinas*

LOCATION	NUMBERS SEEN	DATES SEEN
New Paltz, NY	1	1/26/1895
Georges Bank, MA	1	3/23/77
Stellwagen Bank, MA	1	4/22/91
off Virginia Beach, VA	1	5/30/92
180 mi E of Ocean City, MD	1	7/18/79
off Barnegat Light, NJ	1	7/25/87
Quogue, L.I., NY	1	July 1850
100-150 mi off Virginia	4	8/15/80
Eastham, MA	1*	8/19/91
Wakefield, RI	1*	8/19/91
Oswego, NY	1	8/26/33
Oneida Lake, NY	1*	8/28/1893
Hudson Canyon, NJ	7	8/28/95
Blacksburg, VA	1*	8/30/1893
125 mi ESE of Chincoteague, VA	1	8/30/79
New Hampshire	?*	late Aug 1893
Vermont	?*	late Aug 1893
72 mi E of Chincoteague, VA	1	9/7/75
120-127 mi E of Virginia Beach, VA	1	9/10/81
120-127 mi E of Virginia Beach, VA	1	9/16/81
Hudson Canyon, NJ	1	9/16/91
Horseheads, L.I., NY	1*	9/23/89
Verona, VA	1*	9/23/89
Pennsylvania	6*	9/23 to 9/24/89
Point Judith, RI	2*	9/27/85

LOCATION	NUMBERS SEEN	DATES SEEN
Cayuga County, NY	1*	Sept 1893
Campbell County, KY	1*	10/4 to 10/5/1898
Kenton County, KY	1*	10/4 to 10/5/1898
Bracken County, KY	1*	10/4 to 10/5/1898
Ohio	?*	10/4 to 10/5/1898
Fairfield, CT	1*	10/07/38

Rejected by state BRC
Baltimore Canyon, MD	1	6/14/80

* Following hurricane

Mottled
Petrel

Pterodroma inexpectata

Status and Distribution

You may remember the Mottled Petrel from your old Golden Guide (Robbins 1966) as Scaled Petrel. This species was the first pterodroma found in the western United States (July 25, 1959, Lincoln County, OR; found dead on beach) and was the first species of this genus recognized as a regular visitor to western North America. Since 1959, it has been recorded at least 34 times in the Lower 48, usually between mid-November and mid-April. This is in distinct contrast with Alaskan records, which are mostly from early May to late October (Roberson 1980), and makes little sense given the species' breeding season off New Zealand (October to April; Harrison 1987). It may well be that the Lower 48 records are mostly of subadult and/or nonbreeding birds.

Records of Mottled Petrels span the western coast, but are concentrated in northern California and Oregon. Like other pterodromas, the Mottled Petrel is most often recorded far offshore, though relatively speaking this species is more likely to be found near shore (both dead and alive) than other members of its genus. There are at least four records of live birds seen from shore plus another ten records of dead birds on beaches. Ainley (1979) felt that nearshore Mottled Petrel records coincided with Northern Fulmar invasions, and sightings since 1979 have continued to fit this pattern. There is also one record from the eastern United States. This bird was collected April 1880 at Mount Morris, New York.

Best Bets

Like other pterodromas, Mottled Petrels are best sought from deepwater pelagic trips during the proper season. Once again, boats out of Sausalito have the best record; Mottled Petrels have been seen on two of four November/December trips.

Identification

The Mottled Petrel is distinct from other pterodromas, because it is the only member of this genus with a white throat and undertail coverts that contrast with a gray to blackish belly patch. Be warned, however, that this mark can be indistinct and tough to see at a distance, but the Mottled Petrel's dark underwing ulnar bar is often obvious and may be useful in eliminating a Cook's or Stejneger's Petrel. The Mottled Petrel also has a stockier build with relatively fast, heavy flight when compared with that of the Cook's and Stejneger's. **(See color photo on page 458.)**

Mottled Petrel—*all records*

LOCATION	NUMBERS SEEN	DATES SEEN
2 mi N of Alsea Bay, OR	1(dead)	7/25/59
Mad River Mouth, CA	1(dead)	8/11/76
Clatsop Beach, OR	1(dead)	11/15/89
123 mi SW of San Miguel Island, CA	1	11/15/89
66-90 mi SW of Point Reyes, CA	17	11/16/91
61 mi W of San Miguel Island, CA	1	11/17/89
95 to 123 mi off Point Arena, CA	3	12/8/88
Boiler Bay, OR	1	12/10/87
35-40 mi W of Humboldt/Del Norte County, CA	8	12/10/90
45 mi off Lincoln County, OR	3	12/11/90
Point Pinos, CA	1	12/12/84
80-84 mi SW of Point Reyes, CA	3	12/14/91
Waldport, OR	1(dead)	12/15/86
Point Mugu, CA	1	12/30/81
109 mi W of Santa Barbara County, CA	1	2/11/92
71 mi W of Santa Barbara County, CA	1	2/11/92
Cannon Beach, OR	1	2/13/88
175 mi W of Olympic Peninsula, WA	1	2/23/71
Point Reyes, CA	1(dead)	2/25/76
Cayucos, CA	1(dead)	2/28/76
Ocean Shores Jetty, WA	1	2/28/76

LOCATION	NUMBERS SEEN	DATES SEEN
Moclips, WA	1(dead)	3/6/76
Twin Harbors State Park, WA	1(dead)	3/6/76
S of Newport, OR	2(dead)	3/18/72
Cambria, CA	1(dead)	3/31/76
Ocean Shores, WA	1(dead)	late 3/85
Leadbetter Point, WA	1(dead)	late 3/85
north jetty of Columbia River, WA	1(dead)	late 3/85
60 mi off Waldport, OR	9	3/31/81
Mt. Morris, NY	1(collected)	early 4/1880
40 mi SW of Trinidad Head, CA	1	4/10/86
Bayocean Beach, OR	1(dead)	4/14/93
44-97 mi off La Push, WA to Cape Lookout, OR	62	4/19/85
150-200 mi SW of Cape Mendocino, CA	10	4/20/85
2 ~80 mi off southern WA	2	4/20/77
25 mi off southern WA	1	4/21/77
Bolinas Lagoon, CA	1	5/01/77

all records

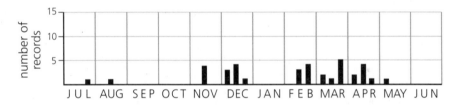

Murphy's Petrel

Pterodroma ultima

Status and Distribution

The "ultimate" pterodroma, as the scientific name *Pterodroma ultima* implies, breeds on South Pacific islands between Australia and South America. Its wintering grounds were formerly thought to be the tropical Pacific up to the equator. Then, in May 1981, several unidentified Murphy's/Solander's Petrels were seen off the coast of Oregon and California. One month later, another of these birds washed up onto the Oregon shore in Lincoln County and was found to be a Murphy's. Birders and professional ornithologists began to wonder if somehow these birds had been overlooked.

As our knowledge and deepwater efforts have increased, so has the number of Murphy's Petrel records. This species is now found annually in the Lower 48 and has been recorded from southern California to Washington. The majority of records are from central California, though this may be partly due to the more intense coverage there.

Like other pterodromas, Murphy's Petrels prefer the deep blue sea. Research vessels studied the waters off central California during April and May of 1989 and 1991. In April they found Murphy's mostly 75-plus miles offshore in waters deeper than 1,800 fathoms. May trips found them a bit closer, mostly in waters 800 to 1,800 fathoms deep. How much this pattern varies from year to year is not yet established. Three Murphy's Petrels seen 16 miles northwest of Fort Bragg on May 6, 1989, provided the record that is closest to the mainland shore.

The vast majority of Murphy's Petrel records are from spring (late March to late June) with a distinct peak from late April to early May.

There are also records from September (Farallon Islands, September 27, 1990), December (36 miles west-southwest of Point St. George, CA, December 10, 1990), and January (west-southwest of San Nicholas Island, January 24 and 25, 1994.

The timing of the Murphy's Petrel's occurrence is a bit puzzling as mid-March to May is when they nest over most of their range (Harrison 1987). Recently, however, the large population on Ducie Atoll (Pitcairn Islands) was found breeding at full blast (thousands of chicks) in mid-November (Zimmer 1992). It may be that our Murphy's Petrels come from Ducie Atoll, although more evidence is necessary for a firm conclusion.

Best Bets

If a Murphy's Petrel is what you seek, then a late April or early May pelagic trip out of Sausalito is what you need. Since these trips were started in 1990, Murphy's Petrels have been found on seven of eight outings. If you cannot make it on a Sausalito boat, try any deepwater trip from mid-April to mid-May. One such trip had success out of Westport on April 25, 1992, but further attempts during 1994 and 1995 failed to find this species.

Identification

The Murphy's Petrel is similar in appearance to the Solander's Petrel. Indeed, their separation has only recently been extensively worked out. Excellent discussions on this topic can be found in Bailey, Pyle, and Spear (1989) and Stallcup (1990). When confronted with a Murphy's or Solander's Petrel, concentrate on the following points:

Hooded Appearance. Solander's Petrels appear hooded because the head, neck, and upper chest are darker than the rest of the bird. Murphy's Petrels do not usually appear this way.

Bill/Head Shape. Murphy's Petrels have a smaller bill and proportionately larger, more rounded head than Solander's Petrels. This difference can be nicely seen in Harrison (1987).

Leg Color. The legs of pterodromas are hard to see. Nonetheless, you can sometimes get a glimpse when the bird is taking off or landing. In Murphy's Petrels, the legs and feet are pink with black on the distal webs only. In Solander's Petrels, the legs and feet are usually black, although they can sometimes have a variable amount of pink. The pink/black demarcation in such birds is still not as sharp as in the Murphy's.

Face Pattern. Though variable, Solander's Petrels have more white on the face than chin whereas Murphy's does not. Indeed, in Murphy's the white is usually restricted to the chin.

Underwing Pattern. There are subtle differences in the underwing pattern involving the secondaries and greater primary coverts, which need illustration for true understanding. See Bailey, Pyle, and Spear (1989) or Stallcup (1990). Some of these differences can be seen in the photos in Harrison (1987).

Flight Style. Murphy's Petrels have a faster flight than Solander's. In comparison with Murphy's, the Solander's Petrel seems to lumber along (somewhat like a Pink-footed Shearwater compared with a Sooty) (P. Pyle, pers comm).

Murphy's Petrel—*all records*

LOCATION	NUMBERS SEEN	DATES SEEN
286 mi WSW of San Nicolas Island, CA	2	1/24/94
174 mi WSW of San Nicolas Island, CA	1	1/25/94
159 mi W of San Miguel Island, CA	1	2/10/92
71-79 mi W of Santa Barbara County, CA	3	2/11/92
Horsefall Beach, OR	1 (dead)	3/6/87
2 mi S of Cape Blanco, OR	1	3/27/88
far off San Mateo/Monterey Counties, CA	122	4/7 to 4/11/91
20 to 120 mi off Cypress Point, CA	100?	4/10 to 4/21/87
35 mi off Columbia River mouth, WA	1	4/10/86
40 mi SW of Trinidad Head, CA	1	4/10/86
40-50 mi NW of Point Conception, CA	4	4/11/86
15-20 mi SW of Cordell Bank, CA	3	4/21/86
15-20 mi SW of Cordell Bank, CA	20?	4/21/86
148 mi WSW of San Nicolas Island, CA	1	4/21/90
55 mi SW of San Nicolas Island, CA	1	4/22/90
70+ mi SW of Point Reyes, CA	5	4/25/93
far off Westport, WA	24	4/25/92
Sausalito to 100 mi SW of Point Reyes, CA	5	4/25/93
40-78 mi W of San Nicolas Island, CA	6	4/25/90
33°10'N-121°30'W, CA	1	4/26/89
149 mi SW of San Nicolas Island, CA	1	4/26/90
32 mi SW of San Miguel Island, CA	1	4/27/90
99 mi SW of San Miguel Island, CA	1	4/27/90

LOCATION	NUMBERS SEEN	DATES SEEN
34°00'N-123°10'W, CA	1	4/29/89
far offshore, Point Reyes to Point Arena, CA	98	4/29 to 4/30/89
Sausalito to 100 mi SW of Point Reyes, CA	34	5/2/92
100 to 300 mi SW of Point Conception, CA	8	5/3 to 5/12/87
Sausalito to 100 mi SW of Point Reyes, CA	78	5/3/91
Sausalito to 100 mi SW of Point Reyes, CA	2	5/3/92
Sausalito to 100 mi SW of Point Reyes, CA	171	5/5/91
16 mi NW of Fort Bragg, CA	3	5/6/89
Sausalito to 100 mi SW of Point Reyes, CA	5	CA 5/7/94
70+ mi SW of Point Reyes, CA	9	5/10/93
100 mi SW of Point Conception, CA	4	5/11/87
Sausalito to 100 mi SW of Point Reyes, CA	47	5/11/91
far off northern California	118	5/16 to 5/21/91
35 to 73 mi SW of Point Reyes, CA	3	5/19/90
55-70 mi off northern Oregon coast	4?	5/20/81
far off Humboldt County, CA	1?	5/21/81
45-70 mi off Cape Mendocino to Point Reyes, CA	19?	5/21/81
15-20 mi SW of Cordell Bank, CA	5?	6/1/86
15-20 mi SW of Cordell Bank, CA	2	6/1/86
12-15 mi W of SE Farallon Islands, CA	1?	6/3/85
15-20 mi SW of Cordell Bank, CA	8?	6/7/86
15-20 mi SW of Cordell Bank, CA	5?	6/13/86
5 mi S of Newport, OR	1(dead)	6/15/81
15-20 mi SW of Cordell Bank, CA	2?	7/4/86
Farallon Islands, CA	1	9/27/90
36 mi WSW of Point St. George, CA	1	12/10/90

? Refers to birds that are best considered Murphy's/Solander's Petrels. Before identification criteria were worked out, many birds were unidentified or were identified (probably mistakenly) as Solander's. There is currently only one record of Solander's that seems likely valid: on September 11, 1983, a Solander's Petrel was carefully observed at close range by an experienced observer over Grays Canyon off of Westport, Washington. For a full discussion, see Bailey, Pyle, and Spear (1989).

all records[†]

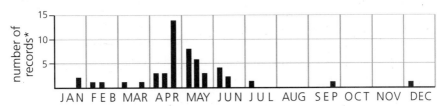

† including birds from 1980s that were Murphy's/Solander's that were most likely Murphy's.

* Sightings of multiple birds counted as one record.

Herald Petrel

Pterodroma arminjoniana

Status and Distribution

With only three North American records prior to 1991, the Herald Petrel was long thought to be strictly a vagrant to the United States. Now, with more than a dozen well documented sightings, this species is known to be rare but regular in the Gulf Stream off North Carolina. Whether this species was previously overlooked or if its status is actually changing is not clear.

The Herald Petrel is widespread in the Pacific Ocean but its range in the Atlantic is more restricted. Atlantic birds [= Trinidade Petrel] breed at Trinidade and the Martin Vas Islands off the coast of Brazil. A nesting attempt in Puerto Rico in 1986 suggests that the Atlantic population may be expanding its range. The distribution at sea is less precisely known, but some birds apparently move north into the Gulf Stream at least as far as North Carolina. North Carolina sightings have all been in warm (79°F or warmer) Gulf Stream water and most have been over water 100-plus fathoms deep. Sightings have occurred between May 22 and September 26 with the bulk of the records in late May and in late July and August. A gap in sightings exists between mid-June and mid-July; however, very few trips have run in this period, so it could be that this gap is an artifact of coverage. Additional sightings of unidentified dark pterodroma petrels off North Carolina fit the same pattern and almost certainly represent this species but have been omitted here.

Best Bets

Any North Carolina pelagic trip from May to September could produce a Herald Petrel, but chances appear to be best in late May and in late July and August.

Identification

The Herald Petrel is a polymorphic species with a nearly continuous gradation of dark to light birds. Off North Carolina, the dark morph accounts for most of the records. Although no other all-dark pterodroma petrels are known to occur in the Atlantic, three similar species—Murphy's, Solander's, and Kermadec Petrels—occur in the Pacific. Given the history of long-distance vagrancy in this genus, some care in identification is urged. For a good discussion of the birds in the Pacific, see Bailey, et al. (1989), but note that Atlantic populations of Herald Petrels lack the white leading edge to the wing present on Pacific birds.

In the Atlantic, a dark morph Herald is most likely to be confused with a Sooty Shearwater. Compared with a Sooty, a Herald Petrel will appear to have a longer tail, a smaller head, and a shorter, thicker bill. Also, the white flash on the underwing is concentrated toward the end of the wing (base of the primaries) like a jaeger in the Herald Petrel but at the center of the wing (primary and secondary coverts) on the Sooty Shearwater. Flight style and wing position tend to be different in the two species, but there is much overlap. The Herald Petrel tends to show a more exaggerated roller coaster flight than the Sooty Shearwater, with higher arcs punctuated by steeper downward glides on more crooked and bowed wings. Despite these average differences, many distant dark birds must be left unidentified.

Dark jaegers also can appear similar to dark Herald Petrels, especially under windy conditions when jaegers (especially Parasitics) usually fly with dynamic arcing glides much like shearwaters and petrels. If seen well, a jaeger should show white primary shafts from above, some sort of central tail projections, and a nontubed bill.

A light or intermediate Herald Petrel may be distinguished from all shearwaters by its extensively dark underwing and shorter, thicker bill.

The Black-capped Petrel differs in its white rump and more extensively white underwings, and in its usually clean white neck and upper breast (typically washed with brown on even the lightest Herald Petrels). Differences from the Soft-plumaged Petrel are discussed under that species. Jaegers again present problems, but in addition to the differences noted above light morph jaegers should show either distinct dark caps (alternate plumage) or barring in the upper- and undertail coverts (basic plumage). **(See color photo on page 458.)**

Herald Petrel—*all records*

LOCATION	NUMBERS SEEN	DATES SEEN
50 mi SE of Hatteras, NC	1 (int)	5/22/91
off Hatteras, NC	3 (2 dark, 1 light)	5/29/94
off Oregon Inlet, NC	1 (dark)	5/29/95
off Oregon Inlet, NC	1 (light)	6/6/92
off Hatteras, NC	1 (dark)	7/23/95
off Hatteras, NC	1 (dark)	7/29/94
off Oregon Inlet, NC	1 (light/int.)	8/2/93
off Oregon Inlet, NC	1 (dark)	8/7/93
off Oregon Inlet, NC	1 (dark)	8/8/92
off Hatteras, NC	1 (dark)	8/8/94
off Oregon Inlet, NC	1 (dark)	8/16/93
off Oregon Inlet, NC	1* (dark)	8/20/78
off Oregon Inlet, NC	1 (dark)	8/21/80
off Oregon Inlet, NC	1 (dark)	8/24/91
storm-driven bird at Ithaca, NY	1* (dark)	8/26/33
off Oregon Inlet, NC	2 (int, dark)	9/3/95
off Hatteras, NC	1 (dark)	9/26/93

*specimen

all North Carolina records through 1995

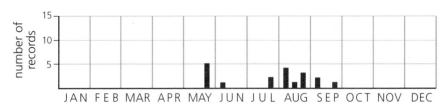

"Soft-plumaged" Petrel

Pterodroma mollis complex

✎ Status and Distribution

One of the most exciting discoveries in recent years is the occurrence of members of the Soft-plumaged Petrel complex off the southern Atlantic Coast. Thirteen sightings (involving 15 to 17 birds) now exist, 11 off North Carolina, 1 off Georgia, and 1 off Virginia. Arguments about which form occurs here continue, but most authorities agree *Pterodroma mollis feae*, also known as the Cape Verde Islands Petrel, is the most likely. This form, which is probably a distinct species, breeds on the Cape Verde and Desertas islands off the west coast of Africa and possibly on the Azores off the coast of Spain (Montiero and Furness 1995). Its movements at sea, however, are still poorly known.

The North Carolina sightings fall between May 24 and September 16, with the bulk of them (eight records involving 10 to 11 birds) from May 24 to June 9. The Virginia record is from September and the Georgia record from November. Most of these birds were over warm and very deep water.

✎ Best Bets

A late May or early June boat trip to the Gulf Stream off North Carolina is the best bet. However, don't ignore the scattering of records through the summer and fall. Effort will be intensive over the next few years, so a clearer pattern should develop.

Identification

Among the locally common species, Black-capped Petrel is the most similar but is easy to distinguish given a good look. Soft-plumaged Petrels are as small as the smallest Black-caps with proportionally longer wings. The dynamic flight style is similar to that of a Black-cap, but the birds may tend to stay closer to the water surface except in high winds. The upperparts are mostly gray, lacking Black-cap's conspicuous white rump, but instead showing a contrastingly pale gray rump and tail and a dark *M* (carpal-ulnar) pattern across the back and wings. From below, the body is white. The wing linings, however, are mostly dark gray and can appear all dark at a distance. Occasionally, the wing linings show a white core.

A light morph Herald Petrel may appear similar to a Soft-plumaged Petrel, but note Herald's dark vent and underside of tail (this region is white in Soft-plumaged) and conspicuous light patches at the base of the primaries' underside (indistinct or lacking in Soft-plumaged). Also note that Herald is more uniformly dark above without a contrastingly pale rump and tail and with little or no dark *M* pattern on the back and wings.

Within the Soft-plumaged Petrel complex, identification becomes much more difficult. Four forms, probably representing three full species, exist worldwide: the nominate *P. mollis mollis* and *P. mollis dubia* (= Soft-plumaged Petrel) which are widespread in the southern oceans, and the two North Atlantic forms with more restricted ranges, *P. mollis madeira* (= Madeira or Zino's Petrel) and *P. mollis feae* (= Cape Verde Islands or Fea's Petrel). The latter two are both quite rare, with populations estimated at about 50 pairs for *madeira* and a few hundred pairs for *feae*. Birds seen at close range in North American waters have shown heavy bills (slightly shorter than a Black-cap's, but just as thick), no white highlight above the black eye patch, no breastband (though some have shown extensive gray smudging at the sides of the breast), pale gray tails and uppertail coverts contrasting with darker rumps, and an overall size that seems to be on the larger end of the scale for the complex. These characters all suggest the Cape Verde Islands Petrel, but more study is needed. To date, the best discussions on these forms can be found in Enticott (1991) and Gantlett (1995).

"Soft-plumaged" Petrel—*all records*

LOCATION	NUMBERS SEEN	DATES SEEN
off Hatteras, NC	1	5/24/81
off Hatteras, NC over 300 fathom line	1	5/24/92
off Oregon Inlet, NC over 1,000 fathom line	1	5/25/91
off Oregon Inlet, NC	2	5/29/95
off Oregon Inlet, NC	1-2	5/30/94
off Oregon Inlet, NC	1	6/3/81
off Oregon Inlet, NC	2	6/4/95
off Oregon Inlet, NC	1	6/9/95
off Oregon Inlet, NC	1	6/27/92
off Oregon Inlet, NC	1	7/30/95
off Virginia Beach, VA	1	9/9/95
off Hatteras, NC	1	9/16/95
off St. Catherines Island, GA	1	11/9/84

Additional published records that are best considered probable

off Hatteras, NC	1	5/20/95
off Hatteras, NC	1	5/28/95

Cook's Petrel

Pterodroma cookii

Status and Distribution

Searching the open seas for Cook's Petrels is to seabirding what seabirding is to birding as a whole. Conditions for viewing are often unfavorable and the chances of success are unpredictable. In other words, you often see nothing except salt spray and feel little other than nausea. Yet when success is met, the taste is all the sweeter and the elation all the grander. It is truly a treat to watch this elegant, pale gray-and-white pterodroma swoop in shallow arcs over the ocean.

Cook's Petrels breed from October to April on islands off New Zealand (Harrison 1987). Some spend their nonbreeding time off South America while others "winter" south of Alaska in the middle of the North Pacific. More important for us in the Lower 48, a significant number spend April to November 60 to 300 miles offshore between southern Baja California and central California.

Currently, all Lower 48 records are from California[1], with the majority being south of Point Reyes. Usually these birds are seen 75-plus miles offshore. However, one was found dead on a Santa Cruz street on November 17, 1983, and twice this species has been found at the Salton Sea: July 24 to 29, 1984, and July 10 to August 6, 1993.

The majority of records are from late April to late November. There are, however, several records from January and February off southern California.

---

[1] Late-breaking news provides a Washington record of one found dead at Grayland on December 15, 1995.

Best Bets

If you are not a researcher and thus unable to spend days a hundred miles out to sea, your best bet for seeing a Cook's Petrel is to ride the *Salty Lady* out of Sausalito. Nine of 15 Sausalito pelagic trips between May and November have found this species.

Identification

A full discussion of Cook's Petrel identification is beyond the scope of this book. The best source for such would be Roberson and Bailey (1991). Of the five members of the subgenus *Cookilaria*, only Stejneger's and Cook's Petrels have been definitely identified in the Lower 48. When trying to separate the Cook's from the Stejneger's Petrel, one should focus on head and tail pattern. The cap and nape of a Stejneger's Petrel is black or blackish, forming a half-hood that contrasts with the paler gray back. In the Cook's Petrel, there is little or no contrast between cap and back; it does have a small dark smudge near the eye. These differences are well shown in Harrison (1987). Also, the Cook's Petrel has white outertail feathers (can be hard to see), which Stejneger's lacks.

When looking at a potential Cook's Petrel, you also need to consider Mottled and Dark-rumped Petrels. In both of these birds, the bold underwing pattern can be seen from quite a distance whereas in a distant Cook's, the underwing usually appears uniformly pale.

(See color photo on page 458.)

Cook's Petrel—*all records*

LOCATION	NUMBERS SEEN	DATES SEEN
172 mi WSW of San Nicolas Island, CA	1	1/16/93
147 mi WSW of San Miguel Island, CA	1	1/21/93
off southern California	20	1/23 to 1/26/94
193 mi W of San Miguel Island, CA	5	2/10/92
110 mi WNW of Santa Barbara County, CA	1	2/11/92
65 mi W of Santa Barbara County, CA	1	2/15/93
150 mi SW of San Nicolas Island, CA	3	2/28/91
40-100 mi off Monterey, CA	15	4/8 to 4/10/91
32 mi W of Cape Mendocino, CA	2	4/10/86
32°00'N-123°00'W, CA	14	4/24 to 4/25/89
Sausalito to 100 mi SW of Point Reyes, CA	1	4/25/93
84-115 mi SW of San Miguel Island, CA	5	4/27/90
90 mi offshore, Point Reyes to Point Arena, CA	113	4/29 to 4/30/89

LOCATION	NUMBERS SEEN	DATES SEEN
Sausalito to 100 mi SW of Point Reyes, CA	1	5/2/92
far off southern California	5	5/2 to 5/8/88
75-78 mi SW of Pigeon Point, CA	5	5/5/91
150 mi SSW of Point Conception, CA	3	5/9/87
75-78 mi SW of Pigeon Point, CA	2	5/11/91
75 mi SW of Point Reyes, CA	1	5/19/91
up to 160 mi SW of Piedras Blancas, CA	9	5/24/94
off Cordell Bank, CA	5	6/23/85
200 mi off southern California	300	7/2 to 7/16/92
between 31°30′N-120°17′W and 30°49′N-121°28′W, CA	21	7/20/89
between 31°43′N-121°18′W and 32°25′N-119°58′W, CA	11	7/23/89
north end Salton Sea, CA	1	7/24 to 7/29/84
32°40′N-121°30′W, CA	9	7/26/89
178 mi WSW of San Nicolas Island, CA	1	7/26/91
33°55′N-121°30′W, CA	2	7/30/89
196 mi WSW of San Miguel Island, CA	1	8/2/91
57-125 mi off Point Sur to Point Reyes, CA	30	8/8 to 11/14/92
far off San Luis Obispo County, CA	35	8/9/92
over 100 mi off northern California	55	8/11 to 8/18/88
85 mi S of Point Conception, CA	1	8/14/84
SW of San Nicolas Island, CA	2	8/16/92
120 to 150 mi WSW of San Diego, CA	40+	8/16/80
120 mi SW of Point Conception, CA	1	8/17/80
65 mi SW of Point Conception, CA	1	8/19/84
far off San Luis Obispo County, CA	8	8/19/92
SSW of Point Conception, CA	3+	9/13/87
36 mi WNW of Point Arena, CA	1	10/3/79
105 nmi W of Point Sur, CA	1	10/7/79
over 100 mi off northern Cailfornia	13	10/13 to 10/14/88
8 mi SW of Cordell Bank, CA	1	11/1/92
Sausalito to 100 mi SW of Point Reyes, CA	12	11/16/91
Davidson Seamount, CA	4	11/17/79
Santa Cruz, CA	1	11/17/83
Davidson Seamount, CA	2	11/24/79
Davidson Seamount, CA	1	12/1/79

all records

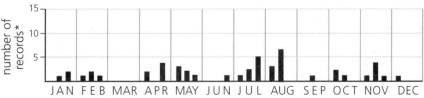

* sightings of multiple birds counted as one record

Flesh-footed Shearwater

Puffinus carneipes

Status and Distribution

The Flesh-footed Shearwater is beautiful in a subtle way. Its plumage is the color of chocolate and seems soft and silky in good light. Perhaps this species should be renamed Chocolate Shearwater, but then again, maybe not—it's not always wise to mention food while at sea.

Flesh-footed Shearwaters breed mainly on islands off Australia and New Zealand during the Austral summer. After nesting, they head northward in the Pacific Ocean. In the Lower 48, they occur along the entire Pacific Coast and tend to grow more numerous as you head northward. Flesh-foots are less than annual off southern California, rare but annual in northern California (except Monterey Bay, where they are uncommon), and uncommon off Washington. The best strategy is to sort through large concentrations of Sooty Shearwaters. When off Washington, pay particular attention to the flocks that commonly attend shrimp trawlers, as this a favored "habitat" for this species.

Flesh-footed Shearwater records span the calendar, and peak times vary from area to area. In Washington and Oregon, Flesh-foots are present in relatively stable numbers from May to November. During this period, boats out of Westport have found this species on almost 50 percent of trips, but this frequency has dropped somewhat in recent years. In northern California, early September into early November seems best. Southern California records are few in number (only 9 in the past 13 years) and seem to fit the northern California pattern. High counts are as follows: 22, off Westport, May 12, 1973; 12, San Pedro Channel, November 22, 1968; 8, 25 miles SW of Point Pinos, September 17, 1979; and 8, off Westport, October 4, 1987.

Best Bets

Westport pelagics, with their 50 percent success rate between May and November, are the best bet. Monterey Bay or Bodega Bay trips from September to November are a good second choice.

Identification

None of our regularly occurring seabirds truly closely resembles the Flesh-footed Shearwater. Sooty and Short-tailed Shearwaters are quickly eliminated by underwing pattern, bill color, and flight style (see NGS guide). The more difficult identification dilemma is posed by dark morph Wedge-tailed Shearwaters, which can have similar wing and bill patterns. The Wedge-tailed Shearwater, however, is a delicate bird with a long tail, slender wings, and graceful flight. The Flesh-footed Shearwater is a heavy plodding bird (for a shearwater) with stouter wings, shorter tail, and heavier flight. Indeed, in shape and flight mannerisms, the Flesh-footed Shearwater is similar to the Pink-footed Shearwater.

Beware the Heermann's Gull. Immatures of this species are also chocolate colored and have a dusky-tipped pink bill. Many a beginner has been beguiled by these similarities. The key is that Heermann's Gulls are indeed gulls. They fly like gulls or like jaegers, but not like shearwaters.

(See color photo on page 459.)

White-faced Storm-Petrel

Pelagodroma marina

Status and Distribution

Veteran pelagic birders will tell you there is nothing like finding a White-faced Storm-Petrel. Few birds have such character and charm, and few create such excitement. Once found, this distinctive little seabird is usually obliging as it single-mindedly skips along the ocean surface in search of food. Solitary by nature, its discovery is always a surprise, though with increasing pelagic effort, it is becoming almost expected in late summer over deep waters off the mid-Atlantic states.

The White-faced Storm-Petrel is a widespread species of temperate and tropical oceans. The ones occurring in North America probably breed on the Cape Verde Islands off the coast of Africa from November to June and then wander west to our offshore waters. Through 1994, there was a total of 45 Lower 48 records involving at least 53 birds. Two outlying records are from May 26 and July 6; the remainder fall between July 24 and October 9, with a peak in late August. Sightings are scattered from Massachusetts to northern North Carolina, mostly from deep water. More than a third of these birds were in North Carolina waters, although intensive coverage there has probably skewed the data somewhat. In addition to these records, there are at least another 15 sightings in the western North Atlantic far out to sea beyond the ABA Area 200-mile limit.

Best Bets

Chances of encountering a White-faced Storm-Petrel are at their best off any port from Massachusetts to northern North Carolina in late August. Early August to mid-September offers a fair chance as well. Most records are in deep (100+ fathoms) water over the slope of the continental shelf. The majority of organized pelagic trips plan to visit these waters, so you need only keep your eyes open. The southern limit of this bird's range in our area seems to be off the northern part of North Carolina where the blue waters of the Gulf Stream veer out to sea allowing cooler blue-green and green water from the north to move in over the continental slope. Good places to look are where warm Gulf Stream water meets cooler water here and, to the north, where Gulf Stream eddies spin off and meet the continental shelf.

Identification

A distinctive bird, the White-faced Storm-Petrel is unlikely to be misidentified if seen reasonably well. Not only is its plumage distinctive (see any field guide), but its flight style also is delightfully unique. Always low to the water, this bird locks its wings in a straight-out position and propels itself by a powerful kick of its huge feet on the water surface. With each kick or "kangaroo hop" it rises slightly and often tilts to one side or the other as if slightly off balance. When it wants to move a little faster it gives several stiff, Spotted Sandpiper-like flaps but then resumes the original flight mode.

Phalaropes are superficially similar but fly very differently. Partial albinism has been noted in Wilson's and Band-rumped Storm-Petrels (M. O'Brien, pers obs), so caution is warranted, but these piebald birds are unlikely to duplicate the White-faced's distinctive face pattern and bold half-black, half-white underwing. The Audubon's Shearwater will often hold its wings outstretched and "kite" into the wind while paddling the water surface. This behavior could cause an identification problem, but the Audubon's larger size, different shape, different face pattern, and shorter legs should prevent confusion on all but the most distant birds. (See color photo on page 459.)

White-faced Storm-Petrel—*all records*

LOCATION	NUMBERS SEEN	DATES SEEN
Hudson Canyon, NJ	1	5/26/76
Oceanographer Canyon, MA	1	7/6/94
off Oregon Inlet, NC	1	7/24/93
6 mi off Avalon, NJ	1	late July 1973

LOCATION	NUMBERS SEEN	DATES SEEN
off Hatteras, NC	1	7/30/94
38° 29'N, 72° 42'W (DE)	1	7/31 to 8/9/84
Milford Point, CT	1	8/10/76
Poor Man's Canyon, VA	1	8/12/91
SE of Oregon Inlet, NC	1	8/14/84
SE of Oregon Inlet, NC	1	8/16/84
near Washington Canyon, VA	1	8/17/91
39° 48'N, 71° 02'W (NJ/NY)	1	8/18/53
Hydrographer Canyon, MA	1	8/19/85
Hydrographer Canyon, MA	2	8/22/83
Baltimore Canyon, MD	1	8/22/93
off Oregon Inlet, NC	1	8/23/85
40° 57'N, 70° 29'W (MA)	1	8/23/93
50 mi ESE of Chincoteague, VA	1	8/24/80
22 mi E of Rehoboth, DE	1	8/26/72
off Oregon Inlet, NC	1	8/27/85
off Oregon Inlet, NC	1	8/27/88
off Oregon Inlet, NC	1	8/27/93
off Hatteras, NC	1	8/28/81
off Hatteras, NC	1	8/28/83
38° 54'N, 69° 30'W (NJ)	1-3	8/29/67
off Oregon Inlet, NC	4	8/29/85
37° 27'N, 71° 55'W (VA)	1	8/30/79
New York	1	8/30/79
38 mi off Oregon Inlet, NC	1	8/31/77
40° 34'N, 66° 09'W (MA)	1	9/2/1885
Hydrographer Canyon, MA	1	9/2/82
off Avalon, NJ	1	9/5/73
off Oregon Inlet, NC	1	9/5/92
Hydrographer Canyon, MA	1	9/7/85
85-100 mi SE of Cape May, NJ	2	9/10/80
40° 00'N, 67° 51'W (MA)	1	9/10/82
40 mi SSE of Block Island, RI	1	9/10/90
Hudson Canyon, NJ	1	9/11/80
Block/Hudson canyons, NY/NJ	1	9/18/87
Hudson Canyon, NY/NJ	1	9/19/79
59.6 mi E of Assateague, VA	1	9/21/85
34 mi NE of Oregon Inlet, NC	1	9/24/77
30 mi N of Cape Cod, MA	1	10/01/46
at Oregon Inlet, NC (storm blown)	2	10/02/71
off Hatteras, NC	2	10/09/83
off North Carolina	2+	fall 1977

all records with dates through 1995

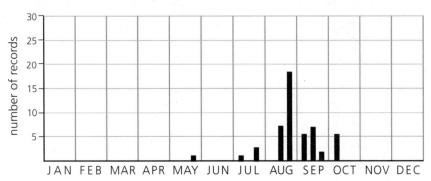

Band-rumped Storm-Petrel

Oceanodroma castro

Status and Distribution

A bird of tropical and subtropical waters, the Band-rumped Storm-Petrel is widely distributed, often occurring in hot, desert-like seas where few other species are found. In the Atlantic, nesting takes place on several islands far off the coast of Africa. Postbreeding dispersal in summer carries some of these birds west to offshore waters of the southeastern United States, where this prize is sought by many birders.

As recently as 15 years ago, the Band-rumped Storm-Petrel was thought to be strictly accidental in the Lower 48, with a scattering of storm-blown individuals at inland as well as coastal sites accounting for most of the records. In fact, the first nonstorm-related record in North America wasn't until the night of August 14, 1975, when one landed on board a ship anchored 73 miles east of Rehoboth Beach, Delaware. Although knowledge of its status is still evolving, this species is now known to be regular—sometimes even fairly common—over warm waters off the southern Atlantic Coast and in the Gulf of Mexico as well. There is also a growing number of records north as far as Massachusetts. This quick change in status is likely the result of improved knowledge about storm-petrel identification combined with increased observer effort in areas favored by this species.

Recent effort off North Carolina has revealed much about Band-rumped Storm-Petrel distribution. Band-rumps normally start to appear in North Carolina waters in late May and reach their peak from about mid-June to mid-August, although this is somewhat variable. The top one-day count is 70 off Oregon Inlet on August 15, 1986, a slightly late date. The last ones are generally gone by early September. The scattering of records north of the Carolinas are mostly from mid- to late August, when water temperatures reach their peak.

In the Gulf of Mexico, Band-rumped Storm-Petrel distribution is less precisely known, but counts such as 25 in deep water off Port O'Connor, Texas, on May 28, 1994, and 31 there on June 24, 1995, indicate that Band-rumps must be fairly numerous. In fact, Band-rumps appear to be the most common species of storm-petrel in the Gulf. Time of occurrence here is not well known, but most records are between mid-April and mid-October. Peak season appears to be late May to early August.

Several reports of Band-rumps off the coast of southern California suggest that a few may occur there, but the species has yet to be thoroughly documented in that state.

Best Bets

North Carolina is the premier locale for the Band-rumped Storm-Petrel. In recent years, most summer boat trips that venture to deepwater areas (500+ fathoms) off Oregon and Hatteras inlets turn up one or more Band-rumps. Peak time there is from about mid-June to mid-August.

A good second choice is a deepwater trip in the Gulf of Mexico. Trips have run regularly in recent years off Port O'Connor, Texas, but other trips may be offered soon. Late May to early August is prime time.

Elsewhere your odds are probably somewhat worse. You may try an August boat trip off any port from Massachusetts to Virginia, but make sure the boat is headed for deep water. At this season, warm-water eddies off the Gulf Stream might harbor a few Band-rumps. On the Atlantic Coast south of North Carolina, very few boat trips are scheduled, but Band-rumps do occur. The timing of occurrence here is from late April to early September (Haney 1985).

Identification

Much has been written about storm-petrel identification, with good accounts in Naveen (1981-82), Harrison (1983), and Lee (1984). Still, the problem is complex and needs to be taken in several steps. To distinguish Band-rumped from Wilson's Storm-Petrels, key points to consider are size, wing shape, foot projection beyond tail, extent of white on flanks and undertail coverts, wing profile during glide, and, to a lesser extent, width of rump patch, prominence of upper wing bar, and flight style. To distinguish Band-rump from Leach's Storm-Petrels, key points to consider are tail shape, wing shape, prominence of upper wing bar, overall color, and, in many cases, rump pattern and flight style. These points are summarized in the table below.

Distinguishing Band-rumped from Leach's is the most difficult task. Flight style, often noted as the best clue, is variable in both species and needs to be used with caution. Classic, distinctive flight patterns are usually evident in light winds. However, in stronger winds or under dead-calm conditions, the flight style of these two species can be almost identical. In light winds, Leach's flight is generally dominated by deep wing strokes with wings held up in a deep *V* at the peak of the upstroke. Leach's also exhibits erratic side-to-side rocking of the body such that the body and wings are not held horizontally for extended periods, thus recalling the flight of a Common Nighthawk. Glides tend to be short and never dominate the flight. Under similar conditions, the Band-rump's flight is dominated by relatively shallow wing strokes (wings only slightly above horizontal at the peak of the upstroke), level body position (little erratic rocking), and long glides that feature prominently in the overall flight. Under windier conditions, both species slip into a dynamic, shearwater-like mode of flight with high arcing glides on motionless, bowed wings. Although a Band-rumped will apparently fly this way in lighter winds than a Leach's, the two may not be safely separable by flight style under these conditions. Likewise, under perfectly calm conditions, both species exhibit a more powerful, direct flight with little gliding and little rocking, rendering flight style a nearly useless identification character. **(See color photo on page 459.)**

ID Summary

Wing Shape

- Leach's: Long and angular with a distinct bend at the wrist obvious on both leading and trailing edges: boomerang shaped.
- Band-rumped: Longer than Wilson's, slightly shorter than Leach's. Distinct bend at the wrist on leading edge but softer angle than on Leach's. Trailing edge very gently curved with less obvious break than

Leach's and sometimes appearing almost straight as in Wilson's: sickle shaped.
- Wilson's: Short with straight trailing edge and curved leading edge. Bend at the wrist is inconspicuous: triangular.

Wing Profile (edge on) During Glide
- Leach's: Bowed
- Band-rumped: Bowed
- Wilson's: Flat

Rump
- Leach's: Variable; typically off-white and V shaped with a distinct smudgy line down the center and no white extending below the level of the tail; a few individuals much whiter without visible dividing line, and with some white extending below the level of the tail; width of rump patch is about 50 to 75 percent of tail length.
- Band-rumped: Small, bright white patch about 50 to 75 percent of tail length and generally straight sided or gently U shaped; white extends slightly below level of tail.
- Wilson's: Large, bright white patch about 75 to 100 percent of tail length and generally straight sided or U shaped; white extends extensively below level of tail, so from side appears to have mostly white undertail coverts. This white on the sides of the rump is obvious even with a bird resting on the water.

Tail
- Leach's: Distinctly notched; no foot projection. (Note: Occasionally a molting Leach's will show a much shallower notch.)
- Band-rumped: Square or very slightly dented in the middle; no foot projection (Note: The generally square tail shape is typical of North Carolina birds. Birds in photos from other parts of the world show distinctly notched tails. Molt may play a major role in tail shape but more study is needed.)
- Wilson's: Square; feet clearly visible beyond end of tail.

Color
- Leach's: Medium brown, often distinctly paler than Band-rumped or Wilson's, but may look dark.
- Band-rumped: Dark brown to blackish but may look paler under harsh light.

- Wilson's: Dark brown to blackish but may look paler under harsh light.

Upper Wing Bar

- Leach's: Usually prominent broad bar reaching the leading edge of the wing.
- Band-rumped: Usually indistinct, narrow bar showing little contrast with remainder of wing and not reaching the leading edge of wing.
- Wilson's: Usually prominent broad bar not reaching the leading edge of the wing.

Size, Proportions, Jizz

- Leach's: Large, long winged, short tailed; rump patch and head inconspicuous; long, bent wings dominate impression.
- Band-rumped: Medium to large, long winged, short tailed; head inconspicuous; long wings and small but bright rump patch dominate impression.
- Wilson's: Smaller with relatively short wings and long tail; head conspicuous in front of wings; since wings are smaller, the overall impression is balanced between wings, big head, large, bright rump patch, and long tail.

Band-rumped Storm-Petrel—*selected high counts, North Carolina to Georgia*

LOCATION	NUMBERS SEEN	DATES SEEN
off Hatteras Inlet, NC	24	5/27/95
off Hatteras Inlet, NC	28	5/29/95
off NC	21	6/18/94
off NC	22+	6/26/84
off Oregon Inlet, NC	26	6/27/92
off North Carolina	21	7/15/85
off Hatteras, NC	36	7/31/94
off McClellanville, SC	5	8/1/93
off Georgia	19	8/1 to 8/2/84
off Oregon Inlet, NC	22	8/6/85
off Oregon Inlet, NC	22	8/8/85
off North Carolina	29	8/14/84
off Oregon Inlet, NC	37	8/14/93
off Oregon Inlet, NC	70	8/15/86
off Oregon Inlet, NC	52	8/21/94
off Oregon Inlet, NC	64	8/24/85
off Oregon Inlet, NC	47	8/25/85
off Hatteras, NC	16	8/28/86
off Oregon Inlet, NC	35	9/2/86

Band-rumped Storm-Petrel—*all records, Massachusetts to Virginia*

LOCATION	NUMBERS SEEN	DATES SEEN
Hudson Canyon, NJ/NY	1	5/26/84
Poor Man's Canyon, VA	1	6/7/86
off New Jersey/Delaware	8	7/31 to 8/9/84
73 mi E of Rehoboth, DE	1	8/14/75
70 mi off VA Beach, VA	7	8/14/88
Poor Man's Canyon, VA	11	8/14/93
Washington Canyon, VA	1	8/17/91
Hydrographer Canyon, MA	2	8/19/85
Hydrographer Canyon, MA	1	8/20 to 8/21/84
Atlantis Canyon, MA	1	8/28/94
Hudson Canyon, NJ	1	8/28/95
Hydrographer Canyon, MA	1	9/4/86
Hydrographer Canyon, MA	1	9/7/85
Carteret Canyon, NJ	1	9/10/90

Band-rumped Storm-Petrel—*all records, Florida and the Gulf of Mexico**

LOCATION	NUMBERS SEEN	DATES SEEN
Palm Beach, FL	1	3/23/93
Rebecca Shoals, FL	1	4/10/93
Rebecca Shoals, FL	1	4/21/92
Dry Tortugas, FL	1	4/24/91
off Jacksonville, FL	1	5/1/84
deep water SE of Key West, FL	1	5/1/92
off Dry Tortugas, FL	1	5/12/91
SE of Key West, FL	8	5/12/94
Mustang Island, TX	1(dead)	5/14/89
60 mi off Venice, LA	24	5/27/95
off Port O'Connor, TX	25	5/28/94
off Sebastian Inlet, FL	1	5/30/92
Upper Matecumbe Key, FL	1	6/1/73
Upper Matecumbe Key, FL	1	6/2/73
Padre Island, TX	1	6/3/69
off Port Aransas, TX	1	6/15/91
off Port Aransas, TX	1	6/11/88
Mitchell Lake, TX	1	6/14/84
50 mi E of Port Aransas, TX	1	6/15/91
Canaveral National Seashore, FL	1	6/16/93
off Port O'Connor, TX	31	6/24/95
Edinburg, TX (after hurricane)	3	6/25/54
New Braunfels, TX	1	6/25/60
off Boynton Inlet, FL	1	7/11/82

LOCATION	NUMBERS SEEN	DATES SEEN
off LA	1	7/16/85
off Port O'Connor, TX	10	7/23/94
north Padre Island, TX	1	7/24/68
off Port Mansfield, TX	a few	8/7/93
off Port Mansfield, TX	a few	8/15/93
Pensacola Beach, FL	1	8/18/69
Pensacola Beach, FL	1	8/20/69
off Port O'Connor, TX	4	8/20/94
Cape Canaveral, FL	1	9/15/74
off Port O'Connor, TX	6	9/24/94
St. Petersburg, FL	1	10/10/75
St. Petersburg, FL	1	10/10/77
Key West, FL	1	10/21 to 10/30/58
off Canaveral, FL	2	10/30/91
off Cape San Blas, FL	1	12/6/58

*Haney (1985) described the Band-rumped Storm-Petrel as rare to uncommon about 18 to 61 mi offshore along the South Atlantic Bight, from Volusia County, Florida, northward, April 29 to September 4.

Band-rumped Storm-Petrel—*all interior records*

LOCATION	NUMBERS SEEN	DATES SEEN
Chambersburg, PA	1	4/15/12
Mitchell Lake, TX	1	6/14/84
Martinsville, IN	1	6/15/02
Edinburg, TX	3	6/25/54
New Braunfels, TX	1	6/25/60
District of Columbia	2	8/28 to 8/29/1893
Great Smoky Mountains National Park, TN	3	9/24 to 9/26/75
Rejected by state BRC		
Los Almos Creek, TX	1	5/30/65
134 to 160 mi SSW of San Nicolas Island, CA	9-13	7/20/89
15 mi W of San Nicolas Island, CA	1	7/25/89
30 mi W of San Diego, CA	1	9/12/70

off North Carolina

seen on about 20% of trips
seen on about 50% of trips
seen on about 90% of trips

JAN FEB MAR APR MAY JUN JUL AUG SEP OCT NOV DEC

Least Storm- Petrel

Oceanodroma microsoma

Status and Distribution

This diminutive storm-petrel is a lover of warm tropical and subtropical waters. It breeds off the sunny coasts of Baja California and then disperses into the Lower 48 as a postbreeding wanderer. The extent to which Least Storm-Petrels enter our waters is highly dependent on water temperature. During years of cool water, this species can be quite scarce, but during El Niño years Least Storm-Petrels are abundant off southern California and may be numerous as far north as Monterey Bay. The northernmost report is of a bird seen off Humboldt County, California, on October 1, 1972.

Least Storm-Petrels have occurred inland as well. During September 1976, Hurricane Kathleen swept 500 to 1,000 Leasts into the Salton Sea and smaller numbers into Lake Mohave and Lake Mead along the Colorado River (Lake Mohave, NV/AZ, on 9/12 and 9/17/76; 50 to 70 at Lake Mead on 9/14/76). The last of the Salton Sea birds was seen on October 21. Other inland records include a bird at Silver City, New Mexico, on August 24, 1992, and another at the northern end of the Salton Sea on July 10, 1993.

Generally, Least Storm-Petrels arrive in southern California by mid to late July. However, in El Niño years, a scattering of birds may appear in June. If Leasts are going to make it to Monterey Bay, they usually have made their appearance there by mid-September. Departure from all areas is during late September or October, although there are a few sightings from November. Out-of-season records include the following: 1, 50 miles west of San Miguel Island, February 9, 1992; and 1, 35 miles south-southwest of San Nicolas Island, April 22, 1990. The record high count of

3,500 comes from the waters off San Diego on September 13, 1992. Narrowly missing this record was a count of 3,200 off San Diego on September 8, 1979. Northern California's maximum count was 500 to 1,000 on Monterey Bay in early October 1983.

Best Bets

Bring the suntan lotion and hop on an August or September pelagic trip out of southern California. Best trips include the early September Western Field Ornithologists trips from San Diego, and Los Angeles Audubon trips from San Pedro. During invasion years, September and early October trips in Monterey Bay can also be worthwhile. If you cannot make an organized pelagic trip, an Island Packer trip or a fishing boat to the Channel Islands may be worth the effort, as may a deep-sea fishing boat out of San Diego County.

Identification

Properly identifying a Least Storm-Petrel depends on some familiarity with Black and Ashy Storm-Petrels. Fortunately, both of these species are usually present when Least Storm-Petrels are about. Like Black Storm-Petrels, Leasts are blackish (Ashys are brownish or grayish in good light). Leasts also fly directly with deep wingbeats, much like a Black Storm-Petrel, and unlike the shallower wingbeats of an Ashy.

The mark that differentiates Leasts from other U.S. storm-petrels is tail shape. The Least Storm-Petrel's tail is wedge shaped and short, giving these birds an almost tailless appearance that is distinct from Ashy, Black, and Leach's Storm-Petrels. This feature is poorly shown in the NGS guide but is well illustrated in Stallcup (1990). Also, the Least Storm-Petrel is truly least, and its small stature can be easily seen in good comparisons with other storm-petrels.

relative abundance

		rare
		uncommon
		fairly common

JAN FEB MAR APR MAY JUN JUL AUG SEP OCT NOV DEC

White-tailed Tropicbird

Phaethon lepturus

Status and Distribution

This nomad of the tropical seas has long been near the top of many a birder's most wanted list. Its stunning beauty and inquisitive nature separate it from other seabirds and make it a specialty of hot summer pelagic trips to the Gulf Stream.

White-tailed Tropicbirds are widely distributed in the tropical and subtropical portions of the Atlantic, Pacific, and Indian oceans. They breed as close as Bermuda, the Bahamas, and Cuba. In the Lower 48, White-tailed Tropicbirds are known to occur primarily off the coasts of North Carolina and Florida, although South Carolina and Georgia would probably produce more records if effort increased. North Carolina records occur primarily between late May and mid-October, but the peak time seems to be from mid-June to mid-August when fishing boat captains report daily sightings of tropicbirds. The timing is slightly different in Florida. There, most records are between early March and early June with an early April to mid-May peak. This is also the time of peak birder activity in Florida, so the records may not fairly represent the White-tailed Tropicbird's true status.

Elsewhere, White-tailed Tropicbirds are strictly vagrants. States with published sightings include California, Arizona, Texas, Alabama, Maine, Vermont, Massachusetts, Rhode Island, New York, Pennsylvania, New Jersey, Virginia, North Carolina, South Carolina, Georgia, and Florida.

No breeding has been documented in North America, but if it were to occur, Florida's Dry Tortugas is the most likely place. For years, the Dry Tortugas was the premier locale to see the White-tailed Tropicbird in North

America. During April and May several birds would often linger around Fort Jefferson for weeks, circling overhead with the frigatebirds and even investigating the fort's many crevices as if searching for nesting sites. Unfortunately, tropicbirds have been much less reliable there in recent years, but it is hoped this is a trend that will reverse itself before long.

Best Bets

Pelagic trips off North Carolina currently offer the best chances for White-tailed Tropicbirds. Sightings seem to be increasing there, and in the past few years organized pelagic trips have been having a high success rate (at least 23 birds in 1995 alone). Peak time is from about mid-June to mid-August. The edge of the Gulf Stream and the Gulf Stream itself are probably the best places, although there are a few inshore records as well.

The next best option would be a trip to the Dry Tortugas. Records there peak from early April to mid-May, but note that tropicbirds have been scarce there in recent years.

Finding a tropicbird is often just a matter of luck. Looking up frequently is a good strategy because tropicbirds are inquisitive and do investigate boats. You can improve your odds a little by scanning any distant dark clouds for a fluttering white speck. Also check for a white dot in the water, but be prepared to be fooled occasionally by floating debris.

Identification

If seen well, adult tropicbirds should not present identification problems, and key points are well covered in the NGS guide, MGB, and in Harrison (1983). Young birds, however, are another story, and much remains to be learned about their identification. The one character that seems to be useful in all plumages is the pattern of black on the primaries and primary coverts. Red-tailed Tropicbird, which is very rare off the California coast, will always be the easiest one to identify. Its primary coverts and primaries are nearly pure white. Fine black shaft streaks in the outer several primaries are barely visible in the field. White-tailed shows a more extensive area of black with a solid black patch on the outer four or five feathers and usually entirely white primary coverts (rarely there will be a few dark marks on the greater primary coverts). Red-billed Tropicbird shows the most black, with a solid black patch on the outer five or more primaries continuous with a solid black patch over most of the greater primary coverts.

In the field, recognizing the precise primary pattern may be difficult without some previous experience, so a close study or good photos may often be necessary for identification. Also diagnostic in Red-billed is a dark nuchal collar connecting the eyestripes around the back of the head, but note that many Red-bills (especially adults) lack this characteristic. Thus, its absence does not necessarily indicate another species.

Another feature that may be useful with some experience is structure. Red-billed Tropicbird is a heavier bird than White-tailed, with a larger head and bigger bill. As a result, Red-billed has a slower, heavier flight that is more direct and less buoyant than White-tailed. **(See color photo on page 460.)**

White-tailed Tropicbird—*Florida records, 1978 to 1995*

LOCATION	NUMBERS SEEN	DATES SEEN
Navarre Beach	1	1/27/89
Dry Tortugas	1	3/6 to mid-May 1986
Key West	1	3/28/85
Dry Tortugas	1+	3/30 to May 1987
Merritt Island NWR	1	4/8/81
Dry Tortugas	3-5	4/22/78
Dry Tortugas	1	4/22 to 5/1/88
Dry Tortugas	1	4/26/94
Dry Tortugas	1	4/29 to 5/10/95
Dry Tortugas	1	5/1 to 5/6/93
Key West	1	5/6/90
off Diana	1	5/9/86
6 mi off Palm Beach	1	5/9/95
Dry Tortugas	1	5/10/94
N Palm Beach	1	5/15 to 5/31/94
20 mi NW of Dry Tortugas	2	5/25/78
off Sebastian Inlet	1	5/30/92
Dry Tortugas	1-3	most of May 1980
S of Sugarloaf Key	1	spring 1979
Dry Tortugas	2+	spring 1982
Dry Tortugas	6	mid-March to mid-May 1983
Dry Tortugas	4-6	April/May 1984
Dry Tortugas	3+	April/May 1985

LOCATION	NUMBERS SEEN	DATES SEEN
Dry Tortugas	2	spring 1990
Dry Tortugas	8-10	spring 1992
Dry Tortugas	1	6/4/79
10 mi E of Fort Pierce	1	7/16/78
25 mi E of Boynton Beach	1	summer 1986
Palm Beach	1	8/15/81
28 mi off Cape Canaveral	1	8/30/87
Marineland	1 (dead)	9/6/79
Hobe Sound	1	9/19/83
St. Augustine	1	9/24/79
Brevard County	8 reports	1980-84

White-tailed Tropicbird—*North Carolina Records, 1978 to 1995**

LOCATION	NUMBERS SEEN	DATES SEEN
Hammocks Beach State Park	1	4/19/86
off Oregon Inlet	1	5/16/92
off Oregon Inlet	1	5/26/90
off Hatteras	1	5/28/95
off Hatteras	1	5/29/95
off Morehead City	1	5/31/88
off North Carolina	2-3	June/July 1980
off Hatteras	1	6/5/94
off Oregon Inlet	1	6/6/78
off Oregon Inlet	1	6/9/95
off Hatteras	1	6/18/81
off Hatteras	4	6/18/94
off Oregon Inlet	1	7/14/90
off Hatteras	4	7/16/95
off Hatteras	1	7/22/95
off Cape Lookout	3	7/23/89
off Oregon Inlet	1	7/24/95
off Oregon Inlet	1	7/25/78
Jordan Lake (after hurricane)	1	7/25/85
off North Carolina	1	7/29/84
off Hatteras	1	7/29/94
off Hatteras	1	7/29/95
off Hatteras	2	7/30/94
off Hatteras	4	7/30/95
off Oregon Inlet	1	7/31/91
off Hatteras	1	7/31/94
off Oregon Inlet	1	7/31/95
off Oregon Inlet	3	8/5/95
off Hatteras	3	8/5/95
off Oregon Inlet	4	8/6/85

LOCATION	NUMBERS SEEN	DATES SEEN
off Oregon Inlet	1	8/8/85
off Hatteras	1	8/8/94
off Hatteras	1	8/10/85
off Hatteras	1	8/13/95
off Cape Lookout	2	8/15/82
off Oregon Inlet	1	8/15/86
off North Carolina	1	8/16/93
off Hatteras	1	8/26/95
off Hatteras	1	8/28/83
off Hatteras	1	9/2/79
off Hatteras Inlet	1	9/2/85
off Oregon Inlet	1	9/2/86
off Beaufort Inlet	1	9/3/79
75 mi E of Cape Lookout	1	9/5/81
Jordan Lake (after hurricane)	1	9/6/79
off Oregon Inlet	2	9/7/91
off Oregon Inlet	1	9/11/78
off Oregon Inlet	1	9/18/88
Shelby (after hurricane)	1	9/22/89
off Hatteras	1	9/25/94

* Many other sightings by fishing boat captains. Seen daily from mid-June to mid-August and sporadically to mid-October.

White-tailed Tropicbird—*records away from Florida and North Carolina, 1978 to 1995*

LOCATION	NUMBERS SEEN	DATES SEEN
125 mi off GA	1	5/11/84
off Charleston, SC	1	5/19/88
70 to 80 mi off GA	1	6/16 to 6/20/83
off South Carolina	1	7/4 to 7/14/84
off South Carolina	3	summer 1993
Norfolk Canyon, VA	1	8/21/93
Scottsdale, AZ	1	8/22/80
Eastham, MA (after hurricane)	1	8/22/91
off Charleston, SC	1	8/24/88
off Savannah, GA	1	8/29/81
off South Carolina	1	Aug 1993
Hydrographer Canyon, MA	1	9/4/86
Poor Man's Canyon, VA	1	9/16/95
off Virginia Beach, VA	1	9/17/88
Chatham, MA (after hurricane)	3	9/27/85
Byfield, MA (after hurricane)	1	9/28/85
Point Judith, RI (after hurricane)	1	9/28/85
Port Aransas, TX	1	10/5/78
Barnegat Light, NJ	1	11/23/85

off North Carolina-1978 through 1995

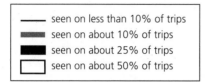

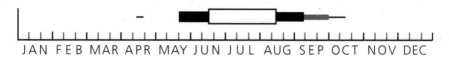

JAN FEB MAR APR MAY JUN JUL AUG SEP OCT NOV DEC

Red-billed Tropicbird

Phaethon aethereus

Status and Distribution

You are standing on the deck of a boat, the hot sun bringing sweat to your brow. As usual, you and your comrades have been scanning with vigilance, but the day has been slow. You break to dab moisture from your forehead, and as you do, you look up. To your total astonishment, a slender white bird with a long flowing tail hangs in the air. Now how did that get there! Welcome to the quintessential tropicbird experience. Many times they seem to appear magically directly above the boat, then after a variable amount of time they seem to just disappear. Poof! Gone!

The Red-billed Tropicbird breeds widely across the tropical seas. In the Pacific, it nests as close to the United States as Baja California. In the Atlantic, Red-bills breed as nearby as the Virgin Islands. In the Lower 48, the Red-billed Tropicbird has occurred in most coastal states and has also wandered inland to Arizona. The pattern of sightings differs from coast to coast. Along the Pacific Coast, this species is seen mostly from mid-July through mid-September, though deepwater research vessels have found Red-bills in smaller numbers at other times of year. East Coast Red-bills, however, are found mostly between early May and late August, with extreme dates stretching from May 6, 1981 (off Cape Lookout, NC) to early November (Martha's Vineyard, MA).

The vast majority of Pacific Coast Red-billed Tropicbirds have been seen in southern California waters, where the species is virtually annual. There are but 11 sightings from central California, north to Bodega Bay, and one record north of Bodega Bay. The latter bird was collected by a fisherman in Grays Harbor, Washington, on June 18, 1941. Along the Atlantic Coast, there have been at least 27 records of Red-billed Tropicbirds. The first occurred on June 10, 1963, when one was found dead at Jamaica Bay, New York. Since then, 13 have been seen off North Carolina, and 5 have been found off Florida. The rest have come from Maine, Massachusetts, Rhode Island, New Jersey, and Georgia.

The remaining Lower 48 records are the most spectacular. These include two sightings from Texas, five from Arizona, and one from inland California (see table for details). There is no particular pattern among these sightings other than coming from the warmer months as a whole.

Best Bets

From the mid-1960s to the early 1980s, Red-billed Tropicbirds could be found with some regularity at southern California's Channel Islands. During this era, you stood an excellent chance of seeing this bird at the proper time of year. Since then, unfortunately, Red-bills have favored the waters farther from shore, remaining outside the islands. Seeing one now requires a certain measure of luck. Nonetheless, you can increase your odds by taking a southern California pelagic trip sometime between early July and mid-September. If you have your own vessel, the San Juan Escarpment, 40 to 60 miles beyond the Channel Islands, has been the best spot during recent research trips.

When looking for tropicbirds, don't look at eye level—they are usually found flying high overhead or sitting in the water with their tail feathers pointed skyward.

Identification

Red-billed Tropicbirds are similar to the other two tropicbirds, White-tailed and Red-tailed. The White-tailed is not rare off the Atlantic Coast and has been recorded in California and Arizona. The Red-tailed has occurred several times off southern California and is being found with increasing regularity far offshore there. (See the White-tailed Tropicbird species account, p. 44, for identification details.)

One word of caution: more than one eager birder has been led to folly by the Caspian/Royal/Elegant Tern complex. Before identifying which kind of tropicbird, be sure it is a tropicbird. **(See color photo on page 460.)**

Red-billed Tropicbird—*southern California records from 1982 on*

LOCATION	NUMBERS SEEN	DATES SEEN
far off San Diego	4	1/9 to 1/10/91
49 mi SW of San Clemente Island	1	1/13/93
46 mi SSW of San Nicolas Island	1	1/17/93
32° 20'N and 120° 30'W	1	1/28/89
79 mi SW of San Nicolas Island	1	3/3/91
52 mi SW of San Clemente Island	1	4/18/90
116 mi SSW of San Nicolas Island	2	4/19/90
47 to 58 mi SW of San Nicolas Island	3	4/22/90
Tanner Bank	1	5/5/87
between Santa Barbara and Santa Catalina islands	1	5/10/87
off San Diego	1	5/17/86
off San Diego	1	5/18/85
10 mi N of Santa Barbara Island	1	5/24/83
84 mi SW of San Clemente Island	1	7/3/92
Palos Verdes Peninsula	1	7/5 to 7/19/92
128 mi W of San Miguel Island	1	7/13/92
5 mi S of Santa Catalina Island	1	7/16/92
44 mi SW of San Clemente Island	1	7/25/91
5 mi S of San Miguel Island	1	7/25/92
161 mi WSW of San Nicolas Island	1	7/26/91
23 mi W of San Clemente Island	2	7/29/91
San Pedro Channel	8	7/31/90
off southern California	8	7/30 to 8/4/90
Imperial Beach	1 (dead)	8/3/84
San Juan Seamount	4	8/22/85
150 miles off San Diego	1	9/9/87
S of San Clemente Island	5	9/10 to 9/12/82
7 mi ENE of Santa Catalina Island	1	9/15/90
SE of Davidson Seamount	1	10/5/87
San Pedro Channel	1	10/17/92
NE of isthmus of Santa Catalina Island	1	10/18/92
64 mi WSW of San Nicolas Island	1	11/13/89

Red-billed Tropicbird—*all central California records*

LOCATION	NUMBERS SEEN	DATES SEEN
near Farallon Islands	1	2/20/92
12 mi NW of Point Pinos	1	7/14/70
18 mi W of Yankee Point	1	7/26/90
3 mi off Cypress Point	1	8/3/91
Pigeon Point	1	8/10 to 12/89
10 mi W of Moss Landing	1	8/14/94
beyond Farallon Islands	1	8/23/87
~10 mi E of Farallon Islands	1	9/20/81
190 mi W of Bodega Bay	1	10/5/79
180 mi W of Point Pinos	1	10/6/79
20 mi W of Point Pinos	1	10/10/82

Red-billed Tropicbird—*all inland records*

LOCATION	NUMBERS SEEN	DATES SEEN
Camp Verde, AZ	1	4/7/84
near Phoenix, AZ	1	4/10/05
Zapata, TX	1	4/29/89
Green Valley, AZ	1	5/22/92
S of Tucson, AZ	1	6/22/90
Morongo Valley, CA	1	9/11/76
Dos Cabezas, AZ	1	9/15/27

Red-billed Tropicbird—*all Gulf of Mexico and Atlantic Coast records*

LOCATION	NUMBERS SEEN	DATES SEEN
20 mi E of Cape Lookout, NC	1	5/6/81
8 mi S of Key West, FL	1	5/12/95
about 40 mi E of Oregon Inlet, NC	1	5/16/79
Seaside Heights, NJ	1	5/23 or 5/24/83
off Oregon Inlet, NC	1	5/29/95
off Hatteras Inlet, NC	1	5/29/95
90 miles E of St. Catherines Island, GA	1	6/7/84
Jamaica Bay, NY	1 (dead)	6/10/63
Martha's Vineyard, MA	1	6/14 to July 1988
Providence, RI	1	7/3/73
31 miles off Cape Canaveral, FL	1	7/9/64
off Hatteras, NC	1	7/9/95
Green Hill Beach, RI	1	7/19/75
Martha's Vineyard, MA	1	7/20 to 8/30/87
out of Cape Hatteras, NC	1	7/24/94
off Hatteras, NC	1	7/29/95

LOCATION	NUMBERS SEEN	DATES SEEN
out of Oregon Inlet, NC	1	Aug 1981
off Hatteras, NC	1	8/13/94
off Cape Lookout, NC	1	8/27/83
off Hatteras, NC	1	8/27/95
Fort Pierce, FL	1	8/27/86
Mt. Desert, ME	1	8/31/86
Martin/St. Lucie county border, FL	1	9/1/79
off Oregon Inlet, NC	1	9/1/81
off Oregon Inlet, NC	1	9/2/95
Martha's Vineyard, MA	1	9/15 to early 11/86
Ponte Verde Beach, FL	1	10/9/75
Houston, TX	1	11/13/85

Red-billed Tropicbird—*high counts*

LOCATION	NUMBERS SEEN	DATES SEEN
off San Diego, CA	9	7/27/68
off Santa Cruz Island, CA	8	9/8/74
San Pedro Channel, CA	8	7/31/90

records in California since 1981

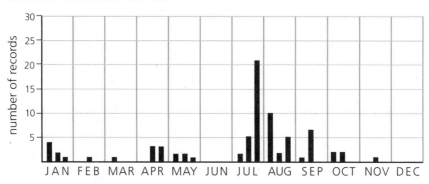

Gulf of Mexico and Atlantic Coast records

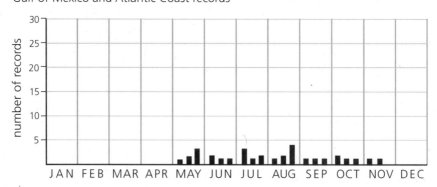

Red-tailed Tropicbird

Phaethon rubricauda

Status and Distribution

The Red-tailed Tropicbird is an angelic vision that lives in the tropical and subtropical regions of the Pacific and Indian oceans. The nearest well-established breeding colonies are in Hawaii, over 2,000 miles from the Lower 48, but the species may nest considerably closer at Las Islas Revillagigedo, Mexico. In any case, the Red-tailed Tropicbird is a true rarity in the Lower 48, with only about 15 sightings on record.

All of these records have been from 1979 on, and about half have been since 1990. This trend is more likely due to changes in observer effort than range expansion. Although all Red-tailed Tropicbirds are born on (or over) land, this bird has a pelagic spirit and leaves the nesting area after breeding to ply deep, warm waters far from terra firma. Accordingly, all but three records are from 80 or more miles from shore, and most have been more than 120 miles out. The only two records from relatively close to land are as follows: one bird near southeast Farallon Island on July 3, 1979, which was the Lower 48's first; one bird 22 miles southwest of Ano Nuevo Point on September 24, 1994.

All Red-tailed Tropicbirds seen in the Lower 48 states have been in the waters off southern and central California. The Farallon Islands' bird is the northernmost, and the bird southwest of Ano Nuevo Point is the next most northerly. Except these two, all records have been south of Monterey Bay. Among the remaining records, five were between Point Conception and Monterey Bay, and the remaining eight have been south of Point Conception.

The 15 Red-tailed Tropicbird records from the Lower 48 show a peculiar bimodal distribution that is likely the result of chance and observer effort. Ten are from mid-August into mid-October and four are during mid- and late January; the remaining sighting is from early July. In reality, the waters far off California, from Monterey south, probably harbor members of this species at various times throughout the calendar year.

Best Bets

If you want to see a Red-tailed Tropicbird in the Lower 48, you'll likely need access to an area that most U.S. birders cannot normally get to—the seas south of Monterey Bay and beyond the edge of the continental shelf. In this region, the Red-tail is probably annual. Even so, your chances of finding one on a one-day visit there would be small. Then again, your odds are worse elsewhere.

Recently, the Los Angeles Audubon Society has tried a few trips to the area described above. None of the trips has produced a Red-tailed Tropicbird, but these voyages would probably be the average birder's best shot. For information on future trips, call (213) 876-0202 or check the most recent January issue of *Winging It*.

Identification

Tropicbird identification is summarized in the White-tailed Tropicbird account, beginning on p. 44.

Red-tailed Tropicbird—*all records*

LOCATION	NUMBERS SEEN	DATES SEEN
130 nmi SW of San Nicolas Island	1	1/14/93
161 nmi WSW of San Nicolas Island	1	1/16/93
160 nmi WSW of San Nicolas Island	1	1/25/94
84 nmi W of San Nicolas Island	1	1/29/94
SE Farallon Islands	1	7/3/79
129 nmi WSW of Point Sur	1	8/8/92
220 nmi SSW of San Nicolas Island	1	8/11/89
145 nmi WSW of San Diego	1	8/16/80
88 nmi SW of Point Piedras Blancas	1	8/19/92
22 mi SW of Ano Nuevo Point	1	9/24/94
100 nmi WSW of Point Arguello	1	9/30/79
147 mi WSW of Point Sur	1	10/7/79
80 nmi SW of Point Piedras Blancas	1	10/8/79
130 nmi off Point Arguello	1	10/8/79
25 mi W of Cortez Bank	2	10/15/93

Masked Booby

Sula dactylatra

Status and Distribution

You are standing atop an old fort made of millions of bricks, and the brilliant tropical sun is beating down upon your brow. For military purposes, the fort was obsolete before it was even finished. For birding purposes, however, it is useful indeed. In the distance you spot a glint of sand—a small isle. You set up your scope, and on the island sits a handful of glistening white objects. One of these stretches its wings and finds the air. Welcome to Fort Jefferson, the Dry Tortugas, and the world of the Masked Booby.

The Masked Booby is a bird of tropical oceans worldwide. In the United States this species is found reliably only in the Dry Tortugas. Elsewhere in the Lower 48, Masked Boobies have been seen along the entire sweep of the Gulf Coast, along the Atlantic Coast north to North Carolina, and in California. As with many other species of such wide distribution, the Masked Booby's status is best discussed in parts.

Though Masked Boobies are now often found in numbers in the Dry Tortugas, they have not always had a strong presence there. The species first appeared at the Tortugas in numbers during May 1982 when 14 were found. The first known nesting attempt occurred in March 1984, but the nest was washed away (Clapp and Robertson 1986). Nesting attempts have been nearly annual since then, and have met with varying success (Stevenson and Anderson 1994). Though most Masked Booby sightings in the Tortugas come from spring, this is also the time most birders visit. In reality, Masked Boobies are likely residents here (Wamer and Pranty 1995). The maximum Dry Tortugas Masked Booby count is 32 seen during April and May 1986.

Masked Boobies are annual in the remainder of Florida as well. From 1972 through 1994 there were 92 Masked Boobies reported from Florida, excluding the Tortugas. Most of these were from the Atlantic Coast north to Cape Canaveral and from the Gulf Coast. Peninsular Florida records are mostly from mid-March to early December, with a peak from late April through mid-May.

Perhaps a bit more surprising is the frequency of Masked Boobies elsewhere along the Gulf Coast. From 1972 through 1994, there have been 136 sightings of Masked Boobies from Alabama through Texas. Though many of these have been from land, pelagic trips have also had fair success, especially around oil platforms. It seems that these structures play an important role in Masked Booby distribution in the Gulf of Mexico (Ortego 1978). Northern and western Gulf Coast records are distributed throughout the year with a lull in February, May, and November. Peak times are from late March through late April and from early June into early October.

Masked Boobies are distinctly less likely to wander up the Atlantic Coast. There are but 27 records from the Atlantic north of Florida since 1972. The majority of these are from North Carolina pelagic trips, and the frequency of sightings there seems to be on the rise. Most records are from early June through early October, but there are also sightings from November and February.

California reports are few, though a small colony exists at Alijos Rocks off Baja California Sur (Stallcup 1990). To date, there have been eight published reports from California, one of which was rejected by the CA BRC. Except for the small flurry of sightings in June 1992, the California records show little temporal pattern.

Best Bets

Without a doubt, your best chance to see a Masked Booby is to go to the Dry Tortugas. Here the birds can usually be found roosting on Hospital Key. Otherwise, Dauphin Island or Fort Morgan in late March and April is worth a try as are pelagic trips out of Texas. Furthermore, given the increase of records from North Carolina, pelagic trips from there may prove fruitful.

Identification

Identifying an adult Masked Booby is straightforward, and key points are well covered in most field guides. Subadults can resemble similarly aged Northern Gannets, but note the gannet's yellowish cast to the head (white in the booby) and blue-gray bill (yellowish with blackish base in the Masked Booby). Younger Masked Boobies can be distinguished from gannets by the combination of a mostly dark head and extensively white underwings.

Juvenile Masked Boobies are also difficult to separate from Brown and Blue-footed Boobies. Key points to note on a juvenile Masked include a partial or complete white hind-collar, white on the underwing extending to the primary coverts, and white on the underparts extending well forward of the wing's leading edge. Juvenile Blue-footed Boobies have a wash of brown across the breast, duskier underwings contrasting with white axillars, and white central tail feathers (tail is all dark in Masked). All ages of the Brown Booby show a brown hood extending down to the breast (even with leading edge of wing), dusky primary coverts on the underwing, and no white on the upperparts (except on adult males of Pacific birds). The best text and illustrations can be found in Harrison (1983). **(See color photo on page 461.)**

Masked Booby–*California and Atlantic Coast (from Georgia north) records**

LOCATION	NUMBERS SEEN	DATES SEEN
California		
SW of San Clemente Island	1	1/10/77
2 mi W of Point Lobos	1	4/5/90
3 mi S of Palos Verdes Peninsula	1	4/30/94
Salinas River mouth	1	6/18 to 6/22/92
Point Mugu	1	6/20/92
Newport Beach	1	6/30/92
Farallon Islands	1	8/9/94
Rejected by CA BRC		
San Elijo Lagoon	1	11/14/87
Georgia		
Cumberland Island	1	2/2/86
off Georgia	1	5/3/83
off Georgia	1	6/6/84
off Georgia	1	mid-6/83

LOCATION	NUMBERS SEEN	DATES SEEN
off Jekyll Island	1	6/29/85
St. Simons Island	1	8/30/83
E of Sapelo Island	1	9/2/84
off Savannah	1	11/14/93
South Carolina		
80 mi E of Hilton Head	1	mid-7/83
off South Carolina	1	1/26/84
62 nmi S of Raccoon Point	1	7/19/85
off Charleston	1	9/23/84
North Carolina		
lower Cape Fear River	1	6 to 10/3/81
off Outer Banks	1	6/6/92
off Oregon Inlet	1	6/22/85
Cape Lookout	1	mid-7/93
off Oregon Inlet	1	7/25/87
off Hatteras Inlet	1	7/29/84
off Hatteras	1	7/31/94
off Outer Banks	2	8/14/84
off Hatteras Inlet	1	8/20/94
off Oregon Inlet	1	8/21/93
off Oregon Inlet	3	8/22/87
off Outer Banks	1	9/1/84
off Hatteras	1	9/18/93
Cape Hatteras	1	10/9/83
40 mi off Oregon Inlet	1	11/30/91

*All records since 1972, except California, for which all records are included.

Blue-footed
Booby

Sula nebouxii

Status and Distribution

You are standing alone along a rocky shore watching a Blue-footed Booby plunge into shallow water. Across the vast expanse of blue, parched brown mountains line the horizon. The heat is searing, the humidity wilting, the sun unrelenting. You crave coolness and fresh air. Are you on some lonely isle in the Sea of Cortez? No, you're on the shore of the Salton Sea during early fall—the best time and place in the United States for Blue-footed Boobies and incomprehensible heat.

In some ways, the Salton Sea is not a surprising place to find a Blue-footed Booby. The water is warm, shallow, and saline, and there are plenty of fish. Furthermore, the sea is not more than 200 miles from the nearest breeding colony at Consage Rock in the Sea of Cortez (a.k.a Gulf of California). What is stunning is that getting to the Salton Sea requires a booby to suddenly launch itself into the most booby-hostile environment imaginable, the Sonoran Desert, and then to somehow find the Salton Sea. Such seemingly unfathomable behavior, however, is not unprecedented. Both Yellow-footed Gulls and Brown Pelicans make the trip in large numbers annually. For these species, going to the Salton Sea is now part of their normal postbreeding dispersal, but for the boobies this adventure is far from normal.

Unlike Yellow-footed Gulls and Brown Pelicans, Blue-footed Boobies do not make the insane cross-desert journey with any regularity. Blue-foots have been seen in the United States (Salton Sea and elsewhere) during only 23 years since 1929 and 16 years since 1960, and their numbers are highly variable. In some years only one is seen, whereas other years produce large numbers. The causes of these invasions remain obscure, but for some reason the 1969-77 period was definitely the era of the Booby in the Southwest, when Blue-footed Boobies were seen every year, with a maximum of 87 reported during 1971. Since 1977, though, Blue-foots have once again become scarce, with but 15 seen during only five years.

With about two-thirds of the approximately 221 U.S. records, the Salton Sea is clearly the preeminent location for Blue-footed Boobies—but not the only spot. There are about 46 records from neighboring locales in the interior of southern California, southern Nevada, and western Arizona. Of these 46 sightings, 17 are from the Colorado River valley (especially lakes along the river, such as Lake Havasu), 27 are from scattered southern California inland lakes and reservoirs (Puddingstone Reservoir, Los Angeles County, is best), and 2 are from isolated lakes in western Arizona (Phoenix and Cameron). Twenty-three of the remaining 28 records are from the Pacific Coast of southern and central California. The origin of these birds is not completely certain, but they probably emanate from the Gulf of California and are part of the same postbreeding dispersal that brings birds to the interior (McCaskie 1970).

The five remaining records are truly extraordinary and are as follows: Everett, Snohomish County, Washington on September, 23, 1935; Point St. George, Del Norte County, California, on January 16, 1981; New Hogan Reservoir, Calaveras County, California, from September 15 to October 18, 1976; South Padre Island, Cameron County, Texas, on October 5, 1976; Lake Lyndon B. Johnson, Burnet County, Texas, from June 2, 1993, into at least October 1994.

Blue-footed Boobies have been recorded in the United States during each month of the year, but records are mainly from late July through late October with peak occurrence from mid-August through late September. Most winter and spring records are of birds that lingered after arriving in the fall. Notably, the pattern along the coast is similar to the pattern inland.

High counts are as follows:

Salton Sea

48, September 6, 1971
40, August 5, 1972
30, September 15, 1969

Inland California (excluding Salton Sea)

6, Puddingstone Reservoir, August 20, 1971

Colorado River

5, Martinez Lake, mid-August, 1971

Pacific Coast

7, Port San Luis, August 22, 1971

Best Bets

The Salton Sea is clearly the place to look for this bird, and the northern end has generally been best (though this was not true in 1990). Other spots to check for Blue-footed Boobies include the western Salton Sea shore from Salton City to Salton Sea Beach and the south end of the Salton Sea between Obsidian Butte and Red Hill.

Identification

The separation of Blue-footed Boobies from Brown Boobies is usually fairly straightforward (see the NGS guide for good drawings; also, see Harrison [1983] and Harrison [1987]). A point to remember is that adult male Brown Boobies from the Gulf of California have pale heads, thereby increasing the resemblance to the Blue-footed Booby. Also, immature Blue-footed Boobies can have rather dark heads. When in doubt, you should look for the Blue-foot's pale nape, rump, and tail patches.

Telling a Blue-footed Booby from immature Red-footed and Masked Boobies can be more complicated. The key marks, once again, are the Blue-foot's nape, rump, and tail patches. In some immature Blue-foots these pale patches can be difficult to see. Secondary marks include head, nape, and upper chest pattern as well as bill size and shape. For more details see Harrison (1983 and 1987). **(See color photo on page 461.)**

Blue-footed Booby—*all records*

LOCATION	NUMBERS SEEN	DATES SEEN
1929		
north end Salton Sea, CA	1	11/1 to 11/11
1933		
Big Bear Lake, CA	1	11/1
1935		
Everett, WA	1	9/23
1947		
Sierra Madre, CA	1	8/18
1953		
Phoenix, AZ	1	7/29
Lake Havasu, AZ	1	9/19
Lake Havasu, AZ[1]	2	10/5
Salton Sea[2]	3	10/18 to 10/31
1954		
Lake Havasu, AZ	1	8/13
Lake Havasu, AZ	1	9/4 to 9/10
1959		
Lake Havasu, AZ	1	late 11/58 to 4/11/59
1964		
Puddingstone Reservoir, CA[3]	2	11/15/64 to 5/9/65
1965		
Lake Matthews, CA	1	5/22 and 7/19
north end Salton Sea, CA	1	7/24 and 8/21
Thousand Palms, CA	2	9/3
near Whitewater, CA	1	9/20
1966		
Salton Sea, CA	1	8/4 to 10/6
1968		
Ocotillo, CA (dead)	1 (dead)	8/4
north end Salton Sea, CA	1	8/10 to 9/1
1969		
Salton Sea, CA (max, 30)[4]		8/31 to 11/23
1970		
Salton Sea, CA	1	8/15
1971		
Lake Mead, NV	3	8/27 to 12/22 (1 to 1/23/72)
Martinez Lake, AZ[5]	5	mid-8/71 to mid-2/72
Pacific Grove, CA[6]	4	10/16 to 10/17
Salton Sea, CA (max, 48)[7]		8/7 to 11/6
near Thousand Palms, CA	2	8/15
North Palm Springs, CA	1	8/21
near Whitewater, CA	1	8/15
near Sunnymead, CA	2	8/23
Mira Loma, CA	1	8/23

LOCATION	NUMBERS SEEN	DATES SEEN
Puddingstone Reservoir, CA[8]	6	8/12 to 11/31
Tarzana, CA	1	8/20
Port San Luis, CA	7	8/22
Goleta, CA	1	9/1
Los Angeles County coast	1+	8/21 to 8/25
Santa Catalina Island, CA	1	8/21
Imperial Beach, CA	1	9/6
Palos Verdes Peninsula, CA	1	11/21
Long Beach, CA	1	11/11 to 11/14
1972		
Salton Sea, CA (max, 40)[9]	1	7/22 to 10/26
Lake San Marcos, CA	1	late 8 to 12/14
1974		
San Gabriel, CA	1	10/15
1976		
New Hogan Reservoir, CA	1	9/15 to 10/18
off Santa Cruz Island, CA	1	6/22
South Padre Island, TX	1	10/5
1977		
Lake Mohave, NV/AZ	1	9/7
Lake Havasu, AZ	1	9/14 to 9/24
San Francisco, CA	1	9/1
Lake Henshaw, CA	1	8/18
north end Salton Sea, CA	11	8/24 to 10/9
1980		
Oceanside, CA	1	3/16/80
north end Salton Sea, CA[10]	5	9/12 to 10/23
1981		
Point St. George, CA	1	1/16/81
1990		
Salton Sea, CA [11]	4	7/12 to 10/3
Lake Havasu, AZ	1	9/16 to 10/20
Huntington Beach, CA	1	9/7
4.3 mi SW of Seeley, CA	1	9/2
1993		
Lake Mead, NV	1	7/23
north end Salton Sea, CA	1	7/25
Cameron, AZ	1	7/27
Lake Lyndon B. Johnson, TX	1	6/2/93 to 10/94
Rejected by state BRC		
between Ventura & Anacapa Island	1	1/8/72
north end Salton Sea, CA	1 (dead)	9/11/73
Manhattan Beach, CA	1	8/30/77
Point Loma, CA	1	8/26/77

[1] different from bird on 9/19.
[2] 3 on 10/18 with 1 to 10/31.
[3] 2 from 11/15 to 11/31 with 1 to 5/9.
[4] 1 on 8/31, 5 on 9/5, 30 on 9/15, 1 on 11/23.
[5] 5 during mid-August with 1 to mid-February 1972.
[6] 4 on 10/16, 2 on 10/17.
[7] 2 on 8/7 going to 48 on 9/6 and decreasing to 2 on 11/6.
[8] 1 on 8/12 increasing to 6 on 8/20, with 1 to 11/31.
[9] 12 on 7/22 growing to 40 on 8/5; 3 still there on 9/24 and 1 to 10/26.
[10] 2 on 9/12 growing to 5 on 9/20 with 1 remaining to 10/23.
[11] 4 on 7/12 with 1 to 10/3.

Brown Booby

Sula leucogaster

Status and Distribution

The Brown Booby is a widespread, common bird of the world's tropical oceans. It is also the most widespread booby in the Lower 48, where it has been recorded in 15 states. It has never bred in the Lower 48 (Stevenson and Anderson 1994), but nests as close as the central Bahamas, Cuba, and the northern Sea of Cortez (a.k.a. Gulf of California) (Nelson 1978). As with other species so widely distributed, the Brown Booby's status is best digested in parts.

The subspecies that reaches the eastern United States is the nominate *S. leucogaster leucogaster*. The adults of this subspecies are the classic chocolate brown booby with a sparkling white belly. In Florida, this bird is fairly common year-round in the Dry Tortugas and at Rebecca Shoals, which lies between the Tortugas and Key West. Elsewhere in the state, the Brown Booby is a year-round visitor in small numbers. Between 1972 and 1994, there were 72 sightings published in *American Birds* and *Field Notes* from Florida (excluding the Dry Tortugas and Rebecca Shoals). Although there is no dramatic temporal pattern, these records do seem to show some peak from early September through early November. There are also two inland records from Florida, both from Lake Okeechobee: November 27, 1980, and January 17, 1983. The maximum Lower 48 Brown Booby count was recorded on April 20, 1994, when 17 were tallied at the Dry Tortugas.

Along the Gulf Coast from Alabama through Texas, Brown Boobies average about 2 birds per year with 45 reported in *American Birds* and *Field Notes* between 1972 and 1994 (excluding rather odd and rejected reports from Texas during spring 1989). Of these, 23 were from Alabama,

18 were from Texas, and 4 were from Louisiana. Northern and western Gulf Coast records are spread year-round but are concentrated between late March and late September. The maximum Texas count is of six birds off Freeport on March 30, 1990. The highest daily count from Alabama was tallied on January 11, 1979, when five were seen offshore.

Along the Atlantic Coast, from Georgia north, the Brown Booby is seen only about once per year. Between 1972 and 1994, there were 24 Brown Boobies reported from this region with 1 in Georgia, 7 in North Carolina, 7 in New York, 7 in New Jersey, and 2 in Rhode Island. There are also older records from South Carolina, Virginia, and Massachusetts. Recent records from this region have been between late May and late October with one record from December (Little Egg Harbor, NJ, December 16, 1990).

The Brown Booby that is found in the southwestern Lower 48 is *S. leucogaster brewsteri* from Mexico. The adult males of this subspecies show extensive gray frosting to the head and neck. This bird is a sporadic visitor to California, Arizona, and Nevada. Between 1972 and 1994, there were 38 sightings reported from this region in *American Birds* and *Field Notes*. Of these, 33 were in California and 5 were from Arizona. The Nevada record was from 1971, when 2 birds were seen on Lake Mead.

What is initially surprising is that most southwestern records of this bird come from inland locations and not the Pacific Coast. Indeed, 29 of California's 40 accepted records are from the interior, mostly from the Salton Sea and lower Colorado River valley. To explain this pattern, you need to consider that the nearest breeding colonies are at Consag Rock and Georges Island at the far northern end of the Sea of Cortez. The Brown Boobies that show up along the Colorado River and Salton Sea are undoubtedly part of the same phenomenon that brings Blue-footed Boobies to these desert regions (see "Blue-footed Booby," p. 61). The northernmost western Lower 48 records come from the Farallon Islands, where Brown Boobies have been seen on several occasions.

Southwestern Brown Booby records occur in two different temporal patterns. Coastal records are scattered throughout the year, with a vague peak from August through October. Inland records are heavily concentrated between mid-July and mid-October. Inland overwintering, however, is not unknown as is amply evidenced by the bird that stayed at Martinez

Lake from September 5, 1958, to October 7, 1960. The maximum Brown Booby count in the southwestern Lower 48 occurred when eight were seen in September 1969 at the Salton Sea and in July 1990, when again eight were found there.

Best Bets

Your best bet for the Brown Booby lies to the southwest of Key West at Rebecca Shoals and the Dry Tortugas. In both places, buoys, lane markers, and other structures are frequently used as perches.

Identification

The adult Brown Booby is a distinctive bird. Only the immature Masked Booby shows any real resemblance. The Masked can be distinguished from an adult Brown by its white neck collar, more limited brown neck and upper chest, and white on the underwing extending into the primary coverts.

Immature Brown Boobies are less distinctive, and you'll need to consider several other sulids. Immature Maskeds can once again be distinguished by their neck collar. The Blue-footed Booby can be separated by its whitish dorsal patches. The immature Red-footed usually has a diffuse breast band and lacks much of an underwing pattern. Also, the Red-footed is smaller and slimmer. Immature Northern Gannets, on the other hand, are larger. With a reasonable view, the spangling on the gannet's upperparts should help identify it. Finally, immature Brown Boobies usually show at least a hint of the breast and belly demarcation seen in adults. This can help eliminate all other boobies and gannets. For more details and good photos, see the MGB and Harrison (1987); see also Howell and Webb (1995). **(See color photo on page 462.)**

Brown Booby—*records excluding Florida**

LOCATION	NUMBERS SEEN	DATES SEEN
Massachusetts		
Chatham	1	5/30/46
Cape Cod	1	9/18/78
Rhode Island		
8 mi SE of Block Island	1	5/25/77
on boat, Cox's Ledge		
to Narragansett County	1	8/19 to 8/26/89
New York		
Mecox Bay	1	9/2/36
off Moriches Inlet	1	9/3/49
Gardiner's Island, Long Island	1	6/2/73
Hudson Canyon	1	6/27/73
Fire Island Inlet, Long Island	1	7/14/91
Shinnecock Inlet to Jones Beach	2	9/28 to 10/13/75
Jones Beach, Long Island	1	10/4/90
off Island Beach	1	10/29/79
New Jersey		
off Manasquan Inlet	3	6/3/73
off Island Beach	2	10/22/79
Cape May	1	5/26/80
30 mi off New Jersey	1	6/3/73
Cape May	1	9/22 to 9/23/89
Sandy Hook	1	9/26/90
Little Egg Harbor Inlet	1	12/16/90
Virginia		
Fisherman's Island	1	6/26/82
Lynnhaven Inlet	1	6/27 to 9/29/68
Smithville	1	7/9 to 7/13/68
Chincoteague	1	9/30/72
North Carolina		
off Oregon Inlet	1	7/9/94
off Hatteras	1	7/24/94
at Hatteras Inlet	1	8/6/94
off Hatteras	1	8/15/94
Cape Lookout	1	8/28/93
off Hatteras	1	9/9/94
off Hatteras		9/17/94
South Carolina		
Charleston	1	1/4/68
Georgia		
off coast	1	5/14/83
Alabama		
off coast	5	1/11/79
off coast	3	1/28/79
Dauphin Island	1	4/11 to 4/14/69

LOCATION	NUMBERS SEEN	DATES SEEN
Mobile Bay	1	4/16/84
Fort Morgan	1	4/23/88
Dauphin Island	4	4/24/79
Fort Morgan	1	4/24/85
Alabama Point	1	4/27/80
Gulf Shores	1	4/30/85
Gulf Shores	1	5/2/85
Mississippi Sound	1	6/18/70
off Dauphin Island	1	6/22/78
Dauphin Island	1	7/1980
Sand Island	1	7/6/69
location?	1	7/15/76
Orange Beach	1	8/5/83
Dauphin Island	1	8/26/61
Fort Morgan	1	9/27/80

Louisiana

well off SE Louisiana	1	3/11/92
SW pass of Mississippi River	1	5/29 to 6/7/85
20 mi SSE of SW pass of Mississippi River	1	6/1 to 6/8/85
Elmer's Island	1	7/18/73

Texas

off Port Aransas	1	3/8/77
Matagorda	1	3/15/89
Freeport	6	3/30/90
North Padre Island	1	5/16 to 5/18/83
Port Isabel	1	5/30/74
Sundown Island	1	6/3/79
off Galveston	1	6/8/72
Calhoun/Aransas County line	1	6/25/48
Galveston County	1	7/25/83
off Galveston	1	7/28/84
off Mustang Island	2	8/10/61
Mustang Island	1	8/11/80
off Sabine Pass	1	8/18/61
Padre Island	1	8/19/67
Port Aransas	2	8/20/77
off Brownsville	1	8/20/79
Port Aransas	1	8/23 to 8/24/80
off Port Aransas	1	8/25/84
off Port Aransas	1	8/30/75
off Port Aransas	1	9/4/76
Port Aransas	1	9/20/71
Padre Island	1	9/23/67
Laguna Madre	1	9/24/88
Boca Chica	1	12/20/87
Galveston	1	12/22/80

LOCATION	NUMBERS SEEN	DATES SEEN
Rejected by TX BRC		
South Padre Island	1	3/27/89
near High Island	170	3/31/89
Gilchrist	4	4/1/89
Matagorda County		4/21/85
Nevada		
Lake Mead	2	8/27 to 9/19/71 (1 to 12/5/71)
Arizona		
S of Yuma	1	7/15/90
Lake Havasu (also in CA)	1	8/19 to 11/?/77
Lake Havasu	1	9/5/53
Martinez Lake (also in CA)	1	9/5/58 to 10/7/60
SE of Yuma	1	9/12/90
Phoenix	1	9/14 to 10/11/90
N of Congress	1	10/21 to 10/26/91
California (also see AZ)		
Pacific Grove	1	12/3/87
Santa Barbara Island	1	3/25/84
Imperial Beach	1	4/2/90
SE Farallon Islands	1	5/25 to 11/13/92
Santa Barbara Island	1	6/2/92
Point Lobos	1	6/15 to 6/19/88
Farallon Islands	1	7/1/84
San Miguel Island	1	7/3 to 7/5/65
Salton Sea	8	7/12 to 7/31/90 (1 until 9/29/90)
near Calexico	1	7/15/72
below Imperial Dam	1	7/25/90
north end Salton Sea	1	7/28 to 8/13/66
north end Salton Sea	2	8/5 to 8/26/72
Santa Barbara Island	1	8/8/91
Farallon Islands	1	8/9/94
Los Angeles Harbor	1	8/14/94
Rock Hill, Salton Sea	1	8/15 to 8/23/70
SE Farallon Islands	1	8/16 to 10/18/93
near Salton City	1	8/23/77
north end Salton Sea	1	8/24 to 9/2/74
north end Salton Sea	1	8/28 to 9/7/71
Rock Hill, Salton Sea	1	8/29 to 9/18/71
Mountain View	1	8/29/92
Salton City	1	9/4/72
Salton Sea (up to 8)	1+	9/6/69 to 4/25/70
Imperial Dam	1	9/20/46
SE Farallon Islands	1	9/24 to 9/28/83
south end Salton Sea	1	10/1967
3 mi SE of Santa Barbara Island	1	10/15/88
near Santa Barbara Island	1	10/29/83

LOCATION	NUMBERS SEEN	DATES SEEN
Headgate Rock Dam	1	11/20/57
San Diego Bay	1	12/14/91
Rejected by CA BRC		
6 mi NE of Point Vicente	1	9/15/90

*All records are given for California, Texas, Alabama, Georgia, South Carolina, Virginia, New Jersey, New York, and Massachusetts. Other states have comprehensive lists from *American Birds* and *Field Notes* from 1972 on.

Atlantic records north of Florida*

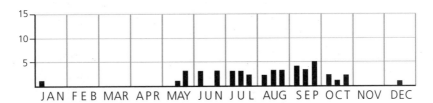

Gulf Coast records west of Florida*

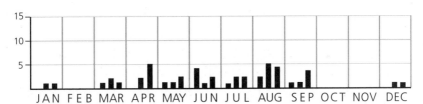

inland Southwest records*

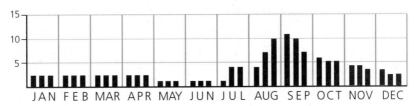

coastal Southwest records*

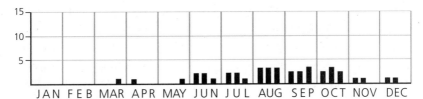

*sightings of multiple birds counted as one

Red-footed Booby

Sula sula

Status and Distribution

The Red-footed Booby is a species with many guises. Some adults are all brown and raise the specter of an immature Brown Booby. Others are mostly white with black flight feathers and appear much like a Masked Booby. Still others are brown with white tail, rump, and tail coverts. All adults do share one feature, however—brilliant red legs and feet.

The Red-footed Booby is a common bird throughout most of the world's tropical oceans. The breeding colonies closest to the United States include Islas Revillagigedo south of Baja California Sur (Howell and Webb 1995) and several islands in the northern Caribbean from just east of the Yucatan Peninsula to Puerto Rico (Nelson 1978). The birds at the Islas Revillagigedo are 95 percent white morph, with the remainder being some combination of brown and white. The Red-foots in the Caribbean are also 95 percent white morph with the remainder being mostly white-tailed brown morph. Birds might also wander to the Lower 48 from Clipperton Atoll off southwestern Mexico, where brown morphs predominate, or from Hawaii, where Red-foots are almost entirely white morph.

Sadly, the Red-footed Booby is rather rare in the Lower 48. There are only about 30 records, the majority from Florida. The first of Florida's roughly 20 records was at Clearwater Beach on September 30, 1963. Since then most Florida sightings have been from the Dry Tortugas. Other non-Tortugas Florida records include the following: off Cocoa Beach, September 18, 1975; 20 miles south of Bahia Honda Key, May 6, 1978; Lake Worth, spring 1980; Dog Island, after Hurricane Juan, October 26, 1985; and Cape Canaveral National Seashore, June 19, 1993.

Most Florida records are from April into September. Extreme dates are March 19, 1991, at the Dry Tortugas and October 26, 1985, at Dog Island.

Other reports from the southeastern United States come from Alabama, Louisiana, Texas, and South Carolina. The Alabama bird was seen at Gulf Shores on January 12, 1979. The Louisiana record was from the mouth of the Bayou Scofield on November 1, 1940. Texas records include a bird off Galveston on March 27, 1983 and a bird at South Padre Island on August 26, 1968. The only South Carolina record was seen on July 27, 1986, at Edisto Island.

Accepted California sightings number approximately 12, all since 1975. These have been fairly evenly scattered along California's coast north to San Francisco. Most have been from mid-August to mid-October, though records also exist for February, May, June, and November.

Best Bets

Without a doubt, the best place to see Red-footed Boobies in the Lower 48 is the Dry Tortugas. Organized tours typically search several of these keys as well as the surrounding waters. Unless you have your own boat, these tours are your best shot. Keep in mind that Red-footed Boobies will hitch rides on boats by standing on elevated perches. More than one has been seen sailing into a harbor in just such a manner.

Identification

The identification problems provided by Red-footed Boobies depend on the morph you're pondering. The white-tailed brown morphs are unique among boobies in their combination of brown body and white tail. The white morph resembles the Masked Booby but has a white tail (except Galapagos birds), white tertials, and a black carpal patch on the underwing (see Harrison 1983 and 1987). Brown morph birds can be separated from immature Brown Boobies by uniform brown underwings (see Harrison 1983). Also, young Brown Boobies typically show a shadow of the adult's underpart pattern. All adult Red-footed Boobies are also separable from other boobies by their red feet and proportionately small bill.

Immature birds are depicted differently in almost every text, which may be due to confusion with various incarnations of dark morph birds. In these birds, structure and size are definitely important. Also, some have dull reddish legs, especially as they approach adulthood. In immatures with some white on the underparts, the dark brown head and neck are separated from the rest of the dark brown upperparts by a whitish hind-collar (Howell and Webb 1995). See photos in Harrison (1987). **(See color photo on page 462.)**

Red-footed Booby—*all records**

LOCATION	NUMBERS SEEN	DATES SEEN
California		
161-141 mi WSW of San Nicolas Island	1	2/1/92
Morro Bay	1	5/27/85
Daly City	1	6/13/94
La Jolla	1	8/13/93
Point San Pedro[1]	1	8/14 to 8/20/87
Redondo Beach	1	8/18/91
SE Farallon Islands	1	8/26/75
San Francisco[1]	1	1st 2 weeks Sep 1987
Moss Landing	1	10/8/87
Santa Barbara Island	1	10/11/87
SE Farallon Islands	1	10/12/75
San Francisco Bay	1	10/13 to 10/18/87
7 mi E of Santa Barbara Island	1	11/15/87
Texas		
near Rockport	1	prior to 1910
off Galveston	1	3/27/83
South Padre Island	1	8/26/68
Louisiana		
mouth of Bayou Scofield	1	11/1/40
Alabama		
Gulf Shores	1	1/12/79
Florida		
Dry Tortugas	1	3/19/91
8 mi S of Dry Tortugas	1	early April 1994
Dry Tortugas	1	4/10 to 5/17/93
Dry Tortugas	1	4/23/91
Dry Tortugas	1	4/24 to 6/5/79
Dry Tortugas	1	5/2 to 5/3/77
Dry Tortugas	1	5/2 to 5/8/82
Dry Tortugas	1	5/4 to 5/5/74
20 mi S of Bahia Honda Key	1	5/6/78
Dry Tortugas	1	5/25/78

LOCATION	NUMBERS SEEN	DATES SEEN
Lake Worth	1	spring 1980
Dry Tortugas	1	6/17 to 6/22/74
Dry Tortugas	1	7/4/78
South Carolina		
Edisto Island	1	7/27/86

*Florida records since 1972 only.
[1]Considered to be same bird.

Greater Flamingo

Phoenicopterus ruber

 **Status and Distribution**

The problem posed by the Greater Flamingo in the United States has not been as much where to look or how to find them, but rather "Are they or are they not wild?" Flamingos, with their spindly legs, long necks, and shocking-pink plumage, are popular birds in captivity. Over the years, there has been that nagging doubt about the origin of any flamingo seen anywhere in the United States, even the ones in extreme southern Florida, where they could easily have wandered from breeding colonies in Cuba or the Bahamas.

There's no doubt, however, that wild flamingos once were part of Florida's avifauna. Flocks in the thousands were reported from Cape Sable and other areas around Florida Bay until at least 1902. At that time, flamingos were also rare to uncommon elsewhere on the Florida coasts. These birds may have come from Andros Island, Bahamas, where the species bred until about 1904. Most records during this era were between June and February.

Thereafter, flamingos were very rare anywhere in Florida until the 1930s, when captive flocks became established. Since the 1950s, small groups have been seen fairly regularly at Snake Bight and its environs in Everglades National Park. This group has had up to 40 individuals, often including both adults and immatures. Sightings from other parts of Florida have remained infrequent and are predominantly coastal. Recent reports are mostly from fall and winter. The lack of sightings from late summer and early fall may well be related to fewer observers in the Everglades at those times.

Regarding that annoying origin question of modern day birds, it's interesting to recall how flamingos have been viewed in *American Birds*:

1983: "We may never be able to recognize true vagrants."

1984: "Origin uncertain."

1988: "It may require nothing less than a national referendum to settle the debate whether these flamingos, and the dozens that have been at Snake Bight in previous years, are wild birds from Cuba or the Bahamas, or escapees!"

1990: "Of uncertain origin."

1992: Florida regional editor J. C. Odgen wrote of birds at Sandy Key, in Everglades National Park, "This flock, like several before it, contained a mix of adults and immatures; my intuitive opinion after watching these flocks come and go for over 25 years is that they are wild birds out of the Caribbean."

A large factor adding to the debate over flamingo origins is the sizable feral flock at Hialeah Park, Dade County. This group numbers in the hundreds, is free-flying, and breeds successfully with some regularity. It is conceivable that some of the adults and young from this flock have been making a yearly jaunt to Florida Bay. On the other hand, birds banded in southern Bahama breeding areas have been found as far west as western Cuba.

At any rate, Greater Flamingos in Florida Bay are considered "countable" by the American Birding Association, which has recognized the tendency of flamingos to wander, and the improbability that a portion of the feral Hialeah flock has established a regular migration route to Everglades National Park. The *AOU Check-list* also recognizes flamingos' wandering instinct, and lists sightings from Texas, Kansas, Michigan, and Nova Scotia, among others, with the caveat that "some of the foregoing vagrant records (especially the northern ones) may . . . pertain to . . . escapees."

In reality, only the Everglades birds can probably be counted with reasonable confidence. Birds elsewhere have a substantial chance of being escapees, especially as one gets farther from known breeding colonies in the the Bahamas, Cuba, and the Yucatan. There is only one accepted U.S. record outside Florida: an individual that appeared at South Bird Island, in Laguna Madre, just south of Corpus Christi, Texas, each year from

1978 to 1982. Typically this bird arrived in March and remained until late summer. Thirteen other reports from Texas have been neither accepted nor rejected.

Best Bets

Almost all U.S. flamingos are seen in Florida Bay, the shallow wedge of island-dotted ocean between the main Florida Keys and the tip of the mainland. There's hardly any sense in looking anywhere else, even for a hotline bird, since the origin of a flamingo seen elsewhere would almost certainly be questioned. Flamingos in Florida Bay are probably best looked for near Snake Bight, Everglades National Park, between July and February. For more details, see the "Site Guide" for the Everglades, p. 384.

Identification

You might think disparagingly, How hard can it be to identify a flamingo? In some ways you'd be right. After all, a Greater Flamingo is half again as tall as a Roseate Spoonbill, and the two birds' bills are as different as a linoleum knife and a spatula. Unfortunately, other species (and subspecies) of flamingos must be considered. Clements (1991) lists five species of flamingos: Greater, Lesser, Chilean, Andean, and Puna. Furthermore, the Greater Flamingo can be separated into New World and Old World subspecies. Before even considering whether you have a wild Greater Flamingo in your sight, you'd best be certain of the correct species and subspecies.

The New World subspecies of Greater Flamingo is best separated from the Old World subspecies by bill color. Whereas an adult of the American persuasion has a tricolored bill (pale yellowish or creamy at the base, pink in the middle, and black at the tip; see NGS guide or Howell and Webb 1995), the adult European's is pink and black (see Jonsson 1993). Immatures also show this pattern but are not as bright. Furthermore, Old World Greater Flamingos are generally paler than New World Greater Flamingos, but color can vary, especially among escaped birds.

Andean, Chilean, and Puna Flamingos are generally paler than the New World Greater Flamingo. In addition, these birds have bicolored black-and-yellow bills. The Chilean can be quickly identified by its dull-colored legs with pink or red "knees." The Puna has all dark brick red legs, and the Andean has dull yellow legs (see Dunning 1987). The Lesser Flamingo, which hails from Africa, can be identified by its black and very dark-red bill that looks all dark at a distance. Lessers also have ragged or blotchy-looking dark pink wing coverts.   **(See color photo on page 463.)**

Emperor Goose

Chen canagica

Status and Distribution

An Emperor Goose is a stunning sight, indeed. Its beautiful plumage is an intense blue-gray that is highlighted by delicate bars of black and white. Its legs are fluorescent orange, and the bill is brilliant pink. As you would expect, such a gaudy goose is a vagrant in the Lower 48. Its normal breeding range is western Alaska (especially the Yukon delta) and extreme eastern Siberia where it nests on coastal tundra. In winter, the majority of birds head for the Aleutian Islands. Fortunately, each year a couple of Emperor Geese find their way to the Pacific Coast of the Lower 48.

In total, there have been about 235 Emperor Geese recorded in the Lower 48, of which 50 or so have been seen since 1981. Of the recent records, approximately half have been from the outer Pacific Coast and half have been from more inland areas. In general, records decrease as one heads south, with the southernmost sighting coming from Anaheim Bay, Orange County, California, from December 15, 1968, to March 18, 1969. There is but one Emperor Goose record away from the Pacific Coast states: Overton National Wildlife Refuge, Nevada, December 11, 1960.

Emperor Geese favor two distinctly different habitats. One cadre occurs on coastal mudflats and rocky shores whereas the other group prefers grassy pasturelike habitats. The coastal birds are not usually in the company of other geese. The inland birds, however, often graze with "Cackling" Canada Geese or Greater White-fronted Geese, both of which are neighbors on the Alaskan breeding grounds.

In the Lower 48, Emperor Geese occur mainly as migrants and winter visitors. Most records have been between early October and mid-May, but a few have summered. Peak occurrence during the past ten years has been from mid-January into mid-March. This corresponds fairly well with Roberson's (1980) summary of earlier records, which shows peak occurrence between mid-December and late February. High counts come from Gold Beach, Oregon, where 17 were seen from April 1 to May 8, 1943 and Tule Lake National Wildlife Refuge, California, where 25 were seen on November 2, 1964.

Inland Emperor Geese, especially those at parks, often incite lively debate. Individuals occurring where wildlife are fed tend to become quite tame; however, this is true of geese in general. For instance, in coastal southern California, Ross', Snow, and Greater White-fronted Geese are all uncommon to rare. Nonetheless, each of these occurs regularly in city parks where they become tame. Even Brant sometimes behave in this fashion. Some of these apparently wild-origin geese grow so comfortable that they never leave. That such has happened with the occasional Emperor Goose should come as no surprise. The wild origin of inland Emperors in general is supported by their strong tendency to occur in the Northwest (from northern California up) and the almost complete lack of records away from the Pacific Coast states. Nonetheless, occasional escapes do undoubtedly occur.

Best Bets

Clearly the best area for Emperor Geese is the Lower Klamath Basin National Wildlife Refuges, in southern Oregon and northern California, where they have been reported 9 of the last 18 falls. Most records from Klamath fall between early October and late November. If you are looking for Emperors elsewhere, a good strategy would be to sort through flocks of "Cackling" Geese.

Identification

Not much needs to be said about the identification of this striking bird. Any resemblance between this species and blue morph Ross' or blue morph Snow Geese is superficial at best. You should note, however, that this is our only goose with dark undertail coverts. You should also be aware that the immature plumage depicted in the NGS guide is briefly held. By late October, the head and neck of most first-year Emperors are largely white, thus resembling an adult. **(See color photo on page 464.)**

Emperor Goose—*records since 1982*

LOCATION	NUMBERS SEEN	DATES SEEN
Smith River mouth/Fort Dick area, CA	1	1/9 to 2/19/82
Lower Klamath NWR, CA	1	10/20/82
Yachats, OR	1	10/29/83 to 2/28/84
0.5 mi W of Dorris, CA	1	11/5/83
Coos Bay, OR	1	11/19/83
Hunter Rock, Prince Island, CA	1	1/13 to 1/16/84
Hunter Rock, Prince Island, CA	1	2/25/84
Portland, OR	1	2/15 to summer 1984
Neah Bay, WA	3	3/9 to 3/16/85
Newport, OR	1	3/20/85
Willapa Bay, WA	1	3/22/85
Dungeness, WA	1	1/20 to 4/5/86
Vancouver, WA	1	10/27 to 12/27/86
Ridgefield NWR, WA (same as above?)	1	11/26/86
Tule Lake NWR, CA	1	10/19/86 to 2/14/87
Ankeny NWR, OR	1	11/23/86 to 3/3/87
Umpqua River Estuary, OR	1	12/10/86
Seattle, WA	1	winter to 3/16/87
Olympia, WA	1	summered 1987
Tule Lake NWR, CA	1	11/6 to 11/13/87
Alameda, CA	1	12/19/87 to 4/17/88
Ocean Shores, WA	1	wintered 1987-8
Seattle, WA	1	wintered 1987-8
Port Susan, WA	1	wintered 1987-8
Hines, OR	1	3/8 to 3/15/88
Glide, OR	1	3/13 to 3/20/88
Tokeland, WA	1	4/1 to 4/24/88
Ridgefield NWR, WA	2	4/7/88
southern Oregon Coast	5	winter 1988-9
Charleston, OR	1	1/20 to 4/8/90
Puget Sound region, WA	3	spring 1990
Clallam County, WA	2	spring 1990
Oceanside, WA	3	early 10/90
Farallon Islands, CA	2	1/25/91
Farallon Islands, CA	1 (1 of above birds)	1/26 to 3/25/91
Point Reyes, CA	1	2/11 to 3/9/91
Seaside, OR	1	5/8/91
Sauvie Island, OR	1	10/16/91
Bay Center, WA	1	11/15 to 11/23/91
Lincoln County, OR	1	12/20/92 to 2/27/93

LOCATION	NUMBERS SEEN	DATES SEEN
Willamette Valley, OR	1	12/6/92 to early 3/93
Snohomish, WA	2	1/93 to 5/93
Snohomish, WA	2	10/3/93 to late 4/93
Everett, WA	1	3/93 to 5/29/93
near Florence, OR	1	12/12/93 to 3/24/94
Rejected by CA BRC		
Tule Lake NWR, CA	1	10/21 to 11/11/91

Emperor Geese —all records from Klamath Basin National Wildlife Refuges*

LOCATION	NUMBERS SEEN	DATES SEEN
Tule Lake NWR	1 with White-fronts	4/18/55
Tule Lake NWR	1 with White-fronts	late 10/55
Lower Klamath NWR	1 immature	date unknown, 1958
Tule Lake NWR, Upper Sump	2 shot from flock of 25	11/2/64
Upper Klamath NWR, Oregon	1 shot by hunter	1/18/65
Lower Klamath NWR, unit 7	1 with Ross' Geese	3/6/65
Upper Klamath NWR, Oregon	1 adult w/ White-fronted Geese shot 10/18/65	
Tule Lake NWR	9	during last half of 11/65
Tule Lake NWR	1	3/10 to 3/25/68
Tule Lake NWR	1	during 11/68
Tule Lake NWR	1 adult with White-fronted Geese	10/10/71
Tule Lake NWR	1 adult	11/23/71
Tule Lake NWR	1	2/17/72
Lower Klamath NWR, unit 8	1 immature shot	10/73
Lower Klamath NWR, unit 12	1 adult w/ White-fronted and Snow Geese 11/73	
Tule Lake NWR, Frog Pond Unit and Lower Sump	1	11/5 to 11/6/73
Tule Lake NWR	2 immatures shot	10/18/77
Tule Lake NWR	1 shot	10/20/77
Tule Lake NWR vicinity	1	3/28/78
Lower Klamath NWR, unit 6	1 adult	10/28/79
Tule Lake NWR, English Channel	1 adult	11/27/79
Tule Lake NWR, Frog Pond Unit	1 adult shot	10/18/81
Tule Lake NWR, lower sump	1 adult with Cackling Geese	10/27 to late 11/81
Lower Klamath NWR	1	10/20/82
0.5 mi W of Dorris	1	11/5/83 (CA BRC)
Tule Lake NWR	1	from 10/9 to early 11/86
Tule Lake NWR	1	from 11/6 to 11/13/87
Tule Lake NWR, Southwest Sump	1	10/19/88
Tule Lake NWR	1 with White-fronted Geese	1/28/89
Tule Lake NWR, Frog Pond Unit	1 immature	10/30/89
Tule Lake NWR, Lower Sump	1 immature with Cackling Geese	10/21 to 11/11/91

*All records are from Lower Klamath National Wildlife Refuges' files or *American Birds*. It should be noted that the refuges' files are unreviewed. Though many birds were shot by hunters or seen by experienced refuge personnel, some of these records may be in error.

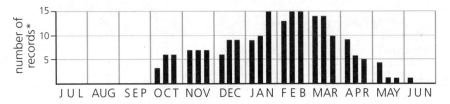

*sightings with multiple birds considered one record.

Barnacle Goose

Branta leucopsis

Status and Distribution

The Barnacle Goose did not get its odd name from any gustatory preference but rather from a peculiar medieval belief that these geese hatched from barnacles in the autumn. Obviously, Britain's ancient inhabitants were unaware of this species' nesting grounds in the high Arctic (Greenland; Svalbard, Norway; and Novaya Zemlya, Russia). After hatching their young from eggs (not barnacles), Barnacle Geese then migrate the short distance to Great Britain, Ireland, and nearby Europe. Occasionally, however, a goose goes awry, thereby providing records for the Mediterranean, Azores, North Africa, Canada, and the United States (AOU 1983).

The first U.S. record occurred on October 31, 1870, when one was found in Currituck Sound, North Carolina. The next occurrence was but six years later at Jamaica Bay, New York. Since then there have been more than 120 sightings, mostly from the northeastern United States. Indeed, New England has produced 24 reports, New York and Pennsylvania have had 28 records, and the Middle Atlantic states (New Jersey to Virginia) have had 26 records. Reports have come, however, from across the United States, including California, Washington, and Texas. States with published sightings include Maine, New Hampshire, Vermont, Massachusetts, Connecticut, Rhode Island, New York, Pennsylvania, New Jersey, Delaware, Maryland, Virginia, North Carolina, South Carolina, Michigan, Ohio, Kentucky, Tennessee, Alabama, Wisconsin, Illinois, Missouri, Nebraska, Oklahoma, Texas, Colorado, and California.

Barnacle Geese breed on coastal tundra and prefer to winter on coastal mudflats and farmland pastures. However, use of inland ponds in Europe is not unheard of and may be increasing (Owen 1977). Birds in the United States are usually seen in similar habitat and are most often in the company of other geese, especially Canadas.

As you would expect, Barnacle Geese in the U.S. are seen mostly during winter. All but three reports fall between early October and mid-May. The exceptions are a bird seen at Kennebunk, Maine, on June 4, 1985, one seen at Naubinway, Michigan, on May 21, 1965, and another at Colorado Springs during the summer of 1993. Peak time seems to be from mid-October through mid-March.

As with all waterfowl, extralimital records of Barnacle Geese are almost always accompanied by nagging doubts regarding origin. The Barnacle Goose, however, has an especially bad stigma. There are several good reasons for this. It is common in captivity, and the wide scatter of sightings across the United States is not consistent with a natural phenomenon.

On the other hand, the Barnacle Goose occurs with as good a temporal pattern as any vagrant waterfowl. Furthermore, it is an excellent candidate for natural vagrancy to the United States. It breeds fairly close to the United States in Greenland, and the population there recently underwent a great expansion (9,000 in 1959 to 28,000 in the mid-1970s; Owen 1977). Also, the Novaya Zemlya and Svalbard populations have a strong westerly component to their migration and could potentially overshoot their wintering grounds, thus ending up in North America. At least one Barnacle Goose from Canada was of proven wild origin: an individual shot out of a flock of three in Newfoundland during October 1981 had been originally banded in Spitzbergen, Svalbard (Montevicci and Wells 1984).

As with any other bird kept frequently in captivity, it's rarely possible to determine the origins of any specific Barnacle Goose seen flying free in the United States. However, some of those found along the Atlantic seaboard south to North Carolina are likely wild. Many are also likely escapees. Inland and more southerly birds are almost certainly escapees.

Best Bets

There is no specific site guide for this species as the records are fairly scattered. Any flock of geese, especially Canadas, from Maine to North Carolina should be carefully perused for Barnacle Geese. Areas with more than one record include Bombay Hook National Wildlife Refuge, Delaware (seven records), Iroquois National Wildlife Refuge, New York (four records), and Long Island, New York (seven records).

Identification

Barnacle Geese look little like any other goose species. However, some hybrid geese, especially Canada x Graylag and Canada x White-fronted, can superficially resemble a Barnacle Goose. Among other marks, note the black chest and neck, the scalloped black-and-gray mantle, and the dark-lored white face. Also, beware of Barnacle x Canada Geese—a hybrid that has been seen on at least one occasion (Szantyr 1985). **(See color photo on page 464.)**

Barnacle Goose—*all records*[1]

LOCATION	NUMBERS SEEN	DATES SEEN
Maine		
Kennebunk	1	6/4/85
Phippsburg	1	3/16 to 3/30/86
Vermont		
Marshfield	1	1878
Maidstone	1	5/15/90
New Hampshire		
Northumberland	2	5/15/90
Massachusetts		
North Eastham	3-4	11/1/1885
Beverly[2]	1	1/23/71
Wachusett Reservoir	1	11/4/79
Acushnet River, New Bedford	1	11/25/88 to 3/11/89
Lexington	1	12/6 to 12/7/90
Osterville[2]	6	1/18 to 3/22/91
South Dartmouth	1	2/6 to 3/20/94
Connecticut		
Westport	1	12/29/68
Norwalk[2]	1	1/5/69
Southbury	1	11/22/84 to 1/10/85

LOCATION	NUMBERS SEEN	DATES SEEN
Connecticut (cont.)		
Mansfield	1	9/15 to 9/21/86
Durham	1	11/20/88
Orange	1	12/12/90
Southbury	1	12/29/91, 2/2/92
Storrs	1	11/10 to 11/28/92
East Haven[2]	6	12/15/93
Westport	1	10/22/94
Mansfield	1	10/24/94
Rhode Island		
Newport	1	2/17/90
West Kingston	1	3/4 to 4/7/89
New York		
Jamaica Bay, Long Island	1	10/18/1876
Money Island, Long Island	1	10/16/19
Farmingdale, Long Island	1	11/28/22
Orient, Long Island	1	12/11/26
Shinnecock Bay, Long Island	1	Dec 1926
Little Neck Creek	1	3/19/33
Wolcottsville	1	March-April 1961
Wolcottsville	1	March-April 1963
Yates	1	3/29/67
Somerset	1	March and 4/1/67
Iroquois NWR	1	3/30/68
Pelham Bay, Long Island[2]	1	1/5/69
Bridgehampton, Long Island	1	3/17/74
Iroquois NWR	1	4/16/78
Cayuga Lake	1	10/31/81
Iroquois NWR	1	3/16/83
Dead Creek WMA	1	fall 1983
Iroquois NWR	1	3/25/84
Hamlin[3]	3	3/11 to 3/15/85
Tyre	1	11/27/86
Iroquois NWR	1	spring 1988
Cold Spring Harbor, Long Island	1	winter 1988-9
Amenia	1	until 3/11/90
East Martinsburg	1	4/7/92
Phoenix	1	4/11 to 4/26/92
Pennsylvania		
Lake Struble	1	3/2/78
Allentown	1	3/2 to 3/3/82
Middle Creek WMA	1	3/13 to 3/14/82
Millersville	1	3/12 to 3/17/86
Lake Galena	1	2/4 to 2/19/89
New Jersey		
Overpeck Creek	1	3/20/26

LOCATION	NUMBERS SEEN	DATES SEEN
Brigantine NWR	2	10/3/86
Mannington Marsh	1	1/31/88
Delaware		
Bombay Hook	1	11/13/65
Bombay Hook	1	11/25/67
Bombay Hook	1	11/13 to 12/26/73
Bombay Hook	1	1/1 to 1/26/80
Bombay Hook	1	2/20/82
Bombay Hook	1	12/14/82 to 1/2/83
Bombay Hook	1	2/6/86
Maryland		
Langford	1	11/12/47
Anacostia River	1	11/10/56
Blackwater NWR	1	11/26 to 11/28/64
Remington Farms	1	late 12/65
Blackwater NWR	1	11/25 to 12/14/66
near Chestertown	1	11/22/75
Blackwater NWR	1	1/9 to 1/10/79
10 mi S of Annapolis	1	1/9+ to 1/10/81
Patuxent Wildlife Center	1	5/8/81
Remington Farms	1	12/19/82
near Bowie	1	11/24/84
Deer Creek	1	2/24/85
Cambridge	1	1/2 to 2/21/86
Fruitland	1	10/13/86
Virginia		
Arlington	1	11/10/56
southeast of Richmond	2	12/23/87 to 1/12/88
North Carolina		
Currituck Sound	1	10/31/1870
Currituck Sound	1	11/22/1892
Ansonville	1	11/3 to 11/13/49
Pea Island	1	11/6/49
Dare County	1	11/23 to 12/28/50
Pea Island NWR	1	11/7 to 11/13/70
Coinjock	1	1/10 to 2/20/72
South Carolina		
Santee NWR	1	11/7/80 to 1/22/81
Michigan		
Naubinway	1	5/21/65
Shiawassee NWR (collected)	1	10/18/73
Shiawassee NWR (collected)	1	10/25/74
Fish Point	1	Oct 1976
Allegan State Game Area	2	10/22 to 10/25/79
Fish Point	1	3/30/80
Muskegon wastewater plant	1	3/7/83

LOCATION	NUMBERS SEEN	DATES SEEN
Michigan (continued).		
Allegan State Game Area	1	late 10 to 11/6/83
Quinicassee	1	4/15 to 4/19/92
Oakland County	1	12/18/93
Wisconsin		
Manitowoc County	1	10/23/77
Horicon NWR	1	late 9/79
Dodge County	1	10/26/85
Illinois		
Lisle Arboretum	2	12/8/68
Union County Conservation Area	1	1/3/81
Durand	1	1/1 to 1/30/83
Kentucky		
Sloughs WMA	1	1/13/83
Sloughs WMA	1	mid-Jan 1987
Tennessee		
Cove Lake	1	2/10 to 3/17/68
Tennessee NWR	1	3/1 to 4/24/70
Cross Creeks NWR	1	1/24 to 1/27/76
Tennessee NWR	1	1/11/83
Alabama		
Wheeler NWR	1	12/20/69
Wheeler NWR	2	11/22/70
Missouri		
St. Charles Marshes	1	3/26/50
Nebraska		
NE Otoe County	1	11/2/68
Oklahoma		
Salt Plains NWR	1	11/21/58
Amorita	1	12/14/63
Tishomingo NWR (up to 5)	2+	11/21/79 to 1/16/80
Caddo County	1	11/20/85
Texas		
Laguna Atascosa	1	11/30/68
Laguna Atascosa	1	11/69
eastern Chambers County	1	3/14/71
near Hagerman NWR	1	11/2 to 11/6/81
Colorado		
Basalt[2]	2	10/26 to 10/27/75
Colorado Springs	1	5/93 to 7/93
Washington		
Skagit WMA	2	9/30/61
Stratford	1	10/12 to 10/13/85
Centralia	1	12/20/93

LOCATION	NUMBERS SEEN	DATES SEEN
California[4]		
Tule Lake NWR	1	early 11/84
Colusa	1	12/7 to 12/10/84
Modesto area	1	12/12 to 12/21/84
Lower Klamath NWR	1	4/5 to 4/15/85

[1]Table based partially on Roberson 1985b.
[2]Known to be an escapee.
[3]Two of these birds were hybrid Canada x Barnacle Geese.
[4]All CA records presumably of same bird.

New England & Atlantic Coast states south to North Carolina

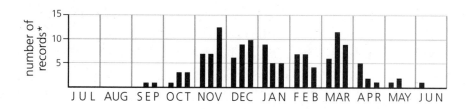

other states

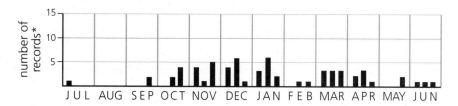

*sightings with multiple birds considered one record. Known escapees are excluded.

Muscovy Duck

Cairina moschata

Status and Distribution

This rather daffy-looking duck with the truly daffy name ("Muscovy" is derived from Moscow, Russia, although the species is found in the New World) is yet another specialty of the lower Rio Grande valley of Texas. As with the Greater Flamingo, the issue with the Muscovy is not where to find it or problematic identification, but rather the origin of individuals being seen in the United States.

Wild Muscovies breed as close to the United States as central Tamaulipas and Nuevo Leon (Howell and Webb 1995). Although they have been extirpated from parts of their range by hunting, a nest-box program instituted by Ducks Unlimited has helped populations recover, and Mexican populations are known within 100 miles of Brownsville. Thus, the Muscovy would certainly not be a surprise vagrant to southern Texas.

The issue is complicated, however, by the Muscovy's abundance as a feral bird. Tame Muscovies and Muscovy hybrids are widespread inhabitants of city parks throughout the Lower 48. Though many are somewhat bizarre in appearance, some look much like their wild forefathers. This is especially true in Brownsville where there is a particularly robust feral population.

The status of Muscovies seen in the Rio Grande valley began to be reconsidered in the mid-1980s. On December 7, 1984, at the famous Santa Margarita Ranch, an individual was observed in an immature plumage "rarely seen in feral birds." The next spring, two adults were seen at Santa Margarita Ranch and nearby Salineño. Since then, wild phenotype Muscovies have been observed regularly along the Rio Grande between Fronton and Falcon Dam, and apparently "good" birds have been seen from as far downriver as Santa Ana National Wildlife Refuge and as far upriver as San Ygnacio. High counts include 13 at Santa Margarita and Falcon Dam during the first week of October 1989, 19 at Salineño on December 17, 1992, and 22 between Chapeña and Fronton on March 12, 1994. Immatures have been seen often, and a nest was found near Bentsen State Park during July 1994. It certainly appears that the wild Muscovy has arrived in the United States. If it continues to spread, however, the issue of origin may once again become muddled when the "good" Muscovies meet the feral ones.

Most Muscovy reports in *American Birds* come from fall through spring, with the peak period being October through April. This may, of course, be an artifact of the seasons birders are most active in southern Texas, and there are several summer records.

Best Bets

As stated above, wild Muscovy Ducks are mostly found along the Rio Grande between Falcon Dam and Fronton (near Roma). This is a stretch of river that spans only about 20 miles. Simply walking down to the river at Salineño or Santa Margarita Ranch and waiting for birds to fly by may be the best strategy. Early morning and late afternoon are the best times to search. Be sure to look up frequently since Muscovies fly fast.

Identification

The Muscovy is a large duck—substantially larger than a Mallard. Wild adults are all black, with a greenish gloss in good light. In adults, white "shoulders" and wing linings are extremely conspicuous in flight, which is nearly always the way the species is seen. A perched bird shows more or less (or no) white in the wing depending on the way its feathers are arranged. Males have a small crest and red warty protuberances at the base of the bill, and both sexes show a light-colored bill with a dark band. Immatures are less glossy, appearing brownish black, and have only a small white spot on the upper wing.

As mentioned above, the only true identification challenge is separating pure wild Muscovies from their feral counterparts. Birds with white in areas other than those described above are almost certainly of domestic origin. So far, the nonferal birds have been wary, and any other behavior argues strongly against a wild bird.

At this writing, the Texas Bird Records Committee is still considering the wild versus feral status of Muscovies. Good documentation is needed for all sightings, including plumage and behavior.

(See color photo on page 465.)

White-cheeked Pintail

Anas bahamensis

Status and Distribution

The White-cheeked Pintail is one of but a few truly neotropical ducks. It breeds in widely scattered locations around South America and is resident throughout most of the West Indies. Like most other dabbling ducks, White-cheeked Pintails are fond of shallow-water habitats, but they are not restricted to either salt or fresh water. The closest breeding population to the United States is as near as the Bahamas, so it is no surprise that there are a number of records from the United States, mostly from Florida.

Indeed, the first U.S. record did come from Florida when a bird was shot at the Banana River, Brevard County, during March 1912. The next sighting was also from Florida, but did not occur until December 23, 1960, when one was found at Everglades National Park. After 1960, there was a virtual outbreak of White-cheeked Pintails, with over a dozen sightings between 1960 and 1974. Since then, however, these birds have grown considerably scarcer, and there are only three records since 1980.

As with all vagrant waterfowl, sightings of White-cheeked Pintails invariably raise the vexing question of origin. This species is particularly troublesome as it is common in captivity. The pattern of occurrence in the United States, however, is consistent with natural vagrancy. In all, there are about 26 U.S. "records" of White-cheeked Pintail. Of these, 24 have been from the Southeast in general and 19 from Florida in specific. Reports away from Florida have come from Texas, Louisiana, Alabama, Virginia, Delaware, Illinois, and Wisconsin. Given this pattern, most Florida White-cheeked Pintails are likely wild. This may also be true elsewhere in the Southeast. The truly worrisome records, with regard to origin, are those from Illinois and Wisconsin. Any proposed wild source for these birds would be extremely speculative.

White-cheeked Pintails have been recorded in every month except September. The bulk of records, however, is from mid-December through late April. Sightings away from Florida follow a similar pattern to those from Florida (which are, of course, more likely of wild origin). Exceptional dates include a bird at Everglades National Park, which stayed from January 12 to July 16, 1974, and a bird seen at Zellwood on August 18 and 19, 1973.

Best Bets

Everglades National Park, with eight records, is undoubtedly the best site for this species in the United States. The best spots to check are the ponds and lakes along Main Park Road (a.k.a. FL 27; see "Site Guide," p. 384).

Identification

The identification of the White-cheeked Pintail is usually a simple affair. One pitfall, however, is pale or leucistic individuals. These are a common variant in captivity (Madge and Burn 1988) and are highly unlikely to be wild. Another possible source of confusion is the Red-billed Teal (*Anas erythrorhyncha*) of southern Africa. Obviously, this species is not a potential natural vagrant to the United States. However, it is kept in captivity and is similar in appearance to the White-cheeked Pintail. The Red-billed Teal can be separated from the White-cheeked Pintail by its entirely red bill, duller plumage, and shorter tail (see Madge and Burn 1988). **(See color photo on page 465.)**

White-cheeked Pintail—*all records*

LOCATION	NUMBERS SEEN	DATES SEEN
Florida		
Banana River	1	3/1912
Everglades National Park	1	12/23/60 to 1/5/61
Fort Lauderdale	1	11/29/61
Everglades National Park	1	4/25 to 5/4/64
Big Pine Key	1	5/24 to 5/25/64
Everglades National Park	1	2/17 to 4/25/65

LOCATION	NUMBERS SEEN	DATES SEEN
Florida (cont.)		
Everglades National Park	1	3/18 to 3/19/67
Loxahatchee NWR	1	2/28/69
Everglades National Park	1	11/1969
Aripeka	2	1/12/70
Hickory Mound Lake	1	2/10/70
West Palm Beach	1	12/19/70 to 1/5/71
Everglades National Park	1	3/29 to 3/31/71
Zellwood	1	8/18 to 8/19/73
Everglades National Park	1	1/12 to 7/16/74
Cudjoe Key	1	3/16 to 3/26/77
Merritt Island NWR	1	10/25/89
Merritt Island NWR	1	3/30 to 4/8/90
9 Mile Pond, Everglades National Park	1	2/5/91
Mt. Dora	1	spring 1991
Delaware		
Assawoman	1	10/25 to 11/1/67
Virginia		
Pungo	1	12/17/37
near Chincoteague	1	11/14/66
Alabama		
Magnolia Springs	1	2/28 to 5/3/70
Louisiana		
date and location? Listed in AOU (1983).		
Texas		
Laguna Atascosa	1	11/20/78 to 4/15/79
Austin (rejected by TX BRC)	1	8/31 to 9/5/91
Wisconsin		
Lake Winnecone	1	9/21/29
Illinois		
Steward Lake	1	11/2/68
Nevada		

Several individuals appeared around Las Vegas during the summer of 1992. Numbers since then have varied from 4 to 20. These are certainly escapees.

Florida records

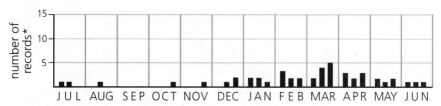

*records with multiple individuals counted as one record.

Garganey

Anas querquedula

Status and Distribution

This handsome duck is among the most migratory of waterfowl. It breeds from Great Britain to Japan and winters from North Africa to Southeast Asia. Given the Garganey's lengthy migration, its regular appearance on our shores is not too surprising. What is surprising is that the first North American record occurred as recently as 1957 (Cape Hatteras, March 25 to 31).

A scan through the Lower 48 Garganey records reveals that Garganey occur regularly, not only on our shores but inland as well. The 45 records from the Lower 48 are scattered among 22 states. Geographic patterns in these sightings are not terribly obvious. For instance, only California has a heavy concentration of sightings (23), and Kansas has as many records as Washington and Oregon combined (see table). The pattern that does exist shows records decreasing from from west to east. The Pacific Coast states have had 27 sightings and the western interior has had 24, while the eastern interior has had but 4 records and the Atlantic and Gulf coasts have had only 10. This distribution of reports implies that most Lower 48 birds are Asian in origin, including perhaps the East Coast records.

Temporal patterns are clearer. Most records are from the spring and, as you would expect, peak dates are earlier in the south than in the north. For instance, in the southern states, most sightings are between mid-March and early May, whereas in the North, spring records are largely between mid-April and mid-May. Canadian spring records are entirely from May and June. Fall records in the Lower 48 are less numerous and lie mostly between mid-September and early November. There are six winter records, five from California and one from Washington.

For most vagrants, fall records outnumber those from spring. The reversal of this trend in the Garganey is most likely due to the difficulty of teal identification in fall. Sadly, the male Garganey holds its dramatic breeding plumage only from early March to midsummer. Most fall and winter birds probably pass unnoticed.

Best Bets

Because Garganey occurrences are so scattered, there are no specific sites to recommend. Seeing a Garganey in the Lower 48 is best accomplished by keeping in touch with hotlines, especially NARBA. Finding a Garganey is largely luck and knowing how to identify females and eclipse plumage males. Also, remember that most Garganeys are found in the company of Cinnamon and Blue-winged Teals.

Identification

The identification of a breeding plumage male Garganey is the simplest of tasks. This is not so, however, for other plumages. In these plumages, Garganeys most resemble the Blue-winged Teal, except the face pattern, which most resembles a Green-winged Teal. The separation of the Garganey from other teals is well delineated in the NGS guide and is covered in more detail (with superb photos) in Jackson (1992). The high points in telling a Garganey from Cinnamon and Blue-winged Teal are as follows.
1. The Garganey has more prominent facial markings, plus a dark cheek bar.
2. The Garganey's greenish speculum is bordered by white, both to the front and rear.
3. The Garganey lacks an eyering.
4. The Garganey's legs are never distinctly yellow.
5. The Garganey's forewing is duller and grayer.

The high points in separating a Garganey from a Green-winged Teal are as follows.
1. The Garganey has a longer, broader bill.
2. The Gargeney has a grayish forewing.
3. Most North American Green-winged Teals have buff (not white) borders to the speculum.

4. The Garganey usually has a bolder face pattern.
5. The Green-winged Teal has whitish stripe near the undertail coverts.
(See color photo on page 466.)

Garganey—*all records*[1]

LOCATION	DATES SEEN
Pacific Coast	
Las Gallinas, CA	1/16/93
Humboldt Bay, CA[3]	1/30 to 2/10/87
Mendota WMA, CA	2/3/90
Long Beach, CA	3/15/72
Long Beach, CA	3/19/75
Lake Elsinore, CA	3/21 to 4/4/79
Bolinas sewage ponds, CA	3/27 to 4/30/90
Watsonville, CA	4/2/91
Long Beach, CA	4/4/74
Modoc NWR, CA	4/10 to 4/28/85
Elma, WA	4/12 to 5/15/91
Mount Vernon, WA	4/27 to 4/30/61
Lower Klamath NWR, CA	4/29/82
Woodland sugar ponds, CA	6/19/88
Mountain View Forebay, CA	8/22 to 9/22/92
Irvine, CA	9/12 to 20/90
Newhalem sewage ponds, OR	9/17 to 9/20/88
Fremont, CA	9/30/90
Arroyo Laguna, CA	10/2/91
Bolinas Sewage Ponds, CA	10/10 to 11/30/90
Furnace Creek Ranch, CA	10/12 to 11/1/90
Santa Maria River mouth, CA	10/15 to 11/4/89
Solano County, CA	10/23/77
Mendota WMA, CA	12/3/89
Kern County, CA	12/10/78
Richland, WA	12/15/94 to 1/1/95
Bolinas sewage ponds, CA	12/29/90 to 1/5/91
Interior	
Tucson, AZ	3/21 to 3/29/92
east of Boulder, CO	3/21 to 4/23/92
Newton, KS	3/29/81
NW of Little Rock, AR	4/1/84
Memphis, TN	4/1 to 4/5/78
Busch Conservation Area, MO	4/2 to 4/3/94
Charlo Pond, MT	4/4/91
Buenos Aires NWR, AZ	4/8 to 4/12/88
John Remond Reservoir, KS	4/14/79
Fermi Lab, IL	4/18 to 4/23/82

LOCATION	DATES SEEN
Jackson Reservoir, CO	4/20 to 4/28/90
Oxford, KS	4/21 to 5/1/82
Bridgeport, MI	4/24/91
Hammond, ID	late 4 to 5/3/90
Goose Lake, MN	4/29 to 5/2/87
Presidio, TX	4/29 to 5/6/94
Sierra Vista Sewage Ponds, AZ	5/1/91
Lakefield, MN	5/1 to 5/5/93
Roger Mills County, OK	5/2/79
Snake River near Hammett, ID	5/2/90
Waterton, CO	5/4/80
Woodbury County, IA	5/11/91
Bismarck, ND	5/12/90
Washita NWR, OK	5/15 to 5/18/81
Benton Lake NWR, MT	5/27/77
Bowdoin, MT	5/93 to 6/26/93
Miami County, KS	10/23/88
Lake Meredith, TX	11/22/85
Atlantic and Gulf coasts	
Gulf Shores, AL	3/11 to 3/19/68
Cape Hatteras, NC	3/25 to 3/31/57
Marshfield, MA	4/1 to 4/18/78
Riviera, TX	4/11 to 5/17/85
Tonawanda WMA, NY	4/16 to 4/19/93
Bombay Hook NWR, DE	4/24 to 5/5/76
Plum Island, MA	5/4 to 5/25/68
Plum Island, MA[2]	5/11 to 7/1/85
Orwell, VT	5/21/88
Chincoteague, VA[4]	5/24/92

[1]All records involve only one individual.

[2]Despite acceptance by the MA BRC, this record is likely a hybrid Garganey x Blue-winged or Cinnamon Teal (D. Sibley, pers. comm.).

[3]Rejected by CA BRC due to identification questions.

[4]Rejected by VA BRC due to origin questions.

all records

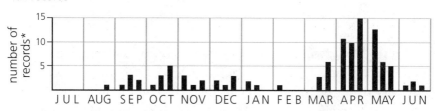

*records with multiple individuals counted as one record.

Tufted
Duck

Aythya fuligula

Status and Distribution

The Tufted Duck wasn't recorded in the Lower 48 until the winter of 1948-49, when one was shot in Alameda County, California. The first eastern Lower 48 record came not much later at Newburyport, Massachusetts, during 1954. Since then, this snazzy Eurasian duck has become a regular visitor. For instance, from fall 1991 through spring 1992, 13 were found in California, 2 were seen in Washington and Oregon, and 4 were seen along the East Coast.

This distribution of sightings is typical for Tufted Ducks. Most are found in Pacific Coast states, especially California, which boasts at least 75 records. Tufteds are also fairly regular at certain favorite locations in the Northeast. Sightings from inland states, however, are few but generally fit the pattern of occurrence found in coastal states. Since 1982, Tufted Ducks have been reported from Washington, Oregon, California, Montana, Michigan (record rejected), Massacusetts, Connecticut, Rhode Island, New York, and New Jersey. Records prior to 1982 have also come from Wyoming, Illinois, Michigan (record accepted), Indiana, and Ohio.

Generally, Tufted Ducks prefer areas that are close to, but necessarily on, the coast. Fresh water seems to be favored, with freshwater outnumbering saltwater sightings by about three to one. Other *aythya* ducks are the favored companions, especially scaup. In fact, Tufted Ducks have been known to hybridize with scaups and there are several records of these as well.

Tufted Duck records span the calendar based on a summering record from Arcata, Humboldt County, California. Since 1982, accepted sightings have ranged from early September into mid-May, but occur more regularly from early October into early May. Peak time is from mid-December through mid-March.

Best Bets

Some places seem to have a magical attraction for Tufted Ducks. These areas have them year after year while other suitable spots lack Tufteds altogether. Part of this phenomenon is due to a distinct wintering site fidelity in this species. It is tempting to attribute this phenomenon entirely to birds returning annually to the same locale; often, however, actual sightings argue otherwise. For instance, a male may be present at a given spot for two years, a female may be there the next year, and then two males may show up the year thereafter. The California Bird Records Committee has estimated that only about 30 percent of records are of returning birds.

The best area for Tufteds is probably the scattered freshwater ponds in San Francisco and Oakland. At least one has been in this area annually, and during some years there have been several in this region. Other places where this species is regular include the Los Angeles County reservoirs, California, Massachusetts, and Central Park, New York.

Identification

The identification of a pure male Tufted Duck is easy. Separating Tufted Duck x scaup hybrids, however, presents a challenge. Formerly, some pale-backed, short-tufted individuals were considered immature male Tufteds. Some of these birds foiled this interpretation by returning year after year to the same spot. Abandoning the theory of prolonged adolescence, birders now realize that these are scaup x Tufted Duck hybrids. When seeing a potential male Tufted Duck, be sure that the tuft length and bill pattern are correct. Also, check the back to confirm that it is *entirely* black and completely lacking fine gray vermiculations. The wing stripe should look like that of a Greater Scaup, but the bill should be distinctly smaller.

Identifying female Tufted Ducks is trickier. Most have at least some tuft. Also, their body color is generally darker than that of a scaup, and they usually have reduced white around the bill, with some birds lacking this mark entirely. Unfortunately, juvenile scaups also tend to be darker and have reduced white on the face. The juvenile plumage, however, is usually held only into November, and these birds can generally be separated from adults by their duller eye color. As with males, female Tufteds have more dark on the bill tip than either scaup and have a wing pattern resembling that of a Greater Scaup. Female Tufteds never have the pale cheek patch present on many Greater and some Lesser Scaups. Hybrid females would presumably appear intermediate and could be a nightmare to distinguish.

For more details on identification see Madge and Burn (1988), Lewington, et al. (1991), and Harris, et al. (1989). Harris, et al., has a particularly excellent discussion of the hybrid problem. **(See color photo on page 466.)**

Tufted Duck—*since 1982*

LOCATION	NUMBERS SEEN	DATES SEEN
Washington		
Everett	1	2/8/82
Ocean Shores	1	3/13 to 3/24/82
near Leadbetter Point	1	4/26 to 4/28/82
Seattle	1	12/23/82 to 3/83
Leadbetter Point	1	10/26 to 10/27/83
Leadbetter Point	1	12/17 to 12/31/83
Leadbetter Point	1	12/15/84
near Leadbetter Point	1	12/30/85
Wenatchee	1	1/17 to 1/19/86
Washougal	1	2/14 to 2/15/87
Ocean Shores	1	3/6/87
Seattle	1	1/15 to 1/16/88
Fort Lewis	1	3/13/88
Methow River, near Pateros	1	3/14 to 3/20/88
Migraine Lake, Columbia NWR	1	3/30/88
Orcas Island	1	1/1 to 1/29/89
Lynden	1	12/11 to 12/13/90
Seattle	1	3/4/92
Turtle Rock, Columbia River	1	11/29 to 12/2/92
Julia Butler Hanson NWR	1	1/23 to 2/6/93
Quilcene	1	2/10 to 2/23/93
Snohomish	1	5/2/93
Puget Island	1	2/10/94
Reardon	1	4/13 to 4/23/94
Oregon		
Finley NWR	1	2/14/82
Wapato Lake, near Gaston	1	12/21 to 12/22/83
near Coquille	1	3/11/84
Warrenton Sewage Ponds	1	2/6/88
Meares Lake	1	2/6/88 to 3/19/88
Cathlamet Bay	1	1/25 to 2/28/89
Kerby	1	3/11/89
Cave Junction	1	2/17/90

LOCATION	NUMBERS SEEN	DATES SEEN
Sheridan sewage ponds	1	1/26 to 3/18/91
Fiddle Creek	1	3/11 to 3/12/91
Bay City sewage ponds	1	3/13 to 5/4/91
Sheridan sewage ponds	1	1/20/92
Bay City sewage ponds	1	3/23 to 4/2/92
Bay City	1	4/9 to 4/17/94
California, Del Norte County		
Smith River estuary	1 (female)	11/16/86
Smith River estuary	1 (female)	2/5 to 2/7/88
Smith River estuary	1 (male)	1/24 to 2/14/88
Smith River estuary	1 (male)	1/17 to 2/11/89
Lake Talawa	1	4/17 to 4/26/93
California, Siskiyou County		
Grenada	1	4/7 to 5/11/85
Grenada	1	3/11 to 4/12/86
Grenada	1	2/15 to 4/13/87
California, Humboldt County		
Ferndale	1 (male)	2/23 to 2/24/82
Arcata	1 (female)	4/29 to 5/4/83
Arcata	1 (female)	11/22/85 to 5/3/86
Arcata	1 (male)	4/13 to 5/3/86
Arcata	1 (female)	4/16 to 4/17/88
California, Shasta County		
Glenburn	1	1/18/86
California, Solano County		
Mare Island	1 (male)	3/15/90
Mare Island	1 (female)	2/11/91
Glen Cove	1 (male)	3/16 to 3/22/91
Lake Dalwigh	1	3/16 to 3/21/91
Mare Island	1	11/27/91
Mare Island	1 (2nd bird)	1/22/92
California, Sonoma County		
Petaluma	1	2/28/87
Petaluma sewage ponds	2	4/9 to 4/23/94
California, Marin County		
Mill Valley	1	2/7 to 3/8/82
Point Reyes*	1	11/7/82
Limantour	1	12/18/82
Mill Valley	1	2/20 to 3/13/83
Tiburon	1	1/19/87
Inverness	1	2/15/87
Larkspur*	1	2/16/87
Belvedere	1	1/2/88
Novato	1	2/12 to 2/20/88
Bolinas sewage ponds	1	12/30/89
Rodeo Lagoon	1	1/10/90

LOCATION	NUMBERS SEEN	DATES SEEN
Richardson's Bay	1	3/6/90
Rodeo Lagoon	1	11/18/90 to 1/21/91
Novato	1	1/29 to 2/8/92
California, San Francisco County		
San Francisco	1	2/13/84
Golden Gate Park	1	1/25 to 3/4/86
Metson Lake	1	3/1 to 3/4/86
Golden Gate Park	1	12/19/86 to 3/20/87
Sutro Baths	1 (male)	11/19/88 to 3/27/89
Sutro Baths	1 (female)	11/26/88 to 3/27/89
Sutro Baths	1	1/9 to 3/2/90
Golden Gate Park	1	2/27/90
Lake Merced	1	4/26/90
Sutro Baths	1	1/18 to 2/28/91
Golden Gate Park/Lake Merced	1	10/23/91 to 3/8/92
Lake Merced	1 (male)	10/23/92 on
Lake Merced	1 (female)	11/26/92
Golden Gate Park	1	11/20/94 on
California, San Mateo County		
Foster City	1	2/20 to 4/2/83
California, Contra Costa County		
Mallard Reservoir	1	12/27/86 to 1/10/87
Mallard Reservoir	1	12/31/88
Mallard Reservoir	1	12/30/89
San Pablo Reservoir*	1	1/15/90
Mallard Reservoir	1	2/13 to 3/14/92
California, San Joaquin County		
Stockton	1	3/17 to 3/22/84
Stockton sewage ponds	1	12/15 to 12/18/90
California, Sacramento County		
Consumnes River Reserve	2	2/13/93
California, Alameda County		
San Leandro Bay, Oakland	1	1/11 to 1/12/87
Lake Merritt	1	3/9 to 4/5/87
Warm Springs	1	11/17/89 to 4/4/90
San Leandro Regional Shoreline	1	1/22/90
Hayward Regional Shoreline*	1	summer to 11/4/90
Hayward Regional Shoreline*	1	summer to 10/5/91
San Francisco Bay NWR	1	12/10 to 12/21/91
Lake Merritt	1	1/6 to 3/14/92
Lake Merritt	1	to 3/28/94
Lake Merritt	1	11/22/94
California, Santa Clara County		
Belmont Slough	1	4/19/87
Alviso	1	to 3/6/94
Alviso and Sunnyvale	6	11/24/94

LOCATION	NUMBERS SEEN	DATES SEEN
California, Merced County		
O'Neill Forebay	1	2/17/86
O'Neill Forebay	1	2/21 to 2/23/88
California, Napa County		
Lake Hennessey	1	1/1 to 1/9/82
Napa sewage ponds	1	12/26/82
Lake Hennessey	1	1/1/90
California, Monterey County		
Elkhorn Slough	1	3/25 to 3/27/87
California, Fresno County		
Fresno	1	12/13/92
California, San Luis Obispo County		
Lopez Lake	1	1/25 to 2/21/86
Lopez Lake	1	(2nd bird) 2/15 to 2/16/86
Lopez Lake	1	1/3 to 3/14/93
Lopez Lake	2	(2 additional birds) 3/14/93
Oso Flaco Lake	1	1/22 to 3/22/94
California, Santa Barbara County		
Lake Cachuma	1 (male)	11/30/87 to 12/6/87
Lake Cachuma	1 (female)	12/18/87 to 2/17/88
near Santa Maria	1	12/27/92 to 3/7/93
California, Kern County		
Lake Isabella	1	1/17 to 1/18/92
California, San Bernadino County		
Hesperia	1	12/6 to 12/11/87
California, Riverside County		
Lake Perris	2 (males)	1/22 to 2/21/83
Lake Perris	1 (male)	11/25/83 to 3/5/84
Lake Perris	1 (2nd male)	1/2/84
Lake Perris	1 (male)	11/8/85
Beaumont	1	2/27 to 3/15/92
California, Ventura County		
Saticoy	2	2/16 to 3/17/85
Saticoy	1 (female)	2/20/86
Saticoy	1 (male)	1/2 to 1/25/86
Saticoy	1 (male)	2/10 to 3/4/87
Saticoy	1 (female)	2/4 to 3/5/89
Saticoy	1 (female)	12/21/89 to 3/10/89
Saticoy	1 (female)	12/23/90
Ventura	1 (female)	1/19 to 3/5/91
California, Los Angeles County		
Quail Lake	1 (male)	12/29/83 to 3/7/84
Quail Lake	1 (male)	10/15/85
Quail Lake	1 (male)	11/25/86 to 1/24/87
Quail Lake	1 (male)	11/19/87 to 3/5/88
Castaic Lake	1 (male)	12/4/88

109

LOCATION	NUMBERS SEEN	DATES SEEN
Puddingstone Reservoir	1 (male)	1/14 to 1/27/90
Castaic Lake	1 (male)	1/28/90
Pyramid Lake	1 (male)	1/28 to 2/28/90
Puddingstone Reservoir	1 (male)	11/17/90 to 1/30/91
Castaic Lake	2 (males)	12/28/90 to 1/28/91
Quail Lake	1 (male)	2/1 to 3/8/91
Pyramid Lake	1 (male)	1/14 to 2/7/91
Quail Lake	1 (male)	11/11 to 11/17/91
Hansen Dam	1	10/24/92
California, San Diego County		
south San Diego Bay	1	2/18/85
Miramar Lake	1	1/13 to 2/9/92
California, Imperial County		
south end Salton Sea	1	2/1 to 2/3 and 2/22/86
Arizona		
Mesa	1	1/8 to 3/31/93
Mesa	1	11/13 to 12/18/93
Montana		
Priest Butte Lake	1	4/17/90
Wyoming		
Casper	1	3/16/94
Michigan		
Belle Isle*	1	1/10 to March 1989
Pennsylvania		
Pymatuning Reservoir	1	9/19/92 to 1/9/93
Massachusetts		
Westport	1	1/27 to 3/13/83
Chatham	1	3/27 to 4/3/83
Monomoy	1	May to 11/30/83
Sandwich	1	12/17/88 to 2/28/89
Brewster	1	4/19 to 4/26/92
Connecticut		
Greenwich	1	3/24 to 4/12/92
Greenwich	1	1/2 to 3/17/93
Greenwich	1	2/12 to 3/21/94
Rhode Island		
Warren	1	1/20 to 2/28/91
Barrington River	1	3/12 to 4/6/92
Bonnet Shores	1	11/21 to 11/25/92
Truston NWR	1	3/24 to 4/6/93
Narrow River	1	1/26 to 2/28/94
New York		
reported nearly annually from Central Park and nearby New Jersey		
Saratoga Lake	1	12/14/91
Jamaica Bay	1	10/12/92 on
Playland	1	11/3/92 on

LOCATION	NUMBERS SEEN	DATES SEEN
Rye	1	12/27/92 to 1/17/93
Manorville	1 (male)	1/12/93
Manorville	1 (pair)	1/13/93
East Hampton	1	1/23/93
Long Island	3	10/93
Read Sanctuary	1	12/23/93 to 1/9/94
Calverton	2 (pair)	12/12/93 on
Jamaica Bay	1	10/23 to 10/29/94

*Rejected by state BRC.

Tufted Duck x Scaup Hybrids—*Since 1982*

LOCATION	NUMBERS SEEN	DATES SEEN
Seattle, WA (returned until 1987)	1	10/21 to 11/7/84
Monmouth sewage ponds, OR	1	winter 1986-7
Monmouth sewage ponds, OR	1	winter 1987-8
Monmouth sewage ponds, OR	1	winter 1989-90
Baskett Slough NWR, OR	1	2/26/89
Inverness, CA	1	1/30/92
Clements, CA	1	1/16 to 1/28/84
Stockton sewage ponds, CA	1	3/17 to 3/22/84
Stockton sewage ponds, CA	1	3/21/86
Stockton, CA	1	11/12/86
Clements, CA	1	1/8/87
San Elijo Lagoon, CA	1	2/20/87
Ceres sewage ponds, CA	1	5/5 to 5/6/91
San Luis River mouth, CA	1	2/16 to 2/29/92
Cleveland, OH	1	4/2 to 4/5/89
New Haven, CT	1	1/28 to 2/10/84

records since 1982

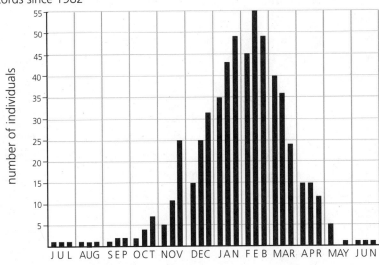

Masked Duck

Oxyura dominica

Status and Distribution

Reclusive yet confiding, nonmigratory yet wide ranging, obscure yet brightly colored—the Masked Duck is best described in apparent contradictions. This neotopical stiff-tail normally ranges from Cuba and Tamaulipas south into Argentina. It favors freshwater marshes, where it skulks in emergent vegetation, often invisible despite its rather bright plumage. At times, for reasons that are likely linked to water conditions, this usually sedentary species bursts forth and is found away, sometimes far away, from its usual haunts.

In the United States, the Masked Duck is a sporadic visitor to southeast Texas and southern Florida. It also has been seen about half a dozen times in Louisiana. Outside of these states, this species is a mega-rarity. Records do exist, however, for Alabama, Tennessee, Kentucky, Georgia, North Carolina, Maryland, Wisconsin, Vermont, Pennsylvania, and Massachusetts.

In Texas, the Masked Duck story is one of low occurrence punctuated by notable invasions. During most years, 1 to 5 Masked Ducks are seen, but during irruptions, over 70 have been found in one year (e.g., 1993). Most of these Masked Duck booms start in fall or early winter. This has usually been followed by three or so years of frequent sightings, which slowly dwindle. Since 1960, large invasions have occurred from fall 1967 into 1970 and from fall 1992 into at least 1995. A smaller incursion was also noted from winter 1975 into spring 1978. Nesting has occurred at multiple locations following irruptions. A distinct nadir of Masked Ducks occurred from 1979 through 1991 with none found in Texas during 1981, 1983, and 1987.

Texan records of this dapper duck have been mostly in counties on or near the Gulf Coast, especially from Aransas County south and from Hidalgo County east. Concentrations have, however, been found as far up the coast as Anahuac NWR, Chambers County (mostly 1967-70) and at McFaddin National Wildlife Refuge, Jefferson County (1993). Records within the Lone Star State have occurred as far north as Dallas County (April 3, 1977; July 18 and August 22, 1970) and as far west as El Paso (July 8 to 17, 1976) and Big Bend National Park (March 29 and April 11, 1978).

Florida has not had as rich a Masked Duck tradition as Texas. Florida's first record was as recent as 1955 when one was retrieved from a garbage can in Key West. Since then, there have been about 27 reports, most of which have been from Loxahatchee National Wildlife Refuge, Palm Beach County. The northernmost record from the state was at Lake Iomonia, Leon County, December 15, 1962. In contrast with Texas, Florida does not have a clear pattern of invasions. Notably, most of Florida's records have been between 1963 and 1984, with only one sighting since. Also, most Florida Masked Ducks have been between late December and early March, though there are reports from every month except June and October. The state's high count is of 9 birds at Loxahatchee NWR from February 12 to 20, 1977.

Best Bets

Your chances of finding a Masked Duck are highly dependent on what year you choose. Beyond picking the right year, your best bet is to check freshwater marshes containing some degree of dense emergent vegetation in the following Texas counties: Hidalgo, Cameron, Willacy, Kenedy, Kleberg, Nueces, San Patricio, and Aransas. You should also be alert for these perky ducks in similar habitats in other coastal (or near-coastal) Texas counties and in southern Florida. Areas with multiple sightings in Texas include Santa Ana, Laguna Atascosa, and Anahuac national wildlife refuges. A stronghold following the most recent invasion has been Brazos Bend State Park in Fort Bend County.

In Florida, the premier spot has been Loxahatchee National Wildlife Refuge. To be successful, it is important to remember that Masked Ducks spend much of their time buried in emergent vegetation. You will rarely find one swimming in wide-open water as Ruddy Ducks frequently do.

Identification

The identification of Masked Ducks is both simpler and more challenging than usually realized. The breeding males are gaudy and unlike any other North American bird. Nonetheless, mistakes have been made. Most of these errors involve birds resembling Ruddy Ducks with black heads. These may be aberrant Ruddies or other stiff-tail species that have escaped from waterfowl collectors. Regardless, a male Masked Duck can be separated from these interlopers by its patterned body, more golden color, and white wing patches (see Madge and Burn 1988; MGB; and NGS guide).

Female/immature/eclipse male Masked Ducks are actually easier to identify than generally realized. The face pattern differences are well known, but the Masked Duck's highly patterned body is at least as obvious. Female Ruddy Ducks are blandly marked birds, with dull flanks and unmarked upperparts. Female-type Masked Ducks, however, have golden or buffy-edged back and body feathers, creating a very different first impression (see NGS guide or MGB).   **(See color photo on page 467.)**

Masked Duck—*records away from Texas/Florida*

Vermont: Alburg, 1858 (rejected by VT BRC due to origin questions)
Massachusetts: Malden, August 27, 1889
Pennsylvannia: Lake Ontelaunee, June 12-14, 1984
Maryland: Elkton, September 8, 1905
Kentucky/Tennessee: Reelfoot NWR, April 11-15, 1974
North Carolina: Lake Ellis Simon, February 20-25, 1982
Georgia: Lowndes Co, April 11, 1962
Alabama: Wheeler Refuge, May 16, 1973
Louisiana: Holly Beach, May 5, 1970; near Holly Beach, January 7, 1971;
    Gum Grove, March 7, 1976; Lafourche Parish, January 19, 1992.
    Other Louisiana records exist.
Wisconsin: has a record per ABA (1990), but the WI BRC did not list this species in their
    communications with us.

Masked Duck—*Texas records away from counties on or near coast*

LOCATION	NUMBERS SEEN	DATES SEEN
Dallas County	1	7/18 & 8/22/70
El Paso	2	7/8 to 7/17/76
Dallas	1	4/3/77
Santa Elena Canyon, Big Bend National Park	1	3/29/78
Hot Springs, Big Bend National Park	3	4/11/78
San Antonio	1	5/22/78
Hays County	1	9/20 to early 10/80
Huntsville	1	6/10/93
Attwater Prairie Chicken NWR	1+ (max, 5)	12/11 to 12/25/93
Attwater Prairie Chicken NWR	24	7/29/94
Attwater Prairie Chicken NWR	10	August into mid-9/94
Attwater Prairie Chicken NWR	1	mid-9/94 to late 10/94

Masked Duck—*all Florida records*

LOCATION	NUMBERS SEEN	DATES SEEN
Key West	1	~4/1/55
Lake Okeechobee	1	early 12/55
Lake Okeechobee	1	11/58
Loxahatchee NWR	1	1/15 to 3/5/63
Loxahatchee NWR	1	12/27/63
near Lantana	1	12/25 to 12/30/66
Loxahatchee NWR	1 (shot)	12/14/68
Loxahatchee NWR	1	2/26/69
Loxahatchee NWR	1	2/13 to 3/2/71
Anhinga Trail, Everglades National Park	1	2/8/73
Loxahatchee NWR	1	1/15 to 1/16/74
Loxahatchee NWR	2	4/18 to 5/14/74
Big Pine Key	1	5/6 to 5/13/75
Key West (female)	1	8/22 to 8/30/75
Key West (male)	1	8/30/75
near Fort Lauderdale	1	1/6/76
5 mi E of Naples	1	7/17/76
Loxahatchee NWR	9 (4 thru 3/77)	2/12 to 2/20/77
Loxahatchee NWR	2	3/10/78
Loxahatchee NWR	4	12/23/78 to 3/79
Loxahatchee NWR	1	9/29/80
Loxahatchee NWR	2	late 2/81
6 mi S of South Bay	2	7/6 to 7/7/83
Highland Park	1	12/20/83 to 2/15/84
Loxahatchee NWR	2	4/8 to 4/11/84
West Lake, Everglades National Park	1	11/27/84
mouth of Suwannee River	1	1/17/90

Hook-billed Kite

Chondrohierax uncinatus

Status and Distribution

Although nominally a kite, the Hook-billed lacks the effortless and graceful flight associated with more typical kites such as the Mississippi and White-tailed. The Hook-billed, flying on rounded wings, is more akin to a Snail Kite, and like that species, it dines on snails. Very little speed or agility is needed to snatch a creeping gastropod off a tree limb.

The Hook-billed Kite is resident, in small numbers, in the lower Rio Grande valley between Santa Ana National Wildlife Refuge and Falcon Lake. Rarely, it has been seen as far south as the Sabal Palm Refuge in Brownsville. Numbers seem to fluctuate in a nonseasonal fashion, and the number present at any given place and time is hard to predict. Nonetheless, a couple are usually present in the area between Bentsen State Park and the Santa Ana refuge.

Since Hook-billeds spend most of their time perched quietly beneath the canopy, they are somewhat more difficult to find than other hawks. This habit can easily lead to making the Hook-billed a "jinx" bird, even if you are expert in knowing where to look.

Best Bets

There are several keys to not having the Hook-billed Kite as your jinx bird. The first key is to walk. The more backcountry in Bentsen State Park and Santa Ana National Wildlife Refuge in Texas you cover, the better your chances. Another important factor is that Hook-billeds do sometimes soar. This happens most often in midmorning when vultures first take to the air, so this is an important time to keep your eyes on the skies. Finding a good vantage point for looking over wooded areas would only aid your cause. Such areas include the dike outside of Bentsen State Park and the marsh overlook at Santa Ana NWR.

Identification

Hook-billed Kites are highly variable in plumage. Females are reminiscent of Red-shouldered Hawks, males can remind you of a Gray Hawk, and black morph birds look like Common Black-Hawks or Zone-tailed Hawks. More important than plumage is shape. Perched birds have an obvious long, hooked bill. Birds in flight have distinctively broad wings with pinched-in bases (almost resembling the wings of a butterfly or moth). The depictions in the NGS guide are adequate, but see Howell and Webb (1995) or Clark and Wheeler (1987) for good in-flight drawings.

Plumage distinctions can, of course, also be helpful. Adult female birds can be distinguished from Red-shouldered Hawks by the rufous nape and presence of only two dark tail bands. The nape color and the underwing's heavily banded primaries eliminate a Broad-winged Hawk. Adult male birds can be told from a Gray Hawk by the generally darker underwing and the heavy banding on the outer primaries' undersurface.

The black morph has been recorded only once in the United States: Santa Ana NWR, March 6, 1986. It can be separated from Zone-tailed Hawk and Common Black-Hawk by tail and underwing pattern. Immature light morph birds can be unbarred or barred on their underparts. The barring, when present, is dark and brownish or grayish. The lack of reddish hues eliminates the Red-shouldered Hawk. The heavily barred primaries eliminates Broad-winged and Gray Hawks. The drawings in the NGS guide are adequate. For more detail, see Clark and Wheeler (1987), Wheeler and Clark (1995), or Howell and Webb (1995). Wheeler and Clark (1995) has wonderful photos. **(See color photo on page 467.)**

Snail Kite

Rostrhamus sociabilis

Status and Distribution

The Snail Kite is one of North America's most aptly named birds, for this raptor dines almost exclusively on the apple snail, *Pomacea paludosa* (Sykes and Kale 1974). The kite hunts this stealthy prey by hovering over the marsh or scanning the marsh from stationary perches. Once a snail is spotted, the Snail Kite plucks it out of the water, flies to a perch, and then uses its finely curved bill-tip to extract the plump morsel.

The Snail Kite was first seen in the United States on April 29, 1844, when one was found in Dade County, Florida. Its status and distribution at that time are not well known. However, more than one-quarter of the Florida peninsula was historically covered by surface water, and the Snail Kite is heavily dependent on such habitats (Sykes 1979, Sykes 1983). Drainage of the peninsula began in the 1880s and 1890s, with major works starting in 1905. This loss of freshwater marsh habitat had a detrimental effect on the Snail Kite population. Nonetheless, scattered flocks of more than 100 kites were still being found in the 1920s and early 1930s. At that time, this species' range included most of peninsular Florida from Lake Okeechobee south, the headwaters of the St. Johns River, and scattered sites northeast to Daytona Beach and northwest to the Wakulla Springs· (Howell 1932).

By 1945, there were probably fewer than 100 Snail Kites left in Florida (Sprunt 1945). This number continued to shrink as did freshwater marshland. By the early 1960s, the population may have been as low as 20 birds and was most likely under 40. During the late 1960s, the number of kites began to rise, and in 1978, 267 birds were censused (Sykes 1979).

Most of these were found around Lake Okeechobee and in Conservation Area 3A in the eastern Everglades (western Broward and northwestern Dade counties) (Sykes 1983). Drought in 1981 caused a dispersal of kites, especially to the north. This resulted in the establishment of viable Snail Kite populations at Lake Kissimmee and Lake Tohopekaliga (Rodgers, et al. 1988). Good water conditions following the drought caused a further rise in kite numbers, and in 1984, 668 birds were counted (Rodgers, et al. 1988). Nonetheless, the Snail Kite's range was still only about 9 percent of what it had historically been. Drought in the late 1980s drove even more kites northward, and this species now occurs mostly from Lake Okeechobee north to East Lake Tohopekaliga. Some are still present, however, in the eastern Everglades, and over the past year or two, numbers there seem to be rebounding strongly. Hopefully, Conservation Area 3A will return to its former glory. Overall, numbers have fluctuated with water levels, but have been basically stable during the past decade or so. The maximum survey number to date was 733 in 1992.

Recent Florida records away from the current breeding range include the following: Tosohatchee State Preserve (eastern Orange County), July 21, 1979; Florida City, January 24, 1981; Levy County, April 1981; Duval County, April 26 to May 1, 1985; Lake Henderson (Citrus County), November 6, 1991; and Lake Jessup (Seminole County), January 2, 1993. There is also one accepted Texas record (plus several rejected reports): Lake Alice, Jim Wells County, from July 22 to 26, 1977. This bird must have come from some distance as the nearest population is in central Veracruz, Mexico (Howell and Webb 1995).

Best Bets

In central Florida, the best spots to check are Lake Kissimmee, Lake Tohopekaliga, and East Lake Tohopekaliga (for further details, see "Site Guide," or upcoming Lane/ABA guide to Florida). In southern Florida, the best spot to check is still the Miccosukee Restaurant along the Tamiami Trail (see Lane/ABA guide). During spring 1996, 20 kites were seen in this area.

Identification

The Snail Kite generally appears little like other North American raptors, but in flight there is some resemblance between the female/immature Snail Kite and the female/immature Northern Harrier. You should note that the harrier has a white rump whereas the kite has a white basal half to the tail. The Snail Kite is well depicted in both the NGS guide and the MGB. Wheeler and Clark (1995) has several fine photos. (See color photo on page 468.)

Short-tailed Hawk

Buteo brachyurus

Status and Distribution

To most ABA birders, the Red-tailed Hawk typifies the genus *Buteo*. In the Neotropics, however, this niche is filled by the Short-tailed Hawk, which is a common resident from northern Mexico into southern Brazil and northern Argentina. Unlike the Red-tail, the Short-tail is primarily a bird-hunter that lives mostly in wooded habitats (usually with nearby prairies, pastures, or marshes). These birds rise out of the forest canopy with the day's first thermals, and from the sky above search for their prey. Once a potential meal is spotted, the hungry Short-tail folds in its wings and dives toward its dinner (for a great description of hunting technique, see Clark and Wheeler 1987).

In the United States, the Short-tailed Hawk is a permanent resident in Florida and is accidental in Texas and Arizona. This is somewhat surprising because this species' range outside the United States does not include the West Indies but approaches Arizona as closely as central Sonora, and Texas as closely as central Tamaulipas. In Florida, the Short-tailed Hawk nests regularly, but locally, from Cape Sable north to Dixie County, Gainesville, and Palatka. On occasion, it has nested north and west to Bay and Holmes counties. Summer records have also come from the Keys as far west as Key West. Short-tails are generally on their breeding grounds from March into September.

During winter, Short-tailed Hawks retreat southward and are uncommon to rare in wooded areas from Lake Okeechobee south into the Keys. Wintering birds occur irregularly north to Orange and Levy counties,

121

and records from this season have occurred as far north as Wakulla, Taylor, Gilchrist, and Putnam counties.

There are eight Texas and two Arizona records of Short-tailed Hawk. The Texas birds were all in the southern part of the state, and the Arizona birds were all in the southeastern portion of that state. Notably, Texas records seem to be sharply on the rise, but there is currently no apparent seasonal pattern in these sightings. The Texas records are as follows: Port Bay, January 24 to March 7, 1954; Santa Margarita Ranch, July 22 to 28, 1989; Bentsen State Park, early November, 1989; Bentsen State Park, March 8, 1994; Santa Ana National Wildlife Refuge, October 4, 1994; Santa Ana refuge, May 30, 1995; Lost Maples, May 23 to June 6, 1995; and Hays County, June 6, 1995. A sighting from September 10, 1957, at Santa Ana was published in Oberholser (1974), but rejected by the TX BRC. The two Arizona records are as follows: near Rustler and Barfoot parks, August 7, 1985; and Sawmill Canyon, July 21, 1988.

Best Bets

There are two strategies to finding Short-tailed Hawk. From late March into September, the best plan is to go to a known nesting area and wait for the birds to soar above the canopy with the first good morning thermals. Short-tails usually first lift off in early to midmorning around the same time as Turkey Vultures, then soon rise up too high to be easily found. For a good look, timing is therefore crucial. At any time of day, however, you may still be able to find a Short-tail by scanning through high soaring flocks of vultures.

During winter, a good approach would be to visit the hammocks and other wooded areas in Everglades National Park. Especially good is the area from Flamingo to Nine Mile Pond. Again, this species is rarely seen perched, so careful attention to soaring birds is important, and the best time to look is when the Turkey Vulture first takes to the sky. Short-tails are most numerous in the Everglades from late October into February.

Identification

The adult light morph Short-tailed Hawk is easy to identify (see NGS guide or Clark and Wheeler 1987). Note the white underwing linings with darker flight feathers and immaculate white underparts. Immature light morph birds are similar to adults, but may have some fine dark streaking on the sides of the breast and pale streaking on the head (see MGB and Clark and Wheeler 1987). Recently fledged birds may have some rufous wash on the chest (Ogden 1973).

The dark morph Short-tailed Hawk is more difficult to identify than the light morph because it resembles most other dark morph buteos. Dark morph Short-tails are also more numerous in Florida, outnumbering light morphs by about four to one (Stevenson and Anderson 1994). Important identification points include shape and size, both of which are similar to the Broad-winged Hawk. The adult's tail pattern is unique, with a dark subterminal band and two to three broken narrow dark bands (see Clark and Wheeler 1987). The immature usually has pale spotting on the belly and vent contrasting with a uniform dark head and chest, creating a dark-hooded effect (see Wheeler and Clark 1995). Furthermore, all Short-tailed Hawks have a white spot above and behind the bill that can be seen with excellent views.

The most difficult challenge in Short-tailed Hawk identification involves adult dark morph Short-tails versus immature dark morph Broad-wings. Since dark morph Broad-wings breed only in Alberta, this is unlikely to be a major concern in Florida. However, for vagrants elsewhere in the United States, this identification question is far more important. Attention should be paid to the above-mentioned tail pattern and pale facial spot. Also note that the undersurface of the secondaries is darker than the inner primaries in dark morph adult Short-tails. In Broad-wings, these feathers are more uniformly patterned. For an excellent discussion, see Clark and Wheeler (1987). **(See color photo on page 468.)**

Gyrfalcon

Falco rusticolus

Status and Distribution

The falcon of kings and of birders' dreams is the Gyr. It is noble in aspect, powerful in form, and sparse in occurrence. The Gyr's usual haunts are in the high Arctic, where it feeds primarily on ptarmigan, waterfowl, and shorebirds. During winter, some head south to the northern Lower 48, where this fleet hunter prefers open country with plenty of fowl, which it usually hunts down in level flight.

In the eastern Lower 48, Gyrs are seen annually (or nearly so) south to northeastern Pennsylvania, across upstate New York, and then down the eastern shore to Barnegat Light in New Jersey. In the Midwest, Gyrfalcons are annual in the upper peninsula of Michigan, across the northern third of Wisconsin, and in the northern half of Minnesota.

Farther west, Gyrs are found regularly south into South Dakota, Wyoming, Montana, and northern Idaho. Finally, in the Northwest, Gyrfalcons occur annually across Washington and almost annually south into Oregon. The river deltas in northwestern Washington, with their huge concentrations of waterfowl and Dunlins, are probably the most reliable location in the country (see "Site Guide").

Occasionally, Gyrfalcons wander even farther from their frigid home. Records have come from as far south as Pamlico County (NC), Jefferson County (TN), Springfield (IL), Oklahoma City (OK), Telesburg (CO), and Alameda County (CA).

The season for Gyrfalcons is late October through late March, but birds are sometimes seen as early as mid-September or as late as early May. There have been no summer records during the past decade. Sightings from early fall and late spring have come from more northerly latitudes, but overall there is little variation in seasonal occurrence from north to south or east to west.

Best Bets

The most reliable place for Gyrs in the Lower 48 is the Skagit Flats in northwestern Washington. One to several winter here every year. Other fairly reliable areas in the Pacific Northwest include Dungeness Spit in northwestern Washington and the Davenport/Reardon area near Spokane (WA). Elsewhere try the Champlain Valley (VT), Sault Ste. Marie (MI), Duluth (MN)/Superior (WI), Sheridan (WY), Fort Peck (MT), and Rathdrum Prairie (ID).

Identification

Gyrfalcon identification is well discussed in the standard guides. For a more in-depth discussion, see Clark and Wheeler (1987) or Dunne, Sibley, and Sutton (1988). For a number of fine photos, see Wheeler and Clark (1995). There are a couple of tips to keep in mind. First, in the extreme western Lower 48, the vast majority of Gyrfalcons are gray morph, whereas both the white and dark morphs are rare. The mixture of morphs changes as one heads east, and in New England, the three morphs are much more evenly mixed. Second, falconers have been known to hybridize Gyrfalcons with other falcons in captivity, so beware of the odd-appearing bird and keep in mind the possibility of a Gyr x Peregrine hybrid. **(See color photo on page 469.)**

Gyrfalcon Records by State—*a summary of records from* American Birds *from summer 1982-1993**

STATE	NUMBERS SEEN
Maine	24
New Hampshire	1
Vermont	33
Massachusetts	23
Connecticut	4
Rhode Island	5
New York	61
New Jersey	19
Pennsylvania	17

STATE	NUMBERS SEEN
Maryland	2
Virginia	1
Ohio	3
Michigan	29
Indiana	1
Wisconsin	30
Illinois	5
Minnesota	45
North Dakota	42
South Dakota	16
Nebraska	8
Kansas	2
Oklahoma	3
Montana (eastern)	53
Wyoming	23
Colorado	4
Utah	3
Idaho/western Montana	15/year (approx)
Washington/Oregon	6/year (approx)
California	5

*Records prior to 1982 have also come from Missouri and Delaware. During the 1990s, there have been two records from Iowa. Additionally, North Carolina has a record: one, Pamlico County, 2/10/92, and Tennessee has an accepted record: one, Jefferson County, 1/13/78.

Whooping Crane

Grus americana

Status and Distribution

Few birds have the pizzazz and grandeur of the Whooping Crane. It is a magnificent bird to look upon, glistening white and standing five feet tall. It is also extremely rare, with fewer than 140 wild individuals on the entire planet (at one time, this number was only 15). You cannot look at this bird without feeling lucky.

The story of the Whooping Crane is one of destruction and rebirth. The former status and distribution of the Whooper are not easy to piece together, for this conspicuous nesting bird of the tallgrass prairies disappeared quickly in front of the plow and the shotgun. It was probably never numerous, and the estimated maximum population prior to 1860 was only 1,300 to 1,400 birds (Allen 1952). At this time, the main breeding range extended from central Illinois north and west through Iowa, Minnesota, Nebraska, and North Dakota into southern Manitoba, Saskatchewan, and Alberta (Johnsgard 1983). There was also an isolated breeding population resident in southwestern Louisiana and eastern Texas (Lowery 1974; Oberholser 1974).

Other scattered nesting areas probably existed, as evidenced by a record from within the present-day boundaries of Yellowstone National Park (Kemsies 1930). Undoubtedly, Whoopers also formerly bred where they breed today—in and around Wood Buffalo National Park, Northwest Territories, Alberta—but this population was not discovered until 1954 (Allen 1956). Historically, the Wood Buffalo National Park nesting area was likely isolated from the core range in the prairies farther south

(Johnsgard 1983).

The historic wintering range consisted of two main groups. One was along the Gulf Coast from northernmost Tamaulipas, Mexico, to Alabama (Johnsgard 1983; Imhof 1976). The other was in the intermountain grasslands of central Mexico from northern Chihuahua south to Jalisco and Guanajuato (Johnsgard 1983; Howell and Webb 1995). There is also a scattering of winter records from elsewhere in the southeastern United States, and it is possible that Whooping Cranes wintered in small numbers in these areas. Southeastern states with a few suggestive old winter records include Florida, Georgia, South Carolina, and North Carolina.

The former migration route of Whooping Crane is even more difficult to discern. Apparently, the Whooper had been seen as far west as the Great Salt Lake, Utah, and as far east as New Jersey. The bulk of migrants probably occurred between 85 and 105° W longitude.

During the latter half of the nineteenth century, the draining of marshes, farming of prairies, and shooting of migrants laid waste to the Whooping Crane population. By 1937, the population wintering along coastal Texas totaled only 15 or 16 birds (Lewis 1995), and the resident group in Louisiana numbered only about 13 (Lowery 1974). In 1940, a hurricane reduced the Louisiana population to 6, and the last surviving individual from this group was taken into captivity in 1950 (Lowery 1974). At the same time, efforts to preserve the birds wintering in Texas produced moderate growth, with about 30 birds extant in 1950 (Lewis 1995). Continued conservation efforts have led to steady increases, and peak population totals during the past decade have been around 145 birds (Lewis 1995). This number is expected to reach 500 by the year 2018 (Mirande, et al. 1993).

The only naturally occurring Whooping Crane population currently breeds in and around Wood Buffalo National Park, Northwest Territories, Alberta, Canada. These birds migrate south predominantly through Alberta, Saskatchewan, extreme northeastern Montana, North Dakota, South Dakota, Nebraska, Kansas, Oklahoma, and eastern Texas. They end their journey at Aransas National Wildlife Refuge, Aransas County, Texas—a trip of 1,600 to 1,800 miles. Members of this group do wander, and since 1950, individuals have been seen as far east as northeastern Illinois and as far west as Morgan County, Colorado.

Whooping Cranes usually begin leaving Wood Buffalo National Park during mid-September and are entirely gone from there by early October. Birds normally start to appear at Aransas in late October and typically have all arrived by mid-November, though occasional stragglers show up as late as early January. Along their migration route, Whoopers are generally rare but regular. In the Dakotas and Montana, they are mostly found from mid-September to early October. In Nebraska and Kansas, mid- to late October is more typical, and in Oklahoma and eastern Texas, migrants are seen mostly from mid-October to mid-November.

The bulk of the Whooping Crane population leaves Aransas between March 25 and April 15, with the last birds usually departing by early May. On rare occasions, however, individuals have lingered later and even spent the summer at Aransas. The first cranes arrive at Wood Buffalo in late April, thus normally covering their spring migration route in only 9 to 23 days (Allen 1952).

Spring migrants are rare but regular along most of their migration route. From Texas to Nebraska, migrating spring birds are seen mostly from late March to late April. In South Dakota, North Dakota, and Montana they are found predominantly between early April and mid-May. On at least one occasion, a spring migrant stopped short of Canada and summered in North Dakota.

In addition to the naturally occurring cohort discussed above, there are currently two introduced groups of Whooping Cranes in the wild. Both of these were created in an attempt to establish additional self-sustaining Whooping Crane populations, thus lowering the risk of extinction. The first trial involved the cross-fostering of Whooping Crane eggs and young by Sandhill Cranes at Grays Lake National Wildlife Refuge in southeastern Idaho. From 1975 through 1988, 289 Whooping Crane eggs were placed in Sandhill Crane nests at Grays Lake; of these, 210 hatched, and 85 chicks were fledged by their foster parents (U.S. Fish and Wildlife Service 1994). Unfortunately, these Whoopers seemed to have an identity crisis, and despite much encouragement, no lasting Whooper-Whooper pair bonds formed (Lewis 1995). In one instance, however, a Whooping Crane did actually pair and breed with a Sandhill, thus producing a hybrid chick (Mahan and Simmers 1992). The lack of pairing and reproduction among cross-fostered Whoopers led to discontinuation of the egg transfers in 1989. The Grays Lake population peaked at 33 birds in 1985 and has declined to 4 birds as of 1995 (Lewis 1995).

The birds raised at Grays Lake winter in central New Mexico. Their migration route carries them through northeastern Utah, southwestern Wyoming, western Colorado, and northern New Mexico (Lewis 1995). The existence of these birds raises questions about the origin of any Whoopers seen west of the normal Wood Buffalo/Aransas migration route. Though it is unfortunate that the Grays Lake experiment failed, the decline in this group will once again allow us to discern western vagrancy patterns in the naturally occurring population.

The second introduction program is taking place at Three Lakes Wildlife Management Area, Osceola County, Florida. Though there is no solid evidence that Whooping Cranes ever bred in Florida, the goal here is to establish a nonmigratory breeding population in central Florida's apparently suitable prairie wetlands. The first birds were released here during January 1993 (Stevenson and Anderson 1994), and through 1995 a total of 52 captive-bred Whoopers had been introduced at Three Lakes. Of these 52, only 25 survived through 1995, with most losses occurring from predation by bobcats (Lewis 1995). The current plan is to release 20 or more birds per year for up to another decade (Lewis and Finger 1993).

Best Bets

Though it is possible to see Whooping Cranes during migration, your most assured path to fulfillment leads through Aransas National Wildlife Refuge in Texas. The best times to look here are from mid-November through late March. There are two basic approaches to seeing the Whooper at Aransas. The first is to look from the observation platform five miles past the visitor center. Any looks obtained from here will be distant, and the bird is far from guaranteed. Many succumb to the temptation to call any distant big white bird (e.g., White Pelican, Great Egret) a Whooping Crane. Do resist.

The other approach is to take one of the many Whooping Crane boat tours. These offer virtually certain success and often provide far better looks. Of the many options, we especially recommend Captain Ted's Whooping Crane Tours (800-338-4551 or 512-729-9589), which leaves out of Fulton. Other tours include Lucky Day Whooping Crane Tours (800-782-bird or 512-749-5760), Sea-Gun Resort (512-729-3292), John Howell (512-729-7525), or the

New Pelican (512-729-8448).

Corpus Christi, about 45 miles south of Aransas, has the nearest major airport. For lodging, Miller (1991) recommends the Sandollar Resort and RV Park (512-729-2381) on State Route 35 in Fulton. This resort offers inexpensive rooms (including some kitchenettes) and is close to Catpain Ted's boat slip. RV hookups are also available here. Campers should try the very pleasant Goose Island State Park (512-729-2858), about 22 miles south of Aransas and 8 miles north of Rockport. For other lodging and camping facilities, call the Rockport-Fulton Tourist Association (512-729-2388) or the Rockport Chamber of Commerce (800-826-6441).

Miller (1991) recommends Charlotte Plummer's Seafood Restaurant on Fulton Beach Road for dinner. For breakfast, you may want to try the Sandollar Pavilion Restaurant, which is adjacent to Captain Ted's. This eatery opens at 7 a.m. and is used to turning out a quick morning meal. A boarding announcement for Captain Ted's is usually made. Not far away the Back Forty Restaurant opens at 6:30 A.M. and provides an earlier alternative.

Identification

There is no North American bird that really resembles the Whooping Crane. Nonetheless, overly excited birders have been known to identify a wide variety of birds as Whooping Cranes, and hunters have shot Whoopers thinking (in their own excitement) that these birds were Snow Geese (*really big* Snow Geese). When looking at a potential Whooping Crane, just remember to check for the field marks so clearly shown in major field guides.

Pacific Golden-Plover

Pluvialis fulva

Status and Distribution

The Pacific Golden-Plover is among the most common species included in this book, yet it is also among the most obscure. This is because until recently the Pacific Golden-Plover was considered a mere subspecies of Lesser Golden-Plover. In 1993, however, the A.O.U. made *P. fulva* a species unto itself. Now, interest in this bird is sharply on the rise.

Pacific Golden-Plovers breed on the Arctic tundra of Siberia and western Alaska. In the fall, most migrate out over the Pacific Ocean to Australasia and islands in the southern Pacific. A few, however, regularly head south along North America's Pacific Coast. In Washington and Oregon, Pacific Golden-Plovers are uncommon to fairly common fall migrants (peak late August through early October), very rare winterers, and rare spring migrants (early April through mid-May). In California, this species is uncommon to rare as a fall migrant (peak mid-September through late October), locally fairly common in winter, and rare as a true spring migrant. This species potentially can be found at any season as is shown by the year-round sightings from California. Only two Lower 48 records exist away from Pacific Coast states: one, Carson Lake, Nevada, August 11, 1988; and one, near Clifton, Colorado, November 12, 1991. Birders on the East Coast, however, should also be on the lookout for Pacific Golden-Plovers, as there is a record from Bermuda (1/25 to 1/31/95).

Pacific Golden-Plovers are mostly found along or near the coast. They prefer a variety of sparsely vegetated habitats and can be found in *Salicornia* marshes, sod farms, pastures, plowed fields, and sandy beaches (especially with scattered grass). During fall migration, Pacific Goldens often mingle with American Golden-Plovers, but winter flocks have so far seemed pure (there are no confirmed winter western U.S. records of American Golden-Plovers). Spring migrants are often single birds.

Best Bets

Some of the best places to find Pacific Golden-Plovers during migration include Ocean Shores (WA), Leadbetter Point (WA), Clatsop Spit (OR), and Bandon (OR). Some regular wintering locations include Point Reyes (CA), Dillon Beach (CA), the Santa Maria River valley (CA), Vandenberg Air Force Base (CA), and Anaheim Bay (CA).

Identification

The separation of the Pacific Golden-Plover is a somewhat complex problem. In all plumages, call, primary projection, toe projection (beyond tail in flight), and wing extension beyond tail are of some help. In juvenile plumage, note the supercilium, and head and breast color. For breeding adults, note the presence or absence of white on the lower flanks and undertail coverts. The differences are summarized below. For a more complete discussion see Hayman, Marchant, and Prater (1986), Golley and Stoddart (1991), and Paulson (1993).

Primary Projection
- American: Longer; three and one-half to four primaries beyond tertials, this distance considerably greater than length of bill.
- Pacific: Shorter; two and one-half to just over three primaries beyond tertials, this distance equal to or a bit longer than the bill.

Wings/Tail
- American: Folded wingtips well beyond tail.
- Pacific: Folded wingtips just beyond tail.

Toes/Tail
- American: In flight, toes reach tail tip.
- Pacific: In flight, toes distinctly beyond tail tip.

Supercilium (juvenile and basic plumages)
- American: White to dull grayish.
- Pacific: Buff to bright golden.

Head (juvenile and basic)
- American: Grayish.
- Pacific: Dull buff to bright gold.

Breast
- Juvenile and Basic: Bright buff to gold in juvenile Pacific only.

Lower Flanks and Undertail Coverts (alternate plumage)
- American: Solid black (beware molting birds!).
- Pacific: White to black with white flecking.

Voice
- American: Call is *quee-eedle*.
- Pacific: Call of *chuwee*, reminiscent of the call of a Semipalmated Plover, more distinctly disyllabic.

Caveats to above notes include the following: molting American Golden-Plovers can have an undertail/flank pattern much like an alternate plumaged Pacific; primary projection and relative wingtip/tail length take much experience to accurately judge; and in fall, worn adults of both species have short tertials and longer apparent primary projection. **(See color photo on page 469.)**

Northern Jacana

Jacana spinosa

Status and Distribution

You're looking over a vegetation-choked pond in southern Texas, hoping to find a Purple Gallinule or Least Bittern, when—whoa, what's that? A dark rail-like bird flutters into the open on screaming neon yellow wings and begins to walk, haltingly, across the lily pads on toes several inches long. Its back is chestnut, and its bright yellow bill is matched by a similarly brilliant frontal shield.

Now *this* is a tropical-looking bird, a colorful stray from the land of macaws and toucans. Common in wetlands from Mexico to Panama, the Northern Jacana sometimes wanders north across the border into southern Texas and Arizona to delight U.S. birders. Though it is somewhat reminiscent of a rail, it's actually a member of the *Charadriiformes*, the order of sandpipers and phalaropes.

The first U.S. record of a Northern Jacana was as long ago as December 10, 1888, when one was collected in Brownsville, Texas. From then until 1958, there were but a handful of reports. Since 1958, however, there have been about 40 sightings in Texas (counting the colony at Maner Lake, Brazoria County, as one record; see below) and two from Arizona. Additionally, the Northern Jacana is hypothetical in Florida (see Stevenson and Anderson 1994). The Texas records are heavily concentrated along the lower Rio Grande valley (up to Falcon Dam) and along the Gulf Coast (north to Brazoria County). Accepted records also come from central Texas (Real, Kerr, Gonzales, Travis, and Bexar counties) and the Trans-Pecos (Brewster County). The Arizona records are of an adult at Kino Springs and Guevavi Ranch from June 7, 1985, to January 3, 1986, and an immature at Mittry Lake from June 3 to June 30, 1986.

The most illustrious incursion of Northern Jacanas into the United States occurred at Maner Lake, Brazoria County, Texas. Here a breeding population was first found in 1967 (Oberholser 1974). At times, this colony reached 35 to 40 birds (late summer 1975 and January 1, 1978). The winter of 1977-78 saw a hard freeze in southern Texas, and apparently only two birds remained thereafter. The last known observation from Maner Lake occurred on April 16, 1978. There is one other breeding record: 3 downy young at San Benito, Texas, on August 24, 1951 (Oberholser 1974).

Northern Jacanas have been recorded during each month of the year, even when the former resident colony at Maner Lake is not considered. Peak numbers, however, have been found from early November through late April.

Best Bets

Santa Ana National Wildlife Refuge has far more records than any other spot in Texas (excluding Maner Lake), but jacanas are still far from regular there. If you hope for the needle-in-a-haystack happenstance of finding a jacana on your own, you should search the proper habitat in southern Texas. The species' enormously long toes are adapted for walking on floating vegetation, and it prefers freshwater ponds, marshes, and riverbanks with abundant lily pads or other plants that will support it while it hunts for small fish and invertebrates. It is also found walking through the grass in flooded fields and pastures.

Identification

With any kind of view at all, an adult Northern Jacana is unmistakable: chestnut body with black head, neck, and upper breast; yellow bill and frontal shield; and those conspicuous pale yellow flight feathers, flashing in flight, and displayed when the bird holds its wings over its back upon landing. The immature looks strikingly different, though similar in structure. It has brownish upperparts (darker on the head and hind neck) and white underparts, with an obvious dark eyestripe. The immature jacana's flight feathers are yellow, as well, though duller than the adult's.

Not much could be mistaken for this bird. The young Purple Gallinule, however, is found in the same habitat and is also vaguely dark on top and light underneath. The gallinule is far less contrasty overall, and its wings are bluish or greenish rather than brownish chestnut. It also lacks the Jacana's yellow primaries and secondaries.

Northern Jacana—*all Texas records**

LOCATION	NUMBERS SEEN	DATES SEEN
Brownsville	1	12/10/1888
Brownsville	1	1/19/1889
Cactus	1	6/15/1890
Mitchell Lake	1	6/25/22
Matagorda	1	10/8/36
Olmita	2	10/2/38
Harlingen	2	12/27/46
San Benito	1-2 (plus 3 downy young)	8/24/51
Santa Ana NWR	1	4/15 to summer 1956
Brownsville	1	5/6 to 5/7/59
Santa Ana NWR	1	5/9 to 5/10/59
Santa Ana NWR	1	10/22 to 11/22/59
Olmito	1	12/1/59 & 1/20/60
Santa Ana NWR	1	12/19/63 to 2/64
Santa Ana NWR	1	11/26/64
Santa Ana NWR	1	7/14 to 7/16/65
Vattmannville	1	8/1 to 9/5/68
near Santa Ana NWR	1	winter 1971-72
Brazoria County	1	3/28/72
Santa Ana NWR	1	7/14 to 8/15/74
Welder Refuge	1	12/20/74 to 3/75
Welder Refuge	1	4/12/75
Santa Ana NWR	1	July 1975
San Benitolate	1	9/76 to 10/76
Santa Ana NWR	1	12/27/78
Matagorda Island	1	late 4/79 to early 5/79
Real County	1	10/79 to 11/79
N of Edinburg	1-2	11/15/80 to 4/26/81
Gonzales	1-2	3/31 to 4/12/81
near Marathon	1	10/7 to 10/11/82
Santa Ana NWR	1	11/10 to 11/30/82
Santa Ana NWR	1	11/7/85 on
Welder Refuge	1	11/24 to 11/30/85
Bentsen State Park	1	11/85 to 12/28/85
Refugio	1-2	3/14 to 3/31/86
Welder Refuge	1	4/11 to 4/22/86
Welder Refuge	2	early fall 1986 to 1/87
Kerrville	1	5/11 to 6/10/86
Austin	1	11/12 to 12/11/89

LOCATION	NUMBERS SEEN	DATES SEEN
Brownsville	1	3/19 to 4/15/93
Falcon Dam	2-3	11/6/92 to 4/15/93
Seadrift	1	12/10/92 to 4/22/93
Pharr	2	1/2/93
Santa Ana NWR	1	2/12 to early 5/93
Brownsville	1	3/15 to 4/18/93
near Gonzales	1	4/25/93
Matagorda County	1	5/22/93
Santa Ana NWR	1	9/25 to 10/16/93
Santa Ana NWR	1	4/5 to 5/10/94

*Except Maner Lake colony. For details on this group, see text.

all records

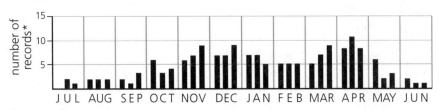

*sightings with multiple individuals considered as one record.

Bar-tailed Godwit

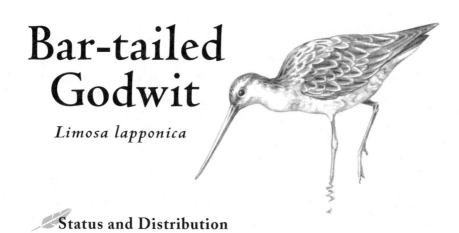

Limosa lapponica

Status and Distribution

The Bar-tailed Godwit is thought of by most birders as an entirely Old World species. This long-billed wader is, however, a common breeder in parts of western Alaska. Indeed, most western and some eastern Lower 48 records likely originate from western Alaska or northeastern Siberia.

Lower 48 sightings of Bar-tailed Godwits are almost entirely coastal because this species has a strong preference for estuarine marshes and tidal mudflats. Since 1982, there have been 54 reports of Bar-tailed Godwits involving about 60 birds, excluding records rejected by BRCs. Of these, 19 records are from Washington, 16 are from California, 3 are from Oregon, and 15 are from the East Coast. There is also a recent seemingly authentic report from Willard Bay, near Ogden, Utah, on October 3, 1994, and an older report from near Palmetto State Park, Texas, on April 9, 1967.

On the West Coast, Bar-tailed Godwits are mainly fall migrants, but eastern records are more evenly split between spring and fall. Fall records stretch from early July to late November, with peak numbers occurring between late August and early October. Spring records fall between early April and mid-June, with peak occurrence between late April and early June. There are also two mid- to late June records, both from the East, and one winter record from the West.

Best Bets

Several locations in Washington and Oregon seem particularly attractive to this species. In Washington, Willapa Bay (especially Tokeland) has accounted for 11 records, Dungeness has had 6 and Ocean Shores has 5. In Oregon,

Bandon is the best spot, having provided 6 sightings. On the East Coast, Monomoy Island is clearly the best spot with 6 records.

Bar-tailed Godwits are often found in the company of local godwit flocks or Black-bellied Plovers, so be sure to check groups of these birds.

Identification

The Bar-tailed Godwit most closely resembles the Marbled Godwit, especially in molting adult and juvenile plumages. Most guides focus on the underwing and rump patterns for identification. Though these marks are important, it should be noted that the Asian/Alaskan race *Limosa lapponica baueri* has heavy gray barring in both areas. Therefore, in the subspecies which accounts for most North American records, neither the rump nor the underwing will give a bright flash of white. The MGB gives the best account among major field guides. Hayman, Marchant, and Prater (1986) do an excellent job in discussing identification, and Chandler (1989) has some nice photographs. Paulson (1993) provides the birder with both: good photos and a fine discussion. For identification of juveniles, which account for most records, focus on the following:

Underwing
- Bar-tailed: White to gray.
- Marbled: Buffy.

Underparts
- Bar-tailed: Pale, grayish.
- Marbled: Darker, buffy orange. Beware of very worn birds, which can appear pale.

Leg Extension
- Bar-tailed: Foot slightly beyond tail in flight.
- Marbled: Foot and distal tarsi beyond tail in flight.

Primary Extension
- Bar-tailed: Longer with wingtips at least one inch beyond tail.
- Marbled: Shorter with wingtips no more than one-half inch beyond tail.

Supercilium
- Bar-tailed: Whitish, prominent.
- Marbled: Indistinct, often absent.   (See color photo on page 470.)

Bar-tailed Godwit—*all records, Pacific Coast*

LOCATION	NUMBERS SEEN	DATES SEEN
California		
Culver City	1	2/11 to 3/2/76
Crescent City	1	6/3 to 6/5/84
Arcata	1	7/11 to 7/17/68
Arcata	1	7/17 to 9/3/74
Berkeley	1	8/11 to 9/22/91
Drake's Estero	1	8/12/93
Pescadero Marsh	1	8/20 to 9/9/89
Abbott's Lagoon	1	8/22 to 9/24/92
MacKerricker State Park	1	8/26 to 10/6/90
Crescent City	1	8/28/93
Point Mugu	1	8/30/90
Mad River estuary	1	9/5 to 9/6/93
Moonglow Dairy	1	9/5 to 9/8/94
Palo Alto Baylands	1	9/9 to 9/24/94
Salinas River mouth	1	9/11/88
Lake Talawa	1	9/14/92
Bolinas Lagoon	1	9/20/88
Point St. George	1	10/2 to 10/8/92
Bodega Harbor	1	10/26 to 11/1/92
Bolinas Lagoon	1	10/27 to 11/30/73
Coronado Island	1	11/4 to 11/27/81
Rejected by CA BRC		
Bolinas Lagoon	1	8/28/91
Washington		
Ocean Shores	1	4/21 to 4/28/91
Leadbetter Point	6	6/8/74
Dungeness	1	6/10/80
Bay Center	1	6/10/83
Dungeness	1	8/1/79
Dungeness Spit	1	8/9/83
Tokeland	1	8/18/87
Ocean Shores	1	8/19/94
Ocean Shores	1	8/20/85
Willapa Bay	1	8/25 to 10/6/90
Tokeland	1	8/26/89
Tokeland	2	9/1/87
Ocean Shores	1	9/3 to 9/4/94
Ocean Shores	1	9/4/73
Ocean Shores	1	9/10 to 9/16/92
Tokeland	1	9/10 to 10/11/88
Tokeland	2	9/11 to 10/29/93
Dungeness Spit	1	9/17 to 9/19/85
Leadbetter Point	1	9/22/84

LOCATION	NUMBERS SEEN	DATES SEEN
Washington (cont.)		
Kennedy Creek	1	10/1/94
Tokeland	1	10/3/87
Tacoma	1	10/11/86
Oregon		
Newport	1	4/25/80
Bandon	4	5/14/88
Nehalem Meadows	1	5/28/78
south jetty of Columbia River	1	6/1/80
Bandon	1	8/27 to 9/2/87
Bandon	1	9/8 to early 10/90
Bandon	1	9/11/77
Newport	1	9/14/79
Bandon	1	9/23/76
Bandon	2	10/4 to 10/5/80
Rejected by OR BRC		
south jetty Columbia River	1	4/27/84

Bar-tailed Godwit—*Atlantic Coast, after 1981*

LOCATION	NUMBERS SEEN	DATES SEEN
St. James, FL	1	4/23 to /25/83
Portsmouth Island, NC	1	4/24 to 5/9/93
Portsmouth Island, NC	1	5/8 to 5/9/92
Longport, NJ	1	5/20 to 5/27/82
East Rockaway, NY	1	6/5 to 6/6/85
North Monomoy Island, MA	1	6/10 to 8/19/90
Chatham/Monomoy, MA	1	6/13 to 6/25/84
North Monomoy Island, MA	1 (2 until 9/5)	7/92 to 10/29/92
North Monomoy Island, MA	1	7/31 to 8/13/88
North Monomoy Island, MA	1	8/11 to 8/14/91
Chincoteague, VA	1	9/7/91
Honeymoon Island, FL	1	9/17 to 9/26/85
Cape May, NJ	1	9/21/85
Portsmouth Island, NC	1	9/22 to 10/10/82
Petit Manan, ME	1	11/21/87

Bar-tailed Godwit—*other selected records*

LOCATION	NUMBERS SEEN	DATES SEEN
near Palmetto State Park, TX	1	4/9/67
Chincoteague, VA	1	12/28/73
Revere, MA	1	4/12/81
Newburyport, MA	1	5/15 to 6/1/76
Monomoy, MA	1	7/4 to 8/31/79
Nauset, MA	1	7/26/37

LOCATION	NUMBERS SEEN	DATES SEEN
Plum Island, MA	1	8/7 to 8/10/79
Chappaquiddick Island, MA	1	8/26 to 8/31/68
Plum Island, MA	1	9/4 to 9/7/78
Chatham, MA	1	9/9 to 9/16/72
Cape Cod, MA	1	9/17/07
Nantucket, MA	1	9/23 to 10/21/78
Moriches Bay, NY	1	5/10 to 5/12/71
Moriches Bay, NY	1	8/17 to 8/18/74
Moriches Bay, NY	1	11/15/46
Brigantine, NJ	1	summer 1937
Beach Haven Inlet, NJ	1	8/1951
Brigantine, NJ	1	summer 1971
Somers Point, NJ	1	5/1972
Longport, NJ	1	5/6 to 5/20/73
Brigantine, NJ	1	6/19 to 6/30/74
Longport, NJ	1	5/14 to 5/19/75
Longport, NJ	1	4/28/77
Willard Bay, near Ogden, UT	1	10/3/94

Pacific Coast records

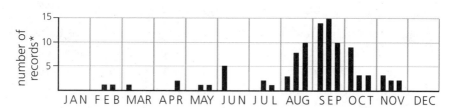

Atlantic Coast records

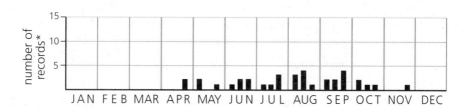

*sightings with multiple individuals considered one record.

Red-necked Stint

Calidris ruficollis

Status and Distribution

The Red-necked Stint is a brilliantly colored peep that breeds in Siberia and, on occasion, in western Alaska. It winters predominantly in Southeast Asia and Australia. Only in the past 15 to 20 years, as midsummer shorebirding has increased in popularity, has it become apparent that this species is an annual visitor to the Lower 48.

The first Lower 48 record occurred when one was found at Walnut Beach, Ashtabula, Ohio, on July 21, 1962. Records since then have been mostly coastal and are about equally split between the Atlantic and Pacific coasts. The Pacific Coast birds are almost certainly coming down from Alaska or eastern Siberia. The origin of the Atlantic Coast birds is harder to discern. Given the extreme rarity of this species in western Europe (only six records as of 1991; Lewington et al., 1991), it seems most likely that the Atlantic birds are taking the transcontinental route across North America, much as East Coast Western Sandpipers do. States with published sightings include Washington, Oregon, California, Nevada, Ohio, Tennessee, Maine, Massachusetts, Connecticut, New York, Delaware, Maryland, and Virginia.

Red-necked Stint records span all of May and stretch from mid-June through mid-October. Peak time is in July as the conspicuous adults, often still in high alternate (breeding) plumage, move south from their nesting grounds. The juveniles, which move later in the fall, are much more difficult to identify and probably pass largely unnoticed.

Like most peeps, Red-necked Stints prefer areas of very shallow water and mud. Most Lower 48 sightings have been in nontidal ponds and pools very near the coast.

Best Bets

There is no reliable place to see Red-necked Stint in the Lower 48, but there are eight records from the Delaware refuges, so this may be the best place to look. There are also three records from the Santa Clara River mouth (McGrath Beach) in southern California. Just about anywhere else that you find concentrations of Semipalmated or Western Sandpipers would be a good place to scrutinize for this species.

Identification

An alternate (breeding) plumage Red-necked Stint is usually quite distinctive. The only likely candidates for confusion are Little Stint, Spoonbill Sandpiper, and Sanderling.

A brightly plumaged Little Stint can nearly match a Red-necked in its bright reddish head and neck, but the throat and breast pattern is distinctly different. On a Red-necked, all spotting is beneath the red/rufous of the upper chest and throat. In Littles, there may not be any reddish color on the underparts. If color is present, all spotting is contained within the colored area. (This throat pattern is also a good distinction from Sanderling.) Another distinction between Little and Red-necked Stints is in the distribution of color in the upperparts. A Little Stint is typically quite reddish throughout the upperparts while a Red-necked is extensively reddish on the mantle and scapulars but mostly gray or gray-brown on the wing coverts and tertials.

Sanderlings are bigger than Red-necked Stints and have longer, thicker bills and longer legs. Like the Little Stint, the reddish color on a Sanderling's breast is usually filled with dark spots. Sanderlings also lack hind toes, a feature present on all peeps.

The Spoonbill Sandpiper has a breast pattern that can resemble that of a Red-necked Stint. The difference in bill shape is dramatic but can be obscured in direct side views. Also beware of color-dyed peeps. Some researchers use colorful dyes to mark shorebirds they are studying. With the right color dye in the right place, some of these can superficially resemble alternate plumage Red-necked Stints. Red-necked Stints in other plumages (and a few odd alternate plumage birds) present much more of a challenge. These birds must be identified with extreme caution and only by observers with much experience with North American peeps. Identifying juvenile Red-necks requires giving close scrutiny to the patterns of the face, breast, back, and scapulars, as well as primary projection, bill shape, and toe webbing. For more details, see Veit and Jonsson (1984), Lewington, et al. (1991), and Paulson (1993). **(See color photo on page 470.)**

Red-necked Stint—*all records*

LOCATION	NUMBERS SEEN	DATES SEEN
Arcata, CA	1	5/5/69
Woodland Beach WMA, DE	1	5/7 to 5/19/94
Ted Harvey Conservation Area, DE	1	5/31/93
Crescent City, CA	1	6/18/74
Tillamook Bay, OR	2	6/20 to 7/3/82
Monomoy Island, MA	1	6/24 to 6/28/80
Bandon, OR	1	6/25/84
Santa Maria River mouth, CA	1	6/28 to 6/29/95
Santa Clara River estuary, CA	1	6/29 to 7/2/94
Jamaica Bay NWR, L.I., NY	1	7/8 to 8/3/94
Santa Clara River estuary, CA	1	7/11 to 7/17/82
Santa Maria River estuary, CA	1	7/11 to 7/15/94
Santa Clara River estuary, CA	1	7/12 to 7/17/81
Santa Maria River estuary, CA	1	7/15/90
Biddeford Pool, ME	1	7/16 to 7/21/77
Scituate, MA	1	7/17 to 7/24/80
Bombay Hook/Little Creek, DE	1	7/17 to 7/25/87
Ashtabula, OH	1	7/21 to 7/22/62
Little Creek WMA, DE	1-2	7/21 to 7/29/86
Little Creek WMA, DE	1	7/22 to 7/29/84
Eureka, CA	1	7/20 to 7/22/84
Craney Island, VA	1	7/22 to 7/25/94
Lancaster, CA	1	7/23 to 7/29/83
Bombay Hook NWR, DE	1	7/26/86
Jamaica Bay NWR, L.I., NY	1	7/27 to 8/11/85
Las Vegas, NV	1	7/27 to 7/28/92
Little Creek WMA, DE	1	7/29/90
Bombay Hook NWR, DE	1	8/3/92
Ensley Bottoms, TN	1	8/7/93
Cedar Beach, L.I., NY	1-2	8/9/92
Salton Sea, CA	1	8/17/74
Tillamook Bay, OR	2	8/19 to 8/28/82
West Ocean City, MD	1	8/19/95
Cedar Beach, L.I., NY	1	8/23 to 8/29/92
Guilford, CT	1	8/25/75
Ensley Bottoms, TN	1	10/8 to 10/20/94

LOCATION	NUMBERS SEEN	DATES SEEN
Rejected by state BRCs		
Santa Clara River estuary, CA	1	7/4/87
Whidbey Island, WA	1	7/18/93
south end Salton Sea, CA	1	7/19/81
Imperial Beach, CA	1	8/10/80
Santa Clara River estuary, CA	1*	9/1 to 9/6/78

*Photos proved it to be a Semipalmated Sandpiper.

all Lower 48 records through 1995

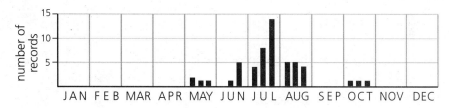

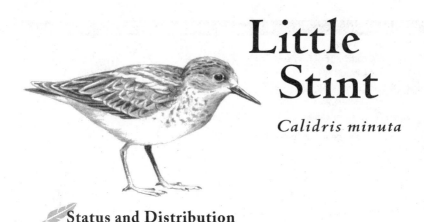

Little Stint

Calidris minuta

Status and Distribution

This common Eurasian peep breeds on the tundra from Norway to western Siberia and winters primarily in Africa, India, and the Middle East. Migrants occur throughout most of Europe and western Asia but are very rare in the Far East. In North America, the Little Stint is a highly coveted vagrant. The challenge of picking one out from vast flocks of Semipalmated and Western Sandpipers draws shorebird enthusiasts to favored locales season after season. Even though success is rare, the pilgrimage and the search are half the fun.

Since the first one was photographed at Little Creek, Delaware, on May 23, 1979, 24 Little Stints have been found in the Lower 48, mostly at coastal locations. About two-thirds of these have been on the Atlantic Coast, suggesting a predominantly European origin. States with published sightings include Oregon, California, Tennessee, Massachusetts, New York, New Jersey, Delaware, Maryland, and North Carolina.

Little Stint records span May to September, with an outlying November record from Harper Dry Lake in California's interior. There is a clear peak in late July and a smaller peak in mid-September. Most records are of adults in various stages of alternate (breeding) plumage, but the small September peak represents mostly juveniles. Sightings have been on tidal mudflats and in nontidal pools and impoundments.

Best Bets

There is no single outstanding site for the Little Stint in the Lower 48. The only real concentration of records is seven from coastal Massachusetts, but each was at a different location. California has six records but, again, each is from a different place. The only sites with multiple records are Jamaica Bay National Wildlife Refuge, Long Island, New York, with three, and Little Creek Wildlife Management Area, Delaware, with two. To search for a Little Stint, the best thing would be to pick your favorite coastal shorebird spot between Massachusetts and North Carolina and scrutinize it from late July to late September.

Identification

Identifying a Little Stint is always difficult, with numerous pitfalls and different key field marks for each plumage. To fully grasp the complexity of the problem, readers are urged to study Veit and Jonsson (1984). Here, we will simply bring up a number of points that should be kept in mind while looking for a Little Stint.

1. Brightly colored birds in breeding plumage can resemble Red-necked Stint (see Red-necked Stint species account, p. 144).

2. All birds in breeding plumage, bright or dull, can closely resemble Sanderling. Be aware of differences in size and proportions between these two and always check for the presence of a hind toe, which rules out Sanderling.

3. The first juvenile Least Sandpipers arrive in the Lower 48 in late July and often look stunningly bright. These birds stand out among the drably colored adults, and unwary observers have called them Little Stints. Always check for the Least's yellowish legs, but be aware that some Leasts have very dull grayish yellow legs that can look quite dark under less than optimal conditions. Also be aware that a Least with muddy legs can look dark legged like a Little Stint.

4. Some Western Sandpipers can be surprisingly short billed. Brightly colored, short-billed Westerns can resemble a Little Stint.

5. Little Stints in juvenile plumage are highly variable, with some individuals being pale and nearly colorless. Duller birds can closely resemble Semipalmated and Western Sandpipers and Red-necked Stints. The brighter ones can resemble Least Sandpipers. Also, unusually bright juvenile Semipalmated Sandpipers can resemble Little (and Red-necked) Stints.

6. A juvenile Little Stint is unlikely to turn up in the Lower 48 before late August. **(See color photo on page 471.)**

Little Stint—*all records*

LOCATION	NUMBERS SEEN	DATES SEEN
south end Salton Sea, CA	1	5/18/91
Little Creek WMA, DE	1	5/23/79
Jamaica Bay NWR, L.I., NY	1	6/5/84
Monomoy Island, MA	1	6/19 to 6/25/80
Jamaica Bay NWR, L.I., NY	1	7/17 to 7/22/83
Brigantine NWR, NJ	1	7/22 to 7/24/85
Cape Hatteras, NC	1	7/22 to 7/25/89
Little Creek WMA, DE	1	7/24 to 7/30/82
Scituate, MA	1	7/25 to 8/16/85
Irvine, CA	1	7/25 to 7/28/92
Plymouth, MA	1	7/28 to 8/8/87
Squantum, MA	1	7/28/90
Duxbury, MA	1	8/6 to 8/14/86
Plum Island, MA	1	8/19/89
Ensley Bottoms, TN	1	8/20/90
Cape May, NJ	1	8/28/86
Jamaica Bay NWR, L.I., NY	1	9/2/87
Bayocean Spit, OR	1	9/7/85
Moss Landing, CA	1	9/10 to 9/21/85
Bandon, OR	1	9/12/86
Bolinas, CA	1	9/14 to 9/22/83
Eureka, CA	1	9/16 to 9/22/92
Hart-Miller Island, MD	1	9/20/87
Bolinas, CA	1	9/22 to 10/10/94
Harper Dry Lake, CA	1	11/21/88
Rejected by state BRC		
upper Newport Bay, CA	1	7/10/88

all Lower 48 records through 1995

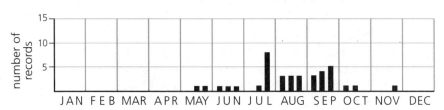

Sharp-tailed Sandpiper

Calidris acuminata

Status and Distribution

While scanning a flock of Pectoral Sandpipers, you glimpse a chestnut cap tilted forward. The bird's plumage is crisp, and its chest is washed with a bright orange-rust. This nifty bird is a juvenile Sharp-tailed Sandpiper winging its way south from its birthplace in eastern Siberia. During an average fall, about half a dozen of these fine birds are spotted in Oregon and Washington, and a similar number are found in California. Elsewhere in the Lower 48, Sharp-tails are considerably rarer, with only one bird per year being typical. States with records of this vagrant include Washington, Oregon, California, Nevada, Colorado, Arizona, New Mexico, North Dakota, Nebraska, Iowa, Illinois, Indiana, Ohio, Tennessee, Massachusetts, Connecticut, New York, New Jersey, Delaware, Virginia, South Carolina, and Florida.

Sharp-tailed Sandpipers are found mostly along the coast in saltwater or brackish marshes and lagoons. Like Pectorals, this species spends much of its time among short vegetation such as *Salicornia* and does not often venture out onto adjacent mudflats.

Sharp-tailed Sandpipers in the Lower 48 occur mostly as juveniles during fall migration, which stretches from early September through late November. Peak time is from mid-September through early November. Adult Sharp-tails are considerably rarer in the Lower 48. The "fall" adults have occurred between late June and late July. The smattering of spring records stretch from late April into mid-June, and the only winter records are from Point Mugu, California, on January 19, 1980, and Alviso, California, from November 11, 1985, to January 5, 1986. The record high count was encountered at Leadbetter Point from October 8 to 13, 1978, when six were seen.

Best Bets

There are three locations in Washington and Oregon where Sharp-tailed Sandpipers are found nearly annually. These are Ocean Shores, Leadbetter Point, and Clatsop Spit. Of these, Leadbetter Point is probably best. In California, no single spot seems to stand out. The key to finding Sharp-tailed Sandpipers is finding the appropriate habitat as described above. Also, Sharp-tails often flock with Pectorals, so check any flocks of these you find.

Identification

The Sharp-tailed Sandpiper most closely resembles the Pectoral Sandpiper, though confusion with a juvenile Ruff is also possible. Among major field guides, the juvenile Sharp-tail is best depicted in the MGB. Hayman, Marchant, and Prater (1986) have an excellent discussion as does Kaufman (1990), Paulson (1993), and Harrop (1993). For good photos see Kaufman (1987) and Harrop (1993). For an example of how similar a juvenile Ruff can appear, see Paulson (1993). Note the Ruff's longer legs, longer neck, and unstreaked breast. For separation of juvenile Sharp-tails from juvenile Pectorals, focus on the following:

Breast
- Sharp-tail: Buffy orange background color fading gradually into white belly. Streaking fine, sparse, mostly confined to sides.
- Pectoral: Whitish to pale buff background, set off sharply from white belly. Streaking heavy, forming band across chest. Rarely, the pale buff ground color can be quite bright.

Cap/Eyeline
- Sharp-tail: Cap bright rust. White supercilium often broadens behind eye giving cap "tipped forward" look.
- Pectoral: Usually duller cap. Supericilium straighter, duller. Brighter-chested birds tend to have brighter caps.

Bill
- Sharp-tail: Shorter, straighter.
- Pectoral: Longer, more decurved.

Voice

- Sharp-tail: A mellow *whit–whit.*
- Pectoral: A coarse *churrrt.*   (See color photo on page 471.)

Sharp-tailed Sandpiper—*records away from Pacific Coast, 1982 on*

LOCATION	NUMBERS SEEN	DATES SEEN
Muscle Shoals, AL	1	4/30 to 5/1/88
Arlington, TX	1	5/17 to 18/91
Jamaica Bay NWR, NY	1	7/16/83
Orangeburg, SC	1	7/24 to 7/31/94
Bombay Hook NWR, DE	1	8/8 to 8/30/93
Sheridan, NE	1	9/8/94
Memphis, TN	1	9/12 to 9/18/92
Hunting Creek, VA	1	9/14 to 9/24/83
Chincoteague, VA	1	9/14 to 9/21/84
Brigantine NWR, NJ	1	9/15/92
Hunting Creek, VA	1	9/16/89
Gibson County, IN	1	9/23 to 10/6/88
Big Lake, IL	1	9/25 to 26/90
Henderson sewage ponds, NV	1	9/26/92
Davenport, IA	1	9/30/88
Minot Lagoons, ND	1	10/4/91
Cleveland, OH	1	10/6 to 10/23/84
Chicago, IL	1	10/6/85
Coralville Reservoir, IA	1	10/14/90
Newburyport, MA	1	10/15/89
Norwalk, CT	1	10/16 to 10/17/85
Phoenix, AZ	1	10/18/85
Monomoy Island, MA	1	10/23/83
Decatur, IL	1	10/29/94
Bosque Del Apache NWR, NM	1	11/3 to 11/27/90
Rejected by state BRC		
Austin, TX	1	5/4/91

Sharp-tailed Sandpiper—*West Coast adult records*

LOCATION	NUMBERS SEEN	DATES SEEN
Point Mugu, CA	1	1/19/80
Leadbetter Point, WA	1	4/26/79
Crockett Lake, WA	1	7/2 to 7/5/95
Lancaster, CA	1	5/5 to 5/9/82
Kern NWR, CA	1	5/8 to 5/10/84
Pescadero, CA	1	5/14/94

LOCATION	NUMBERS SEEN	DATES SEEN
Goleta, CA	1	7/21/88
Batiquitos Lagoon, CA	1	7/24 to 7/25/88
San Joaquin Marsh, CA	1	9/29 to 10/8/92

Sharp-tailed Sandpiper—*other selected records*

LOCATION	NUMBERS SEEN	DATES SEEN
Plymouth, MA	1	6/30/71
Newburyport, MA	1	11/3 to 11/5/73
Jamaica Bay NWR, NY	1	7/18 to 7/21/81
Tuckerton, NJ	1	10/21/75
Avalon Causeway, NJ	1	9/21/80
Tuckerton, NJ	1	8/6/81
Zellwood, FL	1	9/12 to 9/13/73
Long Pine Key, FL	1	10/1/67
Coralville Reservoir, IA	1	10/3/74
Galveston, TX	1	3/21/48
near Lafayette, CO	1	10/26 to 11/6/75
Chandler, AZ	1	10/15 to 10/17/72

Curlew Sandpiper

Calidris ferruginea

Status and Distribution

This prize shorebird is sought as much for its beauty as for its rarity. Happily, it is one of the most regular Old World strays to North America. It has been recorded in 35 of the Lower 48 states with an average of 20 records per year, mostly on the Atlantic Coast. States with published records include Washington, Oregon, California, Montana, Utah, Nevada, North Dakota, Kansas, Texas, Minnesota, Iowa, Louisiana, Wisconsin, Michigan, Illinois, Indiana, Ohio, Kentucky, Alabama, Maine, New Hampshire, Vermont, Massachusetts, Rhode Island, Connecticut, New York, Pennsylvania, New Jersey, Delaware, Maryland, Virginia, North Carolina, South Carolina, Georgia, and Florida.

During the breeding season, the Curlew Sandpiper is confined to the high Arctic tundra of Siberia, but in migration it occurs throughout the Old World, with wintering birds occurring from Africa to New Zealand. With such a wide distribution, it comes as no surprise that a few make it across the oceans to North America. Quite likely, most of the Curlew Sandpipers seen in eastern North America are on a regular path between breeding grounds in Siberia and wintering grounds in Africa.

In North America, the vast majority of Curlew Sandpiper records come from the Atlantic Coast between Massachusetts and North Carolina. They most often associate with Semipalmated and Western Sandpipers and are found equally often on tidal mudflats and in nontidal pools and impoundments. The timing is as predictable as that of any other migrant shorebird. Mid- to late May and mid-July to early August are best for the brightly colored adults as they pass to and from their breeding grounds. A much smaller peak in September and October represents the well-disguised juveniles, which pass mostly undetected.

Best Bets

The refuges in Delaware are probably the best places to see Curlew Sandpiper in North America. Pea Island National Wildlife Refuge and Portsmouth Island, North Carolina, are also very good, but access to the best shorebird areas can be difficult. Other worthwhile spots to check include Brigantine National Wildlife Refuge, New Jersey, Jamaica Bay National Wildlife Refuge, New York, and Newburyport, Masachusetts. Look where Semipalmated or Western Sandpipers are abundant.

Identification

Adults in high breeding plumage are likely to be confused with Red Knot. Note the Curlew Sandpiper's smaller size; longer, blacker legs; longer, more curved bill; and white rump. In early spring, broad white tips to the underpart feathers can give some birds a heavily barred appearance similar to the Stilt Sandpiper. On such individuals, note that the bars are actually red, not black, and the legs are black, not greenish. Birds in juvenile and basic plumages are much more difficult to identify and can closely resemble the Dunlin and Stilt Sandpiper. Stilt Sandpipers' legs are green, not black, making identification straightforward (but beware of birds with stained legs). Also note that Stilt Sandpipers show more streaking on the breast, usually with some streaking extending down the flanks (a feature lacking on the Curlew Sandpiper). The best distinction from a Dunlin is the Curlew Sandpiper's white rump, whiter breast, and more evenly curved bill. For other differences from Dunlin, see Jonsson (1992), Harris, et al. (1989), and Hayman, et al. (1986). **(See color photo on page 472.)**

Curlew Sandpiper—*average number of records per year, 1985 to 1994*

LOCATION	NUMBERS SEEN PER YEAR
Pacific Coast	1
Midwest	1 to 2
Florida and the Gulf Coast	1
Atlantic Coast	17

Curlew Sandpiper—*total number of records by state, 1985 to 1994*

STATE	NUMBERS SEEN	STATE	NUMBERS SEEN
Washington	2	Vermont	2
Oregon	3	New Hampshire	1
California	7	Maine	2
Utah	1	Massachusetts	17
Iowa	2	Rhode Island	5
Minnesota	1	New York	10
Wisconsin	1	New Jersey	27
Michigan	8	Delaware	47
Illinois	3	Maryland	2
Ohio	2	Virginia	8
Kentucky	1	North Carolina	45
Texas	6	South Carolina	3
Louisiana	2	Georgia	1
Florida	6		

Curlew Sandpiper—*all records away from Atlantic Coast, 1985 to 1994*

LOCATION	NUMBERS SEEN	DATES SEEN
Cape San Blas, FL	1	2/23/85
Ottawa, OH	1	5/7 to 5/12/85
Nashua, IA	1	5/10/85
San Antonio, TX	1	5/23 to 5/25/85
Bandon, OR	1	7/25/85
Bayocean Spit, OR	1	8/17/85
Zellwood, FL	1	8/17 to 8/19/85
Bayocean Spit, OR	1	8/20 to 8/25/85
Salinas, CA	1	9/8 to 9/14/85
Vermilion, IL	1	5/16 to 5/19/86
Calumet, IL	1	8/24-8/31/86
south jetty of Columbia River, OR	1	9/23/86
Arlington, WI	1	5/23/87
Salinas, CA	1	7/10/87
Lake Calumet, IL	1	7/18/87
Homestead, FL	1	10/3/87
Oregon and Washington	3	fall 1987
Coralville Reservoir, IA	1	5/13/88
Point Mouille, MI	1	8/22 to 8/24/88
Point Mouille, MI	1	7/16 to 8/14/89
Austin, TX	1	9/1 to 9/9/89
Lake Merced, CA	1	9/17 to 9/20/89
Point Mugu, CA	1	9/26 to 10/9/89
Vincent Wildlife Refuge, LA	1	5/4/90

LOCATION	NUMBERS SEEN	DATES SEEN
Point Mouille, MI	1	9/4 to 9/13/90
Ocean Shores, WA	1	9/19/90
Vincent Wildlife Refuge, LA	1	5/13 to 5/14/91
Ogden, UT	1	spring 1991
Monroe County, MI	1	7/20 to 8/6/91
Erie Marsh Preserve, MI	1	5/10/92
Point Mouille, MI	1	8/15 to 8/23/92
San Mateo, CA	1	8/8/92
Fort Clinch State Park, FL	1	2/22/93
Ottawa NWR, OH	1	8/10/93
Fort Meyers Beach, FL	1	10/14/93 to 5/15/94
Salton Sea, CA	1	4/16 to 4/26/94
Santa Ana NWR, TX	1	5/3 to 5/7/94
Goodhue, MN	1	5/21 to 5/22/94
Bolivar Flats, TX	1	6/24 to early 7/94
McElroy Lake, KY	1	7/9 to 7/11/94
Lancaster, CA	1	7/23 to 7/24/94
Point Mouille, MI	1	7/30 to 8/9/94
Dead Creek, VT	1	8/28/94
Merritt Island NWR, FL	1	10/15/94
Jefferson County, TX	1	11/24/94
Rejected by state BRCs		
Tillamook, OR*	1	9/15/86
Hampton Township Park, MI	1	11/1/91
Austin, TX	1	9/14 to 9/15/92

*Photos proved it to be a Dunlin.

all Atlantic Coast (Maine–Georgia) records with dates—1985-1994

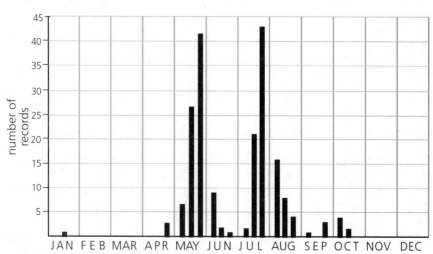

Ruff

Philomachus pugnax

Status and Distribution

This odd but attractive member of the sandpiper family occurs more broadly and more often across North America than any other Eurasian shorebird. Ruffs breed from northern Europe to eastern Siberia and winter primarily in Africa, with a wide scattering in southern Europe, the Middle East, and Southeast Asia. A single breeding record from Alaska in 1976 and a regular migration path through the Lower 48 states raises suspicions that Ruffs may be breeding regularly somewhere in Alaska or Canada.

Ruffs have been found in almost every habitat where there are shorebirds, from flooded fields and freshwater flats to sewage ponds, saltwater marshes, and tidal flats. They are most often seen with Greater and Lesser Yellowlegs, and indeed should be looked for among them. However, they are frequently found off by themselves or in mixed flocks with other shorebirds. Coastal localities seem best for Ruffs, but they are regularly found inland as well.

Of the Lower 48 states, 42 of them have records of Ruffs, and it seems only a matter of time before this species turns up in the other six states. States without Ruff records include Idaho, Montana, Wyoming, Utah, Oklahoma, and West Virginia. As with most birds of such wide distribution, the Ruff's seasonal status is best digested in parts.

Pacific Coast

On the Pacific Coast, fall is the best time to see a Ruff. Fall migration here extends from July to November with a peak from late August to early October. About half of these records come from northern California, with the remainder split evenly between southern California and Oregon and

Washington. During most years, two or three birds winter in California. One Ruff returned to San Diego Bay for at least eight winters, usually arriving between mid-July and early August and leaving in mid-March. Spring migrant Ruffs are unusual on the Pacific Coast, with one or two per year seen between mid-March and mid-May.

Despite the relatively large number of records, few sites are reliable for this species year after year. Perhaps this is because the bulk of the Ruffs on the Pacific Coast are juveniles exploring the area for the first time, thus eliminating site fidelity from the equation. A few of the more consistent localities include Ocean Shores, Leadbetter Point, the South Jetty of the Columbia River, Nehalem Meadows, the south end of San Francisco Bay, Santa Maria, and Point Mugu.

Atlantic Coast

The Atlantic Coast is probably the best place in North America to see a Ruff. Seasonal timing is much different from the Pacific Coast, with spring and late summer being the best times. From late March to early May, showy adult males as well as females can be seen regularly at several sites in New Jersey and Delaware. A few birds, perhaps nonbreeders, often linger through June. Southbound adults pass through most of these same areas, primarily from late June to late July. Juveniles are relatively scarce on the Atlantic Coast, so just a few Ruffs are seen there after mid-August.

Pedricktown, New Jersey, has long been a favored site in early spring, with up to a dozen or more Ruffs seen in a single season. The best time is between late March and late April. By May (and through the fall), vegetation has grown up enough so that habitat is no longer suitable for Ruffs. Numbers of Ruffs at Pedricktown vary from year to year, but unfortunately in recent years numbers have declined (e.g., only one bird in 1994). Overgowth of the marsh vegetation may be the cause for this trend.

With the decline of Pedricktown, Delaware's collection of coastal shorebirding areas (Bombay Hook NWR, Little Creek WMA, and Ted Harvey WMA) is now probably the best place to find a Ruff. In fact, these spots have probably accounted for more Ruff records than any other area in North America. Be sure to check the complex of impoundments, tidal creeks, and tidal flats here. In spring, flooded fields in the large surrounding agricultural areas have also produced many sightings.

Elsewhere on the Atlantic Coast, you may wish to try Newburyport, Massachusetts, where Ruffs are nearly annual.

Gulf Coast

Ruffs are very rare along the Gulf Coast as a whole, but recently they have become more regular in the rice fields of southwestern Louisiana, especially in and around the Vincent Wildlife Refuge. Although birds have been seen along the Gulf Coast in every month but June, a slight peak is evident from mid-August to early September.

Interior West and Midwest

Ruffs are quite rare throughout the interior of the country except in the upper Midwest, where they are annual in small numbers. Interior states where they are annual or semiannual include Minnesota, Wisconsin, Michigan, Ohio, Illinois, and Tennessee. Records span late March to late October with a peak in mid-May and a smaller peak in July. No site is reliable, but both Point Mouille State Game Area, Michigan, and Ensley Bottoms, Tennessee, have multiple records.

Identification

A male Ruff in breeding plumage is more likely to be confused with a chicken than with another shorebird, but juveniles and basic plumage adults can present problems. Because Ruffs are so variable in plumage, shape is often the most useful character for identification. Ruffs have plump, egg-shaped bodies and small rounded heads with short, slightly drooped bills. The feathers on the back often seem very loose and flexible and are easily lifted by a light breeze. It is useful to remember that a male Ruff is about the size of a Greater Yellowlegs whereas a female is about the size of a Lesser Yellowlegs.

Yellowlegs are sometimes confused with Ruffs, but with a good view they should be easy to distinguish. First of all, Ruffs never show the extensive white speckling on the upperparts typical of yellowlegs, and Ruffs have considerably shorter legs than either yellowlegs. Bill length is similar to the Lesser's and much shorter than a Greater's. Also, the bill is more drooped than either. Leg color on Ruffs varies from dull green to dull yellow to bright orangy red. Although a Ruff may show legs that look quite yellow, they never quite match the bright, clear yellow of a yellowlegs.

Juvenile Ruffs, with their rich buffy underparts, may be confused with either the Buff-breasted Sandpiper or Sharp-tailed Sandpiper. Most Ruffs should be obviously larger than either of these, but a few could be nearly identical in size. To assist in your identification, notice the Ruff's long tertials, which all but conceal the primaries on the folded wing. Buff-breasts and Sharp-tails both show two to three primaries clearly past the tertials. Also notice the Ruff's plainer breast, lacking the Sharp-tail's fine necklace of streaking and the Buff-breast's neat rows of black spots at the sides of the breast. If you still have trouble, look for the Sharp-tail's sharply defined dark cap and whitish supercilium (very plain face on Ruff) or the Buff-breast's plain rump (conspicuous white U-shaped rump patch on Ruff). **(See color photo on page 472.)**

Ruff—*average number of records per year, 1985 to 1994*

LOCATION	NUMBER OF RECORDS PER YEAR
Pacific Coast	24
Interior West	1 every 3 to 4 years
Midwest	7
Florida and Gulf Coast	3 to 4
Atlantic Coast	31

Ruff—*total number of records by state, 1985 to 1994*

STATE	NUMBERS SEEN	STATE	NUMBERS SEEN
Washington	19	Texas	10
Oregon	15	Louisiana	15
California	209	Mississippi	2
Nevada	1	Alabama	1
Arizona	1	Florida	7
New Mexico	1	Maine	14
North Dakota	3	Vermont	1
Nebraska	1	Massachusetts	33
Minnesota	10	Rhode Island	3
Missouri	3	Connecticut	4
Kansas	1	New York	19
Arkansas	3	Pennsylvania	5
Wisconsin	6	New Jersey	93
Michigan	9	Delaware	83
Ohio	10	Maryland	20
Indiana	5	Virginia	15
Illinois	12	N Carolina	14

STATE	NUMBERS SEEN	STATE	NUMBERS SEEN
Kentucky	2	S Carolina	6
Tennessee	8		

Ruff—*all records away from Atlantic and Pacific Coasts, 1985 to 1994*

LOCATION	NUMBERS SEEN	DATES SEEN
Acadia, LA	1	1/26/90
Vermilion Parish, LA	1	2/7/88
Vincent Wildlife Refuge, LA	1	2/10/90
Vincent Wildlife Refuge, LA	1	3/13/91
Vermilion Parish, LA	1	3/19 to 3/22/94
Vermilion Parish, LA	1	3/20/94
Lafayette, LA	1	3/28/94
Point Mouille, MI	1	3/29/88
Mercer, KY	1	4/1/89
Delaware WMA, OH	1	4/7/93
Austin, TX	1	4/11/85
Reelfoot NWR, KY	1	4/17/87
Lonoke, AR	1	4/17/88
Chambers County rice fields, TX	1	4/18 to 4/20/93
Phelps, NE	1	4/19/94
Savoy, IL	1	4/20/94
Anahuac, TX	1	4/21/94
Porter, IN	1	4/22/85
Centerton Fish Hatchery, AR	1	4/22/94
Ingham, MI	1	4/23/88
DuPage, IL	1	4/25 to 4/30/92
Erie Power Plant, MI	1	4/27/92
Joliet, IL	1	4/29/88
Minnehan WMA, IN	1	4/29/89
Lac qui Parle, MN	1	4/29/92
Kaplan, LA	1	4/30/88
Schell-Osage WMA, MO	1	5/1/88
Woodburn, IN	1	5/2/93
Ensley Bottoms, TN	1	5/2/94
Ensley Bottoms, TN	1	5/3/93
Ottowa, OH	3	5/4 to 5/11/85
Shiocton, WI	1	5/4/93
Dodge, WI	1	5/5/92
Millwood Lake, AR	1	5/10/89
Austin Springs, TN	1	5/10 to 5/13/89
Dodge, MN	1	5/11/88
Wayne, OH	1	5/11/88
Lac qui Parle, MN	1	5/11/94
Cheyenne Bottoms, KA	1	5/12 to 5/24/86

LOCATION	NUMBERS SEEN	DATES SEEN
Vermilion Parish, LA	1	5/12/90
Seney NWR, MI	1	5/12/92
Willow Slough WMA, IN	1	5/12/94
Theresa Marsh, WI	1	5/14/88
Ensley Bottoms, TN	1	5/14/92
Theresa Marsh, WI	1	5/14 to 5/15/94
Bloomington, MN	1	5/15 to 5/17/88
Cleveland, OH	1	5/16 to 5/20/90
Carver, MN	1	5/16/92
Fargo, ND	1	5/18/91
Kingsbury WMA, IN	1	5/18/94
Ottowa NWR, OH	1	5/23/87
Bay, MN	1	5/28/88
Point Mouille, MI	1	6/1/89
Beaver Dam, WI	1	6/3/93
Madison, WI	1	6/22 to 6/23/87
Point Mouille, MI	1	6/26 to 6/30/88
Decatur, IL	1	6/27/94
Vincent Wildlife Refuge, LA	1	7/2/89
Lake Calumet, IL	3	7/3 to 7/14/87
Nayanquing Point, MI	1	7/7/92
Lake Ardoch, ND	1	7/7/94
Fargo, ND	1	7/9 to 7/17/89
Stoddard, MI	1	7/14/91
Duda/Belle Glade, FL	2	7/19/90
Chicago, IL	1	7/19/92
Cottonwood, MN	1	7/21/85
Ottawa NWR, OH	1	7/22/93
Mitchell Lake, TX	1	7/24 to 12/21/86
Mitchell Lake, TX	1	7/25 to 11/24/87
Duda/Belle Glade, FL	1	7/25/86
Austin, TX	1	7/25 to 8/2/92
Rice Lake Conservation Area, IL	1	7/26 to 7/27/91
Lake Calumet, IL	1	7/28/85
Rice Lake Conservation Area, IL	1	7/30/88
Anoka, MN	1	7/31/91
Riverlands Environmental Area, MO	1	8/3/92
Rice Lake Cons. Area, IL	1-2	8/5 to 9/6/89
Zellwood, FL	1	8/6/88
Hennepin, MN	1	8/9 to 8/14/88
Zellwood, FL	1	8/10 to 8/11/91
Crane Creek, State Park, OH	1	8/16/85
Zellwood, FL	1	8/16/86
Austin, TX	1	8/18 to 8/21/92
coastal Mississippi	1	8/20/88
Austin, TX	1	8/20/88

LOCATION	NUMBERS SEEN	DATES SEEN
Scott, MN	1	8/21/88
Memphis, TN	1	8/21/88
Oxford, MS	1	8/21/89
Cleveland, OH	1	8/24 to 8/25/92
Mitchell Lake, TX	1	8/29 to 10/5/88
Point Mouille, MI	1	9/1 to 9/2/90
Shelby, AL	1	9/2/89
Fort Bliss, TX	1	9/5 to 9/11/93
Shelby, TN	1	9/7/87
High Island, TX	1	9/7/89
West Palm Beach, FL	1	9/7 to 9/8/91
Lonoke, AR	1	9/14/86
Bosque Del Apache NWR, NM	1	9/18/86
Las Vegas, NV	1	9/26/92
Shelby, TN	1	9/27 to 10/12/89
Ensley Bottoms, TN	1	10/1 to 11/28/94
Monroe, MI	1	10/18/85
Phoenix, AZ	1	10/18 to 10/22/85
Vermilion Parish, LA	1	10/23 to 11/4/88
Lakeland State Park, FL	1	10/25/86
Erie, OH	1	10/26/91
Crowley, LA CBC	2	12/16/88

Great Skua

Catharacta skua

Status and Distribution

The Great Skua is a true pelagic thug. It kills and eats any seabird that it can and steals food from the rest of them. Yet watching a Great Skua chase down and beat up a gull or shearwater is an odd thrill. It's nature, bloody and raw. This powerful and aggressive seabird is eagerly sought, even by the most veteran pelagic birders.

Great Skuas breed primarily in Iceland, the Faeroes, Shetland, and Orkney. During the rest of the year, they are known to occur throughout much of the North Atlantic. Off the Lower 48, this species is seen south regularly to Virginia and rarely to North Carolina. From New York to Virginia, Great Skuas are found primarily from December to early March. Their status off New England, however, is somewhat different. Here birds are most numerous from late August to mid-September, with smaller numbers seen through the winter into early March. There are also very rare sightings through summer. Many of the late fall New England sightings are from shore (primarily Cape Cod Bay) after northeast storms, but most of the others are well offshore. Elsewhere, records from shore are few.

Great Skuas were formerly seen in larger numbers off the Lower 48. During the 1970s, when foreign fishing fleets were permitted to fish our continental shelf waters, skuas concentrated off the mid-Atlantic Coast in winter, feeding with the masses of gulls that surrounded these boats. Counts of five or six skuas per day were not uncommon during this period. Since the foreign fishing fleets were forced to withdraw, skua numbers have dropped dramatically. Without these fishing boats to concentrate skuas, numbers will probably remain low, but the recent increase in pelagic effort has proven that the Great Skua is still a regular visitor to our waters.

Best Bets

Probably the best way to see a Great Skua is to go on a winter pelagic trip off the mid-Atlantic Coast. Sightings are most regular off New Jersey, Maryland, and Virginia, and the peak time seems to be December to early March. Trips are organized every year out of Ocean City, Maryland, and Virginia Beach, Virginia. Additionally, most years there is at least one winter trip out of New Jersey, but the port and organizer varies.

Those who don't wish to brave the cold of a winter trip may want to try a late August or September trip in New England waters. The Bluenose ferry, which crosses the Gulf of Maine from Bar Harbor, Maine, to Yarmouth, Nova Scotia, may be the most convenient because it runs at least every couple of days. Cashes Ledge off the Massachusetts-New Hampshire coast may be a better place for skuas, but organized trips there are infrequent. Great Skuas do occur in the winter off New England, perhaps in equal or greater numbers than off the mid-Atlantic Coast. Unfortunately, winter pelagic trips off New England are infrequent and are more likely to be weathered out than more southerly trips.

If you happen to be at Cape Cod, Massachusetts, during a northeast storm (Nor'easter) in fall or winter, head to First Encounter Beach near Eastham. Seabirds blown into Cape Cod Bay by northeast winds fly past First Encounter Beach as they seek to exit the bay. October to December is probably best for Great Skuas under these conditions.

Identification

Skua identification has been problematic over the years and remains so due in large part to the nightmarish state of southern skua taxonomy. This affects U.S. birders because there is a possibility that members of the Antarctic Skua complex (*C. antarctica* subsp.) or hybrid Antarctic x South Polar Skuas are wandering north to our waters. Antarctic Skuas are in many ways more similar to Greats than to South Polars, and hybrids would, of course, look intermediate. That being said, these odd skuas make up a small portion of the skua population. If we resist the temptation to identify every bird, we will still end up with many identifiable skuas.

Most guides cover skua identification adequately, and Harrison (1983) is especially helpful. The following points are worth keeping in mind:

1. The Great Skua can show a contrastingly pale nape like South Polar but usually also shows a contrastingly dark cap, indistinct or lacking in South Polar.

2. Paler Great Skuas will often show a contrastingly darker trailing edge to the wing, which is indistinct or lacking in the South Polar.

3. Many Great Skuas seen off the mid-Atlantic are probably young birds and usually lack the conspicuous pale mottling of adults but still show distinctive rufous hues, especially on the underparts.

4. South Polar Skua always lacks rufous hues.

5. Structure is often helpful. The Great Skua is bulkier with a thicker bill and heavier chest; a South Polar has a slimmer bill and slimmer chest but a fatter belly, giving it a slightly different silhouette than the Great.

Another identification problem faced by seabirders is distinguishing a small skua (especially a South Polar) from a large, dark morph Pomarine Jaeger. The size of the white primary patch is more variable in both Pomarine Jaeger and skuas than might be surmised from most field guides. In fact, there is much overlap in that character. A better feature to look for is barring on the upper- and undertail coverts. Most jaegers show heavy barring there, readily distinguishing them from skuas. However, a few very dark jaegers may lack barring. On these problem birds, tail shape and overall color become very important. A skua's tail will always be shorter and broader than a jaeger's and will show little or no central tail feather projections (obvious on most jaegers). Also, these darkest jaegers are a deep, solid, blackish brown color with a concolorous head, underbody, and underwing. Skuas never get quite that dark, and always show some contrast between a paler head and underbody and darker underwing.

Great Skua—*Maine to Rhode Island, 1975 to 1995*

LOCATION	NUMBERS SEEN	DATES SEEN
20 mi S of Nantucket, MA	1	6/17/79
Georges Bank, MA	1	June/July 1978
Bluenose Ferry, ME/NS²	1	7/22/78
S of Martha's Vineyard, MA	1	July 1980
Bluenose Ferry, ME/NS	5	8/23 to 10/17/90
Bluenose Ferry, ME/NS	2	8/29/85
Cashes Ledge, MA	4	8/31/92
Cashes Ledge, MA	9	9/7/92
Cashes Ledge, MA	1	9/8/91
Bluenose Ferry, ME/NS	1	9/12/93
Cashes Ledge, MA	4	9/13/92
Bluenose Ferry, ME/NS	2	9/17/87

LOCATION	NUMBERS SEEN	DATES SEEN
Provincetown, MA	1	9/19/76
Bluenose Ferry, ME/NS[2]	2	9/19/81
Cox's Ledge, RI	2	9/24/78
Jeffrey's Ledge, NH[2]	2	10/7/78
Provincetown, MA[2]	1	10/18/81
Georges Bank, MA	10	10/20 to 10/30/76
First Encounter Beach, MA	1	10/25/83
First Encounter Beach, MA[1]	4	10/31/91
8 mi E of Block Island, RI	1	11/2/77
First Encounter Beach, MA[2]	1	11/11/91
First Encounter Beach, MA[2]	1	11/19/80
NE Maritime Region (US/Canada)	22	fall 1979
Bluenose Ferry, ME/NS	2+	fall 1984
Gulf of Maine, ME	2	12/6/78
First Encounter Beach, MA[2]	1	12/7/77
First Encounter Beach, MA[2]	1	12/10/78
Barnstable, MA	2	12/13/92
First Encounter Beach, MA	3	12/13/92
First Encounter Beach, MA[2]	5	12/13/92
First Encounter Beach, MA	1	12/14/79
coastal Massachusetts[2]	4	12/17/78 to 2/21/79
First Encounter Beach, MA[2]	1	Dec 1981
Eastham, MA[2]	1	12/25/94
Rockport, MA	1	1/4/92
Georges Bank, MA[2]	1	1/17/78
Gulf of Maine, ME[2]	1	1/20/78
off Nantucket Shoals, MA[2]	2	1/30/77
75 mi S of Block Island, RI[2]	3-5	2/3/78
75 mi S of Martha's Vineyard, MA[2]	4-6	2/4/78
First Encounter Beach, MA	1	2/8/80
Georges Bank, MA[2]	1	3/2 to 3/8/76
Georges Bank, MA[2]	1	4/23/87

[1]After storm, +8 skua spp.
[2]Identification not specified, listed as skua sp., or listed tentatively as Great Skua but believed likely to be Great Skua by present authors.

Great Skua—*New York to North Carolina, 1975 to 1995*

LOCATION	NUMBERS SEEN	DATES SEEN
off NJ	?	9/16/??
off Chincoteague, VA	1	12/3/79
off Ocean City, MD	2*	12/5/76
off Fire Island, NY	1	12/6/75
Hudson Canyon, NJ	2	12/7/78
off Manasquan, NJ	2	12/14/91

LOCATION	NUMBERS SEEN	DATES SEEN
off Ocean City, MD	7	12/30/78
off Oregon Inlet, NC	2+	Jan 1988
Fort Macon State Park, NC	1 (dead)	1/10/89
off DE, MD, and VA	29* (9* on 2/1/75)	1/12 to 3/16/75
off Ocean City, MD	1-6/day	1/12 to 1/21/80
off Virginia Beach, VA	2	1/15/93
off Brielle, NJ	1	1/15/95
75 mi off NJ	5*	1/20/77
off Ocean City, MD	4	1/30/83
off New Jersey	15	Jan and Feb 1976
off Ocean City, MD	6*	2/1/76
Norfolk Canyon, VA	2	2/2/91
shelf waters off DE/NJ	4*	2/4/77
off Virginia Beach, VA	1	2/6/93
off Cape Henlopen, DE	2	2/10/91
off Ocean City, MD	1	2/14/82
Manasquan Inlet, NJ	1	2/15/91
off Virginia Beach, VA	1	2/15/92
off Currituck Banks, NC	3	2/18/95
off Virginia Beach, VA	6	2/18/95
off Bethany Beach, DE	1	2/19/95
off Ocean City, MD	1	2/26/95
off Ocean City, MD	1	3/1/92
off Ocean City, MD	1*	3/1/92
off Virginia Beach, VA	1	3/2/93
off Montauk, NY	1	3/4/95
Hudson Canyon, NJ	5*	3/5/77
off Cedar Island, VA	1	3/25/87
off Cape Lookout, NC	1	4/3/93
off Montauk, NY	1	5/20/78
off New Jersey	?	5/28/??

*Identification not specified, listed as skua sp., or listed tentatively as Great Skua but believed likely to be Great Skua by present authors.

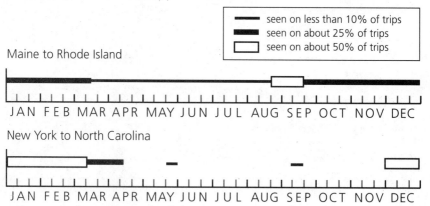

seen on less than 10% of trips
seen on about 25% of trips
seen on about 50% of trips

Maine to Rhode Island

JAN FEB MAR APR MAY JUN JUL AUG SEP OCT NOV DEC

New York to North Carolina

JAN FEB MAR APR MAY JUN JUL AUG SEP OCT NOV DEC

South Polar Skua

*Cataracta
maccormicki*

Status and Distribution

As we have noted, skuas are the thugs of the sea. By comparison, the crimes of gulls are petty larceny. Jaegers are mere hit-and-run artists. After a skua selects its victim, the unfortunate target is pursued with single-minded determination. Immediate compliance is expected. If no tribute is offerred, the skua may well beat the hapless seabird into submission, and occasionally, to death.

The South Polar Skua breeds in coastal regions around Antarctica, feeding its progeny young penguins and other seabirds. After the breeding season, some (mainly immatures) migrate to the northern oceans, especially the Pacific. In the Lower 48, South Polars occur off both the Atlantic and Pacific coasts, but have not been found in the Gulf of Mexico. There are also two records from inland states: Lake Oahe, North Dakota, on July 13, 1989; and Soda Lake, Nevada, on January 1, 1988. A specimen near Sibley, Missouri, from April 3, 1920, is also probably of this species.

Off our Pacific Coast, the South Polar Skua is mostly found from late July through mid-October. During this time, it is uncommon from Monterey Bay north and is a bit rarer to the south. During spring, South Polar Skuas are less numerous, being roughly annual off southern California between mid-May and early June and even rarer elsewhere—there are but a few scattered spring sightings from northern California and Washington. Summer records (mid-June to mid-July) have occurred all along the entire coast, but are few. There are also December, January, and March sightings from northern California and a December record from Oregon.

Off our Atlantic Coast, the South Polar Skua has occurred from March 27 (1989; off Cape May, NJ) to November 28 (1988; Lake Worth, FL) with most records falling between late May and early October, when South Polars are rare to uncommon. Two peak times exist, the larger from late May through early June and the smaller extending from mid-August through mid-September. Though records are scattered from Florida to Maine, several favorite areas seem to exist. These include the waters off North Carolina, Cox's Ledge off Rhode Island, and Georges Bank off Massachusetts. Delaware is the only Atlantic state still lacking a record of this species.

High counts of South Polar Skuas are as follows: 41, just south of Santa Rosa Island, August 11, 1992; 40, Monterey Bay, September 22, 1982; 19, Monterey Bay, October 7, 1961; 17, off Westport, October 3, 1976. The East Coast high count of 7 was tallied on a pelagic trip out of Barnegat Light, NJ, on May 30, 1987.

Best Bets

Several West Coast pelagic trips have success with the South Polar Skua. The Westport pelagics have found this species on about 50 percent of trips during July and August and two-thirds of trips during September and October. Sausalito trips from late September to mid-November also have been excellent; Shearwater Journeys out of Bodega Bay also is another good bet.

If you can't get to the Pacific Coast for a pelagic but can head east, try a late May or early June pelagic out of North Carolina.

Identification

The separation of a South Polar Skua from other members of its genus is not easy. This, however, does not *appear* to be a problem in the Pacific because other skua species have not been recorded there. In the Atlantic, however, separation from other skuas is difficult. For details, see the the Great Skua species account, p. 166. Also, see Harrison (1983 and 1987).

Another bird that needs to be considered is the dark phase Pomarine Jaeger. Though large and barrel-chested, Pomarine Jaegers are still dwarfed by the massively built skuas. Also, the skua's wings are shorter, thicker, and rounder. Furthermore, few Pomarines have white primary flashes as bold as a skua's. Last of all, skuas have shorter, broader tails than Pomarines.

South Polar Skua—*published Atlantic Coast and inland records since 1982*

LOCATION	NUMBERS SEEN	DATES SEEN
70 mi off Cape May, NJ	1	3/27/89
out of Moorehead City, NC	1	5/24/87
out of Oregon Inlet, NC	4	5/25/91
Hudson Canyon, NJ	2	5/28/83
out of Cape Hatteras, NC	1	5/28/87
out of Moorehead City, NC	4	5/29/87
off Montauk, NY	2	5/28 to 5/29/87
out of Barnegat Light, NJ	7	5/30/87
out of Virginia Beach, VA	1	5/30/88
out of Rudee Inlet, VA	2	5/30/92
Cape Hatteras Point, NC	1	6/3/93
out of Outer Banks, NC	1	6/4/94
S of Montauk Point, NY	1	6/9/87
Cox's Ledge, RI	1	6/10/83
95 mi off Charleston, SC	1	6/10/84
Cox's Ledge, NY	1	6/11/83
Cox's Ledge, RI	1	6/12/83
Cox's Ledge, RI	1	6/13/82
70-80 mi off Georgia	1	6/16 to 6/20/83
Melbourne, FL	1	6/17/93
out of Outer Banks, NC	1	6/18/94
30 mi off Charleston, SC	1	6/24/84
32 mi S of Block Island, RI	1	6/27/84
Cox's Ledge, RI	1	7/6/85
Cox's Ledge, RI	1	7/13/87
Lake Oahe, ND	1	7/13/89
Cox's Ledge, RI	1	7/19/85
10 mi NE of Mt. Desert Rock, ME	1	7/22/85
Cox's Ledge, RI	1	7/31/92
S of Block Island, RI	1	8/4/94
off Hatteras, NC	1	8/8/94
off Oregon Inlet, NC	2	8/8/85
S of Block Island, RI	1	8/9/94
15 mi S of Harpswell, ME	1	8/17/88
Long Island Sound, CT	1	8/19/83
Georges Bank, MA	1	8/21/89
off Montauk, NY	1	8/22/87
Cox's Ledge, RI	1	8/23/86
25 mi SE of Block Island, RI	1	8/25/84
Cox's Ledge, RI	1	8/27/90
Cox's Ledge, RI	1	8/28/92
Salvo, NC	1	8/29/88
S of Cox's Ledge, RI	1	9/4/86

LOCATION	NUMBERS SEEN	DATES SEEN
Hydrographer Canyon, MA	1	9/4/86
15 mi off Cape Canaveral, FL	1	9/5/82
off Bluenose Ferry, ME	1	9/5/90
40 mi S of Block Island, RI	1	9/10/90
from Bluenose Ferry, ME	1	9/12/93
30 mi S of Block Island, RI	2	9/14/92
Mt. Desert Rock, ME	1	9/15/91
off New Hampshire	1	9/17/83
Block Canyon, RI	1	9/17 to 9/18/92
Lake Murray Dam, SC (inland record)	1	9/23/89
Chatham, MA	1	9/27/85
Block Island, RI	1	10/5/87
Cape Canaveral, FL	1	10/28/94
Lake Worth, FL	1	11/28/88
Soda Lake, NV	1	1/1/88

Atlantic Coast records

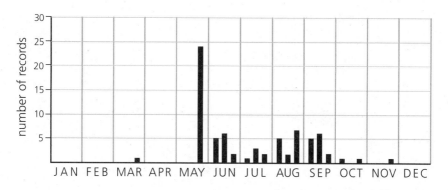

Little Gull

Larus minutus

Status and Distribution

The Little Gull is indeed the world's most petite larid. It resembles a cross between a tern and a phalarope more than it does the hulking brutishness of a Glaucous or Great Black-backed Gull. Undoubtedly, this species' small size and dainty character are part of its charm.

Most of the Little Gull's range is in the Old World, where it breeds from northeastern Europe to eastern Siberia and winters from Britain and west Africa to Japan and the Kamchatka Peninsula. The Little Gull's distribution in the Lower 48 is unusual—virtually nowhere would its occurrence be outlandish, yet nearly everywhere it is noteworthy. The center of its North American range is the Great Lakes and the northern Atlantic Coast. From Lake Michigan and Lake Huron through Lakes Erie and Ontario this species is on the uncommon side of rare. It is of similar status on Lake Champlain and along the coast from Maine to Virginia Beach. Furthermore, Little Gulls are rare but fairly regular along coastal North Carolina, on Lake Superior, around Washington's Puget Sound region, and in northern and central California. Elsewhere in the Lower 48, this species is casual or accidental. Only Nevada, Montana, Wyoming, Utah, Arizona, South Dakota, Nebraska, West Virginia, and Kentucky have not yet recorded a Little Gull.

Little Gulls are not only capable of showing up anywhere but also at any time. In many regions, records of this gull span the calendar. This complex pattern is best considered in parts. In the western Great Lakes (Superior, Michigan, and Huron), the Little Gull is mostly a summer resident and fall migrant. It has bred in Wisconsin and Michigan and has attempted breeding in Minnesota. This species is most numerous in this region during fall migration (late July to mid-December), when an average of 15 to 20 birds is seen (excluding summering birds from Manitowoc). Peak time is from late August into early November. Midwinter records are scarce. In spring a small movement occurs between late April and late May, usually numbering fewer than 5 birds. The summering, breeding birds (typically 8 to 12) near Manitowoc, Wisconsin, normally arrive in early to mid-May, and recent midsummer records (June to mid-July) away from Manitowoc are few. The Manitowoc Little Gulls have usually left that area by early or mid-August.

In the eastern Great Lakes (Erie and Ontario), Little Gull records also span the calendar, but in this region this gull is seen mostly during fall and early winter. Fall arrivals usually appear with Bonaparte's Gulls between late August and mid-September and peak during November. These birds normally linger until the first hard freeze, which most often occurs between late December and mid-January. Peak numbers can be impressive and are usually along the Niagara River or around Rochester, New York. The largest tallies include 55 birds at Rochester on December 24, 1991, and 50 birds at Rochester on January 1, 1992. Not infrequently, one or two birds overwinter in the region, especially on Lake Erie. In spring a small pulse of migrants is normally observed between mid-April and mid-May. There are also a few scattered summer records.

New England has a history of year-round sightings, with most records during migration. Unlike the Great Lakes, however, New England's spring migration roughly equals that of fall in magnitude. Spring migrants occur mostly from early April into early June and normally number between 6 and a dozen birds. Fall migrants occur mostly from mid-August into November and usually total 5 to 15 individuals. Overwintering birds and midsummer records are not too infrequent but are less than annual. The regional high count is of 15 birds on October 17, 1973, at Newburyport, Massachusetts.

The pattern of occurrence along coastal New York and New Jersey resembles that of New England. The big difference is that at least a couple of birds normally overwinter. The regional maximum is 12 at Caven Cove, New Jersey on May 21, 1980.

In the Middle Atlantic states (plus North Carolina), the Little Gull is a migrant and winter visitor. Ten to 15 birds per year are typical. Fall migrants usually first appear from Delaware to Virginia in late November and, in North Carolina, during the latter half of December. These birds usually leave North Carolina by late April and the rest of the region by late May. Summering records are scarce. The region's top counts include 91 off North Carolina's Outer Banks on February 5 and 6, 1993, and 46 birds at Fort Story, Virginia, on February 17, 1989.

Little Gull records from the inland northern Lower 48 (excluding the Great Lakes and Lake Champlain) are few, averaging only two to three a year over this broad area. These records span from late March into early December. Little Gulls in the southern Lower 48 (interior, Gulf Coast, southern Atlantic Coast) occur mostly between late November and early April. There are also a couple of sightings from later in the spring (latest May 12) and earlier in the fall (earliest September 22), but there are no summer records. During a typical year, birders in this far-ranging region find three to four Little Gulls. Notably, more of these are from inland lakes than saltwater habitats.

In Washington and Oregon, the Little Gull has been recorded in every month of the year, though sightings during migration predominate. Fall migration is best with about two to three birds per year, mostly between early September and mid-October. Spring migration averages about one bird annually, usually between mid-March and late April. It is worth remembering that the vast majority of sightings in this region are from Washington's greater Puget Sound area and not the outer coast. Oregon, for instance, has only six records.

In California, Little Gulls have been found year-round, but records from mid-November into early May predominate. About two to three Little Gulls per year is the norm for this state, and the majority of sightings are from Monterey north in saltwater habitats.

Generally, Little Gulls favor the same habitat as Bonaparte's Gulls and are often in the company of this species. The majority are found on the Great Lakes, in sheltered saltwater habitats and at nearby sewage ponds. Breeding birds, however, prefer freshwater marshes and sometimes associate with Black and Forster's Terns during migration.

✒ Best Bets

You have several options when looking for a Little Gull. One is to visit the breeding area in Manitowoc, Wisconsin—a one and one-half hour drive north of Milwaukee (see "Site Guide"). The best time to look here is from mid-May to early August. After leaving Manitowoc, some of these birds stop and dally in Milwaukee at the Coast Guard impoundment. The best time to look at this impoundment is from late July into mid-August, though Little Gulls often linger here later.

During late fall and early winter, the Niagara River area (see Drennan 1981 and Curry 1993) and the Van Lare sewage treatment plant in Rochester are very good spots. During winter, Fort Story north of Virginia Beach has been reliable. Other places with regular sightings include the Cleveland lakefront, Presque Isle State Park in Pennsylvania, the Moses Saunders Dam in upstate New York, Liberty State Park in New Jersey, Indian River Inlet in Delaware, and Ocean City in Maryland.

✒ Identification

The identification of Little Gulls is generally not tricky and is reasonably well covered in major field guides. There are several points to keep in mind, however.

Adult: The slaty gray underwing of the Little Gull is almost unique among gulls. The occasional Ross' Gull, however, can be dark in this area and could cause some confusion. Also, in sufficiently poor lighting, almost any gull could appear to have a blackish underwing.

Juvenile: The juvenile Little Gull is a surprisingly dark-mantled bird. This plumage is well illustrated in the MGB but is completely unaddressed in the NGS guide. This is unfortunate because juvenile Little Gulls are seen regularly in the Lower 48, especially on the Great Lakes.

First-Year Immature: This plumage superficially resembles first-year Bonaparte's and Black-headed Gulls but is more similar to the immature Ross' Gull and Black-legged Kittiwake. Both of these latter species, however, have completely white secondaries and lack the first-year Little Gull's black cap. Furthermore, the kittiwake can sometimes be separated by back pattern. In many first-year Little Gulls, the dark carpal bars of the upperwing are linked by a dark bar across the lower back. In kittiwakes, the lower back bar is always lacking. Little Gulls tend to lose this character by mid- to late winter. Both the MGB and NGS guide fail to show this mark. For a good discussion of this and other plumages, see Grant (1986).

Second-Year Immature: Second-year immatures show characteristics of both adult and first-year birds. Both the NGS guide and MGB cover this plumage adequately.   **(See color photo on page 473.)**

Black-headed Gull

Larus ridibundus

Status and Distribution

The Black-headed Gull is in many ways the Old World counterpart of our Bonaparte's Gull. The Black-headed is, however, a bit bulkier and more gull-like than the ternlike Bonaparte's. Nonetheless, the Black-headed Gull is pleasing to watch and devoid of many of the nastier habits of its larger relatives.

The Black-headed Gull breeds widely across Europe and Asia from Iceland to the Kamchatka Peninsula. In winter, its range expands as far south as central Africa and Southeast Asia. As with Little and Lesser Black-backed Gulls, the Black-headed invaded the New World from Europe during the past century. The first specimen (and first sighting?) in the Lower 48 was not collected until January 27, 1930, at Newburyport Harbor, Massachusetts. Thereafter, sightings of this gull rapidly increased. By the late 1940s, it was a regular winter visitor to the Atlantic Coast south to New Jersey. By the 1970s, it had become uncommon along the coast from Maine to New York and was regular south to North Carolina.

Nesting in the New World was first noted in Newfoundland during the 1970s (Finch 1978) and was attempted for the first time in the Lower 48 at North Monomoy Island, Massachusetts, in 1984 (Holt, et al. 1986). Nesting was again attempted at Petit Manan Island, Maine, during 1991, and a young bird fed by an adult at Kettleson Wildlife Management Area in northwestern Iowa during August 1994 was probably raised locally.

Currently, the Black-headed Gull has the potential to show up almost anywhere in the Lower 48, but is noteworthy just about everywhere. It is on the uncommon side of rare along the Atlantic Coast from Maine to New Jersey and is regular south to North Carolina. Several are also seen annually in the Great Lakes region, especially on Lakes Erie and Ontario and along the Niagara River. Southeastern coastal states from South Carolina to Texas provide one to two sightings a year, while the Great Plains and eastern interior have recently averaged just below one bird per year. Similarly, the Pacific Coast states usually yield one or two Black-headed Gulls annually. The region where this bird is still truly accidental is the western interior from 100° W longitude west to the Sierra Nevada and Cascades. This region has but two records: Cherry Creek Reservoir, Colorado, October 8 and 9, 1988, and Longmont, Colorado, April 9 to 16, 1990.

States with records for Black-headed Gulls include Maine, Vermont, New Hampshire, Rhode Island, Connecticut, New York, Pennsylvania, New Jersey, Delaware, Maryland, Virginia, North Carolina, South Carolina, Florida, Mississippi, Tennessee, Ohio, Indiana, Michigan, Illinois, Wisconsin, Minnesota, Iowa, Missouri, Arkansas, Texas, Oklahoma, Kansas, Nebraska, Colorado, Washington, Oregon, and California.

The Black-headed Gull is primarily a migrant and winter visitor in the Lower 48. As with other species of such wide distribution, this gull's seasonal status is best digested in parts. The northern Atlantic Coast (Maine to New Jersey) is the center of Black-headed Gull distribution in the Lower 48. In this region, this species has occurred year-round but is most numerous from late November to early April in a typical year—25 to 40 are reported during this period from New England and an additional 20 or so are seen in New York and New Jersey. Often a couple birds are found earlier in the fall or later in the spring, but midsummer records are less than annual.

In the Southeast (Atlantic Coast from Delaware south and Gulf Coast states), the Black-headed Gull occurs mostly between mid-December and early March, though sightings as early as late October and as late as mid-April are not unusual. Summer records from this region have occurred but are extremely scarce.

In the Great Lakes states, Black-headed Gull records are scattered year-round without much pattern, but there may be a small concentration of sightings during late fall and winter. Records from the Great Plains are scarce and come mostly from fall and winter. Pacific Coast records come from all seasons, but the vast majority lie between mid-August and late

April with a peak from mid-November into early April.

Black-headed Gulls are most often found with Bonaparte's Gulls, but also sometimes with other species, such as Laughing and Ring-billed Gulls, or by themselves. Since Black-headeds like the company of Bonaparte's Gulls, it's no surprise that the best habitats are those in sheltered saltwater and nearby sewage plants. Inland, large lakes seem to be favored.

There are a few records of hybridization with other species in the Old World. In the United States, an apparent Ring-billed x Black-headed Gull was found in a nesting colony on Little Galloo Island, New York, during May 1982 (Weseloh and Mineau 1986). Furthermore, a Black-headed Gull once attempted to nest with a Laughing Gull on Petit Manan Island, Maine (AB 46:64).

Best Bets

Any large Bonaparte's Gull flock could harbor a Black-headed, but your chances are much better on the northern and central Atlantic Coast than elsewhere. In particular, two places seem to have good concentrations of Black-heads. One of these is Winthrop, Massachusetts, which has harbored 20-plus birds on more than one occasion. The other good spot is Watchemoket Cove, Rhode Island, which has topped 10 birds several times.

Identification

Among North American species, there is only one that is likely to be mistaken for a Black-headed Gull: the Bonaparte's Gull. Fortunately, the main points are well covered by major field guides. All ages can be separated by underwing pattern, bill color, and bill shape. Immatures can also be told apart by differences in upperwing pattern. These are not discussed in detail in either the NGS guide or MGB, but are well illustrated in the NGS guide. For more details see Lewington, et al. (1991) or Grant (1986). **(See color photo on page 473.)**

Slaty-backed Gull

Larus schistisagus

Status and Distribution

The Slaty-backed Gull normally breeds on the Kamchatka Peninsula, around the Sea of Okhotsk, and in northern Japan. During the warmer months a few are also seen annually in the Aleutian Islands and along the Bering coast of Alaska. In winter, some Slaty-backs retreat south to southern Japan and Korea, but others remain near their breeding grounds.

The distribution of the Slaty-backed Gull in the Lower 48 states is, therefore, an enigma. One would expect such a bird to occur only in the Pacific Northwest, if found in the Lower 48 at all, but this is not the case. The first Slaty-backed Gull identified in the Lower 48 was not found near Seattle, but near St. Louis along the Mississippi River. Of the nine or ten subsequent Lower 48 sightings, only four have been from the Pacific Coast. The most likely explanation is that large dark-backed gulls receive much more attention in the interior than they do on the coast. Now that Pacific Northwest birders are starting to scrutinize their Western-type gulls more carefully, Slaty-back records are likely to increase steadily. The current breakdown of records by state is as follows: New York (1), Ohio (1?), Indiana (1), Missouri/Illinois (1), Iowa/Illinois (1), Mississippi (1), Texas (1), Washington (3), Oregon (one record of 3-plus individuals).

No particular habitat is favored. The place to look is anywhere there is a large and diverse concentration of gulls.

The time to look for Slaty-backed Gulls is winter. All Lower 48 records have been between November 24 and March 13.

Best Bets

Unfortunately, there is no reliable site in the Lower 48 as of this time. Again, the place to look is in large concentrations of gulls. Northwest records seem to be at locations where there are concurrent Glaucous Gull sightings.

Identification

Part of the reason for increasing Slaty-backed Gull sightings is undoubtedly improved understanding of this bird's identification. Until Goetz, et al. (1986) was published, there was no good summary of adult Slaty-back identification in print. Now, several good discussions can be found including Goetz et al. (1986), Grant (1986), and Gustafson and Peterjohn (1994). Unfortunately, identification of immature birds seems far less clear at this time (see Grant 1986). A summary of important identification tips for adults is given below.

Mantle Color: The mantle color may be far more variable than alluded to in most texts. According to Gustafson and Peterjohn (1994), the mantle can be nearly as pale as an adult California Gull or darker than a southern Western Gull (*Larus occidentalis wymani*). But this point is controversial. The possibility of a Slaty-backed x Glaucous-winged Gull hybrid should be considered in paler birds. It may be that at this time only darker-backed Slaty-backed-type gulls can safely be identified.

Upperwing Pattern: The famous "string of pearls" primary pattern is not as obvious as many texts imply. The illustration in Harrison (1983), for instance, is clearly exaggerated, and the pattern is also a bit too prominent in the NGS guide. Most birds exhibit the typical upperwing pattern only when the primaries are spread relatively far apart (e.g., when wheeling in flight). For good photos illustrating this variability, see the MGB, Goetz, et al. (1986), and Grant (1986). Also keep in mind that some Glaucous-winged x Western Gull hybrids can appear to have a similar wing pattern.

Underwing Pattern: The undersurface of the Slaty-back's flight feathers shows limited black when compared with most similar species. See Gustafson and Peterjohn (1994) for an excellent photo, and look at the photos in Goetz, et al. (1986) as well; note that the depiction in the

NGS guide is misleading. As with the upperwing pattern, Glaucous-winged x Western Gull hybrids can have underwing patterns similar to Slaty-backs. Also, the underwing pattern is crucial for eliminating Great Black-backed x Herring Gull hybrids in the eastern states.

Eye Color: The eye color of adult Slaty-backed Gulls is usually pale, as depicted in the NGS guide and MGB. However, this is not always the case (see photo 507 in Grant 1986).

Bill Shape: The Slaty-backed Gull has a bill that usually shows a less pronounced gonydeal angle than that of a Western Gull, giving the bill a slimmer and less massive look.

Head Pattern: Basic plumaged Slaty-backed Gulls usually show streaking about the the head and nape resembling that of a Thayer's or Herring Gull. In contrast, Western and Glaucous-winged Gulls are unmarked or have barring or smudging in these areas. Additionally, basic plumaged Slaty-backs normally show a dark smudge around the eye, giving a mascara effect. See Grant (1986), Harrison (1987), and Gustafson and Peterjohn (1994) for good photos.   **(See color photo on page 474.)**

Slaty-backed Gull—*all records*

LOCATION	NUMBERS SEEN	DATES SEEN
St. Louis, MO to Alton, IL	1	12/20/83 to 1/29/84
Elwha River mouth, WA	1	12/31/86 to 1/4/87
Davenport, IA/ Moline, IL	1	12/12/88 to 2/21/89
Brownsville, TX	1	2/7/ to 2/22/92
Niagara River, NY	1	11/24 to 12/20/92
Eastlake, OH	1*	12/28 to 12/29/92
Sauvie Island, OR (at least 3 adults and possibly up to 4 adults and 2 subadults)	1	12/27/92 to 3/13/93
Tunica County, MS	1	2/13 to 2/26/93
Michigan City, IN	1	3/13/93
Tacoma, WA	1	1/1 to 3/11/94
Thurston County, WA	1	winter 1995-96

*The identification of this bird has been questioned, and the published photos do not appear to be of a Slaty-back.

Yellow-footed Gull

Larus livens

Status and Distribution

Admittedly, it can be hard to get excited about yet another large gull, but when looking at your first Yellow-foot, remember the sunny shores and balmy beaches of Mexico from whence it came. Then try to ignore the smell of dead fish that pervades the air around you. That delightful odor is one of the prominent features of the Salton Sea, the preeminent place for this species in the United States.

Yellow-footed Gulls begin life along the shores of the Sea of Cortez (a.k.a. Gulf of California) in Mexico. After breeding, hundreds wander north to southern California's Salton Sea. The influx usually begins in late June or early July, and peak numbers are present by late July. Then in early September, the Yellow-foots start to drift south again. By early October, there are only a few left, and only a small number (maximum 20) of mostly subadults overwinter. The largest number of Yellow-footed Gulls ever tallied in the United States was 1,000 at the Salton Sea during early August 1990.

There are only a handful of Lower 48 Yellow-footed Gull records away from the Salton Sea. These come mostly from the southern California coast, but there are also records from northern California's interior (Crowley Lake), Nevada (Las Vegas), and the lower Colorado River valley (Senator Wash).

Best Bets

Without a doubt, the Salton Sea is the best place to look for this species. Some of the best spots at the sea to look for Yellow-foots include Salton City, Obsidian Butte, and Red Hill.

Identification

Nearly all of the large, dark-backed gulls at the Salton Sea will be Yellow-footed. The Western Gull is, however, a rare but probably annual visitor there and needs to be considered. Fortunately, the differences between the two species are well shown in the NGS guide. Another bird to consider is the Lesser Black-backed Gull, which has been recorded about three times at the Salton Sea. This species is a touch smaller than the Herring Gull and is thus much smaller than a Yellow-foot. Its bill is also relatively long and slim, giving a much different feel than the robust bill of the Yellow-footed Gull.

Also note that unlike most large gulls the Yellow-foot takes only three years to mature. Thus, one-year-old birds (first summer plumage) already have dark backs, and contrary to the NGS guide depiction, most already have yellowish legs as well. For more details, see Grant (1986) or McCaskie (1983). **(See color photo on page 474.)**

Yellow-footed Gull—*all records away from the Salton Sea*

LOCATION	NUMBERS SEEN	DATES SEEN
Mission Bay , CA	1	6/23/66
Tijuana River mouth, CA	1	12/7/78
Otay garbage dump, CA	1	1/19/79
Otay garbage dump, CA	2	2/13 to 2/28/81
Otay garbage dump, CA	1	2/25 to 2/26/84
La Jolla, CA	1	5/21/85
Senator Wash, Colorado River, CA	1	7/27/89
Crowley Lake, CA	1	7/21 to 7/29/91
Lake Mead, NV	1	12/3/91
Lake Mead, NV	1	11/21/92 to 1/9/93
Tijuana River mouth, CA	1	8/24/92
Newport Beach, CA	1	1/9/93
Lake Mead, NV	1	winter 93-94

Note: Mission Bay, the Tijuana River mouth, Otay, and La Jolla are all in San Diego County. Newport Beach is in Orange County, and Crowley Lake is in Mono County. Senator Wash, like most of the Salton Sea, is in Imperial County. The Las Vegas and Lake Mead sightings are of the same bird.

Ross' Gull

Rhodostethia rosea

Status and Distribution

There probably has been no single bird in the history of U.S. birding that attracted the intense attention and fame of the 1975 Newburyport Ross' Gull. An estimated 5,000 to 10,000 birders flooded that Massachusetts town to see this exotic and rare bird. The excitement was so great that the event was covered widely by the national media and even made the first page of *Time*. This gull was dubbed the Bird of the Century.

The fame of this blush-and-ice-colored gull arose from both its beauty and its astounding rarity. The beauty is still there, but Ross' Gulls are no longer as rare in the Lower 48 as they were in 1975. Indeed, there are now at least 19 records from 14 states. The reason for this surge is unclear but may be, in part, linked to the newly found breeding colonies at Churchill, Manitoba, and in the Canadian Arctic (MacDonald 1978; Chartier and Cooke 1980; Balch, et al. 1979). States with records include Massachusetts, Connecticut, New York, New Jersey, Maryland, Minnesota, Iowa, Illinois, Missouri, North Dakota, Nebraska, Colorado, Washington, and Oregon.

The scatter among Lower 48 Ross' Gull sightings is still somewhat mystifying. There are records from the Atlantic Coast, the Pacific Coast, the Great Lakes, the Midwest, and the Rocky Mountain states. Individuals have been seen on the ocean, at sewage plants, on small lakes, and along rivers. Often they are in the company of Bonaparte's Gulls, but sometimes they are alone. Winter and spring records are the norm, but there is a June record from North Dakota.

Despite all of this variance, there are some trends. For instance, the greatest concentration of records is along the central and northern Atlantic Coast, especially Massachusetts. Other sightings come mostly from the

Lower 48 interior between the Rocky and Appalachian mountains. There are but two sightings from the Lower 48 west of the Rockies.

The seasonal distribution of Ross' Gull records is fairly evenly spread from early November through early May without any peak times currently evident.

Best Bets

There is no particular spot for Ross' Gull, partly due to its extreme rarity. Nonetheless, Newburyport, Massachusetts, holds 3 of the 19 Lower 48 records, so it might behoove you to search through the Bonaparte's Gulls there. In reality, flocks of Bonaparte's Gulls anywhere in the northern and central Lower 48 should be carefully surveyed for this species.

Identification

Major field guides are not always accurate or consistent in their treatment of Ross' Gull, and when reviewing these texts, keep several points in mind. First, the Ross' Gull's structure is often its most notable feature. Ross' Gulls almost always appear small billed, round headed, and long winged, but the wedge-shaped tail may or may not be evident. These features are best shown (among field guides) in the MGB. Furthermore, the blushing pink underparts are often present throughout the winter (Grant 1986). Other marks to concentrate on include the wing's trailing edge (see NGS guide), the winter adult's eye smudge (see MGB), and the underwing color (see NGS guide). You should be aware that the Ross' Gull underwing can be dark in some individuals, thus leading to possible confusion with the Little Gull. For an excellent detailed discussion of Ross' Gull identification, see Grant (1986) or Lewington, Alstrom, and Colston (1991). For useful photographs elsewhere, see Harrison (1987), AB 44:379, AB 44:409, and AB 41:211.   (See color photo on page 475.)

Ross' Gull—*all records*

LOCATION	NUMBERS SEEN	DATES SEEN
Newburyport, MA	1	12/7 and 12/28/74; 1/12 to 1/16/75; 3/2 to 5/6/75
Wilmette and Chicago, IL	1	11/19/78; 11/29 to 12/2/78
Newburyport, MA	1	4/26/81
Julesburg, CO	1	4/28 to 5/7/83
Agassiz NWR, MN	1	4/4/84
West Haven, CT	1	4/11 to 4/22/84
Newburyport, MA	1	12/3/84
Reelfoot Lake, TN*	1	12/19 to 12/28/85
Lake Montauk, NY	1	12/11/86
Yaquina Bay, OR	1	2/18 to 3/2/87
East Gloucester, MA	1	2/1 to 2/13/90
Back River State Park, Essex, MD	1	3/3 to 3/12 and 4/13 to 4/24/90
Riverlands Environmental Demonstration Area, MO	1	12/31/91 to 1/11/92
Goose Lake, MN	1	4/16/92
Grand Forks, ND	1	6/5 to 6/6/92
Sutherland Reservoir, NE	1	12/17 to 12/27/92
Red Rock Reservoir, IA	1	10/31 to 11/1/93
5 miles off Manasquan Inlet, NJ	1	11/27/93
Point Lookout, NY	1	3/17 to 3/30/94
McNary Dam, OR/WA	1	11/27 to 12/1/94

*Later rejected by the TN BRC.

Ivory Gull

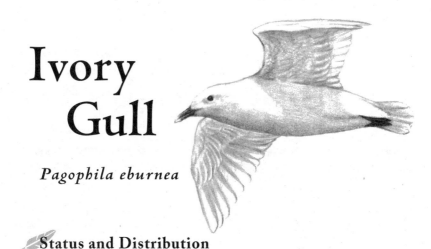

Pagophila eburnea

Status and Distribution

Ivory Gulls are the quintessential Arctic birds. Their color is that of snow. Their range is that of pack ice. In summer, they live in eternal daylight, and during the winter most live in unending darkness. Even the Ivory Gull's scientific name, *Pagophila*, bespeaks its chilly lifestyle, for *Pagophila* means "ice loving." No bird nests farther north than the Ivory Gull (Haney 1993).

There is little doubt that much of this pigeonlike gull's great mystique is tied in with its extremely Arctic origin. Seeing an Ivory Gull without thinking of ice floes is nearly impossible. Consequently, its occurrence in the Lower 48 always creates a stir. Since Newfoundland is the most southerly point of this bird's normal range, the predominance of Lower 48 records from the Northeast is no surprise. Maine, New Hampshire, Vermont, Massachusetts, Rhode Island, Connecticut, New York, and New Jersey have all had records, 17 of them since 1972. Distinctly more unexpected is the number of sightings from the Great Lakes and Midwest. Minnesota, Iowa, Wisconsin, Illinois, and Ohio have all had accepted reports, with 13 since 1972. Other sightings have been from as far south as Delaware and Virginia, as far west as Washington, and as far inland as Colorado and Montana. In addition, the winter of 1995-96 was a stunning one for the Ivory Gull, with two astonishing additional records: one from Orange County, California, and one from western Tennessee.

Most Ivory Gull records have been between late November and early March with a peak between late December and mid-January. There are also two April and two late-October sightings. The two truly startling unseasonable records, however, have to be the bird in Dodge County,

Wisconsin, on July 24, 1972, and another at Fort Peck, Montana, on May 25, 1974. For a good life history of the Ivory Gull, see Haney (1993).

Best Bets

Ivory Gulls occur so sporadically that no particular spot can be recommended. In the Northeast, coastal locations with good supplies of gull food have been the source of most records. Niagara Falls has also produced three sightings. In the Midwest, the confluence of gulls and ice seems to be favorable conditions, but again, records are scattered. You should note that Ivory Gulls usually do not actually flock with other gulls but may be attracted to similar food sources.

Identification

The adult Ivory Gull could only be confused with an albino gull (or pigeon). This species' black legs and yellowish tipped gray bill should eliminate this problem. Immatures have black spotting on the wings and tail as well as a dusky smudged face. For photos and detailed descriptions, see Grant (1986).   **(See color photo on page 475.)**

Ivory Gull—*all records since 1972*

LOCATION	NUMBERS SEEN	DATES SEEN
Dodge Co, WI	1	7/24/72
Lake Anna, VA	1	10/29/80
N of Green Bay, WI	1	11/26/94
Milwaukee, WI	1	11/28/91
Grand Marais, MN	1	12/1 to 12/21/76
Port Washington, WI	1	12/2 to 12/3/91
Rockport, MA	1	12/10/76 to 1/10/77
St. Paul, MN	1 (joined by 2nd bird 12/23)	12/15 to 12/23/91
Cleveland, OH	1	12/17 to 12/19/75
Monhegan, ME	1	late 12/86 to 3/4/87
Rathbun Reservoir, IA	1	12/20/75
Grays Harbor, WA	1	12/20/75
Salisbury, MA	1	12/22/75 to 3/5/76
Red Rock Reservoir, IA	1	12/24/90 to 1/1/91
Chicago, IL	1	12/25/91 to 1/2/92
Addison, ME	1	12/26/77
Ninigret NWR, RI	1	12/29/85
Niagara Falls, NY	1	12/29 to 12/31/73
Portsmouth, NH	1	1/1987
Duluth, MN	1	1/1/76
Niagara Falls, NY	1	1/1/81

LOCATION	NUMBERS SEEN	DATES SEEN
Sodus Bay, NY	1	1/2 to 1/3/94
Cape Neddick, ME	1	1/3/80
Cedar Lake, WI	1	1/7 to 1/10/89
Newburgh, NY	1 (adult)	1/11/81
Newburgh, NY	1 (imm)	1/11 to 1/20/81
Grand Marais, MN	1	1/14/90
Portsmouth, NH	1	1/15/83
Kittery, ME	1 (same as above)	1/17/83
Genesee River, NY	1	1/21/81
Plum Island, MA	1	2/1 to 2/2/85
Chittenden county dump, VT	1	3/3/83
Burlington, VT	1	4/21/82
Fort Peck, MT	1	5/25/74

Ivory Gull—*all other records, except ME, NH, CT*

LOCATION	NUMBERS SEEN	DATES SEEN
Swampscott, MA	1	mid-1800s
Monomoy, MA	1	12/1/1886
French River, MN	1	12/27/48
Grand Portage, MN	1	late 12/66 to late 1/67
Two Harbor, MN	1	early Jan 1956
Waukegan, IL	1	1/1/49
near Strasburg, CO	1	1/2/26
near Sayville, L.I., NY	1	1/5/1893
Newburyport Harbor, MA	1	1/14/40
Cape Ann, MA	2-3	1/14/40
Gloucester, MA	1	1/27/46
Newburyport, MA	1	1/27 to 2/13/49
Manasquan Inlet, NJ	1	1/30/55
Island Beach, NJ	1	2/3/40
Niagara Falls, NY	1	2/10/34
Orient, L.I., NY	1	2/17/45
Duluth, MN	1	2/17/71
Orient Point, L.I., NY	1	2/21/34
off Cape Henlopen, DE	1	2/21/69
Oconto County, WI	1	3/7/47
Manitowoc County, WI	1	3/8/47
Knife River, MN	1	3/14/71
Burnett County, WI	1	4/3 to 4/6/59

records since 1972

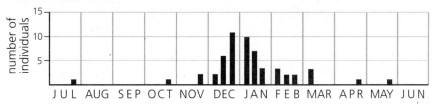

White-winged Tern

Chlidonias leucopterus

Status and Distribution

This striking Eurasian species is a close relative of the Black Tern and is usually found in its company. Although widespread in the Old World, its distribution makes it something less than an obvious candidate for vagrancy to the United States. It has been theorized that a few White-winged Terns regularly join flocks of Black Terns wintering in Africa and then migrate across the Atlantic with the Blacks to that species' North American breeding grounds in the north-central United States and southern Canada. Indeed, the first North American record of a White-winged Tern was not along the Atlantic Coast but at Lake Koshkonong, Wisconsin, on July 5, 1873. What must have seemed like a fluke was followed by several other interior records during this century, as well as confirmed breeding (mated with Black Tern in each case) in Quebec in 1985 and 1989 and New York in 1992.

It is, however, the Atlantic Coast and not the interior that has accumulated most of the White-winged Tern records. To the delight of American birders, the White-winged Tern is becoming regular at several Atlantic Coast sites where Black Tern flocks gather before departing for their wintering grounds. Although records span early May to late September, July and August seem to be the best time. Perhaps this is because birds tend to stick around longer at this season and are thus more likely to be found. The best habitat is coastal impoundments, preferably with pools and nearby tidal creeks for feeding and mud bars for resting.

Best Bets

Without a doubt, the best places to see the White-winged Tern in North America are in Delaware at Little Creek Wildlife Management Area, Ted Harvey Conservation Area, and Bombay Hook National Wildlife Refuge. There are also numerous records from Chincoteague National Wildlife Refuge, Virginia, although none in the past 15 years. Elsewhere on the East Coast and in the Great Lakes region, concentrations of Black Terns should always be scrutinized for a White-winged.

Identification

Most White-winged Tern records are of adults in their distinctive alternate (breeding) plumage. Often they molt rapidly to basic (winter) plumage during their stay, but they almost always retain at least a few telltale black feathers in their wing linings, a feature always lacking on Black Tern.

In full basic plumage, identification is more difficult and requires care. When looking at a White-winged Tern in this plumage you may be reminded of a winter Bonaparte's Gull: a pale bird with a dark eye and a distinct dark ear spot. The White-winged Tern is considerably paler on the back than the Black Tern, and the dark eye is usually well separated from the dark head markings. On a typical White-winged, there will be a distinct dark ear spot and a smudgy or streaky dark cap unlike the more complete and more solidly dark half-cap on a Black Tern. The White-winged also lacks the dark shoulder bar present on Black Tern (but be careful because a Black Tern can sometimes conceal this bar with its wing).

Now that mixed pairs of Black and White-winged Terns have been found breeding in North America, it is just a matter of time before a few oddly plumaged terns show up. As small as it is, the North American White-winged Tern population is more likely to produce hybrids than pure young. Birders should be aware of this possibility and should carefully study any White-winged Terns for plumage abnormalities. In particular, a suspected White-winged Tern in juvenile plumage should be scrutinized because birds in this plumage would likely only come from this continent.

For an excellent, detailed discussion of White-winged Tern identification, see Olsen and Larsson (1995).

(See color photo on page 476.)

White-winged Tern—*all records*

LOCATION	NUMBERS SEEN	DATES SEEN
Chincoteague NWR, VA	1	5/8 to 5/30/65
Perch River WMA, NY	1	5/8/94
Cape May, NJ	1	5/10/83
Cedar Beach, L.I., NY	1	5/12/91
Chincoteague NWR, VA	1	5/16 to early 8/63
Chincoteague NWR, VA	1	5/16 to 8/9/64
Sandy Hook, NJ	1	5/17/83
Bombay Hook NWR, DE	1	5/19 to 9/??/95
Scituate, MA	2	5/25 to 5/27/54
Cape May, NJ	1	6/4 to 8/25/89
White River Junction, VT	1	6/12/87
near Rochester, NY	1	6/19/91
Perch River WMA, NY	1*	6/23 to 7/21/92
Lake Koshkonong, WI	1	7/5/1873
Chincoteague NWR, VA	1	7/7 to 9/17/74
Chincoteague NWR, VA	1	7/7 to 7/13/80
Chincoteague NWR, VA	1-2	7/10 to 8/27/75
Little Creek WMA, DE	1	7/11 to 7/19/87
Little Creek WMA, DE	1-2	7/13 to 9/17/74
Little Creek WMA, DE	1	7/16/94
Hammond, IN	1	7/17/79
Little Creek/Ted Harvey, DE	1-2	7/17 to 8/??/93
Little Creek WMA, DE	1	7/19 to late Aug/1978
Little Creek WMA, DE	1	7/19/80
Little Creek WMA, DE	1	7/22 to 7/29/90
Bombay Hook NWR, DE	1	7/23 to 8/??/89
Little Creek WMA, DE	1	7/24 to 8/6/77
Little Creek WMA, DE	1	7/24 to 9/14/92
Ted Harvey Conservation Area, DE	1	7/30 to 8/28/88
Bombay Hook NWR, DE	1	8/2 to 9/2/94
Bodie Island, NC	1	8/13/94
Point Lookout State Park, MD	1	8/15 to 8/21/94
Jekyll Island, GA	1	9/15/77

*Nesting with Black Tern.

all Lower 48 records through 1995

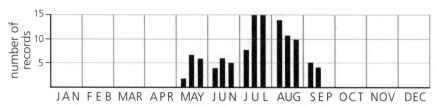

Black Noddy

Anous minutus

Status and Distribution

The Black Noddy is a tern that hails from warm seas and balmy breezes. It is a fair-weather bird that breeds mostly on tropical islands in the Pacific Ocean, Atlantic Ocean, and Caribbean Sea. In the Lower 48, it was first found on Garden Key of the Dry Tortugas on July 13, 1960. Since then the species has been found almost annually at the Tortugas, with sightings from 28 of the 36 years between 1960 and 1995. Most of these reports have been between late April and mid-May. This is, however, when the Tortugas are most carefully scrutinized, and it may well be that Black Noddies are present here over a wider range of dates. During a couple of years, this species has been found as early as late March, and during some years it has been seen through the end of June. The latest sighting was on September 9, 1962. There are no nesting records. The greatest number of Black Noddies distinguished during any one season was four during spring 1995.

Records away from the Dry Tortugas are scarce. There was a sighting of four birds at the "Hump," an upwelling off Islamorada, Florida, on June 4, 1988, and a record from Padre Island, Texas, on June 22, 1975.

Best Bets

The Black Noddy is notable for having the smallest where-to-look target range of any of *America's 100 Most Wanted Birds*: this dark tern roams through most of the world's tropical oceans, but in our area it is found essentially on two tiny islets in the Gulf of Mexico, 68 miles west of Key West, Florida. In other words, to see the Black Noddy in the Lower 48, you must go to the Dry

Tortugas. How's that for narrowing down the search? Your chances are best if you take one of the guided tours that can take you around Bush Key to check roosting sites. The best time of year is late April to mid-May.

If you are on Garden Key, check the old coaling docks because Brown Noddies like to rest on these, and sometimes a Black will join them. Options for birding the Dry Tortugas are covered in the "Site Guide."

Identification

The Black Noddy's color is not as different from the Brown Noddy's as the names imply. The difference is really between blackish gray and blackish brown, and even this distinction is hard to make except during direct comparison. The Black Noddy is also slightly smaller and slimmer, but again this is difficult to be certain of when the two species are not together (fortunately, at the Tortugas they usually *are* together). There are, however, several reliable characters for field separation.

Crown pattern is often easy to see and is quite useful. In the Black Noddy, the black nape contrasts sharply with the rear of the white crown; in the Brown Noddy, the pale brown nape merges gradually into a white forecrown. For a good example, see photo #207 in Olsen and Larsson (1995) and AB 41:220. Another helpful mark is the white under-eye crescent. This is shorter in the Black and longer in the Brown. To use this point of distinction, however, you need a good look and probably a direct comparison.

Bill characteristics are also noteworthy. The bill of the Black Noddy is noticeably slimmer and longer than that of the Brown. Also, the culmen (ridge of the upper mandible) is more curved on Brown, while the Black's is straighter, making the upper and lower mandibles similar in shape.

See the discussion of these points in *Birding* 17:5, October 1985, which also includes photos of the two species taken from similar angles in similar light. Olsen and Larsson (1995) is also a good reference. Finally, there is a fine photo in AB 41:220, showing Black and Brown Noddies perched side-by-side on Garden Key, in which the body and bill shapes are obvious. Pray that you get a look like this one! **(See color photo on page 476.)**

Dovekie

Alle alle

Status and Distribution

The Dovekie, or Little Auk as it is known in Europe, is the only small alcid on the Atlantic Coast. Although common, this endearing little creature remains on the wish list of many a birder due to its Arctic haunts in summer and primarily pelagic distribution in winter. Its small size makes it tough to see in choppy water, adding to the frustration of would-be viewers.

Dovekies breed exclusively in the high Arctic, with southern Greenland being the closest breeding site to the Lower 48. In winter, huge numbers are found in the waters off the Canadian Maritimes, and sightings from shore in those provinces are frequent. During most years, however, a sizable population moves south to feeding areas off the coasts of New Jersey, Delaware, Maryland, Virginia, and even northern North Carolina. Most winter pelagic trips to these waters find at least a few Dovekies, and counts of over 50 are not unusual. These birds are primarily well offshore, and sightings from land in these states are exceptional. Late December to early March is best.

Pelagic waters off New England almost certainly harbor greater numbers of Dovekies in winter than waters off the mid-Atlantic Coast. Unfortunately, little information is available, because pelagic trips here at this season are all too often canceled due to rough seas. New England is, however, a better place to see the Dovekie from shore. Occasionally, after severe storms, especially in November, Dovekies are found scattered along the New England coast and even inland. These "wrecks" were formerly more frequent and more sizable, but a few individuals are still found under the right conditions.

Dovekies have been recorded in all Atlantic Coast states from Maine to Florida, and have been seen in Pennsylvania, Vermont, Illinois, Michigan, Wisconsin, and Minnesota.

Best Bets

The most reliable way to see a Dovekie in the Lower 48 is to take a pelagic trip off the mid-Atlantic Coast (New Jersey to Virginia) in January or February. A winter trip off the New England coast should also produce Dovekies. Sea conditions are critical for finding these birds, and you'll want the calmest seas possible. The mid-Atlantic high count was a healthy 759 off Ocean City, Maryland, on a day when the ocean was like a sheet of glass. Dovekies are inconspicuous and shy, usually diving as a boat approaches, so they tend to disappear in choppy seas.

If the thought of a winter pelagic trip does not appeal to you, you may want to try looking from shore in New England in November or early December. Your success here is even more weather dependent than on a mid-Atlantic boat trip, and here you'll want lousy weather, specifically, several days of strong easterly winds to blow birds in from offshore. Coastal extremities such as Halibut and Andrews points at Cape Ann and the whole Cape Cod sea coast in Massachusetts are probably best. The highest count in the Lower 48 came from Halibut Point, near Rockport, Massachusetts, on November 30, 1957, when an incredible 18,000 were seen passing the point in two hours during a storm. Although most flights have taken place during storms, weather is obviously not the only factor involved. A similar flight of 14,000 Dovekies took place at Halibut Point on November 7, 1950, a sunny day with temperatures in the 60s and light (10 to 12 mph) southwest to west-southwest winds (Veit and Petersen 1993).

Identification

Being the only small alcid in the Atlantic, there is little with which to confuse a Dovekie. In fact, getting a good look is usually the toughest part of the identification. In size, a Dovekie is about a third that of a Razorbill or murre, which are superficially similar in plumage. A distant Dovekie in flight will look like a tiny white speck buzzing along rapidly, low over the water. The flight path will be direct, something like an oversized bumblebee. Red Phalaropes are often seen on winter pelagic trips, especially the more southerly trips, and can resemble Dovekies in flight. On the phalaropes, notice longer, more bent wings, smaller heads, and more erratic flight with rapid changes in direction. Also notice that the phalarope has a pale back and underwing. Dovekie's back and underwings are very dark. A distant Atlantic Puffin in flight can look similar to a Dovekie, especially if no other species are around for size comparison. Compared with a Dovekie, a puffin is larger (about midway in size between a Dovekie and a Razorbill), has a slightly slower wingbeat, a darker head, and a fatter belly. At closer range, look for the puffin's orangish feet (black in Dovekie) and heavier bill, which may be extensively light orange (tiny and black in a Dovekie). **(See color photo on page 477.)**

Dovekie—*selected high counts: Maine to Rhode Island, 1976 to 1995*

LOCATION	NUMBERS SEEN	DATES SEEN
ferry to Monhegan Island, ME	19	10/16 to 10/20/82
coastal MA	59	11/18 to 11/20/90
Pemaquid Point, ME	152	11/24/82
Rockport, MA	23	11/28/93
First Encounter Beach, MA	15	12/13/92
Cape Cod, MA CBC	65	12/19/82
Point Judith, RI	23	12/23/76
Monhegan Island, ME CBC	43	12/27/82
Portland, ME CBC	19	Dec 1976
Eastport, ME CBC	57	Dec 1976

Dovekie—*selected high counts: New York to North Carolina, 1976 to 1995*

LOCATION	NUMBERS SEEN	DATES SEEN
off Cape May, NJ	60+	12/5/82
off Ocean City, MD	51	12/12/76
at Montauk Point, NY	15	12/24/94
off Ocean City, MD	759	12/30/78
off Asbury Park, NJ	13	12/31/77
off Ocean City, MD	319	1/30/83
off Virginia Beach, VA	290	2/2/91
off Virginia Beach, VA	212	2/13/94
off Currituck Bank, NC	257	2/13/94
off Virginia Beach, VA	32	2/15/92
off Brielle, NJ	80	2/18/95
off Cape May, NJ	733	2/19/95
off Ocean City, MD	156	2/23/85

LOCATION	NUMBERS SEEN	DATES SEEN
off Ocean City, MD	139	3/1/92
off Montauk, NY	300+	3/3/95
off Cape May, NJ	24	3/11/95
off Ocean City, MD	59	3/12/94

Dovekie—*other Lower 48 records, 1976 to 1995*

LOCATION	NUMBERS SEEN	DATES SEEN
Plantation Key, FL	1	11/19/92
Fort Worth Pier, FL	1	11/25/88
La Salle nuclear plant, IL	1	11/26/92
Lake Worth Pier, FL	1	11/27/85
Fort Lauderdale, FL	1 (dead)	11/28/88
Indian River, FL	1	12/4/93
Key Biscayne, FL	1 (sick)	12/7/88
off Canaveral, FL	1	1/15/77
Litchfield Beach, SC	1	2/27/94

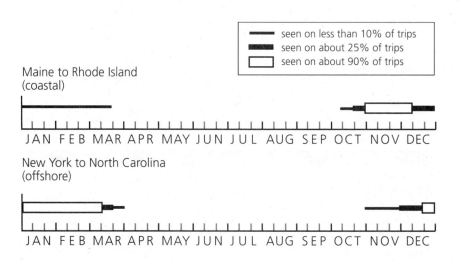

seen on less than 10% of trips
seen on about 25% of trips
seen on about 90% of trips

Maine to Rhode Island
(coastal)

JAN FEB MAR APR MAY JUN JUL AUG SEP OCT NOV DEC

New York to North Carolina
(offshore)

JAN FEB MAR APR MAY JUN JUL AUG SEP OCT NOV DEC

Scrippsi, Xantu's Murrelet

Synthliboramphus hypoleucus scrippsi

Status and Distribution

The "Scrippsi" Xantu's Murrelet, "Hypoleuca" Xantu's Murrelet, and Craveri's Murrelet form a triumvirate of closely related, small, black-and-white alcids that roam the waters off California and Baja California. This trio is so closely related that at one time all three were felt to be races of the same species. Currently, however, the Craveri's Murrelet is held separately, but the Scrippsi and Hypoleuca Xantu's are still together under Xantu's Murrelet.[1] Of these three, the Scrippsi Xantu's is by far the most numerous in U.S. waters. For details on the other two birds, see the next species account.

The Scrippsi Xantu's Murrelet normally breeds on southern California's Channel Islands and on several islands off the coast of Baja California Norte (including San Benitos Island and Los Coronados). The Channel Islands population is well under 10,000 birds, with 2,000 to 4,000 of these at Santa Barbara Island (Sowls, et al. 1980). There is also a record of a pair of Scrippsi with a fledgling in Monterey County, California, on August 8, 1986, and a record of a bird found dead in a crevice on Southeast Farallon Island during May 1971.

The Scrippsi Xantu's Murrelet arrives around the Channel Islands in mid-February and becomes fairly common there by early March. The first individuals leave these breeding grounds in late June, but this murrelet remains common there well into July, and some may be found into early August. Scrippsi Xantu's Murrelets breeding at the Channel Islands are

[1] The "Hypoleuca" and "Scrippsi" Xantu's Murrelets (*S. hypoleucus hypoleucus* and *S. hypoleucus scrippsi*) have potential for separate species status. They both breed on San Benitos Island, Mexico, and interbreeding there is limited (Jehl and Bond 1975; Stallcup 1990).

most commonly seen in the immediate vicinity of the islands but can be found with some frequency as close as halfway to the mainland. Many probably feed at rich areas beyond the Channel Islands as well.

From March into July, the Scrippsi Xantu's is also uncommon to fairly common off San Diego County. These birds may be coming from breeding colonies at Los Coronados (Baja California) or the Channel Islands. North of Point Conception, records from March through most of June are scarce, but there is one record during this season from as far north as the waters off Westport, Washington.

After the breeding season, Scrippsi Xantu's Murrelets become hard to find off southern California. From mid-August on, they are rare to uncommon south of San Luis Obispo County and, from mid-August into October, the Scrippsi Xantu's is typically outnumbered by the Craveri's Murrelet in these waters.

Exactly where most Scrippsi Xantu's Murrelets go after nesting is not entirely clear, but many seem to head north. Most sightings of postbreeding wanderers are from Monterey Bay and offshore San Luis Obispo County, where they are not a rare sight. These murrelets do sometimes go farther north, however, and at least one individual made it as far as Queen Charlotte Sound in British Columbia.

Along offshore San Luis Obispo County and Monterey Bay, the first Scrippsi Xantu's Murrelets usually arrive in early July. By mid-August, they are uncommon to fairly common, and typically they remain this numerous until mid-October, when numbers start to drop. The last individuals are normally gone by mid-November.

North of Monterey Bay, postbreeding Scrippsi Xantu's Murrelets are rare to accidental. There are about 6 records for Oregon and about 15 for Washington. These Pacific Northwest records lie between July 28 and December 6 and, as expected, are mostly from August into mid-October. However, most of these sightings were not identified specifically as *Synthlibotamphus hypoleucus scrippsi*, but just as Xantu's Murrelets; most that were identified to subspecies were *S. hypoleucus scrippsi*, as would be expected. Those identified as *S. hypoleucus hypoleucus* are discussed in the next species account.

Winter records of the Scrippsi Xantu's Murrelet are few. From late November into February, this bird is rare to uncommon from Monterey

Bay south and is accidental farther north. There is some evidence that the bulk of the population at this time is far out at sea and may be surprisingly far north.

Best Bets

The best strategy for finding a Scrippsi Xantu's Murrelet is to go to the Channel Islands off California between early March and early July. Often there is a pelagic trip run by the Los Angeles Audubon Society to this area during this time; call (213) 876-0202 for details. More reliably, however, Island Packers offers trips that leave out of Ventura Harbor, Ventura, California. They are not specifically for birders and may not stop to look at birds. Nonetheless, your chances are good, especially if you go to Santa Barbara Island. If you go to Santa Cruz Island, you can look for Island Scrub-Jay as well. For sailing times, ticket reservations, and directions, call Island Packers at (805) 642-1393. Of note, the ferries to Santa Catalina Island are typically not good for murrelets.

Another good way to look for Scrippsi Xantu's Murrelet is to take a Monterey pelagic trip between mid-August and mid-October. Most of the birding boats out of Monterey have a fair chance for this bird, but the excursions to the albacore fishing grounds are best.

An important point to remember about Scrippsi Xantu's Murrelets (and Hypoleuca Xantu's and Craveri's) is that they are rarely seen from land, except on their breeding grounds. The vast majority of sightings are at least a couple of miles offshore.

Identification

The Scrippsi Xantu's Murrelet needs to be separated from both the Hypoleuca Xantu's Murrelet and Craveri's Murrelet. For details, see the Craveri's Murrelet/Hypoleuca Xantu's Murrelet account on p. 209.

Xantu's Murrelet—*all Oregon and Washington records**

LOCATION	NUMBERS SEEN	DATES SEEN
off Westport, WA	2	5/16/76
~115 mi W of Cape Falcon, OR	1	7/28/69
off Westport, WA	3	7/28/83
off Westport, WA	1	8/4/82
125 mi SSW of Cape Flattery, WA	1	8/7/47
off Westport, WA	1	8/15/84
off Westport, WA	3	8/20/77
12 mi off Lane County, OR	2	8/31/85
100+ mi off OR	6	early 9/70
off Westport, WA	3	9/8/74
off Westport, WA	1	9/8 to 9/9/84
off Westport, WA	6	9/11/78
40 mi off Westport, WA	2	9/11/83
off Westport, WA	1	9/12/87
12-18 mi off Tillamook County, OR	1	9/14/85
off Westport, WA	1	10/4/87
off Westport, WA	2	10/7/79
off Westport, WA	18	10/8/78
off Westport, WA	2	10/9/77
40-45 mi off Westport, WA	6	10/11/70
Boiler Bay State Wayside, OR	1	11/7 to 1/8/87
65 mi off Newport, OR	2	11/19/69
Copalis Beach, WA	1 (dead)	12/6/41

*Most of these sightings were not identified specifically as *S. hypoleucus scrippsi*, but just as Xantu's Murrelets. However, most Pacifc Northwest Xantu's Murrelets that were identified to subspecies were found to be *S. hypoleucus scrippsi*, as would be expected. Those identified as *S. hypoleucus hypoleucus* are listed in the next chapter.

Craveri's Murrelet
Synthliboramphus craveri

Hypoleuca Xantu's Murrelet
Synthliboramphus hypoleucus hypoleucus

Status and Distribution

Alcids have been called the penguins of the Northern Hemisphere. This seems like a flight of wild fancy as you bake in the warm sun and calm seas of a September San Diego pelagic trip. Yet the autumn boat trips off southern and central California are tops for finding two of the Lower 48's rarest alcids: Craveri's Murrelet and "Hypoleuca" Xantu's Murrelet. ("Hypoleuca" Xantu's Murrelet is the nominate race of Xantu's Murrelet. *Synthliboramphus hypoleucus scrippsi* is the race normally found off California. These two have potential for separate species status. On San Benitos Island, where both breed, interbreeding is limited [Jehl and Bond 1975; Stallcup 1990]).

Both birds discussed here breed in Baja California. The Hypoleuca Xantu's nests on San Benitos Island and Guadalupe Island off northwestern Baja whereas the Craveri's Murrelet breeds on islands in the Gulf of California and in the Pacific from San Benitos Island south. After breeding, both murrelets disperse, with some birds heading north into U.S. waters. Their incursion into the Lower 48 is more prominent in years of warmer water.

Oddly, the Craveri's Murrelet, which breeds farther south, arrives earlier and is more numerous. The first individuals often arrive in late July and the last are usually seen in late September or early October. A few have lingered into November, and there is one winter record as well (Monterey Bay, 1/3 to 1/10/81). The rarer Hypoleuca Xantu's has been reported about 30 times from the Lower 48, mostly between early September and mid-October.

Astonishingly, two of the Hypoleuca Xantu's records are of breeding birds (Winnett, Murray, and Wingfield 1979). On April 30, 1977, a Hypoleuca Xantu's was found on a nest on Santa Barbara Island (one of Southern California's Channel Islands). This nest was abandoned on May 15, but found occupied again on April 28, 1978. The original bird's mate was found to be intermediate between *S. hypoleucus scrippsi* and *S. hypoleucus hypoleucus*. This nest was again abandoned on May 23, 1978. Other out-of-season reports include two winter records: two, between Santa Catalina and Santa Barbara Islands, February 28, 1988; and two, 43 miles west of Point Loma, December 4, 1966.

The vast majority of records of both murrelets are from San Francisco south. There are, however, three records of Hypoleuca Xantu's from Oregon and Washington: 65 to 165 miles west of Newport, Oregon, June 1, 1973; 6 off Washington, September 11, 1978; and 2, off Cape Flattery, Washington, August 7, 1947. Craveri's Murrelets have been recorded once north of Sonoma County, California: Siltcoos State Beach, Lane County, Oregon, August 15, 1975.

Best Bets

The best pelagic trips for Craveri's Murrelet seem to be the August or September trips out of Morro Bay. Next best would be the Western Field Ornithologists September trip out of San Diego. In some years, Monterey Bay trips during August and September also can be good, but this is highly variable.

A Hypoleuca Xantu's would be a good find on any pelagic. Your best bet is the September Western Field Ornithologists San Diego special. Trips off Monterey, however, also give you a chance at this murrelet. Try a boat to the albacore fishing grounds or the Cordell Bank.

A novel approach to finding either of these birds would be to take an Island Packers trip to the Channel Islands. The disadvantage of these trips is that the boat usually won't stop to look at a bird. The advantage is that trips go out almost every weekend.

Identification

Craveri's and Xantu's Murrelets have a unique appearance. They are small black-and-white birds that typically sit low in the water with their head held high on an extended neck. This position makes the white sides, so obvious in most field guide depictions, difficult to see. The dark shoulder of Craveri's Murrelet is likewise often obscured.

The Hypoleuca Xantu's Murrelet is the easiest of the three Craveri's/Xantu's Murrelets to identify. It alone has white that comes up in front and then over the eye. However, intermediate forms between *S. hypoleucus hypoleucus* and *S. hypoleucus scrippsi* do exist. In these birds, the white eye mark is much reduced (see Jehl and Bond 1975).

Separating Craveri's Murrelet from *S. hypoleucus scrippsi* is much more difficult. Key points include bill size, chin color, shoulder markings, underwing pattern, and back color.

Bill
- Xantu's: Shorter.
- Craveri's: Slightly longer and thinner.

Face
- Xantu's: Black comes down to gape.
- Craveri's: Black goes to bottom of lower mandible.

Shoulder
- Xantu's: White.
- Craveri's: Black mark extending down from upperparts.

Underwing
- Xantu's: Usually entirely white; may have a few dark flecks.
- Craveri's: Dusky; may have white blotches.

Back
- Xantu's: Grayish black.
- Craveri's: Brownish black.

Despite all of these marks, identification is a challenge. The bill and face marks require considerable experience. The back color needs superb lighting. The shoulder mark of Craveri's is best seen in flight and appears as a partial collar. The underwing is probably the easiest mark to use assuming the bird isn't flying low over the water directly away from you (which they often do). For a good discussion, see Stallcup (1990).

(See color photo on page 477.)

Hypoleuca Xantu's Murrelet—*all records*

LOCATION	NUMBERS SEEN	DATES SEEN
Santa Catalina Channel	1	9/11/28
Santa Catalina Channel	1	9/13/28
off Cape Flattery, WA	2	8/7/47
Off San Diego	2	12/4/66
near San Clemente Island	1	9/4/71
65-165 mi W of Newport, OR	1	6/1/73
off San Diego	12	9/11/76
off San Diego	4	9/12/76
off San Diego	1	9/18/76
well off Point Sur	1	9/20/94
off Anacapa Island	1	8/18/76
Monterey Bay	1	10/2/76
Santa Barbara Island	1	4/30 to 5/15/77
Santa Barbara Island	1	4/28 to 5/23/78
off Westport, WA	6	9/11/78
Monterey Bay	2	10/3/82
Monterey Bay	1	8/24/83
off San Diego	1	9/5/87
near Santa Barbara Island	1	10/11/87
off San Diego	1	9/13/87
between Santa Catalina and Santa Barbara islands	2	2/28/88
off San Diego	1	9/10/89
65 miles SW of Point Reyes	2	9/30/90
72 miles SW of Point Reyes	2	9/30/90
18 miles W of Point Sur	4	10/8/90
20 miles WSW of San Nicolas Island	6	10/5/91
SW of San Nicolas Island	1	8/15/92
85 miles SW of Point Reyes	2	10/17/92
near Cordell Banks	3	11/11/92
Cordell Banks	4	10/9/93
off Point Sur	2	9/20/94

Craveri's Murrelet—*peak counts*

LOCATION	NUMBERS SEEN	DATES SEEN
off San Diego	45	9/11 to 9/18/76
off San Diego	30	9/9/72
off San Diego	30	9/10 to 9/18/77
Monterey Bay	30+	10/2/83
Monterey Bay	20	9/17/82
off Morro Bay	15	9/19/92

Exceptional, unseasonal records
   Spring date: Two, Santa Barbara Island, 4/16 to 4/19/77.
   Earliest fall date: Monterey Bay, 6/27/92.
   Winter date: Monterey Bay, 1/3 to 1/10/81.

Hypoleuca Xantu's Murrelet

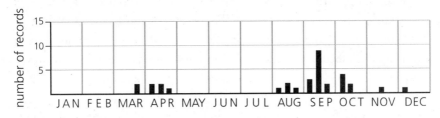

Parakeet Auklet

Cyclorrhynchus psittacula

Status and Distribution

This cute seabird nests on cliffs and rocky shores from the Seward Peninsula to the Aleutian Islands. In winter, it heads out to sea, where its distribution is imperfectly known. The status of the Parakeet Auklet in the Lower 48 is somewhat mystifying. In the early 1900s, nearshore records must not have been too unusual because 14 were collected in Monterey Bay, January 13 to 30, 1908, and several were seen from the Olympic Peninsula on January 15, 1907. Since then, records of live birds have been few and mostly from deep water beyond the edge of the continental shelf. A number of dead or dying birds have also washed ashore.

Between 1982 and 1994, there have been only 18 records involving 45 birds. Of these, 11 records (31 birds) are of live birds more than 20 miles offshore, 5 records (9 birds) are of birds dead or dying on beaches, and only 2 records (5 birds) have been of apparently healthy birds within 20 miles of shore. Surprisingly, sightings have been fairly evenly distributed from Washington to southern California.

The occurrence of the Parakeet Auklet in the Lower 48 fits a definite seasonal pattern. Of the 18 records since 1981, 15 were between November 20 and April 25. Similarly, 36 of the 37 records prior to 1982 were between December 17 and April 17 (Roberson 1980). Out-of-season records include a bird found dead at Westport, Washington, on July 18, 1976; 4 birds 20 miles off Garibaldi, Oregon, on September 7, 1986; a dead individual near the Santa Ynez River mouth, California, on July 4, 1988; and a live bird 11.7 miles west-southwest of Point Ano Nuevo, California, on June 6, 1989.

Best Bets

No pelagic trip offers a real good chance at a Parakeet Auklet. The best opportunities would be on trips that venture out to the continental shelf edge or beyond between late November and late April. Most such trips are out of Sausalito or Westport (April only).

Identification

Close up, a Parakeet Auklet in any plumage is easy to identify (see NGS guide). Real life, however, is rarely so simple, especially out at sea. Parakeet Auklets, like other auklets, look fat and gray as they go whizzing by. A flying Parakeet Auklet is best told from other auklets by underpart pattern. In basic plumage (held into January), the entire underparts are whitish. This differs from both Cassin's and Rhinoceros Auklets, which have dark gray throats, chests, and flanks. In alternate plumage, this distinction blurs as the Parakeet's throat and upper chest become blackish (see MGB).

Breeding plumage birds have a single facial plume which extends directly back from the eye. This is different from all other auklets and is present on many winter birds as well. The oddly shaped orange-red bill is also diagnostic, but beware the occasional Rhinoceros Auklet that has an orange bill. Another useful point is flight posture. Rhinoceros and Cassin's Auklet tend to fly with their necks held in, giving the famous "flying football" appearance. Parakeet Auklets tend to fly with their necks extended, giving them a more enlongated profile (Stallcup 1990).

(See color photo on page 478.)

Parakeet Auklet—*1982 on*

LOCATION	NUMBERS SEEN	DATES SEEN
Wandamere Beach, OR	1 (dead)	4/18/82
Ocean Shores, WA	1 (dead)	1/16/83
Humboldt Bay, CA	1	11/20/83
20 mi from Garibaldi, OR	4	9/7/86
near Santa Ynez River mouth, CA	1 (dead)	7/4/88
78 to 130 mi off Mendocino County, CA	3	12/8/88
Grays Harbor, WA	5 (dead)	12/22/88
11.7 mi WSW of Point Ano Nuevo, CA	1	6/6/89
95 mi WSW of San Nicolas Island, CA	2	3/3/91

LOCATION	NUMBERS SEEN	DATES SEEN
98 mi W of San Nicolas Island, CA	1	3/6/91
off Wesport, WA	1	4/20/91
74 mi SW of Point Reyes, CA	1	12/14/91
140 mi WSW of San Nicolas Island, CA	1	2/1/92
193 mi W of San Nicolas Island, CA	1	2/10/92
off Westport, WA	1	4/25/92
158 nmi SW of San Nicolas Island, CA	1	1/14/93
61-72 nmi W of Point Arguello, CA	18	1/25/93
N of Point Reyes Beach, CA	1 (dead)	11/26/94

Horned Puffin

Fratercula corniculata

Status and Distribution

Puffins are a favorite of birders and nonbirders alike. With their tidy plumage and gaudy bills they look like clowns wearing tuxedos. Seeing a puffin almost always brings a smile. Fortunately, two of the three puffins are easy to enjoy in the Lower 48; unfortunately, the third, Horned Puffin, is not.

Horned Puffins breed predominantly in Alaska and eastern Siberia. Fairly recently this species has expanded its nesting range southward to the Queen Charlotte Islands (British Columbia) and may be breeding as far south as Triangle Island just north of Vancouver Island. In fall, Horned Puffins head out to the deep sea, wintering in the cold currents of the North Pacific.

The status and distribution of this species in the Lower 48 is imperfectly known. The apparent pattern has Horned Puffins wintering mostly well beyond the edge of the continental shelf, where they can be found into May. The majority of these birds probably occur from central California northward. Within this range, Horned Puffins are likely part of the normal avifauna and may be at times numerous. Closer to shore, live Horned Puffins have been seen mostly from May through July. These birds usually occur as singles or in small numbers and are sometimes seen at breeding colonies with other puffins.

A phenomenon apart from the above pattern occurred in 1975 and 1976, when during May and June, a huge number (280+) of these puffins appeared off California. Most of these were found off southern California, with particularly heavy concentrations in the Channel Islands (e.g., 39, San Miguel Island, June 8, 1976). This incursion of healthy birds was likely due to excellent breeding seasons in 1974 and 1975 combined with plummeting food supplies in 1975 and 1976 (P. Pyle, pers comm). There also is an inland record from Coulee City, Washington, in June 1967.

Best Bets

For puffin seekers, the recent success of deepwater trips out of Sausalito is of utmost interest. During 1990 and 1991, four of four May trips had Horned Puffins (maximum: 15, May 19, 1990). Unfortunately, 1992 and 1993 trips failed to find any. Sausalito trips also had Horned Puffins on a September 30, 1990, trip.

For those seeking Horned Puffins closer to shore, the odds are not as good. Northern California, accounting for over two-thirds of sightings during the past decade, is still the area to search, and Monterey Bay, via boat or seawatch, is probably the single best place. You should also look carefully at colonies of breeding alcids because Horned Puffins have visited these now and again (Cape Lookout and Hunter's Island, Oregon; Protection Island, Washington; and the Farallon Islands, California).

Identification

The identification of the Horned Puffin from other Pacific alcids is a straightforward affair. The Atlantic Puffin, an unlikely vagrant to the Pacific, can be separated by bill color and white chin (see NGS guide). **(See color photo on page 478.)**

Horned Puffin—*records since 1981*

LOCATION	NUMBERS SEEN	DATES SEEN
Morro Bay, CA	1	1/2/86
Clatsop Beach, OR	12	2/11 to 2/18/90
100-140 mi W of San Francisco, CA	54	2/17/84
south jetty Columbia River, OR	1	2/17/90
northern California beaches	12	2/17 to 2/28/90
Farallon Islands, CA	2	2/17/90
Pigeon Point, CA	1	2/21 to 2/22/90
5 mi W of Point Reyes, CA	1	2/25/90
San Mateo County, CA	1	late Feb 1990
Monterey County, CA	1	3/4/90
Humboldt Bay, CA	2	3/15/90
northern California beaches	6	3/4 to 3/19/90

LOCATION	NUMBERS SEEN	DATES SEEN
Farallon Islands, CA	4	3/29/90
Pismo Beach, CA	1	4/20/92
70-90 mi W of Point Reyes, CA	136	4/29 to 4/30/89
95-125 mi WSW of San Francisco, CA	7	5/3/91
95-125 mi WSW of San Francisco, CA	3	5/5/91
16 mi NW of Fort Bragg, CA	1	5/6/89
100-170 mi W of Cape Flattery, CA	4	5/8/84
near Santa Rosa Island, CA	1	5/9/88
95-125 mi WSW of San Francisco, CA	8	5/11/91
25 mi off Westport, WA	1	5/15/93
SW of Point Reyes, CA	74	5/19/90
far off Half Moon Bay, CA	1	5/26/88
9 mi SW of Point Reyes, CA	1	5/28/88
6 mi WNW of Point Pinos, CA	1	5/31/85
offshore, northern California	26	5/31 to 7/2/89
SW of Cordell Banks, CA	1	6/1/86
Farallon Islands, CA	3	6/1 to 6/3/90
Monterey County, CA	1	6/2/90
Gulf of Farallones, CA	1	6/9/88
Point Reyes, CA	6	6/9 to 7/21/90
Point Grenville, WA	1	6/11/94
Hunter's Island, OR	1	6/15/88
Farallon Islands, CA	1	6/17/88
5 mi off Point Arena, CA	1	6/21/85
off Monterey, CA	1	6/22 to 6/23/86
Farallon Islands, CA	1	6/22 to 6/24/90
NE of Cordell Banks, CA	2	6/23/85
Monterey, CA	1	6/28/85
off Santa Cruz, CA	1	6/28/86
Monterey Bay, CA	1	6/29/85
Cape Lookout, OR	1	6/30/87
Santa Cruz County, CA	1	7/1/90
Farallon Islands, CA	1	7/6/89
Agate Beach, CA	1	7/9/89
4 mi W of Point St. George, CA	1	7/10/88
Monterey, CA	1	7/17 to 7/24/88
120 mi SSW of San Nicolas Island, CA	1	7/20/89
Gulf of Farallones, CA	1	7/24/88
Gulf of Farallones, CA	2	7/31/88
Hunter's Island, OR	1	8/4/84
Ocean Shores, WA	1	8/7/94
mouth of Siuslaw River, CA	1	8/9/91
Hunter Island, OR	1	8/21/87
6 mi S of Farallon Islands, CA	2	8/23/91
Cape Lookout, OR	6	8/23/81
Whidbey Island, WA	1	9/3/81

LOCATION	NUMBERS SEEN	DATES SEEN
Salinas River mouth, CA	1	9/8/90
Farallon Islands, CA	1	9/17/88
off Bandon, OR	1	9/23/90
7 mi SW of Farallon Islands, CA	1	9/30/90
1/3 mi off Point Pinos, CA	1	9/30/91
N of Waldport, OR	1	11/3/89
15 mi off Cascade Head, OR	2	11/3/89
Edmonds, WA	1	12/15/91
WA coast, from oil spill on	8	12/22/88
OR coast, from oil spill on	5	12/22/88

Horned Puffin—*October to March records of live birds prior to 1981*

LOCATION	NUMBERS SEEN	DATES SEEN
Farallon Islands, CA	1	9/26 to 10/23/74
Farallon Islands, CA	1	10/2 to 10/8/75
80 mi off Westport, WA	1	1/9/77
75 mi W of Grays Harbor, WA	1	1/28/79
San Nicolas Island, CA	1	2/26/78
50 mi W of Point Piedras Blancas, CA	1	3/8/80
Farallon Islands, CA	1	3/18 to 3/19/77

Ruddy Ground- Dove

Columbina talpacoti

 **Status and Distribution**

The Ruddy Ground-Dove is a Neotropical species that was, at one time, a mega-rarity in the United States. It was first recorded as recently as December 23, 1950, in Harlingen, Texas, and as of 1972, there were still only five U.S. records, all from Texas.

During the late 1970s and early 1980s, Ruddy Ground-Dove distribution in the United States began to change. The first non-Texas sighting was in November 1978, when one was found at Fillmore, California, but this bird was considered to be of questionable origin. Three years later, another non-Texan Ruddy Ground-Dove was found. This bird was at Stockton Ranch, Arizona. California then had its first accepted record during August 1984, when one was found at Tecopa. After 1984, sightings of this species began to boom. There area now at least 55 Arizona records involving at least 85 birds (maximum: 5+, Patagonia, winter 1992-3), and California has had 30 or more records consisting of no fewer than 50 birds (maximum: 10, Furnace Creek Ranch, Inyo County, 9/12 to 12/12/92). New Mexico has had 5 records, the first of which was from Owen's Ranch during October 1984, and Nevada had the first of its 4 records on September 25, 1990, at the Amargosa Valley. Finally, Utah has had a record as well: 1 at Beaver Dam Wash on October 30, 1991. Oddly, Texas has not seen the same explosion in Ruddy Ground-Doves, although reports from there have been nearly annual. Most Texas records are from along the Rio Grande either in the lower Rio Grande valley or around Big Bend and El Paso.

The favored habitat of Ruddy Ground-Doves is oases and riparian areas in the desert Southwest.

In California (and Nevada and Utah), Ruddy Ground-Doves currently occur primarily as a fall migrant or wanderer from Mexico. Though records from California span the calendar, late winter and spring records consist mostly, if not entirely, of birds that lingered from the fall incursion. Peak time is from late September to mid-December. What happens to individuals that arrive in the fall but disappear by midwinter is unknown.

In Arizona and Texas the pattern is more of overwintering birds. Like California, Arizona records also span the calender, but the peak occurs from mid-December through mid-February. In Texas, reports extend from October into June, but the peak time is from late December into early May.

Summering, and perhaps breeding, has been suspected at Furnace Creek Ranch in Death Valley, California. The only firm evidence of breeding, however, comes from the Hassayampa River Preserve near Wickenberg, Arizona, where a fledgling was found on May 19, 1993 (AB 47:439).

Best Bets

In Texas, most records come from either Big Bend or the lower Rio Grande valley, but there is no consistent spot. Arizona records are concentrated around Phoenix and the southeastern part of the state without any regular locale, except perhaps in the Pinal Air Park near Tucson. In California, however, Furnace Creek Ranch has proved most reliable for this bird, especially from mid-September to mid-December.

Of note, Ruddy Ground-Doves seem to prefer the company of Inca Doves, when present. Ruddies are only occasionally seen with Common Ground-Doves and have, at least once, been seen with Mourning Doves.

Identification

The identification of adult male Ruddy Ground-Doves is straightforward and well covered in the NGS guide, but beware the occasional brightly colored male Common Ground-Dove with heavy pinkish wash to the breast and head. The females are a bit more confusing. Focus on the following points:

Bill Color
- Common: Pink to red with black tip.
- Ruddy: Dusky, sometimes with darker tip.

Head/Neck/Breast
- Common: Scaling.
- Ruddy: No scaling.

Scapulars
- Common: No spotting (except sometimes one fleck in lower rear-most scapular).
- Ruddy: Spotting.

Lesser Wing Coverts
- Common: 9 to 15 spots.
- Ruddy: 5 or fewer spots.

Underwing Coverts
- Common: Brown.
- Ruddy: Black.

The Ruddy Ground-Dove is also a bit longer tailed and larger than the Common Ground-Dove. For an excellent full discussion on Ruddy Ground-Dove identification, see Dunn and Garrett (1990).

(See color photo on page 479.)

Ruddy Ground-Dove—*all records*

LOCATION	NUMBERS SEEN	DATES SEEN
California		
Tecopa	1	8/31 to 9/29/84
Iron Mountain Pump Station	1	10/11 to 11/3/84
Iron Mountain Pump Station	1	10/9/85
Tecopa	1	9/15 to 9/20/87
Furnace Creek	1	10/17/87 to 1/4/88
Imperial Beach	1 (male)	10/12 to 10/20/88
Furnace Creek	1 (male)	10/21 to 11/3/88
Furnace Creek	3 (female; only 2 past 11/12)	11/3 to 4/2/88
Furnace Creek	3 (2 to 4/1, 1 to 4/7)	10/14/89 to 4/7/90
Imperial Beach	2	10/14 to 10/31/89
Bard	2	11/25 to 12/2/89
Imperial Beach	1	9/8/90
Deep Springs	1	9/26/90
Cantil	1	9/30/90
Iron Mountain Pump Station	1	10/1/90
Point Loma	1	10/14/90
Furnace Creek	1 (male)	10/14 to 10/17/90
Furnace Creek	4	11/17 to 12/14/90
Cantil	1	9/21/91

LOCATION	NUMBERS SEEN	DATES SEEN
Santa Barbara	1	10/5/91 to 1/30/92
Cantil	1	10/17 to 10/18/91
Baker	1	10/25/91
Stovepipe Wells	1	10/26/91
Iron Mountain Pump Station	1	10/28/91
Furnace Creek	6 (3 to 7/21/92)	9/21 to 12/2/91
Earp	1	12/10/91 to 2/1/92
Ridgecrest	1	2/3 to 4/4/92
Iron Mountain Pump Station	1	10/9 to 10/17/92
13.4 mi N of Blythe	1	11/25/92
Furnace Creek Ranch	10	9/12 to 12/12/92
Furnace Creek Ranch	5	to 1/4/93
Furnace Creek Ranch	2	to 6/4/93
near Blythe	1	5/25 to 5/31/93
Furnace Creek Ranch	1	to 12/28/94
Furnace Creek Ranch	1	5/14 to 5/31/94
Iron Mountain Pump Station	1	9/24/94
Rejected by CA BRC		
Fillmore*	1	11/24 to 11/26/78
Imperial Beach	1 (female)	10/22 to 10/29/88
Desert Center	1	11/23/90
Arizona		
Stockton Ranch	1	10/21/81
Rio Verde Ranch	1	12/31/81
Patagonia	1	9/24/83
Green Valley	1	11/17 to 12/27/83
Gila Bend State Park	1	10/14/84
Paloma Ranch	1	9/6/85
Green Valley	2	11/22/87 to mid-4/88
Tucson Mountains	1	12/4/87
Yuma CBC	1	12/17/88
Lukeville	1	1/2 to 1/3/89
Nogales	2	1/15 to 2/19/89
S of Wickenberg	1	10/4/89
Salt River above Roosevelt Lake	1	11/21/89
Fort McDowell	5	12/18/89 to 2/17/90
Avondale	4	early 1/1/90 to 3/21/90
S of Parker	1	12/10/89
E of Sierra Vista	1 (female)	10/22 to 12/18/90
Tucson	1	11/8/90
E of Sierra Vista	1 (male)	2/16 to 2/25/91
Camp Verde	1	6/10/91
Pinal Air Park	1 (female)	10/3 to 10/27/91
Pinal Air Park	1 (male)	10/4 to 10/27/91
SW Phoenix	1	10/31/91
S of Phoenix	2	11/9 to 11/16/91

LOCATION	NUMBERS SEEN	DATES SEEN
Arizona north to Camp Verde	17	fall 1992
Granite Reef Dam	1	12/17/92
Patagonia	5+	winter 92-93
Camp Verde	2	1/5/93
near Wickenberg	2 (fledgling on 5/19)	2/28 to 5/31/93
Picacho Reservoir	2	5/9/93
N of Fort McDowell	1	5/12 to 5/27/93
Painted Rock Dam	1	8/6 to 8/12/93
S of Charleston	1	8/20/93
near Maricopa	4	8/21/93
Paloma	1	10/9/93 to 1/30/94
Tucson	1	11/9/93
Pinal Air Park	1	11/20/93 to 1/2/94
Chandler	1 (male)	11/21/93 to 2/28/94
Chandler	1 (female)	11/30/93 to 2/28/94
S of Ocotillo	2	12/24/93
Pinal Air Park	2	1/2 to 4/10/94
San Xavier Mission	1	2/12 to 3/31/94
San Pedro House, E of Sierra Vista	1	8/23 to 8/24/94
Chandler	1	9/30 to 10/2/94
Green Valley	1	10/15 to 10/22/94
Paloma Ranch	2	11/12/94
Pinal Air Park	1	11/13/94
Nevada		
Amargosa Valley	1	9/25/90
Indian Springs	1	10/24/91
Amargosa Valley	1	10/21/92
Floyd Lamb State Park, Tule Springs	1	1/2/93
New Mexico		
near El Paso	1	10/29 to 10/31/84
Utah		
Beaver Dam Wash	1	10/30 to 11/2/91
Texas		
Harlingen	1	12/23 to 12/24/50
Welder Wildlife Refuge	1	12/5/57
Carrizo Springs	1	4/14/70
Santa Ana NWR	1	1/28 to 3/18/71
Brooks County	1	1/21/79
Santa Ana NWR	1	12/30/80
Santa Ana NWR	1	3/84
Bentsen State Park	1	3/7/84
Santa Ana NWR	1	6/84
Santa Ana NWR	1	10/18 to 22/84
Santa Ana NWR	1	3/22/85
Bentsen State Park	2	3/31/85
Anzalduas County Park	1-2	11/14 to 21/86
Big Bend National Park	2	12/12/87 to early 5/88

LOCATION	NUMBERS SEEN	DATES SEEN
Brownsville	2	1/7/89
Lajitas	1	2/20 to 3/22/90
Big Bend National Park	1	12/24/91 to 5/5/92
Santa Ana NWR	1	1/2/93
La Joya	1	2/13/94
Rejected by TX BRC		
Laguna Atascosa	1	4/21/70
Starr County	1	1/13/88
8 mi S of Rachal	2	4/29 to 5/28/88
Bentsen State Park	1	1/25/89

*Rejected by CA BRC because of origin questions.

California records

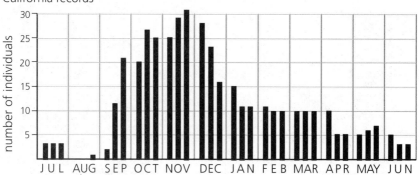

Arizona records

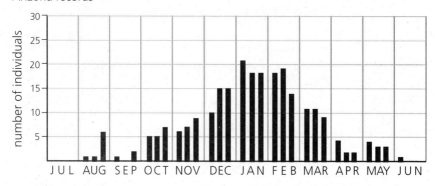

Texas records

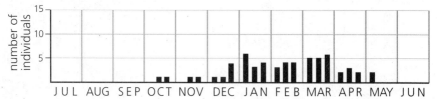

Northern
Hawk Owl

Surnia ulula

Status and Distribution

Sometimes, Mother Nature tempers her stern regime with
a bit of kindness. On the one hand she made the sleekly attractive
Northern Hawk Owl a very rare winter visitor to the Lower 48 and forced
birders to brave frigid weather in Minnesota and Maine. On the other
hand she made it a tame and usually sedentary species: once an individual
is located, it's likely to stay put for days or even weeks. As a bonus, it's
diurnal.

But back to the bad news. *American Birds* and *Field Notes* over the past
dozen or so years reveal the following numbers: approximately 440
sightings, about 300 of which came from northern Minnesota, and 213 of
these came from the fall and winter of 1991-92. About 100 others came
from Michigan (~50), Maine (~22), Wisconsin (~20), and New York (~11);
about 55 of these were also during the fall and winter of 1991-92.

For the rest of the country, it's slim pickings. Vermont, North Dakota,
Montana, and Washington each had a handful of records from these years.
New Hampshire, Pennsylvania, West Virginia, Idaho, and Oregon had only
one each. Older records also exist for Wyoming, South Dakota, Nebraska, Iowa,
Illinois, Ohio, Massachusetts, Rhode Island, Connecticut, and New Jersey.

American Birds and *Field Notes* report three confirmed nests during
the past decade: two in Minnesota (Roseau County, 1987, and Lake
County, 1992), and one near Polebridge, Montana, in 1992.

Hawk owls are seen mostly from mid-November into early March.
Excluding breeding birds, the earliest recent fall record was from September
28, 1990, in Minnesota, and the latest recent spring record was on May
10, 1988, at Whitefish Point, Michigan.

Best Bets

The bottom-line best bet is to check hotlines in winter for Minnesota, Wisconsin, Michigan, upstate New York, and Maine. As mentioned, Northern Hawk Owls are known for remaining in one place for extended periods, which makes them eminently chasable. For instance, the Wayne County, Pennsylvania, bird showed up in late October 1990 and stayed until March 17, 1991.

If you're interested in finding one on your own, northern Minnesota offers by far the best likelihood, followed by the Upper Peninsula of Michigan (especially Whitefish Point and the area around Sault Ste. Marie).

If around, hawk owls are usually relatively easy to spot. They are often found in and around clearings and along roadsides, where they frequently perch high in bare trees, or on the very top of a pole or broken-off tree trunk.

Identification

The Northern Hawk Owl bears some resemblance to other "earless" owls like Northern Pygmy, Boreal, and Northern Saw-whet, but is larger, has horizontally barred underparts, and has a long tail (which gives it a hawk- or falconlike aspect). Its flight is shrikelike, with shallow wingbeats, and it sometimes hovers. It has light eyes, a pale bill, and thick black markings on the sides of its facial disk.   **(See color photo on page 479.)**

Ferruginous Pygmy-Owl

Glaucidium brasilianum

Status and Distribution

The starling-sized Ferruginous Pygmy-Owl, which is simultaneously fierce and cute, is common in the open woods and scrub of Central and South America. North American birders visiting the tropics soon learn to imitate its rapid, slightly upslurred *woot, woot, woot, woot* call—both to attract the owl and to lure in small birds that gang up to mob the predator they believe is nearby.

The Ferruginous Pygmy-Owl ranges into the United States only in southern Arizona and southern Texas. In Arizona, the favored habitat is rather lush Lower Sonoran Zone desert with plenty of saguaros between about 1,500 and 2,700 feet (D. Stejskal, pers comm). The majority of recent records have come from this habitat around northwestern Tucson. Other Arizona records since 1980 have been bounded by Organ Pipe Cactus National Monument and the town of Ajo in the west, Dudleyville in the north, and the Patagonia rest area in the east. Formerly, this species was far more numerous and widespread, having occurred as far west as Yuma County, as far north as the Phoenix area, and as far east as Guadalupe Canyon.

In Texas, the classic site for finding the Ferruginous Pygmy-Owl has been the woodland below Falcon Dam, where the species has nested and where hundreds of birders have seen it. In 1986, Texas regional editors of *American Birds* pleaded with birders not to harass "the only known regular pair" in the state, and wrote that they were "amazed the pair remains in the area" considering the parade of birders continually whistling them into view. They also stated that Ferruginous Pygmy-Owl was "rarely seen or heard away from the Falcon Dam spot."

This changed beginning in 1989, when birders gained access to the Norias division of the enormous King Ranch. Surveys in and around the ranch between 1989 and 1993 revealed that Ferruginous Pygmy-Owls were not rare in the live-oak and mixed live-oak/mesquite woodlands in Kenedy, Willacy, and Brooks counties (Wauer, et al. 1993). Most records fell within an oblong area extending from 6 miles west of Port Mansfield (along State Highway 186) in Willacy County, to roughly 20 miles southwest of Falfurrias in Brooks County, and north to Falfurrias and Sarita (Wauer, et al. 1993). Within this area, surveys garnered 116 nonredundant Ferruginous Pygmy-Owl records. Extrapolations from this data resulted in an estimated 654 pairs in Kenedy, Brooks, and Willacy counties (Wauer, et al. 1993)!

There have been few recent Texas records outside of the population discussed above and the one or two pairs just below Falcon Dam. These reports have come from mesquite woodlands between Falcon Dam and Brownsville.

Best Bets

If you are looking for a Ferruginous Pygmy-Owl in Texas on your own, the best spot is still probably Falcon Dam, or rather the woods reached by walking along the road downstream from the parking lot at the spillway. Other places to check include the rest stop south of Sarita and other oak groves accessible by public roads in Kenedy, Brooks, and Willacy counties (there aren't many). The best time to elicit a vocal response from a Ferruginous Pygmy-Owl is dawn or dusk from January through March (Wauer, et al. 1993).

For those who do not mind tours, Victor Emanuel Nature Tours has begun offering a "Great Texas Ranches Birding Program," allowing access to private ranches where the odds of finding Ferruginous Pygmy-Owls are very good. Field Guides Inc. also offers access to ranches. For pay-per-view birders, this could be a pleasant way to list the owl as well as other Texas specialties such as the Tropical Parula.

In Arizona, the northwest Tucson area has been the most reliable place to find Ferruginous Pygmy-Owl. Most records have come from the tract between Ina Road and Tangerine Road, bounded on the east by the Catalina Mountains and on the west by Thornydale Road.

Identification

The Ferruginous Pygmy-Owl looks quite similar to the Northern Pygmy-Owl (found in Arizona but not in southern Texas) and is not always significantly more rufous. The two species' habitats are usually different, though: the Northern is found in mountain coniferous and mixed coniferous-oak forests, while the Ferruginous lives in deserts and low riparian areas. Records of Ferruginous Pygmys from Sycamore Canyon and Patagonia, however, are from areas where the Northern has been known to occur.

To separate Ferruginous and Northern Pygmy-Owls, concentrate on the following marks.

Tail Pattern: The upper surface of a Northern's tail is almost black and white. On the Ferruginous Pygmy-Owl the tail is usually far less contrasting, though it can be identical to that of the Northern.

Head Pattern: The Northern has a spotted crown and nape whereas the Ferruginous has a streaked crown and nape. The Ferruginous can sometimes be spotted.

Back Pattern: The upperparts of the Northern Pygmy-Owl are spotted whereas the Ferruginous has a plain back. Note: immature Northerns are plain backed and plain headed.

Side Pattern: White with dark streaks in the Ferruginous. Dark with white spots in the Northern.

Voice: A series of toots, usually much faster in the Ferruginous, though an agitated Northern can sometimes sound this way for a short period. Northern's toots are sometimes in pairs.

For further details, see the MGB or Howell and Webb (1995).

Another bird to consider is the Elf Owl, which is found in both Arizona and Texas. It has a shorter tail than the Ferruginous, a dark gray bill (yellowish or pale horn colored in Ferruginous), and lacks the false "eyes" on the nape of pygmy-owls.   **(See color photo on page 480.)**

Great Gray Owl

Strix nebulosa

Status and Distribution

Ghost. Specter. Spirit. Phantom. The aura of mystery that surrounds the Great Gray Owl is reflected in the words so often used to describe it. The Great Gray's specific epithet, *nebulosa*, is derived from its "clouded" color (Terres 1980), but it might just as well indicate the bird's seemingly cryptic and elusive nature. For many, the imperious-looking Great Gray embodies the wild essence of the far northern forests.

The practical side of this fanciful image is that birders can hope to find the owl only in the extreme northern tier of states and a few western locations, and then usually only with a certain amount of searching, patience, and luck.

The Great Gray Owl has been known to nest in the Lower 48 during recent years only in eight states.

• California. It is a rare resident in the Sierra Nevada, most famously in the Yosemite National Park area. A nest at Yosemite in 1986 was said to be only the seventh known from the state (AB 40:1252). The total number of Great Grays in the state is probably around 150 (Small 1994). Most are found between 6,000 and 7,500 feet, but they have been seen between 1,200 and 11,000 feet (Small 1994). There are scattered records outside the Sierras in northern California. The southernmost is from Wolverton Meadow, Tulare County.

• Oregon. It nests mostly on the eastern slope of the Cascade Range north to the 45th parallel and in the mountains of the northeastern portion of the state. Nesting areas in the northeast are bounded by northern Harney County to the south and by Crook County to the west (Contreras, et al. 1994). The Wallowa Mountains near LaGrande are a particularly good spot. There has also been nesting near clear-cuts on the Cascade's western slope.

• Washington. There are scattered records throughout the year from north-central and northeastern Washington. In 1992 two nests were documented in Okanogan County and one in Ferry County for the first confirmed breeding in the state. In northwestern Washington there have been a few winter records.

• Idaho. It is resident in the northern and eastern parts of the state (Bull and Duncan 1993).

• Montana. It has been found in the Bitterroot Range and other parts of the Rockies in the western part of the state (Bull and Duncan 1993).

• Wyoming. It has been documented in the Yellowstone and Grand Teton national parks area (Bull and Duncan 1993).

• Minnesota. Pairs nest in northern counties (see Eckert 1994) including Roseau, Cook, Aitkin, St. Louis, and Lake.

• Wisconsin. Nesting was confirmed for the first time in 1988 in Ashland County near Clam Lake. A second nest was confirmed in 1990 on Stockton Island in the Apostle Island National Lakeshore, and a third was found during 1993, also in Ashland County.

Great Grays are generally nonmigratory, but they wander in winter when prey (almost exclusively small rodents) becomes scarce, or when deep snow makes hunting difficult (Bull and Duncan 1993). Even then, they seldom appear very far south. They have been seen in winter as far south as Long Island, New York, northern Pennsylvania, Indiana, Iowa, Nebraska, Utah, and Tulare County, California.

In occasional invasion winters, Great Grays appear in relatively large numbers from northern Minnesota through northern Wisconsin and into the Upper Peninsula of Michigan. Smaller numbers sometimes also invade into New England. It is during these invasions that most of the far extralimital records occur. During the biggest Midwest invasion to date, 196 Great Grays were seen in Minnesota and 55 were found in Michigan (winter of 1991-92). The largest recent incursion into the Northeast occurred during the winter of 1983-84, when about 50 were seen.

Best Bets

Although the Great Gray Owl is a forest bird, when looking for one it helps to know that the species needs openings—usually bogs or meadows—with scattered tree perches from which to hunt (Bull and Duncan 1993; Quinton 1984). The Great Gray locates its rodent prey by sight and sound. Its hearing is so precise that it can pinpoint prey beneath snow and, rather incredibly, inside earth tunnels, breaking through the surface with its feet to make the capture (Bull and Duncan 1993; Quinton 1984). Great Grays are active at night and during daylight hours, but during the day are most often seen at dawn and dusk.

Winter

In Michigan, the areas around Sault Ste. Marie and the Whitefish Point Bird Observatory are good spots to check. In Wisconsin, most birds have been seen in Douglas, Bayfield, and Ashland counties, east of Superior.

For Minnesota, Jay Strangis's *Birding Minnesota* and Kim Eckert's *Birder's Guide to Minnesota* give details on sites too numerous to summarize, including the Highway 310 bog in Roseau County, Aitkin County, the Sax-Zim bog in St. Louis County, and Highway 61 east of Silver Bay in Lake County.

Because the winter owl outlook in the upper Midwest differs greatly from year to year, timing your trip to go during the right year is helpful. Also, visiting northern Minnesota or Michigan's Upper Peninsula in midwinter is clearly not as simple as flying into McAllen, Texas, and renting a car for a casual birding weekend; sometimes-severe weather conditions must be taken into account (see Fisher, *Winging It*, February, 1993, and Naveen, *Birding*, August 1978, for examples).

In mountainous areas of the West, Great Grays often move lower in winter to places where the snow is not so deep (Bull and Duncan, 1993). In such cases Great Grays are often found in areas of mixed farmlands and woodlots. One spot that regularly hosts Great Grays is the area around Tetonia, Idaho, just west of Yellowstone National Park. In the winter of 1994-95, up to 15 were seen along one mile of South Leigh Creek.

Summer

A handful of pairs nest each year in Minnesota; again, refer to Strangis or Eckert for details about the traditional spots.

In Wyoming, Scott (1993) recommends the Valley Trail in central Grand

Teton National Park, the trail around Two Ocean Lake a bit farther north, and the road between Canyon and Norris in Yellowstone as providing the best chances for finding Great Grays.

An Idaho location from which the species has been reported often is the area around Island Park and Henry's Lake, just west of Yellowstone. Read Harper, *Winging It*, June 1989 for details, and check with personnel of the Targhee National Forest and Harriman State Park for the latest information.

In Montana, the Lolo National Forest near Missoula, and Deerlodge National Forest, to the south, are worth checking; see *Birdfinding in Forty National Forests and Grasslands*, published by the American Birding Association (1994).

In Oregon, the city of LaGrande in the northeast and Jackson and Klamath counties in the south are the centers of Great Gray sightings (see Evanich 1990). In California, Yosemite's Crane Flat, Peregoy Meadow, Westfall Meadow, and McGurk Meadow are well-known locations for Great Grays and have provided many birders with their lifer.

Identification

The Great Gray Owl generally resembles the Barred and Spotted Owls (grayish plumage, round "face") but is usually much bigger, has yellow, not dark, eyes, and displays a prominent white "bow tie" mark just below its bill. **(See color photo on page 481.)**

Boreal Owl

Aegolius funereus

Status and Distribution

For most U.S. birders, the Boreal Owl is a symbol of the Great White North. It is thought of as an impish winter visitor that occasionally wanders to our land. Though small, Boreal Owls are indeed fierce predators, but they are here during more than just the season of snow. In much of their Lower 48 range, these birds are actually permanent residents.

The status and distribution of the Boreal Owl in the Lower 48 is best digested in parts. West of the Great Plains, this species is mostly a permanent resident from the mountains of eastern Washington, northern Idaho, and western Montana, southwest through Wyoming and Colorado, and into northern New Mexico. These owls favor subalpine forests, especially those consisting of subalpine fir (*Abies lasiocarpa*) and Engelmann spruce (*Picea engelmannii*) (Palmer 1986; Hayward, et al. 1987; Garber, et al. 1991). Consequently, Boreal Owls in Idaho and Montana occur primarily above 4,500 feet, whereas in Wyoming they are found above 5,500 feet, and in Colorado, above 9,000 feet (Hayward and Hayward 1993; Garber, et al. 1991). Western records from lower elevations, even in winter, are scarce.

East of the Great Plains, the Boreal Owl nests in northern Minnesota (mostly Cook and Lake counties) in old aspen and mixed forests (Eckert and Savaloja 1979; Lane 1988). During winter, however, eastern Boreals sometimes occur much farther south and in a wider variety of habitats. Accepted records have come from as far south as northern Illinois and New Jersey. These southerly incursions occur sporadically as irruptions and probably are due to scarce food in Canada.

Eastern nonbreeding records show distinct fall and late winter/early spring peaks. The fall peak occurs from late October into mid-November. The late winter/early spring peak is considerably larger and stretches from mid-January into early March. You should note, however, that maximum numbers at the Whitefish Point Bird Observatory (mostly from banding records) are usually in late April. Furthermore, the best years at Whitefish Point do not always coincide with perceived invasions elsewhere in the eastern Lower 48. These discrepancies highlight the current lack of understanding regarding this species' movements. Most of this confusion probably arises out of the difficulty in finding Boreal Owls away from their breeding grounds. Many Boreals seen during the colder months in the eastern United States are probably weak individuals that are forced to hunt during daylight or twilight hours whereas most healthy individuals likely pass undetected.

Boreal Owl nesting dates also vary between the eastern and western Lower 48. West of the Great Plains, Boreal Owls lay their eggs mostly between mid-April and late May (Palmer 1986, Hayward 1989) whereas in Minnnesota, eggs are laid predominantly from late March into mid-April (Lane 1988).

For a good overview of Boreal Owl biology, see Hayward and Hayward (1993).

Best Bets

Several traditional Boreal Owl locations have arisen over the past decade or two. During spring and summer these include the Rogers Lake/Tiffany Mountain area in Okanogan County, Washington; Lolo Pass, Idaho/Montana; the Cameron Pass area west of Fort Collins, Colorado; the vicinity of Jackson, Wyoming; and the Gunflint Trail in Cook County, Minnesota. The optimum time to search varies from place to place and is partly dependent on snow conditions. It is best to contact local birders for details. The best nonbreeding area is probably the north shore of Lake Superior during late winter and early spring. During most winters, this area is a long shot, but during the infrequent "good" winters, your chances are pretty reasonable. Unfortunately, Boreals are hard to see unfettered at the Whitefish Point Bird Observatory, where they are frequently banded.

Identification

Despite what many guides imply, an adult Boreal Owl is easily separated from a Northern Saw-whet Owl. The dark-bordered pale face of a Boreal is striking and most closely resembles that of a Northern Hawk Owl, not a Saw-whet; this is nicely shown in the NGS guide. Immature Boreals and Saw-whets, however, are more similar. The most distinctive mark is the two-toned underparts of the Saw-whet compared with the more uniform underparts of the Boreal (see NGS guide).

Boreal Owl—*all records in AB from 1978 on*

LOCATION	NUMBERS SEEN	DATES SEEN
Washington		
3 locations in Wallowa Mountains		9/93 and 10/93
Mount Rainier	2	10/2/93
Sunrise, Mount Rainier	1	9/11/92
Darland Mountain area	1	fall 1992
Horsehoe Basin	1	7/12 to 7/13/92
Okanogan County	6 (pair w/4 young)	6/11/92
near Snohomish	1	1/14/92
Tiffany Mountain region	3	10/18/91
Columbia County	1	10/11/91
Tiffany Mountain region	9	9/14/91
Rogers Lake	1	8/25 & 11/3/90
Rogers Lake	1	6/30/90
Rogers Lake	1	4/12/90
Conconully	1	12/20/89
Wallowa Mountains	3+	9/9 to 10/14/89
Kittitas County	1	fall 1988
Okanogan County	1	fall 1988
Salmo Mountain	2+	summer 1986
NW of Mazama	1	7/2/86
Panhandle Lake	3	spring 1986
Sherman Pass	1	spring 1986
NE Washington	19	fall 1985
Harrison Lake, W of Bonners Ferry	1	fall 1985
Chumstick Valley, N of Leavenworth	1	1/6/77
Pullman	1	1/10/74
Oregon		
near Waldo Lake	1	7/31/94
Mount Pisgah	1	9/25/93
Waldo Lake, central Oregon Cascades	1	10/18/92
Mount Pisgah	1	10/24/92
Tollgate	1	10/24/92

LOCATION	NUMBERS SEEN	DATES SEEN
Deschutes County	9	10/91
Wallowa County	3	10/12 to 10/15/91
at 5,700 ft near Mount Bachelor	2-3	4/22/91
Blue Mountains, N of Tollgate	1	9/9/90
near Waldo Lake	3	9/28 to 11/4/89
NW Wallowa County	1	fall 1988
Baker, Umatilla, Union, Wallowa counties	17	fall 1987
Idaho		
Nampa	1	11/94
Sawtelle Peak	4	4/6/93
Sawtelle Peak	1	4/10 to 4/14/92
Grays Lake	1	early 4/92
Teton River, near St. Anthony	1	spring 1991
Red River	1	3/15/90
Badger Creek, S of Tetonia	1	1/25/90
near Elk City	1	summer 1989
Lolo Pass, ID/MT	7	2/26/87
Lolo Pass, ID/MT	17 (territorial males)	spring 1987
Ball Creek Road, NW of Bonners Ferry	1	spring 1987
NE of Vernon	1	spring 1987
Boundary County	15	spring 1986
Lolo Pass	1	spring 1986
Montana		
Bitterroot National Forest	12 (singing)	3/93 and 4/93
Cooke City	1	3/4/92
St. Joseph Pass	1	spring 1991
Smith Mountain, W of Troy	1	late 2/90
Lolo Pass	2+ (nest fledged 4 young)	spring 1988
Little Blackfoot River, SW of Helena	1	3/5/88
Lolo Pass, ID/MT	7	2/26/87
Lolo Pass, ID/MT	17 (territorial males)	spring 1987
Fish Creek	1	11/1/86
Glacier Point, Glacier National Park	1	spring 1986
Libby Dam	1	2/16/84
Bull River area	1	fall 1982
Buffalo Fork	1	3/21/80
Lake Abundance	1	3/16/80
Waterton Glacier National Park	1 (nest)[1]	summer 1973
Wyoming		
Paintbrush Canyon, Grand Teton National Park	1	8/13/83
near Jackson	1 (juv)	fall 1993
Medicine Bow NF	15	fall 1991
Yellowstone National Park	5	fall 1991
Teton Pass, near Jackson	1	4/3/91
Yellowstone National Park (territorial)	5	spring 1991
Wilson	1	12/26/89
Yellowstone National Park	1	fall 1988

LOCATION	NUMBERS SEEN	DATES SEEN
Centennial	1 (nest)	8/1 to 8/12/88
Centennial	1	6/15/88
Jackson	17	2/9 to 4/21/88
Jackson	1	winter 1987-88
Yellowstone National Park	1	9/13/87
Jackson	1	spring 1987
Teton Pass	1	spring 1987
Yellowstone National Park	1	9/14/86
Saratoga	1	6/20/86
Yellowstone National Park	1	3/20/86
Jackson	1	4/7/82
Lander	1	11/10/80
Togwotee Pass	1	summer 1979
Jackson	1	12/17/78
Yellowstone National Park	1	6/24/75
Colorado		
Idaho Springs	1	fall 1993
Grand Mesa	many (16 nests)	summer 1993
near Glenwood Springs	1	9/27/92
near Pagosa Springs	1	7/23/92
Ripple Creek Pass	1	6/7/92
Cameron Pass	3	2/19/92
Boulder County	1	1/17/92
north of Craig	1	9/5/89
Cameron Pass	5	8/31/89
Dillon	2	7/30/89
West Elk Wilderness	1	7/28/89
Cameron Pass, nesting	1	3/24 to 5/21/89
Summitville (south-central CO)	1	3/24/89
Grand Junction	1	fall 1988
Gunnison	1	fall 1988
Long Draw Reservoir	1	fall 1988
Cameron Pass	8	3/5 to 4/7/88
Rocky Mountain National Park	1	spring 1988
Eldora County	1	spring 1988
northern Colorado	4	winter 1987-88
Gould	1	11/7/87
Cameron Pass	2-5	3/13 to 5/11/87
Echo Lake, near Evergreen	1	4/26/87
Cumbres Pass	3	4/14 to 4/16/87
Wolf Creek Pass	2	4/13/87
Palisade	1	12/13/85
Grand Mesa	3	10/1/85
Wolf Creek Pass	1	3/17/85
Slumgullion Pass, near Lake City	1	3/17/85
Cameron Pass	25 (singing males)	3/1 to 5/31/84

LOCATION	NUMBERS SEEN	DATES SEEN
Creede	5	April & May 1984
Caribou	1	4/4 to 4/5/84
Coal Creek Canyon	1	4/4 to 4/5/84
W of Fort Collins	9 (territorial males)	April 1983
Cameron Pass	3+ (3 young)	summer 1982
Cameron Pass	1	2/12/82
near Red Feather Lake, Cameron Pass	1+ (nest)	spring 1981
Cameron Pass	4	4/5 to 6/3/80
Rocky Mountain National Park	1	summer 1979
Red Feather Lake	1	7/15/78
Estes Park	1	2/6/78
Evergreen	1	2/2/78
Grand Lake	1	12/2/77
New Mexico		
Pecos Baldy Lake	1 (fledgling)	8/2/93
S of Cumbres Pass	1	8/19/92
Rio de Abiquiu, Jemez Mountains	1	6/9 & 6/23/92
northern Rio Arriba County	2	3/12/92
NE of Santa Fe	1	3/13/92
Pecos Wilderness	1	4/15/89
Carijilon Mountain	1	9/24/88
S of Cumbres Pass	1	6/6 & 7/87
S of Cumbres Pass	1	4/15 to 4/19/87
North Dakota		
Minot	1	12/22/78
Jamestown	1	2/7/78
Robinson	1	11/10/72
Minnesota		
"usual locations"		spring 1993
Duluth	1	1/7/93
Grand Marais	1	winter 1992-3
Biwabik	1	winter 1992-3
Lake County	1 (nested)	spring 1991
Gunflint Trail	1	through spring 91
Minnesota	5	winter 1990-1
Duluth	1	10/24/90
Cook, Lake, St. Louis counties		spring 1990
near Ely and Isabella	2 (nesting)	spring 1990
Duluth	1	2/20/90
one confirmed Minnesota nest		summer 1989
Grand Rapids	1	5/14/89
Kanabec County	1	mid-March 1989
Cook and Lake counties	25+	spring 1989
Cook and Lake counties	3	winter 1989-90
central and northern Minnesota	~80	winter 1988-89
Minneapolis	1	2/18/89

LOCATION	NUMBERS SEEN	DATES SEEN
Cook County	1	11/29/88
Hawk Ridge	1	10/29 & 11/10/88
St. Louis, Lake, & Cook counties	50	spring 1988
Gunflint Trail	1	2/1 & 2/13/88
Hawk Ridge	8	after 10/10/87
Roseau County	2 (young)	summer 1987
central Lake County	12	spring 1987
Roseau County	(nest)	spring 1987
Duluth	2 (dead)	March 1987
Hovland	1	2/27/87
Gunflint Trail	1	2/21/87
Saginaw	1	2/1 to 2/2/87
St. Louis & Cook counties	2+	12/23/86
N of Isabella	1	winter 1986-87
Duluth	1	11/18/86
Duluth	1	10/29/86
Lake County	1	until 8/7/86
N of Isabella	1	summer 1986
Gunflint Trail	1	spring 1986
Murphy Lake	1	5/2/86
N of Isabella	1	5/2 to 5/3/86
Cook County	1	2/16/86
Gunflint Trail	4	spring 1985
Mahnomen County	1	2/14/85
Poplar Lake	1	winter 1984-85
Gunflint Trail	5	spring 1984
Minnesota	7	winter 1983-84
Gunflint Trail	5	4/5/83
Gunflint Trail	1	1/20 to 2/27/83
Itasca County	1	7/1/82
Brule Lake	(nest)	5/3 to 5/26/82
Gunflint Trail	4	April 1982
NE Minnesota	34	3/3 to 4/10/82
Duluth	2 (dead)	late 2/82
Park Rapids	1	12/30/81
Hawk Ridge	1	11/3 to 11/4/81
Gunflint Trail	6 (singing)	3/27 to 4/28/81
Lake County	1	late 1/81
Hawk Ridge	1	10/28/80
Gunflint Trail	1	early May 1980
Tofte	1	2/18/80
Duluth	7	1/19 to 2/9/80
Cook County	1	1/29/80
Hawk Ridge	1	11/12/79
Hawk Ridge	1	10/9/79
Cook County	1	6/17 to 6/19/79

LOCATION	NUMBERS SEEN	DATES SEEN
Knife River	1	3/27/79
Duluth	1	winter 1978-79
Itasca County	1	winter 1978-79
Beltrami County	1	winter 1978-79
Duluth	1	11/8/78
Gunflint Trail	(nest)[2]	summer 1978
Gunflint Trail	15 (singing males)	4/22 to 5/7/78
Duluth	1	3/27 & 4/3/78
Duluth Township	1	3/24/78
N shore of Lake Superior	60+	1/30 to 3/78
Becker	1	Jan/Feb 1978
Koochiching	1	Jan/Feb 1978
northern St. Louis County	1	Jan/Feb 1978
northern Lake County	1	Jan/Feb 1978
Ely	1	11/12/77
Hawk Ridge	5	10/21 to 11/18/77
Agassiz NWR	1	3/10/77
Silver Bay	1	winter 1976-77
Duluth	1	winter 1976-77
Sawbill Trail	1	winter 1976-77
Hawk Ridge	8	10/22 to 11/14/76
Cook County	1	1/1/75
Cotton	1	1/13/73
Pine County	1	11/9/72
Duluth	1	2/28/72
Shelbourne County	1	12/18/71
Wisconsin		
Sawyer County	1	2/24/90
Douglas County	1	3/19/89
Portage County	1	3/8/89
Eau Claire	1	winter 1988-89
near Ashland	1	2/28/89
Rhinelander	1	1/26 to 1/28/88
Dodge County	1	winter 1983-84
Vilas County	1	winter 1983-84
Washburn County	1	winter 1983-84
Douglas County	1	2/26/82
Brown County	1	10/28/78
Michigan		
Whitefish Point Bird Observatory	7	10/2 to 10/11/94
Chippewa County	1	winter 1992-3
Whitefish Point Bird Observatory	1	10/27/92
Whitefish Point Bird Observatory	158	spring 1992
Sault Ste. Marie	1	2/8/92
Gross Pointe Woods	1	2/8/92
Whitefish Point Bird Observatory	22	10/15 to 10/21/91

LOCATION	NUMBERS SEEN	DATES SEEN
Whitefish Point Bird Observatory	25	spring 1991
Whitefish Point Bird Observatory	7	peak count 1991: 4/23/91
Whitefish Point Bird Observatory	1 (only)	spring 1990
Whitefish Point Bird Observatory	16	spring 1989
Delta County	1	winter 1988-89
Emmet County	1	winter 1988-89
Cheboygan County	1	winter 1989-89
Rogers City	1	2/28/89
Whitefish Point Bird Observatory	164	4/1 to 5/23/88
Whitefish Point Bird Observatory	24	peak count 1988: 5/1/88
Whitefish Point Bird Observatory	13	4/13 to 5/4/87
Whitefish Point Bird Observatory	1	4/24/86
Whitefish Point Bird Observatory	4	spring 1985
Whitefish Point Bird Observatory	47	spring 1984
Trout Lake	1	3/7/84
Whitefish Point Bird Observatory	11	spring 1983
Ontonagon County	1	10/14/82
Whitefish Point Bird Observatory	36	spring 1982
Frederick	1	2/27/82
Berkley	1	5/12/78
Whitefish Point Bird Observatory	23	4/24 to 5/7/78
Whitefish Point Bird Observatory	6	peak count 1978: 5/4/78
Rogers City	1	5/13/77
Whitefish Point Bird Observatory	3	10/31 to 11/6/76
Whitefish Point Bird Observatory	7	4/25 to 5/9/75
Whitefish Point Bird Observatory	10	spring 1974
Whitefish Point Bird Observatory	2	April 1972
Maine		
Little Deer Island	1	1/18/87
Oronolate	1	2/79
Boothbay Harbor	1	2/11 to 2/16/79
Franklin	1	2/13/79
Sherman Station	1	late 3/78
Roxbury	1	10/28/76
Vermont		
Enosburg Falls	1	3/5/92
New Hampshire		
Monroe	1	1/16/79
Massachusetts		
Canton	1	12/27/91
south of Boston	5	10/30 to 11/19/91
Boston	1	11/2 to 11/8/83
Chatham	1	11/6/83
Salisbury	1	12/31/78
Connecticut		
Middlebury	1	1/13 to 2/24/92

LOCATION	NUMBERS SEEN	DATES SEEN
New York		
Braddock Bay	1	2/6/92
Rochester	1	3/6/87
Braddock Bay	1	spring 1985
Smoke Swamp	1	winter 1983-84
Rochester	1	3/3 to 3/6/79
Adirondack Mountains	4	Jan & Feb 1979
Rochester	1	2/4 to 2/6/78
Cedar Beach, Long Island	1	1/15/75
Rochester	1	2/26/72

Boreal Owl—*other records of interest*[3]

LOCATION	NUMBERS SEEN	DATES SEEN
Illinois		
Chicago	1	3/5/14
Cicero	1	12/1902
Kenilworth	1	12/26/02
other records	2	prior to 1900
Vermont		
Newbury	1	prior to 1919
Fayston	1	7/18/23
St. Johnsbury	1	1/24/32
Barre	1	winter 1994-95
Rhode Island		
total records	4	prior to 1900
New Jersey		
Bonhamtown	1	11/1/62
Virginia		
near Skyline Drive, Rappahannock County[4]	1	1/16/70

[1]First Lower 48 nesting record.

[2]First Lower 48 nesting record east of Rocky Mountains; female with 5 eggs found on 6/16. Young hatched in early July. All out of nest on 8/3. Nest was 20.8 miles N of Grand Marais.

[3]The Boreal Owl has also been recorded in Nebraska and Pennsylvania.

[4]Considered hypothetical because sight record only.

Antillean Nighthawk

Chordeiles gundlachii

Status and Distribution

When is a Common Nighthawk not a Common? When it goes *killy-ka-dick*. If you hear a nighthawk making this katydid-like noise, you have an Antillean. The Antillean Nighthawk was formerly considered a subspecies of the Common, but these two birds were split from each other based partly on the vast difference in call notes. Visually, the Common and Antillean are similar (see "Identification").

The Antillean Nighthawk was first recorded in the United States during June 1941 at Key West, Florida. It is not clear if this was the beginning of a range expansion into the United States or just the first time a visually difficult-to-identify subspecies (at that time) was noted. By the early 1960s, the Antillean was found to be an uncommon to common summer resident from Key West to northern Key Largo. Recently, however, this species seems to have declined, now being quite uncommon north of Duck Key (near Marathon). The reasons for this decline are not completely understood but may be due to a southward expansion of the Common Nighthawk's breeding range into the upper Florida Keys. Antilleans are still fairly common from Marathon to Key West, as well as a regular spring visitor to the Dry Tortugas.

Outside of the main Florida Keys and Dry Tortugas, there are only about 30 records, most of which are from southeastern Florida. Nesting away from the main Keys may have taken place at Virginia Key and south of Florida City. Truly exceptional sightings come from Merritt Island, Brevard County, Florida, on May 15, 1977, and Cape Hatteras, North Carolina, from August 5 to August 25, 1994. A report from Fort De Soto,

Pinellas County, Florida, on April 13, 1985, was rejected by the FL BRC. Finally, an odd-sounding smallish nighthawk was present near Austin during the spring and summer of 1995. Initial speculation leaned toward Antillean; however, due to a collision with a wire, this bird met its demise, and the specimen is being studied. Current thinking is that it was almost certainly not an Antillean and may possibly have been a Common x Lesser Nighthawk hybrid (G. Lasley, pers comm).

The Antillean Nighthawk normally arrives in the Florida Keys during early to mid-April, with the current extreme early date being April 6. The usual time of departure is unclear because of the difficulties of sight identification. Antilleans have mostly stopped calling by late August (P. W. Smith, pers comm), and records after then are scarce. Nighthawks, however, remain numerous in the lower Keys for another month. Many of these are probably migrant Commons, but the number that are Antilleans is completely unknown. Occasionally, nighthawks of unknown identity have even wintered in southern Florida. Some of these may be Antillean. On the Dry Tortugas, records range from early April to early August, but most have come from April.

Best Bets

The "traditional" areas for Antillean Nighthawk have been the Key West airport, the Marathon airport, and the community college on Stock Island. In reality, however, this bird is fairly widespread in open habitats throughout the lower Keys. It is probably most numerous on Big Pine Key.

Identification

Currently, the Antillean Nighthawk can be reliably identified only by sound. Its *killy-ka-dick* call is dramatically different from the buzzy *peent* or *beerb* of the Common. Methods for sight identification are currently being worked out. Observations by Will Russell, Wes Biggs, P. William Smith, and Michael O'Brien are summarized below.

Underpart Coloration: Both sexes of the Antillean have a buffy lower belly and undertail coverts. Eastern races of Common lack these buffy hues. Female Commons of some western races can be buffy below, but presumably they would be vagrants to Florida.

Primary Extension: Antilleans may have shorter primary extension than Commons; see photo in MGB.

Shape in Flight: Antilleans are a bit smaller than Commons, especially in wing length. This should give the Antillean a short-winged appearance. The wingtip is still pointed like a Common and is, consequently, still useful for separation from Lesser Nighthawk.

Wing Pattern: The white slash on the Antillean's wing is closer to the tip than that of a Common. Usefulness of this mark in the field is unclear.

Buff-collared Nightjar

Caprimulgus ridgwayi

Status and Distribution

The Buff-collared Nightjar is a member of the Caprimulgids, which in the United States are frequently referred to as Goatsuckers. This peculiar title is based on an ancient belief that these birds during the wee hours of darkness suck the milk from goats (Terres 1980). Such reputations are fostered by this group's nocturnal habits and haunting voices. The Buff-collared Nightjar exemplifies this sense of mystery. Many have heard its cry echo in Florida Wash, Arizona, but few know much else about this nighttime spirit.

Early reports of Buff-collared Nightjars in the United States were somewhat sporadic. The first were found in Guadalupe Canyon during the late 1950s. One of these was collected on the New Mexico side of that canyon in 1958, and another was collected in the Arizona portion on May 12, 1960. The next confirmed sighting wasn't until 1971, when one was heard along Sonoita Creek southwest of Patagonia on July 3 and 4. After several more years with no reports, Buff-collars were found again at Guadalupe Canyon on July 1, 1976.

In the years that followed, there were concerted efforts to locate this species, and Buff-collared Nightjars were found to be much more widespread and regular than previously realized. This Mexican species is now recognized as a regular summer resident (and almost certainly a regular breeder) at scattered sites in southeastern Arizona. The favored habitat in the United States is high Lower Sonoran Zone and low Upper Sonoran Zone hilly desert-scrub usually adjacent to desert riparian areas at an elevation of roughly 2,800 to 4,000 feet (D. Stejskal, pers comm). Spots with recurrent sightings include Guadalupe Canyon (Cochise County),

Florida Wash (in Pima County, north of Madera Canyon), Sutherland Wash (in Pima County, on the northwest side of the Santa Catalina Mountains), the west end of Aravaipa Canyon (Pinal County), and California Gulch/Sycamore Canyon (Santa Cruz County). Other records come from Cook's Lake (Pinal County), Tanque Verde Wash (just east of Tucson, Pima County), Chino Canyon (the northwest side of the Santa Rita Mountains, Pima and Santa Cruz counties), and the Baboquivari Mountains (Pima County).

Buff-collared Nightjars have been found in the United States from April 20 to September 7. They are most vocal, and thus easiest to find, from early May into mid-July.

Best Bets

The traditional hot spot for Buff-collared Nightjars has been Florida Wash in southeastern Arizona. Buff-collars have been detected here during each summer from 1985 through 1994 but not during 1995. The reason for this place's popularity is its easy access and proximity to Madera Canyon. However, other known locations (e.g., Guadalupe Canyon) are likely just as reliable. Furthermore, given this species' nocturnal habits, Buff-collars have probably gone undetected from several other locations where they are a regular summer resident. Finding such spots would be a fine task for particularly intrepid birders.

Identification

The resounding *cu-cu-cu-cu-cu-a-chee'a* of a singing Buff-collared Nightjar makes this bird easy to identify. As with most nightjars, however, a quiet bird is far more challenging. The Buff-collar's most famous mark is its distinct buffy hind-collar. Whip-poor-wills usually lack any hind-collar at all, but some males do have an indistinct narrow buffy one. Other marks include the male's tail pattern and the nightjar's overall color. The male Buff-collar's tail has white that is restricted to the inner web of the outer retrices whereas the male Whip-poor-will has white fully across the tips of these feathers. Finally, in good light, the Buff-collared Nightjar should also appear paler than a Whip-poor-will. For further discussion and good drawings, see Howell and Webb (1995). **(See color photo on page 481.)**

Buff-collared Nightjar—*all published records*

LOCATION	NUMBERS SEEN	DATES SEEN
Guadalupe Canyon, NM	1	1958
Guadalupe Mountains(Canyon?), NM	8	6/28/59
Guadalupe Canyon, AZ	1	5/12/60
Sonoita Creek, AZ	1	7/3 to 7/4/71
Guadalupe Canyon, AZ	1	7/1 to 7/2/76
Sutherland Wash, AZ	2	5/19 to 7/18/78
Aravaipa Canyon, AZ	3	spring to 8/12/80
Cook's Lake, AZ	1	8/28/80
Baboquivari Mountains, AZ	3	summer 1981
Tanque Verde Wash, AZ	1	summer 1981
Guadalupe Canyon, NM	1	summer 1981
Aravaipa Canyon, AZ	2	summer to 8/16/81
California Gulch, AZ	4	6/20 to 7/4/82
Chino Canyon, AZ	1	6/21 to late 7/82
Sycamore Canyon, AZ	1	7/3/82
Aravaipa Canyon, AZ	2	summer 1982
Tanque Verde Wash, AZ	1	7/1/82
Aravaipa Canyon, AZ	1	late 5/83 on
Guadalupe Canyon, AZ[1]	2	5/18/83
Tanque Verde Wash, AZ	1	7/17/83
Aravaipa Canyon, AZ	1	5/8/84 on
Guadalupe Canyon, AZ	1	5/20/84
Aravaipa Canyon, AZ	1	5/6/85 on
Florida Wash, AZ[2]	4+	mid-5/85 on
Florida Wash, AZ	4	summer 1986
Florida Wash, AZ	1	7/31/87
Florida Wash, AZ	1	5/17/88 on
Aravaipa Canyon, AZ	1	summer 1988
Florida Wash, AZ	2+	5/2/89 on
Catalina State Park, AZ	2	5/10/89
California Gulch, AZ	2	5/11/89
Guadalupe Canyon, AZ	3	5/18/89
Aravaipa Canyon, AZ	1	May 1989
Guadalupe Canyon, AZ	1	4/20/90
Florida Wash, AZ	2+	early 5/90 on
Aravaipa Canyon, AZ	1	7/4/91

[1]Pair copulating.
[2]1991, 1992, 1993, and 1994 records also exist from Florida Wash.

Green Violet-ear

Colibri thalassinus

Status and Distribution

The Green Violet-ear is a shimmering emerald-and-amethyst nymph that normally inhabits woodlands from central Mexico to northern Bolivia. In Mexico, it usually ranges from southern San Luis Potosi to Jalisco, living in pine-oak habitats between 3,000 and 10,000 feet elevation (Howell and Webb 1995). As this species is not normally very migratory, its regular occurrence in the United States is somewhat of a mystery.

The first U.S. Green Violet-ear was seen at Santa Ana National Wildlife Refuge on July 11, 1961, and remained there until July 2. Since then, there have been 26 additional reports (2 rejected by TX BRC). Twenty-three of these have occurred since 1974, giving this bird its nearly annual status in the Lower 48.

Of the 25 nonrejected U.S. records, 20 are from Texas, 4 are from Arkansas, and 1 is from North Carolina. There are also two Canadian records, one from Thunder Bay, Ontario, and one from Kananaskis Provincial Park, Alberta. The Texan records are entirely from the southeastern part of the state, with concentrations along the lower Rio Grande valley and in the San Antonio/Austin area. All the Arkansas Green Violet-ears have been in the western portion of that state, and 3 of the 4 have been from the northwestern quarter.

The Green Violet-ear seems to occur mostly as a spring and summer wanderer, with peak occurrence from mid-May through late July. Accepted records stretch from April 14 (San Benito, TX) to October 25 (Asheville, NC).

Best Bets

As you can see from the above discussion, U.S. Green Violet-ear records are fairly scattered, and there is no particular spot to search for this species. Indeed, the spread of records implies that a fair number of Green Violet-ears pass unseen by birders' eyes. Thus, it would be worth scrutinizing any hummingbird feeder you come across in southeastern Texas, especially from May through July. Furthermore, considering the previous occurrence of Green Violet-ears in North Carolina, Ontario, and Alberta, birders across the Lower 48 should be aware that a violet-ear may come their way.

Fortunately, many of the Green Violet-ears that have been found have remained for a couple of weeks or more. Therefore, keeping in touch with NARBA or the Texas state RBA would be your best chance of actually seeing this species.

Identification

The Green Violet-ear is a distinctive bird. Its mostly dark green-and-violet plumage is strikingly different from any of the more regularly occurring U.S. hummingbirds (except, perhaps, Magnificent Hummingbird). The male Green-breasted Mango, however, is at least superficially similar and has been recorded in Texas. When confronted with an almost entirely dark green hummingbird, pay special attention to head and tail pattern. For good drawings of Green Violet-ear and Green-breasted Mango, see Peterson and Chalif (1973). For photos of these two species, see Rappole and Blacklock (1994). **(See color photo on page 482.)**

Green Violet-ear—*all records*

LOCATION	DATES SEEN
San Benito, TX	4/14/64
San Benito, TX	4/21/91
Corpus Christi, TX	5/6 to 6/25/95
McAllen,TX	5/6 to 6/13/80
Austin, Travis County, TX	5/12 to 6/9/77
Driftwood, TX	5/14/94
San Marcos, TX	5/14 to 6/21/83
Helotes, TX	5/16 to 5/17/94
Wimberly, TX	5/21 to 7/6/76
Helotes, TX	5/21/91
Lake Jackson, TX	5/26 to 6/19/81

LOCATION	DATES SEEN
Clark County, AR	6/2 to 6/4/89
Brownsville, TX	6/3 to 6/4/89
northwestern Travis County, TX	6/16 to 7/8/95
Sinton, TX	6/22 to 7/11/89
Wimberly, TX	7/3 to 8/13/75
Lost Maples, TX	7/5 to 7/6/95
N of Lurton, AR	7/6 to 7/23/90
Santa Ana NWR, TX	7/11 to 7/28/61
McDade, TX	7/12 to 7/30/95
Conroe, TX	7/14 to 7/17/94
Rogers, AR	8/4 to 9/5/90
Austin, TX	8/25 to 9/18/69
Fort Smith, AR	10/7/84
Asheville, NC	10/21 to 10/25/87
Rejected by TX BRC	
Corpus Christi, TX	3/24/73
Hunt, TX	7/18/93

all records

White-eared Hummingbird
Hylocharis leucotis

Status and Distribution

To those who have walked in the montane forests of Mexico's Sierra Madre, the White-eared Hummingbird is a familiar sight. In the United States, the sight is somewhat less common but far from unheard of. Over the past ten years, this cute hummer has been seen approximately 55 times in southeastern Arizona, 9 times in Texas, and 3 times in New Mexico. Most records have come from pine-oak woodlands and nearby riparian zones located between roughly 4,500 and 6,500 feet.

This species' status has changed dramatically over the years. The first ABA Area record was from Arizona in 1894. Between 1894 and 1919, there were a number of sight records and specimens from the mountains of southeastern Arizona. Then, without obvious reason, the White-eared Hummingbird disappeared. There were only 4 records between 1933 and 1960: 2 from southeastern Arizona and 2 from the Chisos Mountains of Texas. The 1960s produced about 5 records. Then, the number of White-eared Hummingbirds in southeastern Arizona began to boom. There were about 10 records in the 1970s, 30 in the 1980s, and roughly 30 by 1994 in the 1990s. Outside Arizona there has also been a recent increase, but it has not been as dramatic. Texas has 8 records since 1970 and New Mexico has 6.

In southeastern Arizona about 40 percent of the records are from the Huachuca Mountains, 40 percent are from the Chiricahua Mountains, 10 percent are from Madera Canyon, and 10 percent are from Summerhaven in the Catalina Mountains. There are no accepted Arizona records from lowland riparian areas such as Patagonia. Texan records are mostly from the Chisos Mountains, though this trend may shift as shown by the recent spate of records from Fort Davis.

Most records of White-eared Hummingbirds are from mid-May through mid-September, with a distinct peak in July. There are, however, some winter dates: a bird was seen in Ash Canyon (Huachuca Mountains) during December 1987, another stayed at Ramsey Canyon into January 1993, and birds returned to Ramsey on February 20 in both 1992 and 1993.

Best Bets

In Arizona, this species has delighted birders recently by colonizing Ramsey Canyon. During the ten years prior to 1989, Ramsey Canyon had only two White-ear sightings published in *American Birds*. Then, in 1989, a pair bred and raised two young. One to two young were also fledged in 1990 and 1991 (based on the banding of very recently fledged young). At least 17 individuals were banded in the canyon between 1989 and 1995. This recent spurt of activity has made Ramsey Canyon the best place to find White-eared Hummingbird.

It is, however, possible to find this species away from feeders. Carr Canyon, upper Ramsey Canyon, and the Chiricahuas are good places. When walking in any of these canyons, be sure to listen for this hummer's distinctive *tink-tink* call.

Identification

The hummingbird most often confused with White-eared is the Broad-billed. Some immature male Broad-bills retain their white supercilium (ear stripe) after they have already started to attain the adult's blue-green underparts. These can be mistaken for male White-ears. On some female Broad-bills, the white ear stripe is a bit more prominent than usual, prompting confusion with female White-ears.

White-eared Hummingbirds, of either gender, appear chunkier and shorter billed than Broad-bills. The face pattern is likewise different. The NGS guide has excellent depictions. Focus on the White-eared's blackish facial stripe and the shape of the white "ear." The pattern of green spotting on the female White-eared's throat is also diagnostic. For a good discussion of White-eared Hummingbird identification, see Kaufman (1990). (See color photo on page 482.)

White-eared Hummingbird—*all records*

LOCATION	NUMBERS SEEN	DATES SEEN
Texas Records		
Chisos Mountains	1	7/7/37
South Rim, Big Bend National Park	1	7/?/53
Boot Spring, Big Bend National Park	1	4/27/63
near Emory Peak, Big Bend National Park	1	7/17/67
near Emory Peak, Big Bend National Park	1	8/13/67
Chisos Mountains	1	5/6/84
Boot Spring, Big Bend National Park	1	8/4/84
near Rio Grande City	1	7/14 to 7/16/90
Guadalupe Mountain National Park	1	6/7/91
near Fort Davis	1	6/20 to 8/16/93
near Fort Davis	1	7/24 to 8/8/94
El Paso	1	10/12 to 10/20/94
Laguna Meadows, Big Bend National Park	1	6/24/95
Rejected by TX BRC		
Guadalupe Mountain National Park	1	8/8/91
New Mexico Records 1972 to 1995		
Pinos Altos	1	8/29 to 10/3/93
Lake Roberts	1	7/9 to 9/1/93
near Tijeras	1	7/1 to 8/16/94
near Lake Roberts	2	6/10 to 7/31/95
Animas Mountains	1	6/23/95
near Tijeras	1	7/14 to 7/30/95
Arizona Records 1972 to 1994		
Cave Creek Canyon	1	8/18 to 9/11/73
South Fork, Cave Creek Canyon	1	5/17/74
Portal	1	5/18/74
Portal	1	6/20/74
Portal	1	10/5 to 10/16/75
Chiricahua Mountains	1	6/28 to 7/2/76
Ramsey Canyon	1	6/18 to 6/20/77
Ramsey Canyon	1	4/23 to late 6/78
Summerhaven	1	7/4 to 7/31/79
Rose Canyon, Catalina Mountains	1	5/6/81
Summerhaven	1	5/23 to 9/4/81
Ramsey Canyon	1	7/5 to 7/26/81
Portal	1	9/5 to 9/30/81
Portal	1	5/29 to early 6/82
Cave Creek Canyon	1	7/13/82
Portal	1	10/9 to 10/13/82
Chiricahua Mountains	1	9/10/83
Madera Canyon	1	5/24 to 6/2/84
Portal	1	7/27 thru 8/84
Shannon Campground, Pinaleno Mountains	1	7/3 to 7/7/85
South Fork	3-4 (w/nest)	7/11 to 7/13/85

LOCATION	NUMBERS SEEN	DATES SEEN
Madera Canyon	1 (female)	7/12 to 7/27/85
Madera Canyon	1 (imm male)	July 1985 to 11/4/85
Portal	1	5/14/86
Scheelite Canyon	1	6/26/86
South Fork	2	8/3/86
Rustler Park	1	8/21/86
South Fork	1	9/14/86
Mount Lemmon	1	8/12 to early 9/87
Portal	1	9/29/87
Ramsey	1	10/21/87
South Fork	1	7/2 to 7/4/88
Madera Canyon	1	7/7/88
South Fork	1	5/5/89
Ramsey Canyon	1+ (2 young raised)	5/16 to 9/17/89
Cave Creek Ranch	1	5/24/89
Coronado National Monument	1	late 5/89 to 7/8/89
Carr Canyon	1	6/14/89
Carr Canyon	1	9/6/89
Ramsey Canyon	2+ (pair w/2 young)	5/10 to 9/10/90
Ramsey Canyon	1+ (up to 4)	5/1 to 9/25/91
South Fork	1	7/14 to 21/91
Carr Canyon	1	7/17/91
Summerhaven	1	7/19/91
Ramsey Canyon	1+ (up to 3)	3/10/92 to 7/31/92
Madera Canyon	1	5/30/92
Whitetail Canyon, Chiricahua Mountains	1	late 5/92
Carr Canyon	2	7/15 to 7/30/92
South Fork	1	7/16 to 7/18/92
Summerhaven	1	7/22/92
Ramsey Canyon	1	into mid-Jan 1993
Ramsey Canyon	1	from 2/20/93 on
Ramsey Canyon	4	spring 1993 to Sept 1993
Sawmill Canyon	1	4/12 to 4/13/93
Portal	1 (female)	5/13 to 5/22/93
Carr Canyon	1	5/14/93
Portal	1 (male)	5/17/93
Madera Canyon	1	5/17 to 5/18/93
Madera Canyon	1	6/30 to 7/31/93
Comfort Springs, Huachuca Mountains	1	7/19/93
Santa Catalina Mountains	1	7/93
Madera Canyon	1	8/8 to 8/9/93
Ramsey Canyon	1	mid-4/94 to late 7/94
Carr Canyon	1	5/12/94
Southwestern Research Station	1	5/9 to 5/11/94
Portal	1	5/12 to 5/16/94
Cave Creek Canyon	1	5/16 to 5/22/94

LOCATION	NUMBERS SEEN	DATES SEEN
Madera Canyon	1	5/17/94
Carr Canyon	1	7/7/94
Southwestern Research Station	1	8/15/94

records from 1972 on

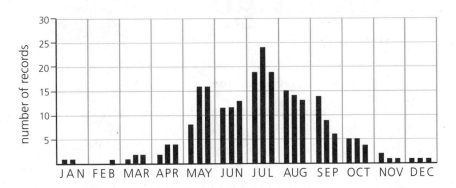

Berylline Hummingbird
Amazilia beryllina

Status and Distribution

This beautiful emerald-and-chestnut hummingbird is appropriately named after a gemstone. It normally ranges across western and southern Mexico down to El Salvador and Honduras. In the United States, it has occurred mostly in southeastern Arizona. There is, however, one record from Texas (Juniper Canyon, Big Bend National Park, 8/18/91), one record from New Mexico (Guadalupe Canyon, 5/24 to 5/25/93), and one record from central Arizona (Prescott, 9/15 to 9/21/90). The preferred habitat is oak woodlands and nearby riparian areas and feeders, especially at about 5,000 feet in elevation.

Berylline Hummingbirds have nested successfully twice in Arizona: two young fledged, Southwestern Research Station, Cave Creek Canyon, July 1976 and two young fledged, Ramsey Canyon, June 1978. Additionally, on September 14, 1984, a female was found feeding two seemingly hybrid young at Chiricahua National Monument. These fledglings were possibly a cross between Berylline and Magnificent hummers. Another female unsuccessfully brooded a nest at Ramsey Canyon during the summer of 1991. When she abandoned the nest, no eggs or young were found.

The best time to see the Berylline Hummingbird is from early June through late July. The extreme dates are from Huachuca Canyon, April 22, 1986, and Madera Canyon, October 21, 1987.

Best Bets

Most Berylline records come from feeders, and the best feeders have been those at Ramsey Canyon, Arizona (nine records). Finding your own Berylline will require considerable luck, even by this book's standards. Nonetheless, you have a fair chance of seeing this species as a "stake-out" during the summer.

Identification

The Berylline Hummingbird is nicely depicted in the NGS guide, and there are no other Arizona hummingbirds that could be easily confused with it. In Texas, however, the Buff-bellied Hummingbird needs to be considered. The Buff-bellied Hummingbird has no chestnut in wings, and the base of both mandibles is red (only the lower mandible is red in the Berylline).

Berylline Hummingbird —*all records*[1]

LOCATION	NUMBERS SEEN	DATES SEEN
Madera Canyon	1	June 1964
Ramsey Canyon	1	late 6 to early 8/67
Cave Creek Canyon	1	6/30 to 8/1/71
Ramsey Canyon	2	6/27 to late 8/75
Southwestern Research Station[2]	4	6/20 to 8/2/76
Ramsey Canyon	1	7/2 to 7/26/77
Ramsey Canyon[3]	4+	6/8 to 9/?78
Carr Canyon	1	6/30/79
Carr Canyon	1	7/31 to 8/7/81
Ramsey Canyon	1	6/22 to 6/27/82
Southwestern Research Station	1	6/26 to 6/28/82
Ramsey Canyon	1	7/18 to 7/19/83
Madera Canyon	1	7/18 to 8/?/83
Garden Canyon[4]	1	8/6/83
Portal	1	6/9/84
Chiricahua National Monument[5]	1	8/18 to 9/5/84
Barfoot-Rustler Trail[6]	1	7/18/85
Patagonia	1	6/8/85
Silver Spring, near Portal	1	7/2/85
South Fork	1	6/29 to 6/30/85
Huachuca Canyon	1	4/22/86
Ramsey Canyon	1	6/22 to 6/26/86
Southwestern Research Station	1	8/5/86

LOCATION	NUMBERS SEEN	DATES SEEN
Ramsey Canyon	2	7/21 to 8/10/87
Madera Canyon	1	7/1 to 10/21/87
Madera Canyon	1	5/13 to 6/5/88
Portal	1	7/18/89
Prescott	1	9/15 to 9/21/90
Big Bend National Park, TX	1	8/18/91
Ramsey Canyon[7]	1	6/21 to 8/31/91
Portal	1	5/4 to 6/11/92
Madera Canyon	1	6/25 to 7/17/92
Guadalupe Canyon, NM	1	5/24 to 5/25/93
Cave Creek Canyon	1	6/29/93
Portal	1	6/18 to 6/21/94
Cave Creek Canyon	1	6/25/94
Paradise	1	6/21 to 6/28/94

[1] All records are from Arizona unless otherwise denoted.
[2] Pair with two young.
[3] Two to five adults with two young.
[4] Huachuca Mountains.
[5] Female Berylline with hybrid young.
[6] Chiricahua Mountains.
[7] Unsuccessful nesting attempt.

all records
(sightings of multiple birds count as one record)

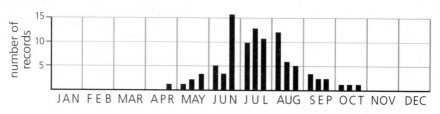

Violet-crowned Hummingbird
Amazilia violiceps

Status and Distribution

Despite its lack of color, the Violet-crowned Hummingbird may be the Lower 48's most dazzling hummer. The brilliant white underparts of a Violet-crown attract attention in a way that the color of other hummingbirds rarely can. Few birders fail to be impressed.

To see a Violet-crown in the United States, you will most likely need to travel to southeastern Arizona, where this species is a locally common breeder. The preferred habitat is cottonwood or sycamore riparian woodlands, but of course many are also found at feeders. Records away from southeastern Arizona (and adjacent Guadalupe Canyon, New Mexico) are few but include the following: Prescott, Yavapai County, Arizona, October 11 to 19, 1975; Santa Paula, Ventura County, California, July 6 to late December 1976; Saugus, Los Angeles County, California, May 25 to 29, 1987; Kenwood, Sonoma County, California, March 28 to 30, 1992; and El Paso, El Paso County, Texas, December 2 to 14, 1987.

The Tucson Audubon Society (1995) lists the Violet-crown as uncommon in southeastern Arizona from early May to late September and rare during the rest of the year. However, careful scrutiny at Patagonia-area feeders has revealed that this species usually arrives in late February and leaves in late October or early November (D. Parker, pers comm). Moreover, there are at least a dozen midwinter records from southeastern Arizona as a whole.

Best Bets

The Violet-crowned Hummingbird is fairly common in Arizona along Sonoita Creek (from Circle Z Ranch to Patagonia) and in Guadalupe Canyon. Individuals occasionally are also found elsewhere (e.g., Ramsey and Madera canyons) at hummingbird feeders. Despite the presence of apparently attractive habitat, there are several southeastern Arizona locales that lack this species.

Identification

The dazzling white underparts contrasting with dark green upperparts make this hummingbird unmistakable. Also note the red bill with dark tip, and yes, violet crown (which is admittedly dull on some individuals). The only truly similar hummingbird is the Green-fronted Hummingbird (*Amazilia viridifrons*) from southern Mexico—a most unlikely vagrant to the United States.   **(See color photo on page 483.)**

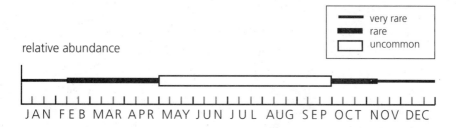

relative abundance

very rare
rare
uncommon

JAN FEB MAR APR MAY JUN JUL AUG SEP OCT NOV DEC

Plain-capped Starthroat

Heliomaster constanti

Status and Distribution

The Plain-capped Starthroat is one of the Lower 48's most sought-after hummingbirds. Not only is it rare (22 records) but it also has the annoying habit of being irregular at feeders. More than one unfulfilled birder has spent days at a hummingbird feeder waiting for a starthroat to reappear.

The Plain-capped Starthroat normally occurs in arid habitats and nearby riparian areas from western Mexico to Costa Rica. In the United States, all records but one have come from Arizona (Animas Valley, New Mexico, 8/25/93), and all but one of the Arizona records are from the southeastern corner of that state (Phoenix, 10/17 to 11/28/78). The favored habitat is the riparian zone of lower canyons (4,000 to 5,000 feet) with plenty of nearby agave.

The bulk of published Plain-capped Starthroat records is spread evenly from late June to early September. The extreme dates are May 20 in the Chiricahuas and November 28 in Phoenix. Notably, in western Mexico, the Plain-capped Starthroat breeds from January into June (Howell and Webb 1995).

Best Bets

There are no specific areas at which to find Plain-capped Starthroats. Records in Arizona are concentrated around Portal (seven sightings) and near Patagonia/Nogales (five sightings). Look carefully around all feeders and agave in these areas. Starthroats also have the habit of flycatching from exposed perches—something to watch for when around blooming agave.

Identification

The separation of the Plain-capped Starthroat from other U.S. hummingbirds should be easy. When you see one, your first impression will be that of a large hummer with a very long, thick-based bill. The white rump markings are diagnostic, but the white flank spots are not. The facial pattern, as shown in the NGS guide, is distinctive, but some immature male Anna's Hummingbirds can have a similar appearance. **(See color photo on page 483.)**

Plain-capped Starthroat—*all records*[1]

LOCATION	NUMBERS SEEN	DATES SEEN
Nogales	1	9/20 to 9/30/69
southwest of Patagonia	1	6/24/78
Patagonia	1	7/15 to 7/20/78
Phoenix	1	10/17 to 11/28/78
near Hereford, San Pedro River	1	6/28/80
Madera Canyon[2]	2	7/17 to 8/14/82 (1 to 9/6)
Sycamore Canyon	1	6/26/83
Copper Canyon[3]	1	8/20/83
White-tail Canyon[4]	2	7/10 to 8/12/85 (1 to 9/2)
White-Tail Canyon[4]	1	6/30 to 7/17/86
South Fork	1	5/20/87
near Paradise/Portal	1	8/21 to 9/2/87
Sunny Flat Campground[4]	1	10/6/87
Coronado National Monument	1	6/13 to 7/14/89
near Portal	1	8/10/89
Sonoita Creek	1	9/2/89
Sabino Canyon	1	9/2/89
Florida Wash	1	9/6/89
Sonoita Creek and Patagonia	1	June & July 1990
Stump Canyon, Huachuca Mountains	1	9/19/90
Portal	1	7/23 to 10/3/92
Animas Valley, New Mexico	1	8/25/93

[1] All records are from Arizona unless otherwise denoted.
[2] Possibly as many as five individuals.
[3] Near Coronado National Monument.
[4] Chiricahua Mountains.

all records (records with multiple birds counted as one record)

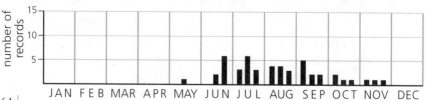

Lucifer Hummingbird

Calothorax lucifer

Status and Distribution

The "Lucifer" in this bird's name has nothing to do with Satan or with this species' preferred desert habitat. Instead, *lucifer* means "light-bringing" in Latin—an appropriate name for this pleasing little hummingbird.

In the United States, Lucifer Hummingbirds occur in isolated pockets from West Texas to southeastern Arizona. The Lucifer's preferred habitat is riparian areas in rocky desert with plenty of century plant (*Agave parryi, Agave havardiana*, and related species). The West Texas population is centered in Big Bend National Park, where approximately 50 females breed (Scott 1993). Records from elsewhere in Texas are scarce but include sightings from Black Mesa, Black Gap Wildlife Management Area, Alpine, and the Glass Mountains, all in Brewster County; the Chinati Mountains, Pinto Canyon, and the Sierra Viejo in Presidio County; Del Rio, Val Verde County; Fort Davis, Jeff Davis County; south of Austin in Travis County; and San Antonio in Bexar County.

The Big Bend population is usually present from late March into early September, with extreme dates being March 8 and November 10. These birds are generally easiest to find from May into September when century plants are in bloom.

In New Mexico, Lucifers have bred since at least 1980 at Post Office Canyon in the Peloncillo Mountains. This population consists of about 10 to 15 adults and is usually present from April to September (Scott 1993). At nearby Skeleton Canyon, there have been a couple birds each summer starting in 1991. Other New Mexico records include one at Clanton Canyon, Peloncillo Mountains, during June, 1989; another at Silver City from August 17 to 31, 1992; and a third bird at Guadalupe Canyon on June 9, 1994.

In Arizona, there were but four records before 1970, but since then Lucifers have been seen in Arizona every year except 1974 and 1981. During 1973, the first (and only) Arizona nest was found at Guadalupe Canyon. Since that time, Portal has been the place for Lucifers in Arizona, and sightings from there no longer even make it to *Field Notes* (a.k.a. *American Birds*). This species is also annual, or nearly so, at Guadalupe Canyon, Ramsey Canyon, the Sonoita area, and Madera Canyon. Records elsewhere in Arizona have come from Coronado National Monument, Tucson, Bisbee, Leslie Canyon (southwestern Chircahua Mountains), California Gulch, Comfort Spring (Carr Canyon), Dragoon Mountains, Fort Huachuca, Hereford, Swisshelm Mountains, and Patagonia.

Around Portal, Lucifers usually appear in early April but then disappear in late May only to reappear during late July and stay into early October (S. Spofford, pers comm). Most Arizona records away from the Portal area are from late June through late August. The latest published record from Portal was on October 23, 1979, whereas the latest Arizona record comes from Tucson on November 7, 1992.

For more details on Lucifer Hummingbird biology, see Scott (1993).

Best Bets

In Texas, Big Bend is the place to look. The prime location in New Mexico is, unfortunately, in private hands. For Arizona Lucifers, try the feeders in the Portal area. Lucifers also show up at other feeders and a check with the Tucson hotline might be worthwhile.

Identification

The identification of an adult male Lucifer Hummingbird is pretty straightforward, and so is the identification of a female, after you've already seen one. Most field guides focus on the buffy underparts and the decurved bill, but it is amazing how many hummingbird species seem to have decurved bills when you look closely. Also, the buffy underparts can be simulated by a dusting of pollen or by reflection from the red parts of feeders. Worst of all, female Broad-tailed Hummingbirds can have a buffy (albeit orange buffy) wash and a distinctly decurved bill.

When looking at a potential female Lucifer, be sure to note the face pattern. The dark ear patch is obviously set off from the dark crown by a (usually) buffy postocular stripe. This stripe widens as it goes back and connects to the sides of the chest and throat. Also, the bill is truly more decurved than other U.S. hummers, and the buff is not concentrated in the lower flanks like a Broad-tail. Probably the best depiction in any major guide is in the MGB. Kaufman (1990) has a good discussion, which is expanded upon (with good drawings) in Kaufman (1992).
(See color photo on page 484.)

Eared Trogon

Euptilotis neoxenus

Status and Distribution

The Eared Trogon is a mystical and elusive species of northwestern Mexico's steep mountain canyons. It had been the nemesis of many serious Mexico listers, so imagine everybody's surprise when one appeared in the United States at Arizona's Cave Creek Canyon in 1977. This bird was first found on October 23, and by late November the number of individuals had grown to four. Surprise turned into astonishment. Then, in early December, another Eared Trogon appeared in Arizona's Ramsey Canyon. Speculation grew rampant. Was this range expansion or merely vagrancy?

The correct answer is probably a bit of both. (For an amusing account of this first record and early speculation, see Zimmerman [1978]). After the last of 1977's invasion disappeared in December of that year, there was a single report during 1978 and just a couple of scattered reports in 1979. Thereafter, no more Eared Trogons were positively identified (a probable Eared Trogon was seen in the Animas Mountains of New Mexico on June 13, 1979) in the United States until 1982, when one was found again in South Fork. Since 1982, however, this wonderful species has been found during 9 of 13 years, and in 1991, another, even bigger, invasion occurred involving at least ten birds at five sites.

The crowning event of the 1991 invasion was a nesting attempt in upper Ramsey Canyon. Young were first found in Ramsey on October 12, but the nest was abandoned on October 26 after a wicked cold front brought snow to the area. The Ramsey pair (plus a lone male) remained in Ramsey and nearby canyons for a couple of years, and one or more were present through at least summer 1995. Scattered reports since 1991 have also come from Cave Creek Canyon through spring 1994.

In Mexico, Eared Trogons are birds of pine forests above 6,000 feet (Howell and Webb 1995). Clearly, a similar habitat is favored in the United States, as almost all records are from above 5,000 feet in moist canyons with pine-oak or pine-fir woodlands. During winter, however, individuals have occasionally strayed lower into oak woodlands. A favored food source in Arizona is the madrone fruit (S. Williamson, pers comm). Many southeastern Arizona canyons have appropriate habitat, especially in the Chiricahua and Huachuca mountain ranges. The preponderance of records from Cave Creek and upper Ramsey canyons probably, in part, reflects the intensity of coverage at these places. At this time, there are no definite records outside of Arizona.

Besides the currently resident bird(s) at upper Ramsey Canyon (and perhaps more widely through the Huachucas), Lower 48 Eared Trogons have been seen between mid-May and early December. Sightings during the past five years have been concentrated between mid-June and early September.

Best Bets

Upper Ramsey and Cave Creek canyons in Arizona should be your destination if you seek Eared Trogons, though many less-covered canyons, such as Miller Canyon, may be equally good. Finding your own Eared Trogon at any of these places is as much a matter of stealth and luck as anything else. Eared Trogons are vocal but shy birds. If one is known to be in a given area, sitting, listening, and waiting is often the best method of searching. Playing recorded calls of this species more often drives these birds away than lures them in.

Identification

Eared Trogon identification is easy if you keep your wits about you. Eared Trogons are much larger than Elegant Trogons. This difference is more than just a discrepency in length, it is also due to a difference in bulk. Furthermore, Eared Trogons lack the Elegant's white chest crescent and have black rather than horn-colored bills. There are other differences as well, such as tail pattern and back color. These are all fairly well represented in the NGS guide. Sadly, the "ears" are rarely visible.

269

Potential pitfalls do exist. One is that moulting Elegant Trogons could possibly lack the white chest crescent. Furthermore, the back and tail color are light dependent.

Eared Trogon—*all records*

LOCATION	NUMBERS SEEN	DATES SEEN
South Fork, Cave Creek Canyon		male appeared on 10/23/77 joined by female on 11/16; 4 present by late November. Last seen 12/2/77.
Ramsey Canyon	1	12/1 to 12/3/77
lower Cave Creek Canyon	1	11/5/78
South Fork, Cave Creek Canyon	1	8/12 to 8/13/79 and 10/22/79
South Fork, Cave Creek Canyon	1	8/22 and 10/1/82
South Fork, Cave Creek Canyon	1	10/22/85
South Fork, Cave Creek Canyon	1	5/26/86
South Fork, Cave Creek Canyon	1	9/1/87
South Fork, Cave Creek Canyon	1	6/21/89
Herb Martyr, Cave Creek Canyon	1	6/22/89
Carr Canyon	1	8/9/89
Rock Creek Canyon, Chiricahua Mountains	1	10/7/91
Ramsey Canyon	3	including pair and lone male, 8/6/91 into 1995. May well account for 1992 to 1995 sightings at other nearby canyons such as Scheelite, Sawmill, and Miller.
Madera Canyon	pair	8/7/91 into 9/91
South Fork, Cave Creek Canyon	female male 1	6/9 to 8/9/91; 6/22 to 8/9/91; 11/22/91. Also, scattered records through spring 1994
Pinery Canyon, Chiricahua Mountains	pair	8/9/91
Gardner Canyon, Santa Rita Mountains	female	8/19/91
Parker Creek, Sierra Ancha Mountains, NW of Globe	1	6/17/92
Black River, Apache County	1	6/13/92

Buff-breasted Flycatcher

Empidonax fulvifrons

Status and Distribution

The diminutive and distinctive Buff-breasted Flycatcher has the most restricted breeding range of any U.S. empidonax. It is currently found almost exclusively in the Huachuca Mountains of southeastern Arizona, where it is fairly common. Formerly, however, Buff-breasts have been more widespread. Prior to the 1900s, Buff-breasts had been recorded as far afield as Prescott and Fort Apache (White Mountains), Arizona (Monson and Phillips 1981), and into New Mexico (DeSante and Pyle 1986). They also were more widespread in southeastern Arizona itself, occurring in the Santa Catalina, Rincon, Chiricahua, Patagonia, and Huachuca mountains (Monson and Phillips 1981). The reasons for their decline is unclear, but by the 1970s Buff-breasts were found only in the Huachucas.

Fortunately, the 1980s and 1990s have brought an increasing number of sightings from other locations. Buff-breasted Flycatchers are now reported nearly annually from the Chiricahua Mountains, and there have been several recent sightings in the Catalina, Whetstone, and Santa Rita mountains. Recent lowland records have come from the upper San Pedro River, Sonoita Creek, and Portal. There is also a report, likely correct, still under review by the Colorado rarities committee: Colorado Springs State Wildlife Area, May 19, 1991. New Mexico has had no recent records, but with the apparent recent range expansion and the proximity of Mexican breeding populations (see Monson and Phillips 1981), such a find is likely just a matter of time. Finally, there is a report of a Buff-breast from Texas (Big Bend National Park, August 12, 1969), which is unsubstantiated and best disregarded.

Buff-breasted Flycatchers arrive in Arizona as early as late March and commence nesting as early as mid-April. In fall, they have usually departed by mid-September (Davis and Russell 1990), and there are no winter records.

Best Bets

As restricted a range as this species has in the United States, it occurs widely in Arizona's Huachuca Mountains. The most traditional spot for this bird has probably been Sawmill Canyon, but access to Sawmill is through Fort Huachuca, which is sometimes closed to civilians. The good news is that Carr Canyon is more reliably accessible and has plenty of Buff-breasts.

If you find yourself elsewhere in the Huachucas and you want to look for your own Buff-breasted Flycatcher, concentrate on dry open Apache and Chihuahuan pine woodlands at about 6,000 to 7,000 feet. Also try whistling like a Northern Pygmy-Owl because Buff-breasts often respond nicely to whistled imitations of this predator (and you might get an owl, too).

Identification

The identification of this petite buffy empidonax should not be a problem. Most major guides are adequate, and Kaufman (1990) has a nice discussion. You should remember, however, that the Tufted Flycatcher, a vagrant to Texas and a potential vagrant to Arizona, is also buffy. Its color, however, is somewhat richer, and it is distinctly crested.

(See color photo on page 484.)

Buff-breasted Flycatcher—*Arizona records since 1977 away from the Huachuca Mountains*

LOCATION	NUMBERS SEEN	DATES SEEN
Chiricahua Mountains		
Cave Creek Canyon	2 (nested)	4/16 to 7/3/81
Whitetail Canyon	1	9/6/81
several west side canyons	summer 1982	
Salisbury Canyon	2+	spring 1983
South Fork	1	4/30/85
South Fork	1	5/12/85
Rustler Park	2	early 5 to mid 7/86
Rustler Park	2	6/8/88
Southwestern Research Station	1	late 4/90 to 5/20/90

LOCATION	NUMBERS SEEN	DATES SEEN
Turkey Creek	1	4/7/90
Turkey Creek	1	4/6/91
Barfoot Park	1	late 4/91
Southwestern Research Station	1	4/11 to 5/12/92
Rustler Park	1	5/21/92
Rucker Canyon	2 (with nest)	6/26/92
Cave Creek Canyon	1	4/12 to 4/16/93
Pinery Canyon	1	5/22/93
Rustler Park	3	8/93
Onion Saddle	1	8/22/93
Southwestern Research Station	1	4/10 to 4/14/94
Rucker Canyon	1	5/94 to 6/5/94
Pine Caynon	(pair nested)	1985-87
Santa Rita Mountains		
Madera Canyon	1	8/17/84
northeast slope of Mt. Hopkins	2	4/19/85
Baldy Saddle	1	early 7/85
upper Madera Canyon	1	8/17/86
Madera Canyon	1	5/23/88
Florida Canyon	1	4/30/89
upper Gardner Canyon	1	9/6/92
Josephine Canyon	1	5/6/93
upper Madera Canyon	1	4/1/94
Santa Catalina Mountains		
Rose Canyon	3	summer 1982
Mt. Lemmon	1	9/26/82
Rose Canyon	2+	spring 1983
Pima Canyon	1	9/9/84
Rose Canyon	1	6/20/85
Whetstone Mountains		
French Joe Canyon	4 (2 pairs)	7/28/93
Lowland Areas		
near Portal	2	9/13/82
Sonoita Creek	1	4/29/84
near Portal	1	4/18/85
Sonoita Creek	1	4/12/86
St. David, upper San Pedro River	1	7/13/89
upper San Pedro River	1	4/20/90

La Sagra's Flycatcher

Myiarchus sagrae

Status and Distribution

The La Sagra's Flycatcher is even drabber than the average *myiarchus*. Its colors are subdued, and unlike the perky Great-crested Flycatcher, the La Sagra's is retiring and lethargic. In the West Indies, it is often known as Tom Fool because of this lackadaisical nature. Yet, despite all of its character flaws, the Tom Fool is certainly a celebrity in the United States.

The La Sagra's Flycatcher was first recorded in the United States in a surprising location: inland Alabama's Dallas County on September 14, 1963. The 19 records since then, however, have all come from southern Florida, mostly along the southeast coast from Islamorada to Riviera Beach. There are also two Dry Tortugas records. The Alabama bird was determined to be of Cuban origin after it was collected. The location of records since then, however, implies a Bahamanian origin for most of these wanderers (Robertson and Kushlan 1974).

In their native lands (Cuba, the Bahamas, and Grand Cayman), La Sagra's Flycatchers prefer tropical hardwood forests (also known as coppice) and mangrove swamps. In the United States, most records have come from similar habitat, especially dense secondary-growth coppice. Unfortunately, the thick cover here, combined with this species' general lassitude, can make the La Sagra's difficult to locate even when present.

Published records of La Sagra's Flycatcher show a bimodal distribution. First, there is a group of winter records, mostly from good coppice habitat, with a peak from mid-December to late January. Then, there is a group of spring records that comes mostly from coastal parks. These records stretch from March 31 to May 30. The spring birds have truly been transients, rarely lingering more than a day or two.

La Sagra's Flycatcher records are so scattered that no particular spot can be highly recommended. In winter, the best area would most likely be north Key Largo and Elliott Key, if they were not largely inaccessible. You could try birding along the road in upper Key Largo or try the land portion of John Pennekamp Coral Reef State Park (phone 305-451-1202). Another area, which just opened to public day use, can be reached by turning left onto County Road 905 from US 1. Drive 0.4 mile and enter through a salmon-colored concrete arch on your right. During migration, try the coastal parks from Miami to Palm Beach County (see "Site Guide"). The La Sagra's tends to vocalize rather incessantly during the spring, so when looking for this flycatcher be sure to listen for its distinctive call (recorded on Reynard and Garrido 1988).

Identification

Finding out how to identify a La Sagra's Flycatcher is challenging. It is not covered in any North American field guide, and if you look in *Birds of the West Indies,* you will be likewise frustrated unless you are aware that La Sagra's Flycatcher was once considered conspecific with the Stolid Flycatcher (*Myiarchus stolidus*). Fortunately, good photos are published in Smith and Evered (1992).

Contrary to the length listed in Bond (1985), the La Sagra's Flycatcher will not strike you as a large *myiarchus*, such as a Great Crested or Brown-crested. Instead, the La Sagra's will appear more like the smaller Ash-throated. The La Sagra's can be separated by its coloration, structure, and posture.

The La Sagra's underparts are duller than the Great Crested and often are even paler than those of the Brown-crested or Ash-throated. The La Sagra's also has less rust in the tail and wings than these species. Its bill is long like a Great Crested, but it is considerably thinner. Perhaps most important, however, is the La Sagra's general shape and attitude. The La Sagra's is relatively short tailed and tends to lean forward on its perch with its crest held flat (Smith and Evered 1992; W. Hoffman, pers comm). This combination gives the La Sagra's a very different feel than its big-headed, big-crested, long-tailed, upright cousins.

Of importance is the La Sagra's call, which can be heard on Reynard and Garrido (1988). Wayne Hoffman (pers comm) describes the call as a series of *whip* notes, clearer, shorter, and less upswept than the harsh, burry *wheep* of the Great-crested.   **(See color photo on page 485.)**

La Sagra's Flycatcher —*all records**

LOCATION	NUMBERS SEEN	DATES SEEN
Dallas County, AL	1	9/14/63
Key Largo	1	10/90 to late 2/91
Treetops Park, Davie	1	11/12/94 to early 1/95
Matheson Hammock	1	12/1 to 12/20/84
Biscayne National Park	1	12/17 to 12/27/91
Elliott Key	1	12/21/82 to 1/24/83
Elliott Key	1	12/22/87 to 1/9/88
Elliott Key	1	late 12/90 to late 2/91
northern Key Largo	1	1/15/88
Miami Canal, Palm Beach County	1	3/31/91
Islamorada	1	4/7 to 4/21/91
MacArthur State Park	1	4/9 to 5/30/93
Biscayne Bay, Miami	1	4/12/95
Boca Raton	1	4/18/92
Lloyd State Park	1	4/20 to 4/21/94
Delray Beach	1	4/20 to 4/21/94
Spanish River State Park	1	5/1/95
Dry Tortugas	1	5/2 to 5/8/94
Dry Tortugas	1	5/5 to 5/8/93
Birch State Park	1	5/14/88

* All records are from Florida unless otherwise denoted.

all records

Fork-tailed
Flycatcher

Tyrannus savana

Status and Distribution

Picture yourself standing at some vagrant hot spot along the Gulf Coast or Atlantic seaboard. In the distance you spy a large flycatcher with a streamerlike tail. Your pulse quickens. A Scissor-tailed Flycatcher—nice find, you think, but something is wrong. As you close in, you notice that the bird has a black cap and not enough white on the tail. You follow it about for 20 minutes as it sallies to and fro, and as you do you become certain that this is *not* a Scissor-tailed Flycatcher. Then, poof, it's gone. The next day, hundreds of birders pour in, but no one can find your flycatcher.

If you were to experience the above scenario, you would be part of a typical Fork-tailed Flycatcher encounter. The majority of Fork-tails are seen only on one day, and many are seen for but a matter of minutes. Some have stayed a little longer, but only a very few have remained at one spot for more than a week. The endurance record holder is a bird that visited Rustic, Virginia, from June 3 to August 1, 1988. The next most stationary Fork-tail remained almost a month near Raymondville, Texas, during the winter of 1984-85. United States records of Fork-tailed Flycatcher are surprisingly far-flung. Records have come from such widely scattered places as Washington, California, Idaho, Minnesota, Maine, Florida, and Texas. There is some pattern, however: 47 of the 93 records are from the Northeast (NJ to ME), and 32 sightings are from the Southeast (TX to FL to VA).

U.S. Fork-tailed Flycatchers appear mostly during fall, with peak occurrence extending from early September through late October. There are records, however, from every month of the year, and there is also a smaller peak from late April through late June. The January, February, and

March sightings are all from Texas and may be of birds that successfully overwintered in the United States. The April records are all from Gulf Coast states.

That Fork-tailed Flycatchers occur in the United States at all is a surprise. Its usual range comes no closer than southeastern Mexico, yet it has been seen over 90 times. Superficially even more amazing is that most U.S. Fork-tails are of the race *Tyrannus savana savana*, which breeds not in Mexico but in southern South America. *T. savana savana*'s occurrence here is mostly explained by its highly migratory habits. Normally, this subspecies spends the austral winter (our summer) in northern South America. Birds overshooting their normal wintering range account for most of our late spring and early summer records. The larger fall peak of sightings probably consists of birds that have engaged in a mirror image migration, flying north instead of south after wintering in the tropics (McCaskie and Patten 1994). Winter records from Texas are more problematical and may consist of *T. savana savana* that have successfully overwintered and *T. savana monachus* individuals that have wandered north from their usual haunts in southern Mexico.

Best Bets

Unfortunately, there is no one site for this species because it rarely gives repeat performances. The most records from one spot is six, stretching back to 1939, from Cape May.

Identification

The Fork-tailed Flycatcher is not likely confused with any U.S. bird other than the Scissor-tailed Flycatcher. The Fork-tail can be identified by its black cap, black tail, lack of rose pink, less-patterned wing, and pointed outer retrices. The NGS depiction is accurate. Note that immatures cannot be reliably aged by tail length. Instead, you should rely on wing covert pattern and rump color. Adults have black rumps and gray fringes to the wing coverts. Immatures have cinnamon brown fringes to the wing and uppertail coverts (McCaskie and Patten 1994).

(See color photo on page 485.)

Fork-tailed Flycatcher—*all records*

LOCATION	NUMBERS SEEN	DATES SEEN
Henderson, KY	1	late Oct, year?
Bridgeton, NJ	1	12/1820
near Natchez, MS	2	8/1822
Camden, NJ	1	6/1832
Fox Chase, PA	1	fall 1873
Lake Ridge, MI	1	7/1879
Vermont	1	1884
Trenton, NJ	1	fall 1900
Marion, ME	1	12/1/08
Martha's Vineyard, MA	1	10/22/16
Cape May, NJ	1	11/1 to 11/3/39
East Quogue, NY	1	9/14/44
north of Uvalde, TX	1	8/10/46
southeastern Cameron County, TX	1	11/19/46
Heckscher State Park, NY	1	9/23/47
14.6 mi W of Okeechobee, FL	1	11/5/52
Clermont, NY	1	10/7/54
near Aransas NWR, TX	1	10/8/58
Rio Grande delta, TX	1	3/20/59
18 mi NNE of Edinburg, TX	1	2/4/61
Martha's Vineyard, MA	1	9/26 to 9/27/61
West Orange, NJ	1	5/29/67
Encinal Peninsula, TX	1	9/25/67
Plum Island, MA	1	5/4 to 5/9/68
Cape May, NJ	1	8/23/68
Biddeford Pool, ME	1	9/6 to 9/11/70
Brigantine NWR, NJ[1]	1	9/4/72
Cape May, NJ[1]	1	9/4/72
Bulls Island, Cape Romain NWR, SC	1	late 10/73 to 11/1/73
Sugarloaf Key, FL	1	7/15 to 7/16/74
Whiting, ME	1	9/14 to 9/25/75
Martinsville, ME	1	9/9 to 9/15/76
Rockledge, FL	1	9/17/76
Kennebunk, ME	1	10/1 to 10/8/76
Chokoloskee, FL	1	10/17/76
Sandy Point, MD	1	9/23/78
Cape May, NJ	1	10/11/78
Queens County, NY	1	10/22 to 10/27/78
Suffolk County, NY	1	10/26/78
Columbia County, WI	1	11/13 to 11/16/78
Chatham, MA	1	9/22 to 10/4/80
East Orleans, MA	1	9/27 to 10/7/80
Big Cypress National Park, FL	1	5/5/81
near Austin, TX	1	5/16/81

LOCATION	NUMBERS SEEN	DATES SEEN
Chatham, MA	1	9/22 to 9/27/81
Nantucket, MA	1	9/16 to 9/18/82
Rumely, MI	1	10/6/83
Cape May, NJ	1	5/18 to 5/20/84
W of Florida City, FL	2	9/15/84
Bailey Island, ME	1	10/24/84
SE of Raymondville, TX	1	12/17/84 to 1/16/85
Dry Tortugas, FL	1	6/6 to 6/8/855
Block Island, RI	1	10/9/85
Monroe, ME	1	10/10/85
east Boston, MA	1	10/11 to 10/12/85
Port Mahon, DE	1	10/19/85
Merritt Island, FL	1	11/11/85
Cape Carteret, NC	1	6/1 to 6/7/86
Brooklyn, NY	1	7/17/86
Falmouth, MA	1	6/13/87
Marshfield, MA	1	6/20 to 6/21/87
Fort Morgan, AL	1	4/24/88
Rustic, VA	1	6/3 to 8/1/88
Douglas County, WI	1	6/24/88
south Colleton County, SC	1	10/23/88
Ricardo, TX[2]	1	12/18 to 12/26/88
Oak Beach, NY	1	5/7/89
Camden, DE	1	9/27/89
Aransas NWR, TX	1	12/4/89
Concord, MA	1	5/2 to 5/3/90
Chincoteague NWR, VA	1	5/17 to 19/90
Shark Valley, Everglades National Park, FL	1	6/16 and 6/25/90
Ledyard, NY	1	9/26/90
Hamlin, NY	1	10/7 to 10/16/90
Gilchrist, TX	1	4/23 to 4/25/91
Castellow Hammock Park, FL	1	6/14/91
east of Picabo, ID	1	8/25 to 9/7/91
Duluth, MN	1	9/6/91
Cape May, NJ	1	9/29/91
Wellfleet, MA	1	10/3/91
False Cape SP, VA	1	10/21/91
Dauphin Island, AL	1	4/20/92
Grand Marais, MN	1	5/3 to 5/14/92
Loxahatchee NWR, FL	1	7/13 to 7/14/92
Bridgehaven, CA	1	9/4 to 9/8/92
Fire Island, L.I., NY	1	10/13/92
Sabine Pass, TX	1	4/25/93
Ram Island, Mattapoisett, MA	1	6/29/93
Ellisburg, NY	1	9/8/93
Kittery, ME	1	5/18 to 5/31/94

LOCATION	NUMBERS SEEN	DATES SEEN
Charlestown, RI	1	10/20 to 10/29/94
Robert Moses State Park, NY	1	10/23 to 10/29/94
Chinook River, WA	1	9/12 to 9/13/95
Rejected by state BRC		
Santa Monica, CA		summer 1883

[1]These two records may well be of the same individual.

[2]This individual was reportedly of the northern subspecies, *T. savana monachus,* which breeds from southeastern Mexico to Colombia, Venezuela, and Suriname.

Fork-tailed Flycatcher—*records by state*

STATE	NUMBERS SEEN	STATE	NUMBERS SEEN
Maine	8	Vermont	1
Massachusetts	13	Rhode Island	2
New York	12	Pennsylvania	1
New Jersey	10	Delaware	2
Maryland	1	Virginia	3
North Carolina	1	South Carolina	2
Florida	11	Alabama	1
Mississippi	2	Texas	12
Kentucky	1	Michigan	2
Wisconsin	2	Minnesota	2
Idaho	1	California	1

all records

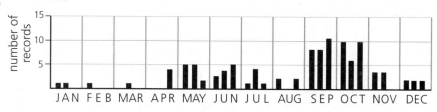

Rose-
throated
Becard

Pachyramphus aglaiae

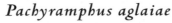

Status and Distribution

The becards form a genus of Neotropical flycatchers of which only the Rose-throated occurs in the United States. This rather frumpish bird breeds from northern Costa Rica to Arizona. It also occurs with some regularity in Texas and has been recorded in New Mexico.

In Arizona the Rose-throated Becard is a summer resident along sycamore-lined streams in the southeastern corner of the state. It breeds regularly only along Sonoita Creek (between Patagonia and Lake Patagonia), in Sycamore Canyon (Pajaritos Mountains), and near Arivaca. It has also nested at Guadalupe Canyon (1957 and 1982). Away from these areas, this species is a true vagrant. The few such records have come from Box Canyon (Santa Rita Mountains), Harshaw Canyon (Patagonia Mountains), Madera Canyon, the San Pedro River at Fairbank, upper Aravaipa Canyon, and the Huachuca Mountains.

Arizona becards usually start arriving in mid-May and the last have usually gone by mid-September. There are, however, a couple of winter records: Arivaca, December 23, 1986, and Harshaw Canyon, near Patagonia, December 18, 1983.

In Texas, Rose-throated Becards are almost annual winter visitors to the lower Rio Grande valley, with ten records since 1982. Formerly, however, this species was a permanent resident, albeit in small numbers. The last summer/nesting record came from Santa Ana National Wildlife Refuge in 1978. Recent (since 1982) winter records have come from Bentsen-Rio Grande State Park (4 records), Santa Ana National Wildlife Refuge (5 records), Anzalduas County Park (1 record), Big Bend National

Park (1 record), King Ranch (1 record), and Salineño (1 record). The published New Mexico records come from lower Guadalupe Canyon, just across the border from Arizona: June 9, 1978, and June 10, 1984.

Best Bets

The classic place for Rose-throated Becards is the Patagonia Rest Stop. During most years, a pair nests at this location. Other places to look include Circle Z Ranch (must stay here to bird here) and Sycamore Canyon. Becards are generally secretive. Listen for their calls as this is often a great aid in finding this species. Also, the becards' large bulky hanging nests can sometimes bely their presence.

Identification

One look at your field guide and you will realize that there is no other U.S. species that resembles the Rose-throated Becard. You should note, however, that some male Rose-throateds do not, in fact, have any rose on the throat.

The only similar species that approaches the United States is the Gray-collared Becard (*Pachyramphus major*), which breeds as far north as southern Sonora and central Nuevo Leon (Howell and Webb 1995). The Gray-collared is thus a potential vagrant to the Lower 48, especially in Texas. The male Gray-collared is strikingly different in plumage. The female Gray-collared can be told by its undertail pattern, more patterned wings, and pale supraloral stripe. For good drawings, see Peterson and Chalif (1973) or Monson (1986).

Rose-throated Becard—*Arizona records away from known breeding sites*

LOCATION	NUMBERS SEEN	DATES SEEN
Box Canyon, Santa Rita Mountains	1	6/16/73
Madera Canyon	1	5/16 to 5/18/79; 6/1/85
San Pedro River at Fairbank	1	6/2/89
Upper Aravaipa Canyon E of Graham County line	1	7/6/79
Huachuca Mountains	1	6/20/1880
Harshaw Canyon	1	12/18/83

Rose-throated Becard—*Texas records since 1982*

LOCATION	NUMBERS SEEN	DATES SEEN
Big Bend National Park	1	2/7/82
Bentsen State Park	2	10/82 to mid 1/83
Bentsen State Park	1	11/28 to 12/6/85
Santa Ana NWR	1	12/28 to 29/87
Salineño	1	early 12/87 to 1/28/88
Santa Ana NWR	1	12/24/88
Bentsen State Park	1	12/26/88 to 3/30/89
Bentsen State Park	1	9/14/89 to 3/3/90
Santa Ana NWR	1	2/18/90
Anzalduas County Park	1	1/15 to 2/9/90
King Ranch	1	1/20/92
Santa Ana NWR	1	1/2 to 3/18/93
Rejected by TX BRC		
Santa Ana NWR	2	12/20 to 12/31/86

Eurasian Skylark

Alauda arvensis

Status and Distribution

The Eurasian Skylark has the dubious distinction of being the only introduced species in this book. We've included it because some birders are unaware that the skylark has extended its range from Vancouver Island (British Columbia) to San Juan Island (Washington). More important, however, skylarks are fun. It is truly a treat to watch them pronounce their larkish love by climbing skyward and unleashing a torrent of song. The jagged Olympic Mountains and glistening Pacific add even more delight to the magnificent scene.

The European race (*Alauda arvensis arvensis*) of the Eurasian Skylark was first successfully introduced into North America on Vancouver Island during 1903, but the first Lower 48 record was not until August 15, 1960, when one was seen at Friday Harbor, San Juan Island. Ten years later, the first U.S. nest was located at American Camp on San Juan Island (5/17/70), and American Camp remains the premier spot for this species. The only records of this introduced population away from San Juan Island come from nearby Iceberg Point on Lopez Island.

Notably, a northeast Asian race of Eurasian Skylark, *A. arvensis pekinensis*, occurs with some regularity as a spring migrant on the outer Aleutians. A vagrant showing characteristics of one of the northeast Asian races also returned for seven consecutive years to Point Reyes, California. The dates were 12/16/78 to 2/19/79, 10/27 to 11/1/79, 10/25/80 to 2/21/81, 11/3/81 to 1/3/82, 10/31/82 to 1/29/83, 11/3 to 11/8/83, and 10/27/84 to 2/17/85.

Best Bets

The birds at San Juan Island are present year-round and the easiest spot to find them is at the rabbit barrens of American Camp. The skylarks are most easily seen when singing, from March through July, but they are rarely difficult to locate.

Identification

The Eurasian Skylark looks as much like certain sparrows (e.g., the Savannah Sparrow) as anything else in North America. Attention to shape and structure should make that separation straightforward. Telling the race introduced from Europe (*A. arvensis arvensis*) from *A. arvensis pekinensis* and other Asian subspecies is not so easy. Important points found on the northeast Asian races include the following:

Face and Breast Color: Buffy yellow, unlike duller European birds.

Back: Darker streaks with brighter colored feather edgings.

Nape: Narrower streaks.

For more details, see Roberson (1980) or Morlan and Erickson (1983).

(See color photo on page 486.)

Bahama
Swallow

Tachycineta cyaneoviridis

Status and Distribution

The elegant Bahama Swallow is native to the northern Bahamas, where it breeds in the Caribbean Pine barrens of Grand Bahama, Abaco, New Providence, and Andros Islands (Smith and Smith 1990). It is generally a sedentary species, though a few do wander south to Cuba in winter. Nonetheless, Bahama Swallows have been found in the United States at least 29 times. The Bahama Swallow was one of the earliest vagrants to be described from the United States, with the first record coming from the Dry Tortugas on April 7, 1890. All records since then have also been from Florida, and most have come from the Florida Keys.

During the 1970s and 1980s, a pattern seemed to form when Bahama Swallows were seen nearly annually on pine-forested keys. Nesting probably occurred in 1974 when a pair of adults was seen around Sugarloaf Key from May 3 into July, at which time a juvenile bird appeared. Unfortunately, the trend ended in 1986, and there have been no Bahama Swallows seen on the Keys since.

Surprisingly, the most celebrated Bahama Swallow occurred not in the Keys but in Cutler Ridge of southern Dade County. This cooperative bird was first found with a colony of "West Indian" Cave Swallows on May 18, 1988, and it thrilled countless birders for four consecutive summers. Sadly, it met its end as a traffic casualty in late April 1992.

Bahama Swallows have been recorded every month except September, October, November, and February; most sightings, however, have come from May and June. Some of this may be due to observer bias, and if birding activity in July and August were to increase, records then might do so as well.

287

Best Bets

There is no specific site for Bahama Swallows. If you were desperate and absolutely had to search for Bahama Swallows, try the areas around Big Pine and Sugarloaf keys in Florida in May and June (and perhaps July and August). Use the Rand McNally Florida Keys map for navigation.

Identification

The adult Bahama Swallow is reasonably well shown in the NGS guide. Note, however, that the deeply forked tail is not always so obvious and that the wings and rump are more purplish and less green. Also, the snowy white wing linings are diagnostic despite no mention in the text.

Immature Bahama Swallows pose more of a problem. They lack both the deeply forked tail and white underwing of the adult. However, they can be told from Tree Swallows by their immaculate white breasts and whiter face pattern. For details, see Smith and Smith (1990).

Bahama Swallow—*all records*

LOCATION	NUMBERS SEEN	DATES SEEN
Dry Tortugas	2	4/7/1890
Fisheating Creek	1	3/19/53
New Smyrna Beach	1	6/6/55
Little Duck Key	1	12/11/55
Virginia Key	1	1/6/58
Dry Tortugas	1	7/9 to 7/10/60
Naples	1	4/24/62
Ramrod Key	1	6/30/74
Sugarloaf Key	2 (adult)	5/3 to 7/14/74
Sugarloaf Key	1 (immature)	7/74
Cudjoe Key*	1	5/15/76
Boca Chica Key*	1	5/16/76
Key Haven*	1	5/22 to 5/23/76
Sugarloaf Key*	1	6/23/76
Cudjoe Key*	1	6/28/76
Big Pine Key	2	5/7/77
Big Coppitt Key	1	6/30/79
Big Pine Key	1	5/5/82
Stock Island	1	8/16/83
Key West	1	8/19/83

LOCATION	NUMBERS SEEN	DATES SEEN
Big Pine Key	1	12/21/85
Big Pine Key	1	7/27/86
Flamingo	1	8/26/86
Cutler Ridge	1	5/18 to 6/11/88
Flamingo	2	6/21 to 6/22/88
Cutler Ridge	1	3/30 to 7/31/89
Homestead	1	8/11/89
Cutler Ridge	1	3/2 to 5/31/91
Cutler Ridge	1	3/25 to 4/30/92

*Note: 1976 Florida Key records involve an unknown number of birds (perhaps only one).

all records (sightings of multiple birds counted as one record)

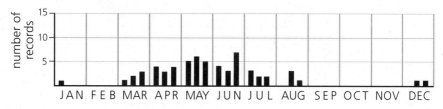

West Indian Cave Swallow

Hirundo fulva fulva

Status and Distribution

T h e "West Indian" Cave Swallow has yet to sue for independence from the rest of the Cave Swallow complex, but it may do so soon. The ranges of *Hirundo fulva fulva* and *H. fulva pelodoma* (the subspecies in Texas and New Mexico) are expanding so rapidly that we may be able to watch them breed sympatrically soon. At that time, whether these two species should be split will likely be easy to decide, but for the time being, *H. fulva fulva* will have to remain just another "bank bird."[1]

The West Indian Cave Swallow is largely a permanent resident of Jamaica, Hispaniola, Cuba, Puerto Rico, and the Vieques Islands, but during the past two decades this species has begun a range expansion. Prior to the 1960s, there were two records of West Indian Cave Swallow from the United States, but starting in the 1970s it became an annual find at the Dry Tortugas. Records from elsewhere in Florida multiplied as well, and in 1987 a breeding colony was found in southern Dade County near Goulds (a.k.a. Cutler Ridge). Since then, this subspecies has been found nesting under several bridges in southern Dade County.

Sightings from elsewhere in Florida also are on the rise, and there are currently about 20 scattered additional records away from the Dry Tortugas and known nesting areas. These records are concentrated in southern Florida and along the Gulf Coast.

The West Indian Cave Swallow boom, however, has not been limited to Florida. *H. fulva fulva* has now been identified as far west as Alabama

[1] A bank bird is a species or subspecies that is not currently countable but has a chance of being countable in the future. Therefore, you bank these uncountable birds hoping that they will accrue "interest" by being split.

290

and as far north as Nova Scotia. Records of Cave Swallows, possibly West Indian, also exist for New Jersey, New York, North Carolina, and Mississippi. Even some Louisiana records may refer to *H.f. fulva*. On the other hand, it is certainly not outrageous for *H.f. pelodoma* to have wandered as far east as the Florida panhandle, and some records from Florida may be of *H. fulva pelodoma*.

The seasonal distribution of U.S. West Indian Cave Swallows is best digested in parts. In Florida, *H. fulva fulva* is mainly a spring migrant and breeder. The Dry Tortugas account for most of the migration records. Birds are sometimes seen as early as late February and as late as June, but peak time is from late February through early May. The nesting population usually arrives in late January and departs in September (Robertson and Woolfenden 1992).

Oddly, there's no real fall movement, evidenced by only a handful of fall records (away from the nesting areas) with no real pattern. One interesting report, however, consists of hundreds of birds near Homestead on August 18, 1989. Winter (i.e., December and early January) records of West Indian Cave Swallow are likewise widely scattered and with no real pattern.

Outside Florida, the West Indian Cave Swallow occurs mostly during migration. There are about ten records of Cave Swallow from Alabama, all from April or early May, but not all of the Alabama Cave Swallows have been identified to subspecies; those that were have been *H. fulva fulva*.

There are but five cave swallow records from New Jersey and New York, all during spring or fall. There is one non-Florida winter record that likely pertains to this subspecies: New Bern, North Carolina, on December 16, 1991.

Best Bets

The West Indian Cave Swallow is best sought from February to August at its nesting site at Cutler Ridge, Florida. To get to this nesting site, take the Florida Turnpike south from Miami to the Cutler Ridge exit (exit #11). From here, go south on the frontage road, which runs along the west side of the turnpike. At 216th, turn left and go a short distance to a bridge over a creek.

The swallows nest under this bridge and under the turnpike a short distance to the north.

The next best place to look is the Dry Tortugas. Here this species is rare to uncommon from February to June.

Identification

In order to identify a West Indian Cave Swallow, one has to first separate the Cave Swallow from a Cliff Swallow. Fortunately, the NGS guide does a fine job in illustrating the salient points; however, a rare Cave Swallow of race *H. fulva pelodoma* or *H. fulva fulva* will have some black throat markings (Turner and Rose 1989), thus complicating the issue.

Telling a typical *H. fulva fulva* from *H. fulva pelodoma* is almost easier than separating *H. fulva pelodoma* from Cliff Swallow. In *fulva*, the orange of the throat extends down onto the sides, flanks, and upper chest. This mark will also distinguish *fulva* from Cliff Swallow. Furthermore, *fulva* has a darker rump and darker undertail coverts than *pelodoma*. But there is some concern that these characters are variable and may not be absolutely reliable. For more information on the subspecies of *Hirundo fulva*, see Turner and Rose (1989).   **(See color photo on page 486.)**

West Indian Cave Swallow—*all records since 1977*[1]

LOCATION	NUMBERS SEEN	DATES SEEN
Flamingo, FL	3	2/11 to 2/12/78
Mullett Key, FL	1	3/25 to 27/79
Dry Tortugas, FL	1	3/29/79
Big Pine Key, FL	1	4/29/79
Cedar Key, FL	3	9/9/79
Dry Tortugas, FL	1	5/3 to 5/5/80
Eastpoint, FL	1	12/26/80
Eastpoint, FL	1	3/7/82
Tallahassee, FL	1	5/21/83
Dry Tortugas, FL	1	4/25/85
Dry Tortugas, FL	1	3/15 to 16/86
Horn Island, MS[2]	1	3/25/86
Fort De Soto Pk, FL	1	4/4/87
Dry Tortugas, FL	1	5/3/87
Loxahatchee NWR, FL	1	12/12/87
Carteret County, NC[2]	1	12/17/87

LOCATION	NUMBERS SEEN	DATES SEEN
St. Marks Light, FL	2	1/8/88
St. Marks Light, FL	1	2/7/88
Key West, FL	1	9/13/88
Fort Morgan, AL	1	4/20/89
Dry Tortugas, FL	1	4/24 to 4/25/89
Homestead, FL	1	8/11/89
near Homestead, FL	hundreds	8/17/89
Dry Tortugas, FL	2	2/26/91
Cape May, NJ	1	4/20 to 6/5/90
Dauphin Island, AL	1	4/21/90
Dauphin Island, AL	1	5/9/90
Jamaica Bay, NY	1	5/23/90
New Bern, NC[2]	1	12/16/91
Fort Morgan, AL[2]	1	4/12/92
Fort Morgan, AL[2]	1	4/19/92
Cape May, NJ[2]	4	11/7/92 (1 to 11/15)
St. Marks, FL	1	3/14/93
Cape May, NJ[2]	1	11/20/93
Wildwood, NJ[2]	1	11/8/94
Cape May, NJ[2]	1	11/8 to 11/19/94

[1]All records published in *American Birds*.
[2]Subspecies not known.

West Indian Cave Swallow—*Cutler Ridge/Southern Dade County breeding records*

nested 4/18 to 5/31/87—first U.S. breeding record
2 first seen on 2/15/89—further info not published
16 first seen on 2/18/90—remained until?
30 first seen on 2/21/91—remained until?
75 first seen on 1/30/92—15 still present on 7/29/92

Island Scrub-Jay

Aphelocoma insularis

Status and Distribution

The Island Scrub-Jay is a distinctive bird that is found only on Santa Cruz Island, California. Santa Cruz Island is one of southern California's famous Channel Islands, which are well known for their unique fauna and flora including many endemic species and subspecies. The Island Scrub-Jay is different enough from other scrub-jays that it, too, was initially considered a distinct species, *Aphelocoma insularis*. Early observers were impressed by this jay and referred to it as "the most interesting bird on the island" (Howell and van Rossem 1911) and "the most sharply differentiated of any of the island species" (Swarth 1918). However, in Pitelka's landmark review of scrub-jays (Pitelka 1951), the Island Scrub-Jay was relegated to subspecific status as part of Scrub Jay, *Aphelocoma coerulescens*. In 1957, the A.O.U. Check-list Committee followed suit. In 1995, however, the Check-list Committee reversed its previous decision and once again gave the Island Scrub-Jay full species status. Now the United States is considered to have three species of scrub-jays: Western Scrub-Jay (*A. californica*), Island Scrub-Jay (*A. insularis*), and Florida Scrub-Jay (*A. coerulescens*).

The Island Scrub-Jay's full-species status is based upon morphological and genetic differences between it and *A. californica californica* (formerly *A. coerulescens californica*), which occurs along the mainland Pacific Coast from Washington to Baja California. The most striking visible feature of the Santa Cruz Island birds is their size. They average about 35 percent heavier than *A. californica californica*, with proportionally similar increases in bill size and tarsus length (Pitelka 1951; Atwood 1979). Santa Cruz Island jays are also darker and more intensely blue than *A. californica*

californica, which is otherwise the darkest and bluest of the scrub-jays (Pitelka 1951).

The genome of the Island Scrub-Jay differs from that of Western Scrub-Jay as much as the genome of Western Scrub-Jay differs from those of Unicolored Jays and Gray-breasted Jays. This finding does not mean that Gray-breasted Jays and Island Scrub Jays are equally close in evolutionary terms to Western Scrub-Jays, but these data do suggest that Island Scrub Jays have diverged substantially from the rest of the scrub-jay complex.

How the Island Scrub-Jay came to be a separate species is a matter of considerable speculation. Western Scrub-Jays have never been seen on any of the Channel Islands, including Anacapa, which is only 13 miles from shore (Johnson 1972; Jones 1975). Furthermore, despite intense coverage, there is only one record from the Farallon Islands, which are 19 miles from shore, and no records from the Los Coronados Islands, which are located 8 miles from the Baja Peninsula. The Island Scrub-Jay is even more homebound. It has never been recorded from the mainland (18 miles away) or from any other Channel island, including Santa Rosa, which is only 5 miles from Santa Cruz Island and has apparently suitable habitat. Given the tendency of these birds not to wander across water, it is hard to imagine that scrub-jays emigrated to the Channel Islands during recent times. Johnson (1972) postulates that scrub-jays first came to the Channel Islands during the Pleistocene, when the northern Channel Islands were probably attached to the mainland. More recent colonization via short overwater vagrancy is also possible because glacial lowering of sea level may have decreased the gap between island and mainland as recently as 10,000 years ago.

The Island Scrub-Jay occurs only on Santa Cruz Island, where it is fairly common in oak woodlands and somewhat less common in eucalyptus groves. The total population has never been carefully studied, but Pitelka (1951) estimated it to be around 4,000 to 6,000 whereas Collins (pers comm) estimated the current number to be about 10,000. This discrepancy is probably more reflective of observer differences than actual population changes. Current studies should give us a much better idea regarding this species' true numbers.

Best Bets

By now you know that you need to go to Santa Cruz Island, California, to see an Island Scrub-Jay. The easiest way to travel to the island is to take one of the Island Packers tours, which offer trips to three Santa Cruz Island destinations. The odds of seeing an Island Scrub-Jay are excellent if you go to Prisoner's Harbor and take the 6-mile (round-trip) walk to the "main ranch." Your odds are still good if you go to Pelican Bay and take the scenic semistrenuous 2-mile hike to Prisoner's Harbor (the boat picks you up there). The third trip goes to Scorpion Ranch. Here your chances are not so good (less than 50 percent), but you can wander down a eucalyptus-lined canyon that is home to at least a couple of jays.

Island Packers sails out of Ventura Harbor, Ventura, California. For sailing times, ticket reservations, and directions, call Island Packers at (805) 642-1393. Trips to Pelican Bay and Prisoner's Harbor are offered from April through November and go out a couple times per month. Trips to Scorpion Ranch are year-round several times per week. The cost is roughly fifty dollars per person. Remember to keep your eyes open on the boat ride over—you have a good chance for some of southern California's pelagic specialties including Xantu's Murrelet (April through June is best) and Black-vented Shearwater (September through March).

There are a number of places to stay in Ventura, including a Motel 6 near the harbor. You need to take your own food and water to Santa Cruz Island. Camping is allowed only at Scorpion Ranch.

Identification

The problem of separating Island Scrub-Jays from mainland scrub-jays is unlikely to be a big issue. Just remember that size is important, especially if direct comparison with other scrub jays is available. Western Scrub-Jays are roughly the size of a Sharp-shinned Hawk or Steller's Jay. The Santa Cruz Island birds are about 20 percent longer. Island Scrub-Jays are also darker and richer blue than *A. californica californica*. See Madge and Burn (1994) for a good depiction. **(See color photo on page 487.)**

California Gnatcatcher

Polioptila californica

Status and Distribution

If you are walking through the coastal sage-scrub of southwestern California and hear a kittenlike mew, there could be a California Gnatcatcher flitting about in the bushes near you. With a bit of patience, and perhaps a bit of pishing, you will be able to see this secretive gnatcatcher.

Prior to 1970, this resident species of southern California and Baja California would not have been a candidate for this book because of the California Gnatcatcher's subspecific status at that time. The more important factor, however, would have been its actual numbers, because this gnatcatcher was not historically an uncommon species. Massive habitat destruction, however, has made this bird increasingly difficult to locate.

California Gnatcatchers now occur in suitable habitat in California's Los Angeles, Orange, Riverside, and San Diego counties. Such habitat consists of coastal sage scrub, especially those tracts below 800 feet in elevation that are dominated by California sagebrush. All such habitat is west of the peninsular ranges (e.g., Laguna and San Jacinto mountains).

Best Bets

Unfortunately, the best sites for California Gnatcatcher are disappearing more quickly than we can write about them. One good area that is unlikely to be destroyed and is excellent for this species is San Pasqual Battlefield State Historic Park (San Diego County). Not only is this park good for California Gnatcatchers but it is also a great spot for other coastal sage scrub birds such as Rufous-crowned Sparrow and Cactus Wren. Another location, closer to Los Angeles, is Pelican Point State Park just south of Newport Beach in Orange

County. This area has fewer gnatcatchers and other sage scrub birds than San Pasqual, but it does have an excellent view of the ocean and can be good at times for seabirds, especially the Black-vented Shearwater.

When looking for California Gnatcatchers, your most important tool will be your ears. This little bird is usually heard before it is seen. The most distinctive call is its high, thin, kittenlike mew, but these birds do make other sounds. Some of these are scold notes, which sound more like the calls of other gnatcatchers or like House Wrens (see Dunn and Garrett 1987 for details). You should also note that California Gnatcatchers tend to be considerably less vocal during their breeding season (mid-March to mid-August), and are thus harder to find then.

Identification

In the United States, the only other gnatcatcher likely to be seen side-by-side with a California is a Blue-gray. This occurs during winter and migration when the Blue-gray moves into the California's coastal sage scrub home. Fortunately, these two species are easily separated, and their differences are well shown in the NGS guide.

The species most similar to the California Gnatcatcher is the Black-tailed, with which it was once considered conspecific. These two birds' ranges do not usually overlap in the United States, but you may find yourself needing to tell them apart. They can be separated by underpart color and tail pattern. These differences are fairly well shown in the NGS guide, but for a more detailed discussion see Dunn and Garrett (1987).

(See color photo on page 487.)

Black-capped Gnatcatcher

Polioptila nigriceps

Status and Distribution

The unimposing Black-capped Gnatcatcher attracts little of the attention showered on gaudier vagrants such as Eared Trogon and Aztec Thrush. Nonetheless, the sight of this mousy little insectivore has gladdened the heart of more than one birder.

Usually Black-capped Gnatcatchers occur in the thorn forest of northwestern Mexico from northeastern Sonora south to Colima. In the United States Black-caps have occurred irregularly in Arizona and have been reported from Texas.

The first Arizona (and U.S.) Black-capped Gnatcatcher was seen along Sonoita Creek some 12 miles northeast of Nogales on June 26, 1970. Unfortunately, it was misidentified as a Black-tailed Gnatcatcher, and consequently this species was not fully verified until the following spring when a pair was found at the same location. Black-caps were then seen sporadically at this spot until 1976, when they suddenly disappeared. The ensuing gnatcatcher drought ended in 1981 when a pair of Black-caps was observed raising eight young (two broods) in Chino Canyon. Thereafter, Black-capped Gnatcatchers were seen every summer through 1986 at either Chino or Sycamore canyons.

Arizona Black-capped records after 1986 have been somewhat more sporadic. There was a male at Kino Springs in January 1987, and a pair at Chino Canyon in August 1991.

Texas has had three published reports, all from Big Bend National Park. Two of these have not been reviewed by the Texas Bird Records Committee (April 29, 1985; and May 2, 1985), and one has been rejected by that committee (April 11, 1984). Thus, the species remains unverified from this state.

Most Black-capped Gnatcatcher records are from March through July, but some of this trend may reflect observer effort. Records from January, February, August, and December imply that this species may actually occur year-round. The true scenario may well be that Black-caps colonize an area and then inhabit that place throughout the year until some factor causes the colony to die out.

The habitat favored by Black-capped Gnatcatchers in the United States is similar to that used in nearby Mexico: desert riparian woodlands around 3,500 to 4,000 feet with dense stands of velvet mesquite and canyon hackberry (D. Stejskal, pers comm).

Best Bets

The best places to look for Black-caps are Chino Canyon and the lower end of Sycamore Canyon, where this species has nested in the past. There also may be small ephemeral colonies in suitable habitat elsewhere near the Mexican border that have not been found by birders.

Identification

In the United States, the range of Black-capped Gnatcatcher overlaps that of two other gnatcatcher species—the Black-tailed Gnatcatcatcher and the Blue-gray Gnatcatcher. In its breeding plumage (held February into August), the male Black-capped Gnatcatcher is similar only to an alternate male Black-tailed Gnatcatcher. In other plumages, both Black-tailed and Blue-gray Gnatcatchers need to be considered. For alternate plumage males, consider the following points, which are well shown in the NGS guide.

Undertail Pattern: In the Black-capped, this area closely resembles the Blue-gray Gnatcatcher, showing considerably more white than a Black-tailed. Molting birds may show less white than is typical.

Cap Pattern: The black cap extends below the eye on the Black-capped Gnatcatcher but not on the Black-tailed. Also note that the Black-cap shows only the bottom half of the eyering if any at all. The Black-tail has a complete eyering.

Bill: The Black-capped Gnatcatcher has a noticeably longer bill than the Black-tailed.

Identifying females, juveniles, and basic plumage males is more difficult. Black-capped and Black-tailed Gnatcatchers can still be told apart by using the above-mentioned tail and bill characteristics, but telling Black-capped from Blue-gray Gnatcatcher is now an issue. The Blue-gray Gnatcatcher has a bolder eyering and a shorter, thinner bill. Male Blue-grays are usually obviously blue-gray in color, but females and juveniles can be plain gray, like a Black-capped. Other marks for separation include the following.

Bill Color: Blue-gray Gnatcatchers (except alternate plumage males) have a flesh-colored base to the lower mandible. The bill is all dark in Black-capped Gnatcatchers.

Upperpart Color: Many Black-capped Gnatcatchers have a brownish wash, especially on the wings. This is lacking in Blue-grays.

For a more complete discussion, see Dunn and Garrett (1987) or Howell and Webb (1995).

Black-capped Gnatcatcher—*all records*[1]

LOCATION	NUMBERS SEEN	DATES SEEN
12 mi NE of Nogales	1	6/26/70
12 mi NE of Nogales	5 (pair w/3 young)	5/22 to 6/22/71
just S of Lake Patagonia	1	March 1973
12 mi NE of Nogales	1	6/26/75
Chino Canyon	2+ (pair, 2 nestings, 8 young)	5/17 to 9/?/81
Chino Canyon	6+ (3 pairs, 1+ young)	3/5 to 9/4/82
NE of Nogales	1 (male)	5/30/82
Chino Canyon	2+ (pair, 2 nestings, 5+ young)	early 5/83 to 7/25/83
Chino Canyon	3	mid-Jan to 2/11/84
Florida Canyon (male)	1	3/3/84
Sycamore Canyon	2 (pair)	6/13/84
Chino Canyon	3	summer 1984
Sycamore Canyon	2	12/26/84
Chino Canyon	2 (pair)	4/4 to late 5/85
Sycamore Canyon	8	mid-5/85 to summer 1985
Sycamore Canyon	1	3/19/86
Chino Canyon	1-2	mid-April to 5/26/86
Sycamore Canyon	2+ (pair w/4 young in nest)	7/27 to 8/2/86
Kino Springs	1 (male)	1/10/87
Chino Canyon	2 (pair)	8/28/91
Sabino Canyon[2]	1	2/21/93

[1]All records are from Arizona.

[2]Will likely be rejected by the AZ BRC.

Northern
Wheatear

Oenanthe oenanthe

Status and Distribution

This hardy, energetic little thrush spends its summers on the barren Arctic tundra where it ranges nearly around the globe. North American breeding areas are extensive, and two distinct races are involved. The nominate *Oenanthe oenanthe oenanthe* breeds throughout much of northern Alaska, the Yukon, and the northwestern Mackenzie District. The Greenland race *O. oenanthe leucorrhoa* (Greenland Wheatear) breeds from Baffin Island east to Labrador. In winter, however, the Northern Wheatear retreats to the Old World, and only rarely does it make an appearance in the Lower 48.

Clearly, the status of the Northern Wheatear in the Lower 48 States is changing. Prior to 1975, there were fewer than 40 records, but since then at least 130 have been reported, primarily from the Northeast. The change began during 1976 when a seemingly unique "flight" took place, bringing 14 wheatears to the Northeast; but in 1988 another flight occurred, and since then all but two years have seen substantial numbers of this species in this area. The best year was 1993, with 16 in the Northeast plus a sprinkling elsewhere in the Lower 48. It is no coincidence that the timing of this increase parallels a breeding range expansion of the Greenland race (*O. oenanthe leucorhoa*) in northeastern Canada (Koes 1995). This population is almost certainly the source of wheatear records in New England and elsewhere in the eastern United States. The steady increase in birders over the same period may also have something to do with the increase in records.

Most Lower 48 records are from the northeastern United States, with disproportionate numbers in Massachusetts and New York. States with published records include Oregon, California, North Dakota, Nebraska,

Texas, Minnesota, Arkansas, Louisiana, Wisconsin, Michigan, Illinois, Indiana, Ohio, Alabama, Maine, New Hampshire, Vermont, Massachusetts, Rhode Island, Connecticut, New York, Pennsylvania, New Jersey, Delaware, Maryland, Virginia, North Carolina, South Carolina, and Florida.

Northern Wheatear records span the entire year, but the best time is mid-September to mid-October.

Best Bets

Although the Northern Wheatear is now an annual visitor to the Northeast, your chances of setting out and finding one yourself are very slim. Your best bet is to listen to the New England and mid-Atlantic hotlines in September and October. More than half of the wheatear records are of single-day sightings, but the average stay is three days, and some birds are around for more than a week.

If you want to look for your own wheatear, the best place is right on the coast from Massachusetts to New York. In this region, check any open areas such as vacant lots, parking lots with weedy margins, lawns, dunes, or shorelines. Also the margins of sewage ponds or dredge-spoil ponds may be attractive habitat to a wheatear.

Identification

Identifying a Northern Wheatear is a straightforward task and most guides do a more than adequate job of outlining the characters. Most birds that show up on the East Coast are presumed to be of the Greenland race, which tends to be larger and more richly colored than the nominate race, but subspecific identification may not be possible in the field in fall.

(See color photo on page 488.)

Northern Wheatear—*total number of records by state, 1975 to 1994*

STATE	NUMBERS SEEN	STATE	NUMBERS SEEN
Oregon	2	Maine	9
California	5	New Hampshire	3
North Dakota	1	Vermont	8
Texas	1	Massachusetts	22
Minnesota	1	Rhode Island	5
Arkansas	1	Connecticut	4

STATE	NUMBERS SEEN	STATE	NUMBERS SEEN
Louisiana	2	New York	18
Michigan	3	Pennsylvania	1
Illinois	1	New Jersey	6
Indiana	1	Maryland	2
Ohio	1	Virginia	2
Alabama	3	North Carolina	2
Florida	2		

Northern Wheatear—*all records, 1975 to 1994*

LOCATION	NUMBERS SEEN	DATES SEEN
Ottawa, OH	1	1/4 to 1/21/88
New Branford, CT	1	2/15/81
Chincoteague NWR, VA	1	3/23/78
Gibson County, IN	1	3/31 to 4/6/91
Nantucket, MA	1	4/1 to 4/3/94
Rye, NY	1	5/7/88
Lostwood NWR, ND	1	5/23/94
Thomson Beach, NJ	1	6/1/81
Baxter State Park, ME	1	6/13/92
Malheur NWR, OR	1	6/22/77
Scarborough Marsh, ME	1	8/15 to 8/17/79
Duxbury, MA	1	8/23 to 8/30/76
Quabbin, MA	1	9/1 to 9/7/78
Cedar Beach, L.I., NY	1	9/5/94
Massachusetts	7	9/5 to 10/17/94
Charleston, RI	1	9/7/76
Stonington, CT	1	9/7 to 9/11/76
Bristol, NH	1	9/7/90
Mackinaw City, MI	1	9/7 to 9/8/94
Rosedale Park, NJ	1	9/8 to 9/11/93
Maine	3	9/8 to 9/22/94
Damariscove, ME	1	9/10/78
Bridgeport, VT	1	9/10 to 9/11/93
Cape May, NJ	1	9/11/88
Hog Island marsh, MD	1	9/11 to 9/13/90
Plum Island, MA	1	9/11/93
Martha's Vineyard, MA	1	9/11/93
Tobay Sanctuary, L.I., NY	1	9/11/94
South Wellfleet, MA	1	9/12/88
Coles County, IL	1	9/12/90
Accabonack, L.I., NY	1	9/13 to 9/16/82
Cornwall, VT	1	9/13 to 9/17/83
Shelter Cove, CA	1	9/15/77
Brigantine, NJ	1	9/15/83
Chatham, MA	1	9/15/90
Eastham, MA	1	9/15 to 9/18/92
Monhegan, ME	1	9/16 to 9/17/76

LOCATION	NUMBERS SEEN	DATES SEEN
Bald Eagle State Park, PA	1	9/17/85
Schoodic Point, ME	1	9/17/88
S of Lincoln, VT	1	9/17/94
Hammonasset State Park, CT	1	9/17 to 9/18/94
Nantucket, MA	1	9/18 to 9/19/76
Peterborough, NH	1	9/18 to 9/22/88
Nantucket, MA	1	9/18 to 9/27/90
Block Island, RI	1	9/18/93
Northampton, MA	1	9/18/93
Jones Beach State Park, L.I., NY	1	9/18/93
Great Gull Island, L.I., NY	1	9/18/93
St. Ignace, MI	2	9/19/80
Groton, CT	1	9/19/93
Nantucket, MA	1	9/20 to 9/23/75
Madison, CT	1	9/20/90
Montgomery, AL	1	9/20 to 9/22/93
Vanderbilt Island, NY	1	9/21 to 9/25/93
Annisquam, MA	1	3rd week of Sept 1976
Grand Isle, VT	1	9/22/92
Cape Hatteras, NC	1	9/22 to 10/29/94
Captree State Park, L.I., NY	1	9/23/76
Raymond, ME	1	9/23/78
Cape May, NJ	1	9/23/78
Fort Edward, NY	1	9/23 to 9/27/93
Long Point State Park, NY	1	9/24/76
Lamoine, ME	1	9/24 to 9/28/76
Warren, NY	1	9/24/90
Jones Beach State Park, L.I., NY	1	9/24/92
Beltsville, MD	1	9/25/80
Dixfield Notch, NH	1	9/25/81
Block Island, RI	1	9/25 to 9/29/92
S of Monomoy Island	1	9/25/93
Burlington, VT	1	9/25 or 9/26/93
St. Joe Peninsula, FL	1	9/26/76
Farallon Islands, CA	1	9/26/92
Block Island, RI	1	9/27/75
Roseville, MN	1	9/27/82
Nicasio Reservoir, CA	1	9/27 to 9/29/92
Petit Manan NWR, ME	1	9/27/93
Manhattan, NY	1	9/27 to 9/28/93
Lake Placid, NY	1	9/28 to 9/29/84
Jones Beach State Park, L.I., NY	1	9/28/86
Monomoy Island, MA	1	9/29/77
Wellfleet, MA	1	10/1/76
Finley NWR, OR	1	10/1/88
Milton, MA	1	10/2 to 10/6/76
Nauset Beach, MA	1	10/2 to 10/14/76

LOCATION	NUMBERS SEEN	DATES SEEN
Chincoteague, VA	1	10/2/82
Avon, NC	1	10/2/87
Fort Morgan, AL	1	10/2 to 10/3/88
Fort Morgan, AL	1	10/2/93
Colchester, Point, VT	1	10/3/80 on
S of Harwich, MA	1	10/3 to 10/4/88
Robert Moses State Park, L.I., NY	1	10/7 to 10/10/91
Grand Isle, VT	1	10/7/92
Block Island, RI	1	10/8/89
Montauk Point, L.I., NY	2	10/9/87
Nantucket, MA	1	0/13/76
Orland, CA	1	10/13 to 10/15/88
Salisbury, MA	1	10/15 to 10/17/78
Whitefish Point, MI	1	10/15/93
Westhampton, L.I., NY	1	10/16 to 10/23/77
Westchester, NY	1	10/17/86
Ogunquit, ME	1	10/18 to 10/23/77
Lake Millwood, AR	1	10/18 to 10/22/90
Robert Moses State Park, L.I., NY	1	10/19 to 10/20/78
Key Biscayne, FL	1	10/19 to 10/23/94
Freemont, MI	1	10/20 to 10/23/89
New Orleans, LA	1	10/23/91 on
Plymouth, MA	1	10/27/84
Laguna Atascosa NWR, TX	1	11/1 to 11/6/94
Fullerton, CA	1	11/5/94
Farallon Islands, CA	1	11/6 to 11/10/88
Cape May, NJ	1	11/12/85
Acadia, LA	1	12/17/92 to 2/27/93

Maine to New Jersey—1975-1995, all records with dates
(some records span more than one time period)

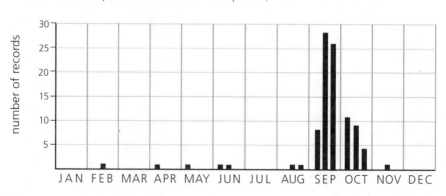

Clay-colored Robin

Turdus grayi

Status and Distribution

Clay? Well, that may be as good a description as any for the main coloration of this handsome *Turdus*, which even a beginning birder can see is a kissing cousin of our familiar American Robin. Not Georgia pinewoods red clay, but tawny-buff is the hue of its breast and belly.

The NGS guide describes the Clay-colored Robin as "very secretive," but in its main range from Mexico through northern Colombia, it's a familiar yard and garden bird, found in towns, woodlands, pastures, and cultivated areas. In Costa Rica the Clay-colored Robin is well known and well liked enough to be considered the national bird. Even on their first trip to the Neotropics, most birders quickly come to think of it as an "Oh, it's just another Clay-colored Robin."

In the United States, of course, it's another story.

The Clay-colored Robin is a specialty of the lower Rio Grande valley of Texas—not one that can be counted on, like Brown Jay or Audubon's Oriole, but regular enough that an occurrence doesn't cause a shortage of rental cars at the McAllen airport. Since 1940, there have been documented records of more than 40 individuals in Texas plus nearly another 40 sightings for which documentation was not submitted to the Texas Bird Records Committee. Most sightings have come from the lower Rio Grande valley between Brownsville and Bentsen State Park, but a few have also occurred along the lower Gulf Coast. Rio Grande records have occurred as far north as San Ygnacio (2/21/88), whereas Gulf Coast records have occurred as far north as Victoria (2/28 to 4/3/88). The most surprising Clay-colored Robin, however, is one that was present from February 2 to February 7, 1973, near Huntsville, Walker County, Texas.

The preponderance of Clay-colored Robins have been seen from December through March, with lesser numbers in April. This is probably due, in part, to greater coverage at these times. Indeed, Clay-coloreds have been seen during every month and have even nested at Bentsen State Park. The maximum number ever recorded at one spot was five during January and February 1990 in Laguna Vista.

Best Bets

Most Clay-colored Robin records have come from the heavily birded parks from Brownsville to Bentsen State Park. Much of this is likely due to the intense coverage at these places. Records such as the five in Laguna Vista indicate that this species probably also occurs with some frequency in lusher residential areas. Places to check outside of the usual parks and refuges include Laguna Vista, the vicinity of Dallas and McColl in McAllen, and the vicinity of Honeydale and Los Ebanos in Brownsville.

Identification

The Clay-colored's shape and actions identify it as a thrush, yet its color is so different from the American Robin's that confusion with that species is nearly impossible. Other marks for separation include the Clay-colored's buffy undertail coverts and lack of eyering.

The White-throated Robin (*Turdus assimilis*), another Neotropical thrush, approaches the United States as closely as southern Tamaulipas and has been officially recorded once in this country: February 18 to 25, 1990, at Laguna Vista, Texas, associating with Clay-colored Robins. (There is also an entirely believable sight report from nearby San Benito dating from March 13 to March 15, 1984.) Whereas the White-throated's coloration is somewhat more like a Clay-colored's than an American Robin's, its upperparts are much darker olive brown than the clay-colored, its underparts lack the buff (clay) color, it has a clearly marked white throat with black streaks (which can appear all dark from certain angles), and its yellow eyering is strikingly obvious against the dark face.

During your searches for Clay-colored Robins, you should be aware that this bird can be located by call-note and song. The Clay-colored's lilting whistled song is of the same pitch and quality as the American Robin's, but has been described as mellower, richer, smoother, and clearer and more melodic, all of which may be because it is often slower. Its notes are more clearly enunciated, and for the musically inclined, may be given more in duple than triple time (segments in two-beat phrases rather than three-beat).

The Clay-colored has a *tock* (Stiles 1989) or *cut-cut* (Davis 1972) note similar to the American Robin's, but a distinctive call is a whining, catlike, slurred, ascending *me-a-wee* that has been aptly described as "querulous" (Stiles 1989). A good example of this call is found on the recording "A Bird Walk at Chan Chich," by John V. Moore. **(See color photo on page 488.)**

Clay-colored Robin—*all records**

LOCATION	NUMBERS SEEN	DATES SEEN
Brownsville	1	3/10 to 3/17/40
Bentsen State Park	1	5/14 to 6/8/59
Bentsen State Park	1	3/2 to 3/5/62
Bentsen State Park	1	2/24/63
Anzalduas County Park	1	6/72
Laguna Atascosa NWR	1	12/10/72
near Huntsville	1	2/2 to 2/7/73
Santa Ana NWR	1	7/9 to 8/24/73
Santa Ana NWR	1	1/3/74
Santa Ana NWR	1	2/28/74
Santa Ana NWR	1	spring & summer 1974
Santa Ana NWR	1	winter 1974-5
Santa Ana NWR	2	3/30/75
Brownsville	1	winter 1975-6
Santa Ana NWR	1	2/76 to 3/27/76
Bentsen State Park	1	3/24/76
Santa Ana NWR	1	6/23/77 to 7/77
Pharr	1	1/78
Santa Ana NWR	1	4/27/79
Brownsville	1	2/24/80
Bentsen State Park	1	5/20/80
Bentsen State Park	1	late 12/80 to early 1/81
Sarita	1	12/31/81 to 2/5/82
La Feria	1	1/7/82
Weslaco	1	1/9 to 1/31/82
Santa Ana NWR	2	2/3/82
Bentsen State Park	1	1/18 to 3/13/82
Corpus Christi	1	3/28/82
several lower Rio Grande locations		winter 1982-83
Brownsville	2	summer 1983
McAllen	1	late 12/83
Brownsville	1	winter 1983-4
Brownsville	1-2	spring 1984
Brownsville	1+ (up to 6)	9/84

LOCATION	NUMBERS SEEN	DATES SEEN
Bentsen State Park	1+ (up to 6)	winter 1984-5
Santa Ana NWR	1	1/18/85
Bentsen State Park	1+ (up to 4; nested)	1/26/85 to 5/90
Nueces County	1	12/25/85
Santa Ana NWR	1	1/15 to 1/22/86
San Ygnacio	3	4/12/86
San Ygnacio	1	6/5/87
Sabal Palm Sanctuary	1+ (up to 3)	12/5/87 to 4/28/88
Sarita	1	12/8/87
Santa Ana NWR	2	12/5/87 to 4/5/88
Laguna Atascosa	1	12/18/87 to 3/24/88
McAllen	1	12/28/87 on
Falfurrias	1	1/15 to 3/3/88
near Ricardo	1	1/21/88
Aransas NWR	1	2/7 to 2/12/88
Corpus Christi	1	1/15 to 4/1/88
Laguna Vista	1	2/88
S of Falfurrias	1	2/20/88
San Ygnacio	2	2/21/88
Victoria	1	2/28 to 4/3/88
Santa Ana NWR	1	fall 1988
Santa Ana NWR	1	12/11/88 to 2/5/89
Santa Ana NWR	1	5/19/89
North Padre Island	1	1/14/90
Kingsville	1	1/14 to 1/28/90
Santa Ana NWR	1	3/15 & 4/22/90
Anzalduas County Park	1	6/22/90
Anzalduas County Park	2+ (up to 4)	6/12/91 to 8/11/92
Santa Ana NWR	1-2	11/30 to 12/31/91
Zapata	1	5/1/92
Santa Ana NWR	1	1/2 to 1/28/93
McAllen	1	2/1/93
McAllen	1	6/26 to 7/17/93
Bentsen State Park	1	2/94

*All records are in Texas.

all records (only records with specific dates used, sightings of multiple birds counted as one record)

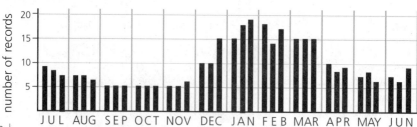

Rufous-backed Robin

Turdus rufopalliatus

Status and Distribution

A Rufous-backed Robin may be even more cheering on a winter's day than an American Robin. It is at least as attractive, and a vagrant always warms the spirit. Fortunately, Rufous-backed Robins are not too rare. During the past 15 years there have been an average of about three sightings per year, although in some years none were seen. Records were more numerous during the mid-1970s (34 records between 1973 and 1978), but the reasons for this are unclear.

Rufous-backed Robins "normally" occur on Mexico's Pacific slope from southern Sonora/Chihuahua to Oaxaca. In the United States most sightings have been in Arizona, but there are also records from New Mexico, southern California, western Texas, and the lower Rio Grande valley. Like American Robins, Rufous-backs prefer moist green habitats such as lush riparian zones, fruit orchards, and dense plantings. Unlike American Robins, however, Rufous-backs are secretive and spend much of their time concealed in thick foliage. Sadly, this tendency has frustrated many a birder. This is not a bird that you will find hopping about on the front lawn. Likewise, you will probably not find your Rufous-backed Robin actually in a flock of Americans, although the two species do occasionally consort with each other, and American Robins are often nearby.

Rufous-backed Robins occur mostly between mid-October and late April, with peak occurrence from late November through early April. There are, however, several summer records: one, Madera Canyon, July 15, 1968; one, Patagonia, July 4 and 5, 1974; one, Patagonia, June 27, 1975; and one, Guadalupe Canyon, June 3 and 4, 1980. Records away from Arizona fall mostly between mid-October and late April.

Best Bets

The majority of Rufous-backed Robin records are from southeastern Arizona, and these are somewhat scattered. No one area is vastly better than any other. However, there is a concentration of sightings along the drainages of Sonoita Creek and the Santa Cruz River between Nogales and Patagonia. Areas especially worth checking would be Kino Springs, the Sonoita Creek Nature Conservancy Sanctuary, and collections of fruit trees along north River Road (near Kino Springs). Closer to Phoenix, the Boyce Thompson Arboretum has had several records. Remember, with this species patience is a particularly important virtue.

Identification

The rufous back of the Rufous-backed Robin is diagnostic. Other marks to consider include the pattern of color on underparts, the rufous on the wings, and the lack of white around the eye. For decent drawings see the NGS guide or Peterson (1990). **(See color photo on page 489.)**

Rufous-backed Robin

LOCATION	NUMBERS SEEN	DATES SEEN
Arizona records, 1978 on		
Boyce Thompson Arboretum	1	11/18 to 11/21/78
Guadalupe Canyon	1	6/3 to 6/4/80
Hereford	1	3/28/81
Aravaipa Canyon	1	3/7/82
Tucson	1	11/6 to 11/12/82
Parker	1	11/15 to 12/?/82
Sun City	1	late 12/82
Nogales CBC	2	12/17/82
Green Valley	1	12/27/82 to 2/?/83
Hereford	1	12/31/82 to 1/16/83
Patagonia	1	1/17 to 2/6/83
Cibola NWR	1	1/19/83
Tucson	1	2/21/83
Tucson	1	3/7 to 4/4/83
Tucson Desert Museum	1	3/8/83
Tanque Verde Ranch	1	3/10/83
Canoa Ranch	1	4/17 to 4/22/83
Madera Canyon	1	4/29/83
Sonoita Creek Sanctuary	1	5/17 to 5/21/83
Guadalupe Canyon	1	5/20/84
Patagonia	1	11/12/84

LOCATION	NUMBERS SEEN	DATES SEEN
Buenos Aires Ranch	1	mid 10/85
Canoa	1	11/24/85
Kino Springs	1	12/14/86 to 4/1/87
E of Tucson	1	11/5/87
Organ Pipe Cactus National Monument	1	11/22/87
Boyce Thompson Arboretum	1	11/22/87 to 12/?/87
Sonoita Creek Sanctuary	1	2/26 to 3/21/88
Sonoita Creek Sanctuary	2	1/14 to 4/10/89
S of Phoenix	1	early 1/90 to
Tucson Desert Museum	1	1/17 to 4/5/90
Babocomari Creek	1	10/25/92
near Patagonia	1	12/20/92 to 1/1/93
north of Nogales	1	1/1/93 to 3/11/93
Boyce Thompson Arboretum	1	10/28 to 11/1/93
Boyce Thompson Arboretum	1	11/6/94 on
Patagonia	1	11/19/94
Kino Springs	1	11/26/94
New Mexico records		
Percha Dam	1	7/3/87
S of San Antonio	2	12/9 to 12/21/89
Socorro	1	12/16/91 to 1/15/92
Santa Teresa	1	10/16/94
Texas records		
Rio Grande Village, Big Bend National Park	1	10/23 to 10/31/66
Santa Ana NWR	1	8/15/72
below Falcon Dam	1	12/29/75
Langtry	1	11/11 to 11/18/76
near Fort Davis	2	2/9/92
El Paso	1	10/27/93
California records		
Saratoga Springs	1	11/19/74
Imperial Dam	1	12/17/73 to 4/6/74
Newport Beach	1	1/1 to 4/11/83
Newport Beach	1 (2nd bird)	2/23 to 3/5/83
Furnace Creek Ranch	1	11/5/83
Desert Center	1	11/24 to 11/26/89
Snow Creek	1	3/1 to 3/20/92

records from 1978 on

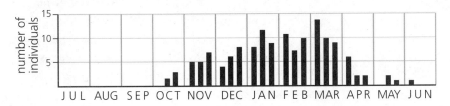

Aztec Thrush

Ridgwayia pinicola

Status and Distribution

The Aztec Thrush is a mystical skulking visitor from the Mexican Sierra Madre. Its known breeding range extends north to central Chihuahua and Sonora. Viewing this elusive thrush somehow carries you to a more distant, secluded landscape where parrots and odd jays lurk. Fortunately, Aztecs are being seen with more frequency in the United States, and more of us may be able to enjoy them.

The first U.S. sighting came as recently as 1977 from Big Bend. Since then, there have been about 20 reports, all from Arizona or Texas. Sightings between May and October have mostly come from moist wooded canyons between 5,000 and 8,000 feet in the Chisos, Santa Rita, Chiricahua, and Huachuca mountains. One winter record was from a lower elevation at Port Aransas, Texas.

Except for two January records, sightings of Aztec Thrushes have occurred entirely from May 13 to October 26, with a distinct peak from late July through late August. This peak accounts for 15 of the 22 reports. For a more detailed discussion of U.S. sightings, see Zimmerman (1991).

Best Bets

In the warmer months, the Chisos, Chiricahua, Huachuca, and Santa Rita mountains in Arizona are clearly the places to look for Aztec Thrushes. During this time, they are usually in moist areas with good cover between 5,000 and 8,000 feet in elevation. Summer Aztecs do not seem to fraternize with other species.

In winter, however, Aztecs have been seen with robins in both the United States and Mexico (Zimmerman 1991). Thus, checking winter Robin flocks in southern Arizona, New Mexico, and Texas is probably not a bad idea. You should remember that at any time of year Aztec Thrushes are not shy but are skulkers. They distinctly prefer to stay in or near dense vegetation. For call notes, listen to *Voices of the New World Thrushes* published by the Florida State Museum at the University of Florida.

Identification

The identification of the Aztec Thrush generally is easy. However, you need be wary of the occasional partially albinistic Hermit or Swainson's Thrush that can mimic the white and buffy wing and tail markings of the Aztec Thrush. Another bird that can superficially resemble an Aztec Thrush is the juvenile Spotted Towhee; the towhee's shape and bill structure are, of course, very different. The Aztec Thrush female and juvenile are best depicted in the NGS guide whereas the adult male is most accurate in Peterson (1990). Also, see Howell and Webb (1995).

(See color photo on page 489.)

Aztec Thrush—*all records*

LOCATION	NUMBERS SEEN	DATES SEEN
Portal, AZ	1	1/26 to 2/3/91
Port Aransas, TX	1	1/30/79
Madera Canyon, AZ	1	5/20/78
Huachuca Canyon, AZ	1	5/30 to 6/13/78
Garden Canyon, AZ	1	7/23/82
Madera Canyon, AZ	1	7/23/92
Madera Canyon, AZ	1	7/28/82
Carr Canyon, AZ	2	7/29 to 9/6/89
Boot Canyon, TX	1	7/31 to 8/7/82
South Fork, Cave Creek Canyon, AZ	1	8/11/86
Madera Canyon, AZ	1	8/13 to 8/17/86
Ramsey Canyon, AZ	1	8/13 to 8/15/94
Lost Mine Trail, TX	2-3	8/14/83
Madera Canyon, AZ	1	8/16/85
Cave Creek Canyon, AZ	1	8/17 to 8/22/94
Madera Canyon, AZ	2	8/21/94
Boot Canyon, TX	1	8/21 to 8/25/77
Madera Canyon, AZ	1	8/27 to 8/30/89
Madera Canyon, AZ	1	8/30 to 9/13/83

LOCATION	NUMBERS SEEN	DATES SEEN
Cave Creek Canyon, AZ	1	9/4/93
Ramsey Canyon, AZ	2	9/25 to 9/27/91
Madera Canyon, AZ	1	10/26/91
Rejected by state BRC		
Big Bend State Park, TX	1	5/13/90
Del Rio, TX	1	10/11/89

all records

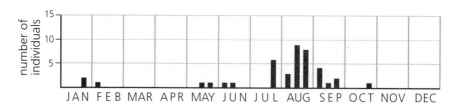

Bahama Mockingbird

Mimus gundlachii

Status and Distribution

The Bahama Mockingbird is an inhabitant of arid habitats in the Bahamas, Jamaica, and several obscure cays off the northern coast of Cuba. The first U.S. record was at that tropical vagrant trap extraordinaire, the Dry Tortugas, in 1973. Although this first record was unexpected, the true surprise is the rapidly accelerating number of sightings: There were 3 more records in the 1970s, 8 in the 1980s, and 16 so far in the 1990s (as of 12/1/94). This explosion is due in part to increased observer awareness, but other likely factors remain obscure.

All current records except one have been limited to the narrow strip extending from the Dry Tortugas, through the contiguous Florida Keys, and up the southeastern coast to West Palm Beach. Within this region, the records are evenly distributed. There does not seem to be any particularly favored habitat, but most records come from coastal parks and other relatively disturbed settings. The remaining sighting was from Flamingo.

Bahama Mockingbirds have occurred in Florida from April 8 to September 7, but these sightings show a dramatic peak from mid-April into late May. June to August records are scarce but include an individual at Key West that summered during 1991, 1992, 1993, and 1994. Other summer dates are June 10, at the Dry Tortugas; July 5, 1987, at Plantation Key; and August 3, 1976, at Stock Island. So far, there have been no records of fall migrants or wintering birds.

Best Bets

From 1991 to 1994, a Bahama Mockingbird was repeatedly seen in southwestern Key West. Most sightings were from May into July, but this bird may have been around all year. The neighborhood in question is bordered by Flagler Avenue, Reynolds Street, White Street and Atlantic Boulevard. To get there from the east, take US-1 to FL-A1A. Turn left (south) on A1A and go a short distance to Flagler. Turn right on Flagler and go roughly 2 miles to White Street. (For navigating the Florida Keys, try the excellent Rand McNally Florida Keys map.) When searching this area, beware! There may be several hybrid Bahama x Northern Mockingbirds in the vicinity. You should also note that no pure Bahamas were seen at Key West in 1995.

Two other places with multiple Bahama Mockingbird sightings are Cape Florida (four records) and the Dry Tortugas (five records). As an alternative, you might want to try the Fort Lauderdale and Boca Raton vagrant traps, which have also had several records (see "Site Guide").

Identification

The Bahama Mockingbird does not look as much like a Northern as you might expect. You should note, however, that the Bahama can hold its wings so that much of the side streaking is hidden. Also, juvenile Northern Mockingbirds are streaked underneath, but the streaking is of a different character and in a different location. Bahamas are streaked mostly on the flanks and undertail coverts whereas immature Northerns have most of their streaking on the chest. Other important marks include tail and wing pattern. The NGS guide illustrates these differences nicely. Also, the jizz of a Bahama Mockingbird is as much that of a thrasher as a mockingbird.

Be sure to look carefully. As the Key West birds show, hybridization between Northern and Bahama Mockingbirds is a very real possibility. These apparent hybrids have less or no streaking and intermediate wing, tail, and face patterns. **(See color photo on page 490.)**

Bahama Mockingbird—*all records*[1]

LOCATION	NUMBERS SEEN	DATES SEEN
Dry Tortugas	1	5/3/73
Dry Tortugas (Garden Key)	1	5/16 to 5/18/76
Stock Island	1	8/3/76
Elliott Key	1	4/22/79
Dry Tortugas (Long Key)	1	6/10/82
West Palm Beach	1	4/14 to 4/18/85
Elliott Key	1	5/19/86
Islamorada	1	5/18 to 5/20/87
Plantation Key	1	7/5/87
Flamingo	1	3/9/88
Hypoluxo Island	1	4/21 to 5/14/88
Cape Florida	1	4/8 to 4/11/89
Fort Lauderdale	1	5/20/90
Cape Florida	1	5/20/90
Cape Florida	1	4/14 to 5/11/91
Hypoluxo Island	1	5/11/91
Key Largo	1	5/25/91
Key West[2]	1	6/14 to 8/21/91
Cape Florida	1	4/25 to 5/4/92
Birch State Park	1	4/25 to 5/20/92
Dry Tortugas	1	4/25/92
Key West[2]	1	4/30 to 9/7/92
Key West	1	4/13/93 to 8/14/93
Dry Tortugas	1	4/25/93
Fort Lauderdale	1	5/21 to 5/24/93
Key West	1	2/20/94 to 7/10/94
Hypoluxo Island	1	4/23 to 4/30/94
Lloyd State Park	1	4/27/94
Spanish River Park	1	5/1/95

[1]All records are in Florida.
[2]Built nest but no eggs were laid.

all records

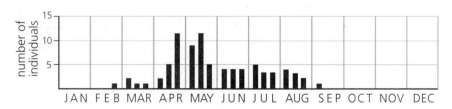

White *and* Black-backed Wagtails

Motacilla alba and
Motacilla lugens

Status and Distribution

Wagtails are an almost entirely Old World genus that looks little like any New World counterpart. Therefore, the sight of one cannot help but get the adrenaline pumping— you *know* you're looking at a vagrant.

The White and Black-backed Wagtails are no exception. They are elegant black-and-white birds that stand out among the North American avifauna. Formerly these two species were considered conspecific but were split by the AOU in 1983. Since then, their identification has still not been fully worked out (see "Identification"), and many records remain nonspecific.

The first White/Black-backed Wagtail in the Lower 48 was seen during October 1972 in Ventura, California. Thirty-one more have occurred in the years since, but only 13 have been identified to species. Of these 13, 3 were White Wagtails and 10 were Black-backs. Two of the Whites were in California, and the third was in Washington. Of the Black-backs, 5 were in California, 3 were in Washington, 1 was in Oregon, and 1 was in North Carolina. Unidentified wagtails have come from California (9), Oregon (2), Washington (2), Arizona (1), New York (1), and Michigan (1). The North Carolina Black-back sighting (Cedar Island, 5/15/82) stands as one of the most amazing Lower 48 records of any species.

An intriguing seasonal pattern starts to emerge as wagtail records accumulate. Black-backs seem to be warmer-weather birds, their records concentrated from late July through late September and from mid-May through late May; there is one winter record. White Wagtails, on the other hand, have occurred only between October 5 and May 5 with two of the three individuals overwintering. Most of the unidentified birds have occurred as late fall migrants or overwinterers, implying that they are more likely Whites. Any firm conclusion is premature, but this is something to watch as more records accrue.

Best Bets

Records of these species are too widespread to provide any specific recommendations. Their preferred habitat is moist barren areas such as the edges of mudflats, shallow pools, and coastal lagoons. River and creek mouths seem particularly favored. At most West Coast shorebird areas, keep an eye out for these birds.

Identification

The separation of a Black-backed from a White Wagtail can be extremely difficult. There exists no reliable mark for field identification of immatures. Fully adult Black-backs can be separated from White Wagtails by back pattern and the amount of white on the flight feathers. A special problem arises in telling first alternate plumage female Black-backs from adult female Whites. For this dilemma, pay careful attention to the exact rump, chin, and scapular patterns. For excellent discussions of Black-backed and White Wagtail identification see Morlan (1981) and Howell (1990).

This identification discussion would be remiss without some mention of other wagtails. Immature Yellow Wagtails superficially can look surprisingly like an immature Black-back or White. Yellows can be told from these by their dark foreheads, dark cheeks, and shorter tails. Immature Citrine and Gray Wagtails (*Motacilla cinerea* and *citreola*) can also have a slight resemblance, but neither of these has a black breast band, and Gray Wagtails always have yellow undertail coverts.

(See color photo on page 490.)

White Wagtail—*all records*

LOCATION	NUMBERS SEEN	DATES SEEN
Arroyo de la Cruz, CA[1]	1	10/9/83
Arroyo de la Cruz, CA[1]	1	10/5 to 10/8/84
Crockett Lake, WA	1	1/14 to 5/5/84
Saticoy/Oxnard, CA[2]	1	11/22/87 to 3/06/88
Saticoy/Oxnard, CA[2]	1	10/16/88 to 3/04/89
Saticoy/Oxnard, CA[2]	1	11/08/90 to 3/09/91
Rejected by CA BRC		
Saticoy/Oxnard, CA	1	2/8/92

[1]same bird returning.   [2]same bird returning.

Black-backed Wagtail—*all records*

LOCATION	NUMBERS SEEN	DATES SEEN
Eugene, OR	1	2/3 to 3/31/74
Watsonville/ Pajaro River mouth, CA	1	8/7 to 9/22/79
Watsonville/ Pajaro River mouth, CA	1	7/20 to 9/21/80
Tiburon, CA	1	5/22/80
Cedar Island, NC	1	5/15/82
Mad River estuary, CA	1	5/13/85
Azwell, WA	1	5/19/85
Ocean Shores, WA	1	5/11/86
Port Hueneme, CA	1	8/2 to 9/7/87
Point No Point, WA	1	5/5 to 5/7/93
Crescent City, CA	1	9/6 to 9/7/94

Black-backed/White Wagtail—*all records*

LOCATION	NUMBERS SEEN	DATES SEEN
Santa Clara River mouth, CA	1	10/18 to 10/29/72
Southeast Farallon Islands, CA	1	10/10/74
Umatilla NWR, OR	1	2/9/75
Goleta, CA	1	10/9 to 10/11/78
Harris Beach State Park, OR	1	6/4/80
Seattle, WA	1	11/8 to 11/9/81
Los Angeles River, Long Beach, CA	1	11/4/82 to 1/18/83
Muskegon, MI	1	4/14 to 4/24/85
Eel River bottoms, CA	1	9/1 to 9/3/94
Grand Canyon, AZ	1	10/6/85
Rodeo Lagoon, CA	1	10/1/89
Pajaro River mouth, CA[1]	1	12/3 to 12/11/89
Pajaro River mouth, CA[1]	1	11/7 to 12/3/90
Moss Landing area, CA[1]	1	12/23/88 to 1/21/89
Moss Landing area, CA[1]	1	12/21 to 1/19/91
Coyote Creek Riparian Station, CA	1	12/15/91
Plumb Beach, Brooklyn, NY	1	12/21/92
Ocean Park, WA	1	4/26/94
Rejected by CA BRC		
San Joaquin Marsh, CA	1	10/27/85

[1]These four sightings are likely of the same bird. If this is the case, then this bird was a White Wagtail. The controversy is still under consideration by the CA BRC.

Red-throated Pipit

Anthus cervinus

Status and Distribution

Pipits are a largely Old World group of mostly highly migratory species that have a distinct tendency to wander. Four predominantly Eurasian species have been seen in the United States, and two of these, Olive Tree-Pipit and Red-throated Pipit, have made it to the Lower 48. The Red-throated Pipit, which actually breeds in northwestern Alaska as well as in Asia, was first found in the Lower 48 in October 1964, when Guy McCaskie saw at least 12 in San Diego's Tijuana River valley. Since then, birders' familiarity with this species has grown, and so has the number of sightings. Red-throats are now found regularly south of the Canadian border and are the most frequently seen Asian landbird in the Lower 48. Between 1982 and 1994, at least 166 individuals were recorded, including a stunning 96-plus in 1991 alone.

Red-throated Pipits are most often found with American Pipits in fields of short green vegetation within a mile or so of the coast. Favored areas include sod farms, golf courses, and certain agricultural fields. Unlike American Pipits, Red-throats generally shun beaches and mudflats. This species does sometimes occur inland, and there are several records from oases in the California deserts plus two records from Arizona.

California has accounted for all but three Lower 48 Red-throated Pipit records: Kayenta, Arizona, October 12 to 17, 1989; Snyder Hill sewage ponds, Tucson, Arizona, May 2, 1989; and American Camp, San Juan Island, Washington, September 14 to 16, 1979.

Red-throated Pipits provide searchers with a nice tight pattern of occurrence. Virtually all records fall between September 9 and November 11, with a distinct peak from early to late October. This pattern is reinforced

323

by the top 1991 numbers: 8, Moss Landing, October 4 to 20; 8, Point Reyes, October 6 to 14; and 20, Tijuana River valley, October 10. You should note, however, that Washington's record is from mid-September, suggesting that Red-throats may move through that state a bit earlier. Currently there is only one Lower 48 spring record of this species: male, Snyder Hill sewage ponds, Tucson, May 2, 1989.

Best Bets

In California, Goleta, southeast Farallon Island, Point Reyes, the Oxnard Plain, the Santa Maria River valley, and the Tijuana River valley have all played host to multiple Red-throated Pipits. Of these, the Tijuana River valley has clearly been exceptional. Red-throats have been found there in at least seven of the past ten years, with an astonishing maximum of 20+ on October 10, 1991. Unfortunately, changes in land use here may well make the Tijuana River valley less attractive to this species in the future. When looking for Red-throated Pipits, be sure to listen for their thin explosive *speeew* or *spreee* call, which is usually given in flight. This may be your first clue that there is a Red-throat in a flock of Americans.

Identification

When you first see a Red-throated Pipit, you will be surprised how little it looks like an American. The differences are probably best shown in the MGB, which has good photographs. You should note the Red-throat's high-contrast back pattern and its darker streaking on the underparts. The bright pink legs can also be helpful, but these are present on some Americans as well, especially those of the race *japonicus*. If you're lucky, you'll actually see a red throat, but this is present only on some adults.

When looking at a potential Red-throated Pipit, remember that other pipits are possible. Olive Tree-Pipit is nearly annual in Alaska and has been recorded once from the lower 48: Reno, Nevada, May 16, 1967. In addition, Pechora Pipit has been recorded in Alaska at least a dozen times and Brown Tree-Pipit has been found twice.

The Olive Tree-Pipit is striking and well-depicted in the NGS guide. The Pechora Pipit, however, is similar to the Red-throated Pipit. To distinguish the two, concentrate on the following points.

Nape
- Pechora: Distinctly streaked, as is head and back.
- Red-throat: Indistinct streaks, differing from sharply streaked head and back.

Chest
- Pechora: Background color creamy yellow, contrasting noticeably with white belly and throat.
- Red-throat (immature): Faint buff, contrasting little with belly and throat.

Back
- Pechora: One pair (usually) of white to whitish buff stripes; when second pair present, shorter and darker.
- Red-throat: Two pairs of pale buffy stripes.

Primary Extension
- Pechora: Short, but distinct.
- Red-throat: No extension of primaries beyond tertials.

For a full discussion of pipit identification, see King (1981), and for a detailed discussion on the separation of Pechora and Red-throated Pipits, see Heard and Walbridge (1988). The comments and drawings in Lewington, et al. (1991) are also useful. (See color photo on page 490.)

Red-throated Pipit —*all records*[1]

LOCATION	NUMBERS SEEN	DATES SEEN
Imperial Beach[2]	12	10/12 to 10/27/64
Imperial Beach	10	10/9 to 10/30/66
Imperial Beach	10	10/22 to 11/4/67
SE Farallon Islands	1	11/3/68
Imperial Beach	1	10/17/70
Santa Cruz Island	1	10/10/74
Imperial Beach	1	10/13 to 10/15/77
Imperial Beach	6	10/19 to 10/27/74
San Nicolas Island	2	10/20 to 10/21/74
Carson	1	10/20 to 10/21/77
San Nicolas Island	1	9/28/78
Point Reyes	1	9/30/78
Point Reyes (same as above)	3	10/7 to 10/13/78
Oxnard Plain	1	10/4 to 10/9/78
Goleta	1	10/12/78
Oxnard Plain	3	10/13 to 10/15/78
Goleta	2	10/26 to 10/27/78
American Camp, WA	1	9/14 to 9/16/79

LOCATION	NUMBERS SEEN	DATES SEEN
Imperial Beach	1	10/8/79
Goleta	1	10/11/79
Imperial Beach	1	10/11/79
Imperial Beach	1	10/22/79
Goleta	1	9/24/80
Santa Clara River mouth	1	9/28/80
Goleta	1	9/9 to 9/11/81
Imperial Beach	2	10/10 to 10/25/81
Point Loma	1	10/25 to 10/28/81
Goleta	1	11/1/81
Imperial Beach	1	10/4 to 11/7/82
Goleta	1	11/6/82
Humboldt County	1	10/10/82
Salinas sewage ponds	1	9/29/84
Furnace Creek Ranch	1	10/5/85
Imperial Beach	1	10/6 to 10/11/85
SE Farallon Islands	1	9/24 to 9/27/86
Santa Maria River valley	1	10/5 to 10/6/86
Point Reyes	2	10/6 to 10/11/86
Bolinas	1	10/7/86
Imperial Beach	3	10/14 to 11/2/86
Goleta	1	10/14 to 10/15/86
Goleta	1	11/4 to 11/15/86
Moss Landing	1	10/12 to 10/18/86
Virgin Creek	1	10/10 to 10/13/87
Carmel River Mouth	1	10/11/87
Morro Bay	1	10/9 to 10/17/87
Goleta	1	10/6/87
Goleta	1	10/15/87
Imperial Beach	2	9/19 to 9/20/87
Salinas River mouth	1	10/3/88
SE Farallon Islands	1	10/6 to 10/7/88
SE Farallon Islands	1	10/27/88
Santa Maria River valley	2	10/16/88
Goleta	4	10/2 to 10/27/88
near Oxnard	1	10/11 to 10/15/88
Imperial Beach	2	10/23/88
100 mi SW of Santa Barbara	1	10/21/88
Tucson, AZ	1	5/2/89
SE Farallon Islands	1	9/27/89
Kayenta, AZ	1	10/12 to 10/17/89
SE Farallon Islands	1	10/14/89
SE Farallon Islands	1	9/24 to 9/27/90
near Oxnard	3	9/30 to 10/7/90
Goleta	1	10/1/90
Santa Maria River valley	1	10/6 to 10/7/90
Santa Catalina Island	1	10/26/90

LOCATION	NUMBERS SEEN	DATES SEEN
China Lake NWR	1	9/20/91
Furnace Creek Ranch	1	9/21/91
California City	1	9/22/91
Cow Creek, Death Valley	1	9/23/91
San Pedro	1	9/28/91
Arroyo Laguna	1	10/2/91
Furnace Creek Ranch	1	10/4 to 10/5/91
Tijuana River valley	20+	10/6 to 11/11/91
Goleta	3	10/6 to 10/28/91
Furnace Creek Ranch	1	10/11 to 10/24/91
Sepulveda Basin	2	10/16 to 20/91
Oxnard	2	10/13 to 10/19/91
Santa Maria River valley	1	10/20 to 10/26/91
Oxnard	1	10/26/91
northern California[3]	58+	
Point Reyes	1	10/10 to 10/11/92
near Imperial Beach	1	10/17 to 10/20/92
Point Reyes	8	9/26 to 10/23/93
Farallon Islands	3	9/30 to 10/13/93
Purisima Creek mouth	1	10/24/93
Goleta	1	9/16/93
Hansen Dam	1	9/16 to 9/19/93
Irvine	1	10/9 to 10/23/93
Imperial Beach	1	10/13 to 10/14/93
Lake Mendocino	1	9/26 to 9/29/94
Table Rock	1	10/23/94
Tijuana River valley	2	10/4 to 10/10/94
Rejected by CA BRC		
near Oxnard	1	10/11/87
Arroyo de la Cruz	1	10/2/91

[1]All records are from California unless otherwise denoted.
[2]Imperial Beach usually refers to lower Tijuana River valley.
[3] 58+ birds from 9/20 to 11/2/91 from multiple locations; maximum: 8, Moss Landing, 10/4 to 10/20/91 and 8, Point Reyes, 10/6 to 10/14/91.

all records (excluding 1991 invasion and spring record from Arizona)

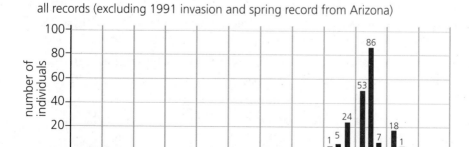

Yellow-green Vireo

Vireo flavoviridis

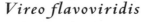

Status and Distribution

The Yellow-green Vireo is a woodland sprite that breeds from northern Mexico into Central America and then migrates south to winter in South America. In the United States, this species has occurred in Texas, California, Florida, Louisiana, New Mexico, and Arizona. In Texas, Yellow-green Vireos have been recorded approximately 50 times. The vast majority of these sightings are from the Rio Grande valley and Gulf Coast in Cameron, Hidalgo, and Starr counties. There are also scattered records elsewhere in southern Texas north to Chambers and Travis counties. Outside this area, Texas has but one record: Big Bend National Park, July 13, 1972.

In the Lone Star State, the Yellow-green Vireo is mostly a late spring migrant (and summer resident?). Records are concentrated between early May and mid-June, but there are sightings from every month except January and March.

Outside Texas, most U.S. Yellow-green Vireos have been seen in California, which has had about 40 records (excluding rejected reports). California's vireos have occurred mostly along the coast from Marin County south. There are, however, two inland records and one more northerly record. The inland records come from Riverside (9/29/1887) and Harper Dry Lake (10/2/88). The northernmost record comes from Fairhaven, Humboldt County, on October 9 and 10, 1984.

Unlike Texas, California's Yellow-green Vireos appear in fall. Indeed, California's records lie entirely between September 8 and October 30, with peak time from late September through mid-October. These birds are most likely reverse migrants that headed north after breeding instead of south.

Florida has had six Yellow-green Vireo records, which is surprising since Bond (1985) lists no records from the West Indies. Four of these six records are from Gulf Breeze in the Florida panhandle. The other two records are from Hypoluxo Island on the southeast coast and Fort De Soto near St. Petersburg. All Florida records are between April 18 and June 13. The Louisiana records fit this pattern as they were both seen along the Gulf Coast during spring in Cameron Parish. The Florida and Louisiana birds undoubtedly are lost spring migrants, and some may have even made a trans-gulf journey.

The remaining records are from Arizona and New Mexico, which have had 4 and 5 published reports, respectively. These have all been between late April and late August and several have been from mid-summer. These birds may well be individuals that overshot their Mexican breeding grounds and then spent the summer in the southwest. At this time there seems to be no sign of the California pattern spilling over into these nearby southwestern states.

This discussion would not be complete without mentioning an old specimen collected at Godbout, Quebec, on May 13, 1883. This bird was the second North American record north of Mexico and highlights the possibility of this species showing up almost anywhere in the Lower 48. For further details on this Canadian record, see Holder (1996).

Best Bets

There is no consistent spot for this species. This bird should be on your mind, however, if you are birding the southern or central California coast in fall or the lower Rio Grande valley in late spring or early summer.

Identification

The Yellow-green Vireo closely resembles the Red-eyed. The Red-eyed, however, has blackish lores and a black border above the supercilium, both of which the Yellow-green lacks. The Yellow-green Vireo has whitish underparts that are heavily washed with lemon yellow on the undertail coverts and the sides of the breast and belly. Red-eyeds can show yellow in this distribution, but are never as bright. Another useful mark is that Yellow-green Vireos have brighter feather edges to their folded flight feathers. This difference exists in the tail feathers as well but is much harder to see in the field. For more details, see Holder (1996).

Philadelphia Vireos also superficially resemble Yellow-greens. The

Philadelphia, however, is a smaller bird with a proportionately smaller bill. It also has a yellow throat and yellow completely across the breast. For details, see the NGS guide or Howell and Webb (1995).

(See color photo on page 491.)

Yellow-green Vireo—*all records*

LOCATION	NUMBERS SEEN	DATES SEEN
Texas		
Brownsville	1	8/23/1877
Brownsville	1	6/7/1892
Matagorda	1	5/9/38
Harlingen	1	6/20/43
Harlingen	1	9/5/43
Harlingen	1	12/27/47
Santa Ana NWR	1	7/12/52
Santa Ana NWR	1	12/31/53
Laguna Atascosa NWR	1	12/31/55
Santa Ana NWR	3+	summer 1960
Austin	1	7/3/60
Cove	1	9/8/60
Santa Ana NWR	1	12/20/61
Austin	1	9/14/62
Santa Ana NWR	1	July-Aug 1963
Bentsen State Park	1	12/23/65
Santa Ana NWR	1	5/6/66
Ingleside	1	5/10/66
Santa Ana NWR	1	9/11/66
Falcon Dam	1	5/13/72
Big Bend National Park	1	7/13/72
Falcon Dam area	1	6/11/73
Bentsen State Park	1	6/12/73
South Padre Island	1	9/29/73
Bolivar Peninsula	1	4/26/74
Brownsville	2+	6/1/74
Starr County	1	9/21/76
Santa Margarita Ranch	1	5/11/78
Santa Margarita Ranch	1	4/27/79
Santa Ana NWR	4	5/20 to 6/1/81
Santa Ana NWR	2+	summer 1982
Bentsen State Park	1	8/1982
Bentsen State Park	1	10/30/84
Corpus Christi	1	12/21/85
Santa Ana NWR	1	fall 1986
Santa Ana NWR	1	11/5/86
Brownsville	1	2/11/87
Laguna Atascosa	2	7/2 to 8/6/88
Laguna Atascosa	2	5/25 to 9/10/89
Santa Ana NWR	1	spring 1989

LOCATION	NUMBERS SEEN	DATES SEEN
Brownsville	1	6/22 to 7/10/89
Laguna Atatscosa	1	5/6 to 8/24/90
Laguna Atascosa	1	5/11 to 7/13/91
Brownsville	1	summer 1991
Santa Ana NWR	1	summer 1991
Bolivar Peninsula	1	5/1/92
Webberville Park	1	5/3 to 7/5/92
Laguna Atascosa NWR	1	7/5 to 7/10/92
Webberville Park	1	5/3 to 9/8/93
Laguna Atascosa NWR	2	5/15/93

Rejected by TX BRC

Kerr County	1	9/19/76

California

Riverside	1	9/29/1887
Dana Point	1	9/22 to 9/27/64
Tijuana River valley	1	9/23/67
Costa Mesa	1	10/3/67
San Diego	1	10/7/67
Tijuana River valley	1	9/19 to 9/20/74
Tijuana River valley	1	10/25/76
Point Loma	1	10/15 to 10/19/77
Point Loma	1	9/13/78
Lake Merced	1	10/22 to 10/25/78
Gaviota State Beach	1	9/8/79
SE Farallon Islands	1	10/30/80
Point Loma	1	10/1/81
Goleta	2 (only 1 on 10/12)	10/11 to 10/12/82
SE Farallon Islands	1	10/19/82
Point Loma	1	9/16 to 9/18/83
Oxnard Plain	1	10/3 to 10/4/83
Fairhaven	1	10/9 to 10/10/84
Stinson Beach	1	10/27 to 10/30/85
Little Sur River mouth	1	10/3/86
Big Sycamore Canyon	1	9/21 to 10/5/87
Goleta	1	9/24/88
Tijuana River valley	1	9/25 to 9/26/88
Nunes Ranch, Point Reyes	1	9/30/88
University of California, Irvine	1	10/1/88
Harper Dry Lake	1	10/2/88
Pacific Grove	1	10/9 to 10/12/88
Point Loma	1	10/12/88
La Jolla	1	10/21/88
SE Farallon Islands	1	10/25/88
Morro Bay State Park	1	10/14/89
Golden Gate Park	1	9/23 to 9/26/90
Point Loma	1	10/7 to 10/17/90
Costa Mesa	1	10/18/90

LOCATION	NUMBERS SEEN	DATES SEEN
Point Loma	1	9/29/91
Palomarin	1	10/11/91
SE Farallon Island	1	9/29/92
Carmel River mouth	1	10/20/92
Bolinas Lagoon	1	10/16 to 10/19/93
SE Farallon Island	1	10/26/93
Mendoza Ranch, Point Reyes	1	10/28/93
Consumnes River Preserve	1	10/5/94
Wilmington	1	10/16 to 10/17/94
Farallon Islands	1	10/17/94
Florida		
near Gulf Breeze	1 (collected)	5/4/58
near Gulf Breeze	1	5/11/58
near Gulf Breeze	1	4/18/60
Gulf Breeze	1	6/13/83
Hypoluxo Island	1	5/25/84
Fort De Soto	1	5/11/86
Louisiana		
Willow Island	1	6/3/90
Smith Ridge	1	5/2/92
New Mexico		
Red Rock	1	7/20/83
Embudito Canyon	1	4/24/85
Bosque del Apache NWR	1	8/29/86
Rattlesnake Springs	1	8/11 to 8/19/91
Rattlesnake Springs	1	7/8/92
Arizona		
Sonoita Creek	1	6/18/69
Guadalupe Canyon	1	5/11/75
Patagonia rest stop	1	6/19 to 6/27/75
Paloma	1	7/13 to 7/15/80

Texas records (excluding those without specific dates)

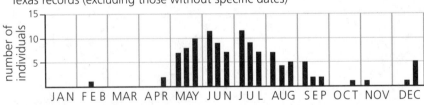

California records

Tropical Parula

Parula pitiayumi

Status and Distribution

As its name implies, the Tropical Parula is a close relative of the Northern Parula, a familiar warbler that nests in the eastern United States and southeastern Canada. The two at times have even been classified as the same species. The Tropical looks very much like the Northern at first glance, and its habits are much the same (Howell and Webb 1995). It often builds its nest of Spanish moss in humid Mexican forests, just as Northern Parulas do in the bald cypress swamps of the southern United States.

In the States, the Tropical Parula is another southern Texas specialty, with sightings almost exclusively confined to that birding mecca. The species does wander, though. An immature female at Sabine National Wildlife Refuge in southwestern Louisiana in mid-December, 1983, was the first U.S. record outside Texas. Shortly thereafter, Arizona acquired its first record when a male was at Madera Canyon from July 14 to September 13, 1984. A female was also seen at Madera Canyon on July 18, 1984.

Within Texas, the Tropical Parula is regular along the Rio Grande north through Starr County and is found in coastal prairies north into Kenedy County. Throughout much of this range the Tropical Parula is uncommon, although it is probably more numerous in the Norias division of King Ranch. Vagrants within Texas have strayed as far north as the upper coast (Lake Jackson, February 1, 1988; Brazos Bend State Park, September 17 to 26, 1993); and Austin (April 8, 1983). There is also one record from Big Bend National Park (April 30 to May 1, 1994).

Tropical Parulas are year-round residents in southern Texas. Most sightings, however, come from spring (March through May) when the species is singing.

Best Bets

South of Sarita, Highway 77 passes the entrance to the Norias area of the famous King Ranch, where Tropical Parulas have bred and been seen with great regularity in recent years. Victor Emanuel Nature Tours takes visitors onto the King Ranch, and a spring VENT tour may well be the most surefire way to find this species. Another important spot near the King Ranch is the often visited Highway 77 rest area south of Sarita. This rest stop has long been known for Tropicals, though occurrence varies from year to year.

In the valley, Santa Ana National Wildlife Refuge, Bentsen State Park, and Brownsville's Sabal Palm Sanctuary are the spots that most frequently host Tropical Parulas. One or two are staked out most winters at one of these locales.

Identification

Finding the Tropical Parula in southern Texas during spring and fall (and even winter) can be complicated by the presence of migrating Northern Parulas. With a good look at a male, there should be no problem in distinguishing the two, but as is the case so often with warblers, flitting birds in thick, dark vegetation often don't cooperate by giving good looks. For good drawings, see the NGS guide.

Important marks are as follows.

Eyering
- Northern: Eyering is broken and white.
- Tropical: No eyering.

Face:
- Northern: Black, if present, restricted to lores.
- Tropical: Males usually with noticeable black mask; yellow farther up.

Breast
- Northern: Male with blue and orange bands.
- Tropical: Male with broader orange band only.

Belly
- Northern: Yellow to uppermost belly only.
- Tropical: Yellow down to legs.

(See color photo on page 492.)

Kirtland's Warbler

Dendroica kirtlandii

Status and Distribution

The Kirtland's Warbler was named after Dr. J. P. Kirtland, because it was on this respected naturalist's land that the presumed first specimen was collected on May 13, 1851. It was later found, however, that the first specimen was actually collected by Dr. Samuel Cabot on a ship near the Bahamas in October 1841 (Pearson 1936). Perhaps, therefore, this bird should be named Cabot's Warbler, or maybe we should forgo attaching the name of a person and instead use an adjective that actually says something about the bird. The colloquial name Jack Pine Warbler would do nicely, for the survival of the Kirtland's Warbler is intimately dependent on the jack pine (*Pinus banksiana*).

Jack pine stands between 8 and 22 years old are necessary for Kirtland's Warbler breeding success. Good ground cover and sandy soil are also important because the Kirtland's is a ground-nesting species (Mayfield 1960). During historical times, Kirtland's Warbler numbers probably peaked between 1870 and 1900, due to foresting and fires, both of which created the proper habitat.

The first formal survey was performed in 1951 and revealed 502 singing males. This number was stable through 1961, but during the next decade the population crashed and the 1971 survey found only 201 singing males. Some of this decline was due to fire control, which actually decreased the amount of suitable habitat, but another factor, Brown-headed Cowbirds, was at least as important. Between 1931 and 1955, 24 percent of surveyed Kirtland's Warbler nests were parasitized by cowbirds, but between 1963 and 1971 this attack rate rose to a frightening 67 percent. During 1972, however, measures were instituted to control these pests, and by the mid-

1970s, the parasitization rate was less than 5 percent. Since then, Kirtland's Warbler numbers have rebounded. The 1992 summer survey revealed 397 singing males, and the 1995 breeding census produced 765 singing males.

The Kirtland's Warbler's refined taste in habitat has led to a limited breeding range. The vast majority of these warblers nest in the north-central (lower peninsula) Michigan counties of Crawford, Iosco, Kalkaska, Ogemaw, Oscoda, and Roscommon, and as of 1992, 63 percent of singing males were in the 1980 Mack Lake Burn area of Oscoda County.

Not all territorial Kirtland's Warblers have been in Michigan's lower peninsula, however. In 1978, two singing males were found in appropriate habitat at Black River Falls State Park, Jackson County, Wisconsin. Singing males were again found in Jackson County on June 7, 1979, and on June 14, 1980. Perhaps due to lack of effort, Wisconsin did not have its next summer record until June 1988, when a total of eight singing males were at scattered locations in the jack pine woods of Douglas, Washburn, and Jackson counties. One to two singing males have been found in at least one of these counties each year since (through at least 1992 and again in 1995). There are also summer records of singing males from Michigan's Upper Peninsula (Gwinn, June 9 to 17, 1983; Delta, Marquette, and Schoolcraft counties, summer 1995) and Ontario.

As August wanes and September waxes, Kirtland's Warblers begin their fall migration to the Bahamas. The first Kirtlands leave their breeding grounds during mid- to late August, and departures peak in early September. Some birds are usually still around into mid-September, but few if any are around in late September. The latest lingerer on record was seen on October 6, 1992.

Kirtland's spend little time making their way south. Peak occurrence in the northeastern United States is during late September and peak occurrence in the Southeast isn't much later, with most birds seen between late September and mid-October. By mid-October, most have already arrived in the Bahamas.

Most Kirtland's seem to take a direct route to the Bahamas; the 50 or so fall records are mostly around the straight line connecting northern Michigan to these islands. Notably, this line has these birds departing the States from coastal South Carolina, and there are several fall records from this region. However, there are a number of records from Florida as well, and some birds may travel down the Florida peninsula before making the hop to the Bahamas.

When Kirtland's Warblers arrive at their winter destination, they spend most of their time in the widespread broadleaf scrub habitat. Kirtland's Warbler's extreme dates of occurrence in the Bahamas are August 5 and May 5. Of great interest is a report of two birds about 20 miles south of Veracruz, Mexico, on November 11, 1974 (Bond 1975). How many others winter this far afield?

Spring sightings of Kirtland's Warblers are far more numerous than those from fall and follow a vastly different pattern. In spring there is no nice line connecting the Bahamas with Michigan. Instead, there is a handful of early (mid-April through early May) records from the Southeast and a huge number of later (early May through late May) records from the Midwest. This pattern, especially in contrast with that from the fall, strongly suggests that spring migration is made in one giant leap. Supporting this theory is the timing of arrivals on the breeding grounds. These start in early May, peak in mid-May, and taper off toward the end of the month.

For an excellent overview of Kirtland's Warbler biology, see Mayfield (1992).

Best Bets

The two major areas in Michigan for public viewing of this endangered gem are near Mio (Oscoda County) and Grayling (Crawford County). Organized tours are led out of Grayling by the U.S. Fish and Wildlife Service and out of Mio by the U.S. Forest Service. Generally, tour season begins in mid-May and ends in early July, but dates and times do vary from year to year, so call the Fish and Wildlife Service at (517) 337-6650 or the Forest Service at (517) 826-3252.

To maximize your chances of seeing a Kirtland's, you should avoid the first and last week of the season. Also, the Mio tours have a slightly better success rate than the Grayling tours, though both offer excellent chances.

In Mio we recommend the moderately priced Mio Motel (phone 517-826-3248), which has microwave ovens and refrigerators in each room. Reservations should be made at least one month in advance. For breakfast try the Au Sable River Restaurant, which opens at 6:30 a.m. Both the motel and the restaurant are located at 4th and MI 33, which also happens to be the location of the Forest Service headquarters from whence the warbler tours originate.

Identification

The Kirtland's Warbler is a mostly blue-gray and yellow warbler that is adequately described in the NGS guide and the MGB. You should pay careful attention to the almost incessant tail wagging of this species, but beware! Prairie Warblers do this, too. Also note that dull females and immatures can look surprisingly like a Yellow-rumped Warbler (without the yellow rump, of course); see page 150 of the MGB, volume 3.

(See color photo on page 492.)

Kirtland's Warbler—*fall migration records**

LOCATION	DATES SEEN
Michigan	
Davisburg	8/7/73
near Grand Haven	8/17/63
Imlay City	8/31/46
St. Clair County	9/1/91
Bloomfield Hills	9/24/65
Muskegon	9/29/51
Ohio	
Ironton	8/28/02
Buckeye Lake	9/1928
Columbus	9/11/25
Toledo	9/22/29
Cincinnati	9/27/75
Bowling Green	9/28/69
Cleveland	10/7/34
Cleveland	10/14/1886
Cleveland	10/25/69
Illinois	
Winnebago County (2 males)	9/2/48
Chicago	9/4 to 9/5/66
Chicago	9/26/78
Lake Chat	10/9/92
Indiana	
Whiting Park	9/24/94
Pennsylvania	
Somerset County	9/21 to 9/22/74
Rector	9/21 to 10/2/71
near Ligonier	9/24/65
Wellersburg	9/26/72
Lewisville	9/27/64

LOCATION	DATES SEEN
Virginia	
Arlington	9/25/1887
Arlington	10/2/1887
Kent Reservoir	9/1/74
Tennessee	
Greeneville	9/28/56
North Carolina	
10 mi N of Statesville	8/29/82
South Carolina	
Eastover	9/1/51
Simpsonville	9/17/86
Eastover	9/22/67
Christ Church Parish	10/4/10
Aiken	10/5/60
Chester	10/11/1888
Eastover	10/14/49
Mt. Pleasant	10/29/03
Georgia	
Savannah	8/27/09
Pendergrass	9/7/81
Blairsville	10/5/90
Jekyll Island	10/17/75
Florida	
Lower Saddlebunch Key	8/1/81
20 mi W of St. Mark's	9/9/19
Miami	9/21/58
Chokoloskee	10/11/15
Princeton	10/25/15
Dickenson State Park	10/27/78
Fort Pierce	11/1/18
West Palm Beach	11/2 to 11/3/61
Alabama	
Jacksonville	10/5/66

*All records involve one bird unless otherwise denoted.

Kirtland's Warbler—*spring migration records**

LOCATION	DATES SEEN
Florida	
Gainesville	4/12/70
West Jupiter	4/19/1897
Indian River County	4/22/93
Gainesville	4/26/34
West Jupiter	4/27/1897
Hypoluxo Island	4/29/82
Duval County	5/1/32

LOCATION	DATES SEEN
Georgia	
Cumberland Island	4/12/02
Cumberland Island	4/14/03
Camden County	4/16/02
Cumberland Island	4/27/04
Athens	5/12/69
Alabama	
Birmingham	5/7/36
Woodbine	5/10/08
South Carolina	
St. Helena Island	4/27/1886
Lugoff	5/1/90
St. Helena Island (3)	5/3/1886
Irene Mills Park	5/5/25
Virginia	
Wise	5/7 to 5/9/94
Kentucky	
Danville	5/15/68
West Virginia	
Boaz	5/17/83
Pennsylvania	
Franklin County	5/14/94
Indiana	
Wabash	5/4/1893
Wabash	5/7/1895
Richmond	5/7/06
near Richmond	5/13/05
Chesterton	5/17 to 5/18/81
Richmond	5/18/08
Michigan City	5/22 to 5/23/83
Ohio	
Tiffen	4/30/75
Cleveland	5/1860
Rockport	5/1878
near Columbus	5/1917
Cincinnati	early 5/1872
Lorain County	5/2/06
Avondale (2 birds)	5/4/1872
near Cleveland	5/4/1880
near Oberlin	5/9/00
Oberlin	5/9/04
Seneca County (2 birds)	5/11/06
near Cleveland	5/12/1880
Oak Openings Park	5/12/66
near Cleveland	5/13/1851
near New Bremen	5/14/08

LOCATION	DATES SEEN
Willoughby	5/15/94
Catawba (2 birds)	5/16/09
Lakeside	5/16/64
near Columbus	5/17/21
near Columbus	5/20/20
Magee Marsh Wildlife Area	5/21/80
Pearson Park	5/22/52
Lakeside	5/23/62
near Columbus	5/24/24
Put-in-bay Lighthouse	5/24/54
Illinois	
Blue Island	4/28/32
Glen Ellyn	5/7/1894
Bird Haven	5/3/08
Chicago	5/10/79
La Grange (6 birds!?)	5/12/47
La Grange	5/16/08
Jackson Park	5/18/34
Chicago	5/21 to 5/22/1899
Winnebago County	5/25/1894
Glen Ellyn	6/3/10
Wisconsin	
Milwaukee	5/14/83
Madison	5/19/17
Door County	5/20/56
Redgranite	5/21/71
Rhinelander	5/23/46
Douglas County	5/21 to 5/22/89
Minnesota	
near Minneapolis	5/13/1892
St. Cloud	5/22/44
Michigan	
Ann Arbor	4/30 or 5/1/1888
Ann Arbor	5/6/05
near Ann Arbor	5/9/16
Ann Arbor	5/10/11
Saginaw	5/10/55
Erie Game Area (2 birds)	5/10/69
Battle Creek	5/11/1883
Grand Haven	5/11/63
Ann Arbor	5/13/07
Ann Arbor	5/14/02
Ann Arbor	5/15/1875
Kalamazoo	5/15/1886
Tawas Point State Park	5/15 to 5/16/91
Ann Arbor	5/16/1879

LOCATION	DATES SEEN
Ann Arbor	5/16/07
Ann Arbor	5/18/05
Spectacle Reef	5/21/1885
near Ann Arbor	5/21/15
Fish Point	5/21/26
Clear Lake (12 birds)	5/21/60
Holland (3 birds)	5/22/38
Wayne County	5/30/07
Presque Isle County (3 birds)	5/31/64
Missouri	
St. Louis	5/8/1885

*All records involve one bird unless otherwise denoted.

Kirtland's Warbler—*out-of-range "summer" dates*

LOCATION	DATES SEEN
Black River Falls State Forest, Jackson County, WI	6/10 to 7/18/78
Jackson County, WI	6/7/79
Jackson County, WI	6/14/80
Gwinn, MI	6/9 to 6/17/83
Douglas County, WI (2 singing males)	6/88
Washburn County, WI (2 singing males)	6/88
Jackson County, WI (4 singing males)	6/88
Jackson County, WI	summer 1989
Jackson County, WI	6/10 to 6/14/90
Jackson County, WI	5/23 to late 6/91
Washburn County, WI	6/8 to 6/21/92
Jackson County, WI	6/4/95
Delta County, MI	summer 1995
Marquette County, MI	summer 1995
Schoolcraft County, MI	summer 1995

Note: Most old (pre-1970) records of Kirtland's Warblers were obtained from the monumental unpublished work by Amy E. Stone: *Migration and Wintering Records of Kirtland's Warblers: An Annotated Bibliography.* This report was written while at the Georgia Cooperative Fish and Wildlife Research Unit, School of Forest Resources, University of Georgia, Athens, Georgia. All previously published records were included unless there was substantial reason to doubt their validity.

southern states (FL, GA, AL, SC, NC, VA, TN)

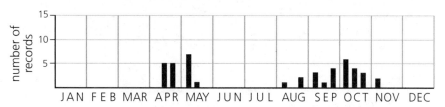

northern states (MI, OH, MN, WI, IL, IN, PA, WV, MA)

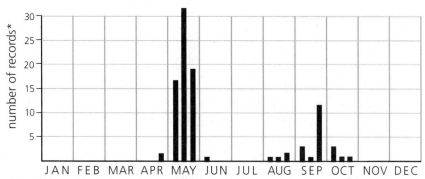

*excluding records of birds from breeding grounds.

Rufous- capped Warbler

Basileuterus rufifrons

Status and Distribution

The perky Rufous-capped Warbler is a common resident of dry scrub, secondary growth, and woodland edge habitats in Mexico and Central America. Its normal range closely approaches the United States in northern Sonora and northern Nuevo Leon. Thus, it is no great surprise that all U.S. records of this warbler come from Texas (14 birds) and Arizona (9 birds).

Given the Rufous-capped Warbler's usual range, you would expect most of the Texas Rufous-capped Warbler sightings to come from the lower Rio Grande valley. Instead, fully half of Texan Rufous-caps have been seen at Big Bend National Park, which lies as far from this species' known Mexican range as any point along the southern Texas border. Other Texas records come from Val Verde, Uvalde, Webb, Starr, Kenedy, and Nueces counties. Texan records from Uvalde to Big Bend span the calendar year but come mostly from mid-March into early August. The few lower Rio Grande and lower coastal sightings are mostly from winter.

In Arizona, records are fewer but the pattern is better defined. All Arizona sightings are from the southeastern part of the state between mid-March and mid-August.

Best Bets

As the discerning reader has no doubt figured out, there is no particular spot (in the U.S.) to go looking for a Rufous-capped Warbler with any real expectation of finding one. Nonetheless, birders have been lucky enough to happen onto a Rufous-cap about 23 times in the past 22 years. The best way

344

of maximizing your chances is to learn this bird's song. Many of the current records are of singing birds, and on at least several occasions, the happy discoverers first located their prize by hearing it.

But despite the poor odds of finding your own Rufous-capped Warbler, your chances of seeing one found by somebody else are reasonable. Singing male Rufous-caps have had a tendency to stick around for a while, thus giving the traveling birder an opportunity to track them down. When looking for this bird, remember that it tends to stay low in the foliage, usually coming up onto bushtops only to sing.

Identification

There is no U.S. bird that resembles the Rufous-capped Warbler. For a good depiction, see the NGS guide.

There is one Mexican species that looks like the Rufous-cap and is also a potential vagrant to the United States—the Golden-browed Warbler, *Basileuterus belli*. This bird approaches the United States as closely as southern Tamaulipas and could possibly turn up in south Texas. Unlike the Rufous-cap, the Golden-brow prefers moist woodlands. The Golden-brow can be separated from the Rufous-cap by its bright yellow supercilium (a.k.a. brow) and the narrow black border above the brow. Also, the Rufous-capped Warbler subspecies that wander to the United States have whitish bellies. The Golden-browed has a bright yellow belly. For details on subspecific variation in Rufous-capped Warblers and identification of Golden-browed Warblers, see Curson, et al. (1994).

Rufous-capped Warbler

LOCATION	NUMBERS SEEN	DATES SEEN
Arizona records		
Sycamore Canyon	1	3/16 to 5/?/94
Comfort Spring, Carr Canyon	1	4/7/85
lower Cave Creek Canyon	1	4/8/78
lower Cave Creek Canyon	1 (male)	5/9/77
French Joe Canyon	1 (male)	5/25 to 8/?/95
French Joe Canyon	1 (2nd male)	5/28 to 8/?/95
lower Cave Creek Canyon	1 (female, nest, 4 eggs)	7/17 to 7/23/77
California Gulch	1	7/24/93
Coronado National Monument	1	8/14/83
Texas records		
Cibolo Creek near Boerne	1	1/3 to 1/12/82

LOCATION	NUMBERS SEEN	DATES SEEN
Dolan Creek	1	1/10 to 3/9/93
Falcon Dam	1	2/10/73
Lost Mine Trail, Big Bend National Park	1	3/12 to 3/13/86
Santa Elena Canyon, Big Bend National Park	1	3/23 to 6/?/79
Santa Elena Canyon, Big Bend National Park	1	4/15 to 4/28/77
NW of Uvalde	1	4/20 to 7/31/95
Dugout Wells, Big Bend National Park	1	5/8/93
Webb County	2	5/17 to 5/19/80
Campground Canyon, Big Bend National Park	1	7/? to 8/?/75 & 11/23/75
Santa Elena Canyon, Big Bend National Park	1	8/3 to 8/4/76
Campground Canyon, Big Bend National Park	1	9/9/73 to 6/29/74
Corpus Christi	1	12/19/92

Bananaquit

Coereba flaveola

Status and Distribution

The tiny and delightful Bananaquit is a widespread Neotropical species that occasionally wanders to Florida from the Bahamas. These birds feed heavily on nectar using their curved bill and specialized tongue. Some of these traits once placed the Bananaquit among the honeycreepers, hence its old name, Bahama Honeycreeper. The honeycreepers, however, have been disbanded, and the Bananaquit now has its very own subfamily, *Coerebinae*, which is considered to be closely related to the wood warblers.

All of the approximately 30 U.S. records are from Florida, and all Florida records have come from the Keys (west to Key West) and along the Atlantic Coast (north to Fort Pierce, St. Lucie County). The distribution of sightings accepted by Stevenson and Anderson (1994) is as follows: St. Lucie County (2), Palm Beach County (5), Broward County (5), Dade County (9), and Monroe County (8).

In the West Indies, the Bananaquit occupies a wide variety of habitats and is frequently found near human development. Indeed, in some places, this association has led to a distinct fondness for sugar and sugar water leading to the nickname, Sugar Bird. In Florida, Bananaquits have been found in parks, gardens, and hardwood hammocks. They are especially attracted to flowering trees and shrubs and do occasionally treat themselves to sugar water, when available.

The earliest fall or winter Bananaquit record comes from John Lloyd State Recreation Area on December 19, 1993, and the latest spring date is of a bird seen near Cape Sable on May 19, 1922. The vast majority of reports have been between early January and mid-March, with a distinct peak between mid-February and mid-March. There are no breeding records of Bananaquits from the United States, but three times they have built nests that were used for roosting purposes (Stevenson and Anderson 1994).

Best Bets

No one spot seems to be a particular favorite among this species. However, a fair number of records are scattered among the coastal parks from Miami to Palm Beach County, Florida, and these are probably the best places to check. Many sightings have also come from heavily landscaped suburban neighborhoods, and one should be on the lookout when in these areas during the proper season.

Identification

The identification of an adult Bananaquit is simplicity itself. Immature Bananaquits are not so obvious. See the NGS guide for a drawing, and remember the decurved bill.   **(See color photo on page 493.)**

Bananaquit —*all records*

LOCATION	NUMBERS SEEN	DATES SEEN
John Lloyd State Recreation Area	1	12/19/93
Key Largo	1	12/29/71 to early
West Palm Beach	1	1/1967 to 4/4/67
Fairchild Tropical Garden	1	1/4 to 1/6/85
Key Biscayne	1	1/7 to 1/8/67
Fort Lauderdale	1	1/18 to 3/10/72
Pompano Beach	1	1/22/91
east of Princeton	1	1/22/67
Palm Beach	1	1/27/55
Indian Key	1	1/31/1858
Palm Beach area	2	2/1965 to 3/1965
Lake Worth	1	2/4/94
Miami Beach	1	2/7/21
near Dania	1	2/8 to 3/6/89
John Lloyd State Recreation Area	1	2/8 to 3/6/89
Hollywood	1	2/10 to 2/19/76
Fort Capron (Fort Pierce Inlet)	1	2/11/1874
Lantana	1	2/14 to 2/28/64
Fort Lauderdale	1	2/18 to 3/17/61
Key Biscayne	1	2/18/68
Homestead	1	2/24/54

LOCATION	NUMBERS SEEN	DATES SEEN
Fort Pierce	1	2/25 to 3/15/70
Palm Beach	2	2/26 to 3/15/82
Key Biscayne	1	3/1967
Key West	1	3/1 to 3/5/60
Big Pine Key	1	3/7/80
Virginia Key	1	3/19/85
Homestead	1	3/21/54
Marathon	1	3/22/49
Palm Beach	1	3/23/55
Key Largo	1	4/10/88
Boca Raton	1	4/21 to 5/3/94
Coral Gables	1	5/11/77
near Cape Sable	1	5/19/22

all records

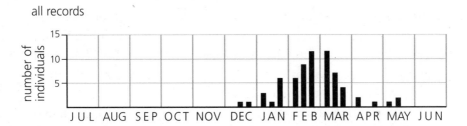

Stripe-headed Tanager

Spindalis zena

Status and Distribution

The Stripe-headed Tanager is a dazzling vagrant from the West Indies, where it can be found in the Bahamas and through most of the Greater Antilles. In its native habitat this species is a secretive bird of shrubbery and forest, especially in hilly or mountainous areas. In the United States, this nifty tanager has occurred only in Florida, where it is has been found skulking about hardwood hammocks and thick ornamental plantings seeking small fruit, emergent leaves, and flower buds.

The first U.S. record occurred when Mr. and Mrs. Roy Dickie found one near Cutler, Dade County, on December 28, 1957. The next one wasn't located until May 12, 1961, in Marathon. The almost 40 records since then have all been from southern Florida and the majority have been within proximity to the coast. The records in Stevenson and Anderson (1994) are distributed, as follows, among several south Florida counties: Palm Beach County (10), Broward County (2), Dade County (14), Monroe County (10), Dade and Monroe County (1).

The origin of U.S. records is likely Bahamanian by virtue of the preponderance of Atlantic Coast records alone. Additionally, male Stripe-headed Tanagers show a great deal of subspecific variation, and all U.S. records identified to subspecies have indeed been from the Bahamas.

Stripe-headed Tanagers come to Florida as migrants and winter visitors. The earliest fall record comes from Cape Florida on September 5, 1988, and the latest spring date was recorded on June 17, 1963, at Key Largo. The high count is a stunning seven birds that were present during April or May 1973 at Hypoluxo Island. Although there are records in every month from September through June, the majority of sightings are from mid-December through mid-May.

Best Bets

The area with the greatest number of records is Cape Florida, with a total of nine sightings. Cape Florida's vegetation, however, was erased by Hurricane Andrew in 1992. Though this locale may once again become a top vagrant hot spot, such is unlikely in the immediate future. A good substitute, however, would be the parks near Fort Lauderdale and Boca Raton (see "Site Guide").

Identification

The male Stripe-headed Tanager's brilliant coloration and striking pattern have spawned a multitude of nicknames such as Markhead, Orange Bird, and Spanish Quail. This bird is unlikely to be confused with any other species. The female, however, is dull green or olive and could be mistaken for the female of a number of species, especially the Painted Bunting. Note the pale edging to the greater wing coverts and tertials and the white mark at the base of the folded primaries, which resembles that on a Black-throated Blue Warbler. Any head markings are subdued. Also the bill is stouter and more finchlike than that of other tanagers. Unfortunately, the drawings in the MGB, the NGS guide, and Peterson (1980) differ dramatically, and none is totally accurate. The drawing in Bond (1985) illustrates the vastly different Jamaican subspecies.

As to identifying subspecies, focus on the male's back and rump color and on the pattern of the underparts. The two Bahamanian subspecies are depicted in the MGB, and the Jamaican race is shown in Bond (1985). The females of the two Bahamanian races are indistinguishable. Females from other islands differ in rump and underpart coloration (see Bond 1985)
(See color photo on page 493.)

Stripe-headed Tanager—*all records**

LOCATION	NUMBERS SEEN	DATES SEEN
Cape Florida	1	9/5/88
Cape Florida	1	10/14/85
Cape Florida	1	10/17/83
Greynolds Park	1	11/22/65 to 2/26/66

LOCATION	NUMBERS SEEN	DATES SEEN
Delray Beach	1	11/30/92
Matheson Hammock	1	12/1976 to 4/29/77
Key Biscayne	1	12/2/67
Fort Lauderdale	1	12/11/75 to 1/6/76
Snake Bight Trail, Everglades	1	12/14 to 12/25/90
Fort Lauderdale	1	12/14/75
West Palm Beach	1	12/15/79
Marathon	1	12/21/71 to 3/26/72
Key Largo	1	12/22/62
West Palm Beach	1	12/27/63
near Cutler	1	12/28/57
Key Largo	1	12/28/79
Key Largo	1	12/29/71
Tavernier	1	early 1/63 to 3/19/63
north of Homestead	1	1/3 to 3/3/92
Islamorada	1	2/1973
Miami	1	2/13 to 2/20/77
Hypoluxo Island	1	2/22 to 2/23/83
Hypoluxo Island	1+ (up to 7)	3/19 to 5/28/73
Hypoluxo Island	1	3/28 to 4/3/67
Plantation Key	1	3/30 to 4/6/63
Cape Florida	1	4/1 to 4/6/91
Key West	1	4/12 to 4/16/67
Spanish River Park	1 (female)	4/16 to 4/20/94
Spanish River Park	1 (male)	4/18 to 4/20/94
Cape Florida	1	4/28/88
Cape Florida	1	4/29/83
Key Biscayne	1	5/1962
Hypoluxo Island	1	5/3/76
Hugh Taylor Birch State Park	1	5/5/95
Palm Beach	1	5/11/63
Marathon	1	5/12 to 5/28/61
Delray Beach	2	5/17/83
Key Biscayne	1	6/3/67
Key Largo	1	6/17/63

*All records are from Florida.

all records

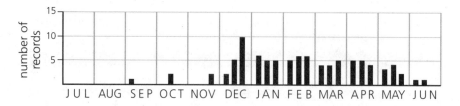

Blue Bunting

Cyanocompsa parellina

Status and Distribution

The Blue Bunting is a Mexican and Central American species that normally comes no closer to the U.S. border than central Tamaulipas and Sinaloa. Thus, it is odd that the first confirmed U.S. record came from neither Texas nor Arizona, but from Louisiana, where one was photographed in Cameron Parish on December 16, 1979.

Prior to the Louisiana bird, there had been just one report—a bird in Hidalgo County, Texas, from February 4 to 5, 1978. Since 1979, there have been 20 more published reports, involving at least 25 birds, and all of these are from Texas (3 have been rejected by the TX BRC). Records have come mostly from the lower Rio Grande valley, but exceptions include one at Big Bend National Park on July 29, 1993, and two in Freeport during the winter of 1987-8.

Excluding the Big Bend sighting, all records have been between October 18 and April 8, with most between late December and mid-February. Notably, the vast majority of records are between 1984 and 1990. Since then there has been one published report—the sighting from Big Bend. Only time will tell whether the spurt we saw in the 1980s was a short-lived aberration.[1]

Best Bets

Blue Buntings in the United States have tended to frequent pie plates, cut-open milk jugs, and similar homemade bird feeders. The premier location for this habitat in the lower Rio Grande valley is Bentsen State Park near McAllen. Once they have shown up here, they have stayed around for a while.

[1] One or two Blue Buntings once again graced Bentsen State Park during the winter of 1995-6.

Identification

The male Blue Bunting is distinctly reminiscent of a male Indigo Bunting. The main coloration of a male Blue Bunting, however, is much darker than that of an Indigo, almost black in many light conditions; its most striking feature is areas of lighter blue on the forehead, face, shoulder, and rump, which contrast strongly with the rest of the body.

Female Blue Buntings resemble both Indigo and Varied Buntings. Blues are a richer brown than Indigos, verging on rusty or chestnut. They are also are more uniformly colored, lacking the diffuse streaking on the underparts of an Indigo. The Indigo has a smaller, straighter bill, as well. The bill of a Varied Bunting is also smaller than that of a Blue. Furthermore, female Varieds often have a bluish cast to the folded primaries and tail (see Howell and Webb 1995). **(See color photo on page 494.)**

Blue Bunting—*all records**

LOCATION	NUMBERS SEEN	DATES SEEN
Hidalgo County	1	2/4 to 2/5/78
Cameron Parish, LA	1	12/16/79
Bentsen State Park	1	3/12 to 3/16/80
Anzalduas County Park	1	1/31 to 2/1982
Bentsen State Park	1	1/24 to 2/16/84
Santa Margarita Ranch	2	3/15/84
Bentsen State Park	3-4	12/3/84 to 4/1985
Santa Ana NWR	1	10/18/85
Bentsen State Park	1-3	early 12/85 to 4/8/96
Santa Ana NWR	1	12/13/87 to 1/9/88
Bentsen State Park	3	mid-12/85 to 4/7/88
Freeport	1	12/20/87 to 2/12/88
Freeport (different bird)	1	12/20/87 to early 1/88
Bentsen State Park	2	12/29/87
Salineño	1	1/5 and 1/30/88
Santa Ana NWR (different from below)	1	1/12/88
Sabal Palm Sanctuary	1	2/7/88 on
Bentsen State Park	1-2	1/5 to 3/15/90
Big Bend National Park	1	7/29/93
Rejected by TX BRC		
Santa Ana NWR	1	1/5/88
Bentsen State Park	1	12/20/88
Aransas NWR	1	12/21/89

*All records are from Texas unless otherwise denoted.

all records

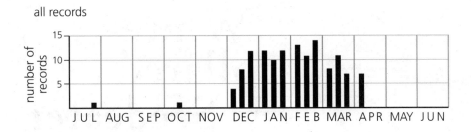

White-collared Seedeater

Sporophila torqueola

Status and Distribution

The generic name *Sporophila* means "seed lover," and seedeaters are just that. Unlike the "winter" finches that we North Americans so often associate with a lust for seeds, the seedeaters are a Neotropical group of birds. Only one, the White-collared, ventures into the United States. From northern Mexico into western Panama, the White-collared Seedeater is a common, gregarious resident of a variety of scrubby habitats: abandoned pastures, weedy fields, waste areas in towns, and cropland. These birds are so numerous that they can be pests in grain fields.

Seedeaters were once common in southern Texas as well, but vast amounts of Rio Grande valley brush country have been cleared and converted to orange groves, cabbage fields, grazing land, and trailer parks. The species is now rare in the United States, or at least very local, and it's not always a cinch to find.

Recent records of White-collared Seedeaters have been mainly from San Ygnacio and Zapata. Sightings away from these areas are less than annual and are mostly from around Falcon Dam and Salineño. Reports have come from as far afield as Sarita (spring 1984) and Laredo (January 8, 1987).

Seedeaters have been seen in southern Texas year-round, but at times these birds seem completely absent north of the Rio Grande. Most sightings are from December through May—but then, that's when most birders are in the area. Usually only a handful of individuals is seen at one time, so 17 at San Ygnacio on October 8, 1993, was exceptional and is probably a modern-day high count.

In 1986, San Ygnacio was the site of the first probable breeding of seedeaters in recent U.S. history, with singing males remaining through the breeding season and a probable juvenile seen on July 4. Nesting may have also occurred in 1989 when three singing males, two or three females, and six or more possible immatures were found in San Ygnacio on July 22.

Best Bets

The most reliable place to see the White-collared Seedeater in recent years has been the tall cane along the Rio Grande at San Ygnacio, Texas, 35 miles south of Laredo. Check the areas accessible from the southern ends of Washington and nearby streets. Informal trails lead around and through this habitat in the floodplain of the river (which, because of dams and agricultural exploitation, doesn't flood much anymore). It's also possible to look down on the cane from the riverbank above, although houses and businesses can impede access in places. Formerly, habitat remained around the cemetery just east of San Ygnacio, but visits in 1994 and 1996 showed that it had been plowed down to the bare earth. Various roads lead to the river both east and west of town and to possible good habitat; whenever possible, ask permission before poking around.

In Zapata, 14 miles south of San Ygnacio, seedeaters have been seen in the reeds at a small wetland in a park beside the city library. (This area is easy to reach, just a couple of blocks off Highway 83; ask for directions.) Birds were first found there in the fall of 1991.

The Rio Grande valley hotline (or the local birders' grapevine) usually has information about seedeaters. So many birders visit the valley, and so many of them look for the seedeaters, that news of their presence or absence at San Ygnacio is nearly always in circulation.

More important than the time of year may be the time of day. Experienced observers say very early morning and late afternoon are the times to find seedeaters at San Ygnacio; the birds leave to forage during the day, returning to the cane near dusk to roost for the night. Many visiting birders, concentrating their efforts farther downriver at hot spots such as Santa Ana and Bentsen, make a quick midday trip upstream and arrive at just the wrong time.

Identification

Clue number one: seedeaters are tiny. Really tiny. Almost kinglet tiny. With their stubby curved bills they have a chunky silhouette that is all by itself quite distinctive. Goldfinches are similar but can be easily separated (see MGB and NGS guide).

A concern when viewing a seedeater away from the usual Zapata and San Ygnacio haunts is other subspecies/species of seedeaters. The typical Texan subspecies is *S. torqueola sharpei*. The males of this subspecies are duller and less contrasty than other varieties of *S. torqueola*, but the females are similar. For further details, see Howell and Webb (1995). Other seedeater species that are possible as escapees but are not likely as vagrants include the Ruddy-breasted, Variable, and Slate-colored. The females of all three resemble the female White-collared. Focus on overall color and bill color. For further details see Howell and Webb (1995).

Large-billed
(Savannah)
Sparrow

Passerculus (sandwichensis) rostratus

Status and Distribution

The Savannah Sparrow (*Passerculus sandwichensis*), like so many other sparrows, shows a great deal of geographic variation. This variability has provided considerable grist for the taxonomic mill, leading to many energetic debates. The Savannah Sparrow is currently the only member of the genus *Passerculus*, but this was not always so. Baird, Brewer, and Ridgway (1874) listed four species of *Passerculus*: Savannah Sparrow (*P. sandwichensis*), Ipswich Sparrow (*P. princeps*), Belding's Sparrow (*P. beldingi*), and San Diego (a.k.a. Large-billed) Sparrow (*P. rostratus*). Though this taxonomy held for a while, Belding's Sparrow was eventually lumped with Savannah, followed next by the Large-billed Sparrow, and finally the Ipswich Sparrow in 1973 (AOU 1973).

The debate regarding Large-billed Sparrow was quiescent until Zink and friends (1991) took a close look at Savannah Sparrow mitochondrial DNA. They found a substantial difference between the DNA of *P. sandwichensis rostratus* and "typical" Savannah Sparrows wintering in southern California and Louisiana. Their data strongly suggest that the Large-billed Sparrow is, indeed, a distinct species, but before final conclusions can be drawn, intermediate birds (between the Large-billed and Belding's) from western Baja need to studied. For an excellent discussion (with color drawings) of northwestern Mexico's Savannah Sparrows, see Van Rossem (1947). For other discussions on the taxonomy and distribution of these races, see AOU (1983), Grinnell (1939), and

Byers, et al. (1995).

The definition of a Large-billed Sparrow typically includes those populations that breed along Baja California's Pacific coast from El Rosario through Magdalena Bay (including San Benito Island) and the populations that breed from northeast Baja south through coastal Sonora to northern Sinaloa (to latitude 25°N). As implied above, there is some variation between these groups. Fortunately, in the United States we have only the distinctive "nominate" race of Large-billed Sparrow to deal with (formerly *P. rostratus rostratus*). This bird breeds from the tidal marshes at the Colorado River mouth south along the coast of Sonora to Puerto Lobos (Van Rossem 1947). After breeding, it disperses radially with some birds wandering north or northwest to the United States. These Large-bills can be found reliably in small numbers around the Salton Sea and, with a bit more difficulty, along the southern California coast from San Diego to Ventura. In recent years, a few birds have even made it north to Morro Bay, and one was found as far north as Princeton Marsh in central California's San Mateo County (September 8, 1991). Surprisingly, there are only two Arizona records: near Yuma on August 15, 1902, and Bill Williams River delta, La Paz County, January 1977. At the Salton Sea, Large-billed Sparrows prefer moist low alkalai scrub marshes at or near the edge of the sea. On the coast, this species gravitates toward salicornia marshes, especially those with nearby sandy or grassy areas.

Large-billed Sparrows start to appear in the Lower 48 during late July and depart mostly in February or early March. When this species was more common, it was seen into April and may still occasionally occur this late. The earliest recent record is from the Salton Sea on July 7.

Best Bets

The preeminent place to find Large-billed Sparrows in the United States is undoubtedly the southeastern portion of the Salton Sea. Especially good places to look there include the Niland boat ramp, the mouth of the New River, and along Davis Road. If you spend several hours intently searching the above areas during the proper season, you should be able to find a handful of Large-billed Sparrows.

If you find yourself in coastal southern California and can not make the drive to the Salton Sea, do not despair. You still have a fair chance. Try the Tijuana River estuary, Kendall Frost Marsh, the "Silver Strand" in San Diego County, or McGrath Beach.

Identification

When compared with other western Savannah Sparrows, the once (and future?) *P. rostratus rostratus* is a paler and larger-billed bird with more diffuse markings. It can be separated from mainstream Savannah Sparrows and Belding's Savannah Sparrow by using the following marks (for a good photo, see *Birding* 28:60. The depiction in the NGS guide also is fairly good).

Back streaking: This is markedly reduced or absent on *P. rostratus rostratus*.

Bill: As the name implies, Large-billed Sparrows have a strikingly larger bill than Savannah Sparrows. In *P. rostratus rostratus*, the culmen is convex.

Supercilium: The supercilium of *P. rostratus rostratus* lacks, or has but the faintest, yellow.

Call: The call of the Large-bill is briefer and not quite as sibilant as that of "typical" Savannahs and *P. sandwichensis beldingi*.

(See color photo on page 494.)

Shiny Cowbird

Molothrus bonariensis

Status and Distribution

The Shiny Cowbird is probably America's most unwanted bird. Like other cowbirds, the Shiny is a brood parasite, and its addition to the U.S. avifauna has given our native songbirds just one more threat to overcome. During the 1800s, Shiny Cowbirds seemed like an implausible invader, but at that time this species was restricted mostly to South America. In the early 1900s, however, Shinies began to spread into the Lesser Antilles. During 1972, this species first appeared on Hispaniola (Post and Wiley 1977), and by 1982, Shiny Cowbirds were in northern Cuba (Garrido 1984). Their advance northward was due to the clearing of land for farming, with its attendant increase in cowbird food supply (Post, et al. 1993).

The first Shiny Cowbird beachhead on U.S. soil was at Lower Matecumbe Key, Florida, on June 14, 1985. This bird left in late July 1985, but less than a year later three others were found at Islamorada, Florida (July 5, 1986). The invasion then began to pick up steam. In 1987, there were at least nine Shinies scattered across three locations in southern Florida. During 1988, over two dozen were seen, with one as far north as Jacksonville. In 1989 Shinies invaded North Carolina, South Carolina, Georgia, and Louisiana, and well over 100 were seen in Florida that year. In 1990, the expansion continued as Alabama, Texas, and Oklahoma added the Shiny Cowbird to their state lists. The tide stemmed a bit in 1991 and 1992, however, when only Maine was added to the Shiny Cowbird's list of states.

The pattern of Shiny Cowbird occurrence was similar from 1990 through 1993, and for at least the time being the distribution of these cowbirds seems stable. In their current pattern, the bulk of Shiny Cowbirds is found in Florida, especially southern Florida. A few, however, are found annually along the Gulf Coast between the Florida panhandle and eastern Texas and along the Atlantic Coast between Jacksonville and North Carolina.

In southern Florida, Shiny Cowbirds are year-round residents, but peak numbers are present during spring from late April through early June. Record high counts include 52 on the Dry Tortugas on May 25, 1989, and 44 at Key West on May 16, 1989. Winter records have occurred as far north as Tierra Verde, Pinellas County, Florida. Winter high counts include 30 to 40 during the winters of 1991-2 and 1992-3 at Rookery Bay in Collier County, Florida.

Outside south Florida, spring records also predominate with peak time from mid-April through mid-June. The earliest (non-Florida) spring sighting is one from Johnson's Bayou, Louisiana, on March 13, 1994, and the latest fall report is from Fort Morgan, Alabama, on November 29, 1991. There is also a midwinter record from Wilmington, North Carolina. There are about four spring records away from Florida and about one such fall record annually. The highest tally away from Florida is of 28 birds at Dauphin Island, Alabama, on May 11, 1990.

Shiny Cowbirds, like most other cowbirds, prefer open lands and are not averse to feeders. It is not a surprise, therefore, that Shinies are often found with Brown-headed Cowbirds or other blackbirds. Keep in mind, however, that Shinies are not uncommonly by themselves as well.

Best Bets

There are many places in southern Florida that attract Shiny Cowbirds, especially in spring. The spring Dry Tortugas tours, for instance, usually find some. Flamingo and the lower Keys also often have a few. In Flamingo be sure to look around the campground. Another decent spot is 209th Street, southwest of Homestead.

In winter, the location of choice is the Briggs Nature Center at Rookery Bay, Collier County. Shiny Cowbirds usually arrive here in mid-November and stay into early March but have been seen as early as late October and as late as late April.

Identification

The male Shiny Cowbird is distinctive if seen well. No other similarly sized blackbird is glossy purplish black with dark eyes. The most likely confounding species is the Brown-headed Cowbird, which is common in winter (but rare to uncommon in summer) in southern Florida and common all the time just about everywhere else. Aside from the obvious brown head, the male Brown-headed Cowbird is duller greenish black and shows minor structural differences from the Shiny (see below). For a good photograph of a Shiny, see the "Pictorial Highlights," summer 1992 in *American Birds* (46:1195).

Identifying a female Shiny Cowbird is far more challenging. The two most similar species are the female Brown-headed Cowbird and the female Brewer's Blackbird. With experience, bill shape is diagnostic, but several other characters are useful as well. As with many identifications, it is safest to use a combination of marks. The most useful ones are listed below. For more discussion and an excellent photo, see "Answers to June Photo Quiz" in *Birding* (23:233-234) and Smith and Sprunt (1987).

Bill
- Brown-headed: Relatively thick-based and conical; usually at least partially gray but occasionally all black.
- Shiny: More slender, slightly longer, and slightly sharper than Brown-headed; usually all black.
- Brewer's: Shorter and even more slender than Shiny; color varies from mostly gray to all black.

Face Pattern
- Brown-headed: Usually conspicuous dark jaw stripe, contrasting with paler throat and partially paler cheeks.
- Shiny: Cheeks solidly dark, contrasting with paler throat but not contrasting much with faintly darker jaw stripe.
- Brewer's: Plain with no jaw stripe and no contrastingly paler throat.

Breast Streaking
- Brown-headed: Usually conspicuous though blurry.
- Shiny: More uniformly colored breast but often with faint blurry streaks.
- Brewer's: Streaks usually lacking.

Overall Shape
- Brown-headed: Larger head, rounder crown, plumper body than Shiny.

- Shiny: Smaller head, flatter crown, and more slender body than Brown-headed. Heavier chest than Brewer's.
- Brewer's: Smaller head, slimmer chest than Shiny.

Overall Color
- Brown-headed: Usually dull gray-brown but warmer yellowish brown on young birds. No gloss.
- Shiny: Averages warmer brown than Brown-headed. No gloss.
- Brewer's: Dull grayish brown with dull green gloss on wings, rump, and tail of at least adults.   **(See color photo on page 495.)**

Shiny Cowbird—*all citations in* American Birds*

LOCATION	NUMBERS SEEN	DATES SEEN
1985		
Lower Matecumbe Key	1	6/14 to late July
1986		
Islamorada	3	7/15
1987		
Flamingo	2	5/25 to 5/31
Islamorada	1	6/19
Flamingo	6	6/20
1988		
Dry Tortugas	7 (1 until 5/5)	4/25 to 4/26
Flamingo	1	5/4
Flamingo	1	5/17
Big Pine Key	1	5/19 to 5/21
Fort De Soto	4	5/25 to 5/31
Flamingo	3	5/27
Mahogany Hammock, Everglades	1	6/12
Flamingo	2+	through summer
S of Homestead	2	6/16
Jacksonville	1	6/22 to 8/31
Everglades National Park	6+	8/12
Key West	11	8/31 to 10/9
W of Homestead	2	11/88 to 1/20/89
E of Homestead	1	12/23
1989		
Florida City	6 (3 pairs)	April and May
Big Coppitt Key	1	4/9
Dry Tortugas	42+	4/24 to 5/7
Cape San Blas, Florida panhandle	1	5/1
Delray Beach	1	5/8
southwest Palm Beach	2 (pair)	5/10
Big Pine Key	5	5/11 to 5/31
Flamingo	2	5/14

LOCATION	NUMBERS SEEN	DATES SEEN
Key West	44	5/16
Cumberland Island, GA	2	mid-May to early June
Point Fourchon, LA	1	5/20 to 5/21
Dry Tortugas	52	5/25
Warner Robins Air Force Base, GA	1	late May
W of Homestead	2 (pair)	all spring
Key West	13	6/1
Cameron Parish, LA	1	6/4 to 6/6
Key West	9	(none past 6/27) 6/8
too numerous to count elsewhere in south Florida		summer
Anclote Key	3	6/30
Sullivan Island, SC	2	7/16 to 7/28
Sullivan Island, SC	1 (male)	8/23 to 8/24
Sullivan Island, SC	1 (female)	8/25
near Aurora, NC	1	11/16
Monroe, Dade, Broward, Palm Beach counties		winter 1989-1990

1990

LOCATION	NUMBERS SEEN	DATES SEEN
Lake Harbor	1	3/4
Key West	12	spring
Homestead	2 (pair)	all spring
Bon Secour NWR, AL	1	4/25
Gulf Shores, AL	1	4/26
Fort Morgan, AL	3	4/26
Fort Morgan, AL	7	(some until 5/12) 4/27
Dauphin Island, AL	1+ (max, 28 on 5/11)	4/30 to mid-June
Levy County	1	May
Dry Tortugas	5	5/1
Pinellas County	1	5/1
N of Gulf Shores, AL	4	5/3
Islamorada	2 (pair)	5/5
Lee County	1	5/5
Fort Pickens, Florida panhandle	1	5/9
Grand Isle, LA	1	5/14
Flamingo	12	5/16
Taylor County	1	5/20
Wakulla County	1	5/23
Fort Hood, TX	1	5/23
James Island, SC	2	6/3 to 6/26
Wichita Mountains, OK	1	6/12
Eastpoint	1	6/23
Fort Johnson, SC	1	6/25
Key West	12	through summer
Cooper City	2	7/4
Eastpoint	1	7/10
Key West	3	8/23 to 10/22
Lake Seminole	1	10/2 to 11/31
New Bern, NC	1	10/9 to 10/12

LOCATION	NUMBERS SEEN	DATES SEEN
New Bern, NC	1	10/29
Weedons Island	2	October
St. Petersburg	1	11/4
Homestead	1+ (up to 6)	winter 1990-91
1991		
Fort Morgan and Dauphin Island, AL	small flocks	arriving on 4/12
Dry Tortugas	(max, 14)	4/23
Sullivan Island, SC	5	4/30 to 7/13
Fort Walton, Florida panhandle	1	5/4
Monhegan Island, ME	1	5/24 to 5/26
Hancock, MS	1	6/12
ort Morgan, AL	1	11/29
Florida, winter 1991-1992	max = 30 to 40	at Rookery Bay; northern-most = Tierra Verde, Pinellas County. Also, a few individuals at four other scattered locations.
1992		
Dry Tortugas	decreased numbers spring 1992	
Fort Morgan, AL	1+ (up to 8)	4/11 to 4/26
Dauphin Island, AL	2	4/17 to 4/26
Grand Isle, LA	2	mid- to late April
Fort De Soto	1	4/25
Hillsborough County	1	5/9
Fort Hood, TX	1	6/12
Cape Carteret, NC	1	fall 1992
Cameron Parish, LA	1	10/25
Cameron Parish, LA	1	11/28
Rookery Bay winter	30-40	1992-93
1993		
Florida City	2	1/4
A few at Dry Tortugas; Key West; Levy, Wakulla, and Franklin counties, spring 1993		
Goliad County, TX	1	3/5
Fort Pickens, Florida panhandle	1	4/9
Dauphin Island, AL	1	4/10
Dauphin Island, AL	1	4/24
Figure Eight Island, NC	1	mid-May to 6/12
Cape Lookout, NC	1	6/10
St. Marks NWR	2	7/10
St. Marks NWR	1	8/22
1994		
Wilmington, NC	1	Jan and Feb
Rookery Bay	20	1/11
Johnson's Bayou, LA	1	3/13 to 4/2
Port Bolivar, TX	1	4/16
Gulf Breeze, Florida panhandle	1	8/19
Grand Island, LA	1	10/9 to 10/10
St. Marks NWR	1	10/25/94

*All records pertain to the Florida peninsula unless otherwise denoted.

Brambling

Fringilla montifringilla

Status and Distribution

You might think that a Brambling was named after its fondness for brambles, but in this case you'd be wrong. The name Brambling is actually a bastardization of Brandling, a name that refers to this beautiful species' heavily brindled markings. Indeed, the Brambling's exotic beauty and unpredictable rarity have made it a show-stopper whenever it is found in the Lower 48.

Bramblings are native to the Palearctic, where they breed in the pine and beech forests of northern Eurasia and winter south to the Mediterranean Sea and southern China. This is a species famous for nomadic behavior. Birds banded during winter in Britain have been found in subsequent winters as far away as Italy and Yugoslavia. In North America, this species is most often found in the Aleutian Islands, where it is a regular spring and fall migrant in small numbers. The first Lower 48 record of a Brambling, however, wasn't until December 15, 1958, when a bird showing no signs of captivity "consorted unamiably with House Sparrows" at Stanton, New Jersey (Banks 1970). Since then, Bramblings have been recorded about 50 times in the Lower 48. As you would expect, most of these records are from more northerly states, especially the Pacific Northwest (San Francisco through Washington), which accounts for approximately 19 records. Records also come from Montana, Wyoming, Utah, Colorado, Nevada, North Dakota, Minnesota, Wisconsin, Michigan, Indiana, Ohio, Pennsylvania, New Hampshire, Massachusetts, New York, and New Jersey.

When Bramblings are found in the Lower 48, they are indeed sometimes in brambles. They are also fond of woodland edges (especially birch and alder), farmyards, and of course, feeders. Often they are alone or only loosely associated with other seed-eating birds, but occasionally Bramblings do flock with other species such as Golden-crowned Sparrows and Dark-eyed Juncos.

As you would expect, the Brambling is predominantly a winter visitor to our area. Dates range from October 20 (Colorado Springs, CO) to April 22 (Branchville, NJ), with the bulk of records occurring from mid-December through early March. You should note, however, there are several dates as early as late October and as late as early April.

Best Bets

As you might imagine with a species that has such widely scattered records, there is no particular top spot. A staked-out bird, preferrably at a feeder, is your best bet. Keep in touch with NARBA for such finds. As an aside, however, keep in mind that should you find a Brambling in a place far from feeders and human residence, you may want to spread bird seed around. During January 1993, intrepid birders near Ferndale, Washington, did exactly that, making that Brambling easy for many a joyous birder to find.

Identification

The identification of the Brambling is no real problem, and the drawings in the NGS guide are fine. A female or immature Chaffinch could be temporarily misleading, but note the Brambling's white rump, orange breast, and orange scapulars. The white rump really stands out in flight and should be looked for in flushed flocks of ground-foraging birds in the Pacific Northwest and elsewhere. **(See color photo on page 496.)**

Brambling—*all records*[1]

LOCATION	DATES SEEN
Washington	
Aberdeen	winter 1969
Issaquah/Lake Sammamish	1/6 to 3/22/82
Tenino	1/11 to 1/18/84
Steilacoom	12/28/88 to 1/1/89
Sedro Wooley	11/6 to 11/10/90
Elma	1/20 to 2/26/91
Port Angeles	12/14/90 to 2/28/91

LOCATION	DATES SEEN
Westport	12/15/91 to 2/8/92
Walla Walla	2/20 to 2/24/92
Richland	1/30/92
near Ferndale	1/1 to 1/20/93
Newhalem	4/9 to 4/12/93
Oregon	
Portland	11/22/67 to 4/3/68
La Grande	12/9/83 to mid-2/84
Florence	10/25 to 10/31/90
Umapine	2/8/92
California	
Crescent City	2/5 to 3/28/84
Arcata	11/20/85
Chico	2/11 to 2/19/86
Santa Cruz	12/15/90 to 2/16/91
Ferndale	12/29/91 to 2/28/92
Montana	
Swan Lake	11/19 to 12/3/78
Kalispell	11/8 to 11/9/90
Swan Lake	10/26/91
Kalispell	12/19/93 to 3/30/94
Wyoming	
Dubois	11/10 to 11/26/85
Sheridan	11/18 to 11/30/85
Nevada	
Sutcliffe	10/31 to 11/1/78
Utah	
Brighton	11/28/85 to 1/22/86
Logan	12/12 to 12/30/83
Colorado	
Colorado Springs	10/20 to 11/4/83
Pueblo Reservoir	12/16 to 12/19/83
Boulder	12/17/83 to 3/3/84
North Dakota	
Bismarck	12/15/79 to 2/29/80
Minnesota	
Owatonna	mid-1/84 to 3/25/84
East Grand Forks	12/26/88 to early 4/89
Sawbill Trail	10/22/93
Wisconsin	
Neenah	1/17 to 1/25/94
Michigan	
Kalamazoo County	11/25 to 11/29/91
Indiana	
Indianapolis	11/10/85

LOCATION	DATES SEEN
Ohio	
Bath	3/31 to 4/7/87
Pennsylvania	
Allegheny County	2/2 to 4/1/78
New Hampshire	
Plymouth	10/23/87
Massachusetts	
near Hadley	11/29/61 to 3/18/62
near Richmond	2/18 to 4/6/62
Mansfield	12/78 to 3/79
Groveland	11/8/93
New York	
Tupper Lake[2]	4/6/62
Kennedy airport	2/11/65
Pleasant Valley	3/13 to 3/27/84
New Jersey	
Stanton	12/15/58
Branchville	4/20 to 4/22/65

[1]Each record involves one bird.
[2]Rejected by NY BRC, due to origin questions (?).

all records

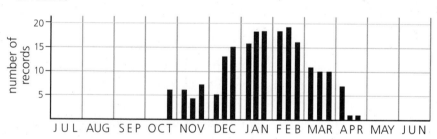

Hoary Redpoll

Carduelis hornemanni

![leaf] Status and Distribution

The status of the Hoary Redpoll in the Lower 48 is among the least understood of any regularly occurring species due to the difficulties of separating this species from the Common Redpoll (see "Identification" for details). The muddle is made worse by variation among regional editors for *American Birds* (now *Field Notes*). Some approach Hoaries with great cynicism, publishing but a small percentage of sightings. Others, meanwhile, simply print the number of individuals reported, even if the species is less then annual in their region.

Some of the conflicts regarding the Hoary Redpoll arise out of the existence of individuals that are intermediate between "typical" Commons and Hoaries. These birds at times have been assumed to be hybrids. However, no actual hybridization between these two species has been convincingly witnessed (Knox 1987). Some confusion may be due to feather wear. Freshly plumaged Common Redpolls in fall are likely to look paler than expected whereas worn Hoaries in spring may appear darker than usual (Granlund 1994). Most of these intermediates are, however, probably Hoaries (Knox 1987 and Seutin, et al. 1992).

Despite this confounding situation, some conclusions can be drawn. First and foremost is that the Hoary Redpoll is an irruptive species in the Lower 48. Some winters it is absent while during others it is uncommon across much of the far North. Hoary Redpoll invasions are almost always part of a larger incursion of Common Redpolls, but not all irruptions of Commons include an increased number of Hoaries.

It is impossible to predict a good Hoary winter, but when Common Redpolls start to appear in waves, it is time to start searching. Hoary-poor winters are easier to predict because these typically occur the year after an invasion. Since 1977, there have been five irruptions: 1977-78, 1981-82, 1986-87, 1991-92, and 1993-94. Winters particularly bereft of Hoary Redpolls include 1978-79, 1982-83, 1990-91, and 1992-93.

Even in poor winters, there are usually a couple of Hoaries found in northern Minnesota. They are also seen most years in North Dakota, extreme northern Wisconsin, and the Upper Peninsula of Michigan. In these areas, Hoaries typically constitute about 1 percent of all redpolls. During invasions, however, the proportion of redpolls that are Hoaries can go as high as 10 to 20 percent (Eckert 1982).

Most invasions bring Hoary Redpolls to Montana, South Dakota, New England, and New York. Extreme southern records include Grant County, Oregon; Verdi, Nevada; St. Louis, Missouri; Ashton, West Virginia; and Middleton, Virginia. States with records for the Hoary Redpoll include Washington, Oregon, Idaho, Nevada, Montana, Wyoming, North Dakota, South Dakota, Nebraska, Minnesota, Iowa, Missouri, Wisconisin, Michigan, Illinois, Indiana, Ohio, Maine, New Hampshire, Vermont, Massachusetts, Rhode Island, Connecticut, New York, Pennsylvania, West Virginia, New Jersey, Delaware, Maryland, and Virginia.

Redpoll invasions often start rather late in the winter, with large numbers often not arriving until January. This is reflected in Hoary Redpoll occurrence as well. Typically, even in good winters none are seen until the latter half of December, and the bulk of sightings are usually from mid-January through early March. In better years, a few do sometimes linger into early April. Extreme dates since 1977 are October 10, 1991 (Whitefish Point, MI) and May 11, 1982 (Duluth, MN).

Best Bets

Probably the best region for Hoary Redpolls is northwestern Minnesota, but this area is difficult to access. Duluth and its environs, however, is probably almost as good and much easier to get to. Once you have reached the great white North, the most important factor in finding Hoary Redpolls is finding Common Redpolls. During an invasion winter, this is easy because redpolls seem to be everywhere there is suitable habitat (e.g., weedy fields, patches of alder or birch, and feeders). During noninvasion winters, the task is more difficult. The first step should be checking the Duluth Rare Bird Alert for any hot leads. If this fails, try finding feeders in Duluth and searching weedy fields or alder/birch stands nearby. Be sure to check Lester Park, which is between US 61 and MN 23 in northeastern Duluth.

Identification

The identification of a "classic" Hoary Redpoll in North America is probably not nearly as confounding as some believe. Any redpoll lacking streaking on the rump or undertail coverts is a Hoary, except some adult male Commons. In these birds, the rump is strongly washed with red, as is the chest, thus eliminating the Hoary.

The converse is not necessarily true. Some Hoaries can have fine streaks on the rump. Also, many Hoaries have a fine streak on the longest undertail coverts. Heavy streaking in either area, however, does eliminate Hoary. There is a variety of other marks that can be helpful. For a summary of these, see below. For a more detailed discussion and numerous photos, see the superb articles by Czaplak (1995) and Lansdown, et al. (1991). Also see Balch (1978) and Lewington, Alstrom, and Colston (1991).

Bill
- Hoary: Averages shorter bill with straight culmen.
- Common: Averages longer bill with curve to culmen.
- Note: There is much overlap in this feature, but it is useful in typical Hoaries.

Scapulars
- Hoary: Often has whitish-edged lower rear scapulars, creating contrasting whitish braces.
- Common: Almost always lacks above feature.
- Note: Probably a quite useful field mark.

Breast Color
- Hoary: Males with pale frosty pink, usually more limited in extent than Common.
- Common: Males with pink-red to intensely red chest.
- Note: Breast color intensifies in spring and is palest in fall.

Overall Color (including flank streaks, background underpart, and back colors).

- Hoary: Paler background color with wispy flank streaks.
- Common: Darker with more distinct flank streaks.

Finally, you need to consider subspecies. The usual subspecies of Hoary in the Lower 48 is *C. hornemanni exilipes,* and it is this nasty bird that looks so much like the Common Redpoll. If you are very fortunate, you will see the larger whiter nominate race, *C. hornemanni hornemanni,* which breeds in northern Greenland, Baffin Island, and Ellesmere Island. This bird will leave no doubt that it is a Hoary.

In summary, a classic Hoary Redpoll with an unmarked rump or undertail coverts can be easily identified. Intermediate birds are likely Hoaries but require more attention to whole body plumage, and many of these may not be identifiable with certainty.

(See color photo on page 496.)

Hoary Redpoll—*records of interest since 1977*[1]

LOCATION	NUMBERS SEEN	DATES SEEN
several locations in NJ		winter 93-94
Meadville, PA	1	3/19/94
King's Mountain, PA	3	3/94
Narvon, PA	1	3/1 to 3/14/94
Caernarvon Township, PA	1	3/1/94
Monterey, VA	1	2/27/94
Hockessin, DE	1	2/26/94
Dan's Rock, MD	1	2/5 to 2/28/94
Hanover Park, IL	1	2/2 to 2/6/94
Cordova, MD	1	1/24 to 2/5/94
Middleton, VA	1	1/23 to 1/31/94
Germantown, MD	18 (up to 4 in a day)	1/94 to 4/1/94
Columbia, MD	1	1/15/94
Hart-Miller Island, MD	1	1/4 to 1/9/94
Ashton, WV	1	12/21/93
Elkhorn Village, ID	1	2/3/93
Kootenai NWR, ID	few	winter 91-92
south of Troy, ID	2	2/16/92
Minot, ND[2]	32	12/29/91
Whitefish Point, MI[3]	1	10/10/91
9 mi NW of Bates, OR	1	1/19/90
Whitefish Point, MI[3]	1	10/30/88
Lock Haven, PA	2	1/29 to 3/22/87
Umatilla County, OR	1	1/21 to 2/5/86
Grant County, OR	1	winter 85-86
Walla Walla, WA	1	winter 85-86

LOCATION	NUMBERS SEEN	DATES SEEN
Verdi, NV	flock	winter 85-86
Sheridan, WY	2	11/7 to 11/9/84
Stone Harbor Point, NJ	1	1/27/82
Butler, PA	2	1/8/82
Eldora, IA	1	1/23 to 1/30/82
Gary, IN	1	2/6/82
Akron, OH	1	2/12 to 2/28/82
Lorrain, OH	2	2/15 to 2/28/82
Joliet, IL	1	1/30 to early 2/82
Blue Island, IL	1	2/24/82
Bridgeport, WA	1	2/11/82
Twisp, WA	1	1/20/82
Tonasket, WA	1	1/31/82
Kingston, PA	1	3/5/82
Slippery Rock, PA	1	until 4/11/82
Blue Island, IL	1	4/8/82
Duluth, MN[3]	1	5/11/82
Toledo, OH	1	3/22/82
Laurens, IA	1	3/2/82
Presque Isle, PA	1	12/20/80 to 1/10/81
Waterloo, IA	1	12/27/80 to 1/3/81
Wayne County, OH	1	2/19/81
Moose, WY	1	late 2/81
St. Louis, MO	1	3/6/78
Iowa City, IA	1	3/10/78
Davenport, IA	1	2/12/78
River Forest, IL	1	into 4/78
Chesterton, IN	5	2/14 to 3/18/78
Indianapolis, IN	1	4/12/78
Burtonsville, M	1	2/11 to 2/16/78
Baltimore, MD	1	1/29/78
Valparaiso, IN	1	2/25 to 3/2/78
Porter County, IN	3	2/18 to 19/78
Marion, IA	1	1/22 to 2/15/78
Lake Calumet, IL	1	1/15/78
Jacksonville, IL	1	2/78
Nampa, ID	1	winter 77-78
Chewelah, WA	1	winter 77-78
Sheridan, WY	1	winter 77-78
Jackson, WY	1	winter 77-78

[1]Most records are from states where this species is considered very rare in DeSante and Pyle (1986).

[2]Included because of unusually high count.

[3]Included on basis of unusual date.

Site Guide

In the pages that follow, you will find places to search for most of the birds covered in this book. Among these are many of the Lower 48's finest birding locales—legendary sites that are savored by even the most experienced birders. Visiting most of these hot spots will be a treat that you will remember for a long time, even if you don't see any of America's 100 Most Wanted Birds. A trip to the Salton Sea is guaranteed to inspire awe. A July or August journey to Delaware Bay will be spectacular, even without a White-winged Tern or Red-necked Stint.

Of course, since many of the locations we cover are famous, there are already bird-finding guides that cover most of them. We are not trying to reproduce the information given in quality local guides. Instead, we focus on providing advice relating specifically to America's 100 Most Wanted Birds. Also, to make your trip more enjoyable and easier to plan, we often make suggestions on where to stay and eat. For some particularly remote areas, we even tell you where you can get gas.

Read on and enjoy. Also, remember that some locations that are good for one species only are covered under that species' account.

—LEGEND—

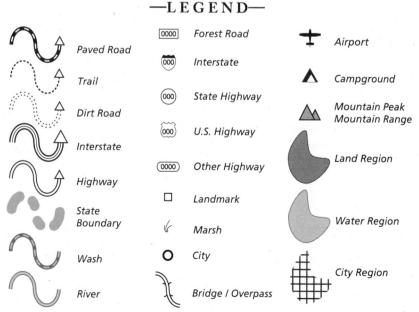

Paved Road	[0000] Forest Road	✈ Airport
Trail	(000) Interstate	▲ Campground
Dirt Road	(000) State Highway	Mountain Peak / Mountain Range
Interstate	(000) U.S. Highway	Land Region
Highway	(0000) Other Highway	
State Boundary	□ Landmark	Water Region
	Marsh	
Wash	O City	City Region
River	Bridge / Overpass	

Massachusetts

- ### NEWBURYPORT

One of the better places on the East Coast to find a Ruff is Newburyport, Massachusetts, where records are nearly annual in spring and late summer. To reach Newburyport, take I-95 north from the Boston area and exit at Route 113 (exit 57) east. In about a mile, turn right on High Street, then in about 1.5 miles, go left on State Street. Follow State Street to the end and turn right onto Water Street. After about a mile you will come to a long seawall on the left bordering Newburyport Harbor. There are several places to stop over the next couple miles, and each should be checked. Midtide offers the best viewing. Other rarities to keep an eye out for while birding at Newburyport include Little and Black-headed Gulls and the Curlew Sandpiper. Also, keep in mind that Ross' and Ivory Gulls have been recorded here, and the Bar-tailed Godwit has been seen a number of times. The most convienient place to stay in Newburyport is the Morrill Place Inn (508-462-2808).

For more information about birding Massachusetts, see *A Birder's Guide To Eastern Massachusetts,* published by the American Birding Association.

New York

- ### JAMAICA BAY NATIONAL WILDLIFE REFUGE

Jamaica Bay National Wildlife Refuge is an oasis in the middle of New York City and is well known for its concentrations of shorebirds. The Curlew Sandpiper is nearly annual there and such rarities as Little Stint, Red-necked Stint, and Sharp-tailed Sandpiper (two records each) have been found. Ruff has also been seen from time to time.

To reach Jamaica Bay from northern New Jersey, take exit 13 off the New Jersey Turnpike onto I-278 East. You will soon cross the Goethals Bridge onto Staten Island and, about 8 miles later, the Verrazano Bridge into Brooklyn. While crossing the Verrazano Bridge, stay in the left lane and exit at the Belt Parkway. Follow the Belt Parkway for about 14 miles to exit 17, where you will head south on Cross Bay Boulevard. Follow Cross Bay Boulevard for about 3 miles to the visitor center and parking area on the right. (If you are coming from Kennedy Airport, head west on the Belt Parkway for about 2 miles to Cross Bay Boulevard, then south on Cross Bay to the refuge.) Stop at the visitor center to check the sightings sheet and get an access permit to walk the trails. You may wish to walk the trail around West Pond which begins at the visitor center, but the East Pond (across the road) is usually better for shorebirds. High tide is best.

Motels in New York City are numerous but pricey. Of the motels near Kennedy Airport (which borders the refuge), Jade East Motel (718-723-5100) is the least expensive. Another option is to stay in the Newark, New Jersey, area. In Linden, the Benedict Motel (201-862-7700) and the Swan Motel (201-862-4500) are reasonably priced, as is the Motel 6 in Piscataway (908-981-9200).

New Jersey

• PEDRICKTOWN

The marsh along Oldman's Creek near Pedricktown is well known to area birders, primarily for its early spring gathering of Ruffs. Peak time for this spectacle is late March to late April, but note that numbers of Ruffs have declined here in recent years. To reach Pedricktown from the Philadelphia or Wilmington areas, take I-295 to exit 10, Center Square Road. Follow Center Square Road to the northwest for about a mile and turn left onto Pedricktown Road. The road sign has sometimes been missing here in the past, but Pedricktown Road will be the first crossroad you come to after leaving I-295. Follow Pedricktown Road for about a mile until it crosses the half-mile stretch of marsh along Oldman's Creek. Ruffs are most often seen here during a rising or falling tide. The most convienient and affordable motel is probably the Motel 6 in Wilmington, Delaware (302-571-1200).

Delaware

• DELAWARE REFUGES

In central Delaware, along the coast of Delaware Bay, lies one of North America's most impressive birding areas. During migration, huge numbers of shorebirds rest and refuel here. Mega-rarities seen here include Whiskered Tern, Northern Lapwing, and Eurasian Golden-Plover. Among *America's 100 Most Wanted Birds*, this region is tops for the Ruff, Curlew Sandpiper, and White-winged Tern (the latter has been seen eight out of the past nine years). The Sharp-tailed Sandpiper, Red-necked Stint, and Little Stint have also been seen.

This area consists of a complex of refuges (including Bombay Hook National Wildlife Refuge, Little Creek Wildlife Management Area, and Ted Harvey Conservation Area) plus a long stretch of beach with several access points. The patchwork of impoundments, marshes, and shoreline offers a wide variety of shorebird habitats. Note that lighting conditions will be best in the morning at Bombay Hook but better during the afternoon almost everywhere else.

Bombay Hook is the northernmost in this complex. To reach it, take US 13

Delaware's Shorebirding Hotspots

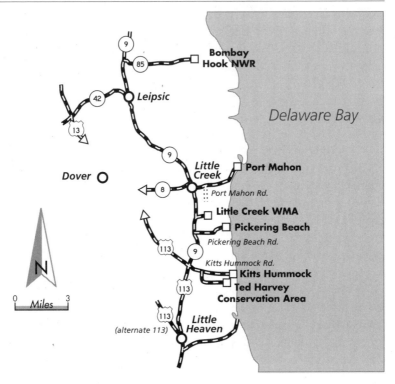

north from Dover for four 4 miles to DE 42. Turn right (east) on DE 42 and go 3.5 miles until it dead ends in the town of Leipsic. From there, go left (north) on DE 9 for 1.5 miles to Road 85 on the right where you will see a sign announcing the refuge. Turn right (east) on Road 85 and follow it 2.2 miles to the refuge entrance. After a heavy rain in spring, check any pools along this road for shorebirds. This is sometimes a good place for Ruffs. Actually, any farm road from the Bombay Hook area west to the Maryland line may be worth checking for Ruffs in flooded fields. Pay special attention to the large flocks of yellowlegs.

Before entering the wildlife drive, be sure to stop at the headquarters building to check the sightings sheet. Birders tend to log in observations here from all the Delaware refuges, not just those from Bombay Hook. The wildlife drive takes you past three impoundments: Raymond Pool, Shearness Pool, and Bear Swamp Pool. The Ruff is found regularly at all three, but Curlew Sandpiper is most often seen at Raymond or, at low tide, in the extensive mudflats opposite Shearness. The latter areas are also the best places to look for Red-necked Stint, which has been seen three times at the refuge. White-winged Tern has been seen several times as well.

After leaving Bombay Hook, turn left (south) on DE 9 and go 8.3 miles to the town of Little Creek. Here, take the only road to the left, Port Mahon Road, and follow it for 0.9 mile to a dirt road on the right (opposite some large oil storage tanks on the left). The dirt road will lead you to the huge northernmost impoundment of Little Creek Wildlife Management Area, popularly called the Port Mahon impoundment. From here you may want to walk about halfway out the dike along the northern edge of the impoundment. If water levels are right, this is an excellent shorebird area. Ruffs are seen here regularly, and Red-necked Stints and White-winged Terns have been seen here several times.

Turn right off the dirt road and continue east along Port Mahon Road for less than a mile until you reach the point where the tidal creek on your right empties into Delaware Bay. At low tide, the flats here can be packed with shorebirds, especially peeps and Short-billed Dowitchers, and close study is usually possible. From this spot, the Curlew Sandpiper is seen regularly, the Ruff is seen occasionally, and a Little Stint was seen in May 1979 and July 1982. Other rarities will no doubt be found here in the future.

To get to the main entrance of Little Creek Wildlife Management Area, return to the town of Little Creek and turn left (south) on DE 9. After 1.6 miles, you will reach the main entrance on the left. Follow the entrance road 0.8 mile to a small parking lot on the left opposite a boardwalk that leads to an observation tower. The tower is a good vantage point to scan for White-winged Terns, but most shorebirds will be frustratingly distant, so your chances of a rare one are slimmer than elsewhere. For a closer look at some of the shorebirds, continue on foot down the road past the parking area (the "No Entry" sign here refers to cars). If water levels are good, this can be excellent for shorebirds including Ruffs and Curlew Sandpipers.

To get to the south impoundment of Little Creek Wildlife Management Area, return to DE 9 and turn left (south). In 0.8 mile, turn left again on Pickering Beach Road and follow it 1.6 miles to the sign for Little Creek Wildlife Management Area on the left. From the parking area, the walk to the impoundment is 0.5 mile but is worthwhile. In recent years, this has been one of the best places for White-winged Tern, and the 1993 Whiskered Tern spent some of its time here. If you return to your car and continue down to the end of the road, you will reach Pickering Beach. Park along the shoulder before the end of the road and walk straight ahead to a narrow path in the dunes that brings you to Delaware Bay. At low tide the beach is usually packed with shorebirds, primarily peeps. The Curlew Sandpiper is seen here occasionally, and this may be a good place to look for Little or Red-necked Stints. This is a private community, so please obey the "No Trespassing" signs.

Return once again to DE 9 and turn left (south). In 2 miles, turn left at Kitts

Hummock Road and continue for another 2 miles to the sign for Ted Harvey Conservation Area on the right. Turn right (south) here and follow the dirt road 2 miles to the parking area at the end. (Note that at 0.5 mile you will come to a gate that is sometimes locked, and at 1 mile you will need to follow the main road sharply left where a smaller road continues straight.) The impoundment here is a traditional spot for Curlew Sandpipers and has hosted White-winged Terns several times, as well as the 1993 Whiskered Tern for much of its stay. When you return to Kitts Hummock Road, turn right and continue 1.1 miles to the end of the road at the town of Kitts Hummock. The beach here can be as good as at Pickering Beach but the birds are often more distant, so a rising, falling, or even high tide may be preferable. A Red-necked Stint was once seen here.

If you want to get a sandwich or a cold drink, the most convenient place is the Little Creek Deli and Market (open until 5 P.M. Sunday and 7 P.M. the rest of the week), which is located on Route 9, 0.4 mile south of Port Mahon Road. For an authentic Delmarva crab feast, Sambo's Tavern is a must. Sambo's is located on Front Street in Leipsic, 0.1 mile east of DE 9 and is open Monday to Saturday from 11 A.M. to 10:30 P.M., April to November. Along US 13 in Dover there is an abundance of eateries as well as motels. The most affordable motels are the Arborgate Inn, Dover (302-674-8002) and the Econo Lodge (302-678-8900).

Louisiana

Although there are relatively few records, Ruffs have been annual over the past five years in the rice fields of Vermilion Parish and vicinity. Especially productive is the Vincent Wildlife Refuge. To reach Vincent from Lafayette, head west on I-10 for about 17 miles to LA 35. Go south on LA 35 for about 13 miles to the refuge on the right (or, go about 5 miles north of Kaplan on LA 35). This area is also known for its concentrations of rails, most notably Yellow Rail and Black Rail. These rails can be seen as they are flushed by combines harvesting rice in late fall. For more information about birding in the Louisiana rice fields, see "Birds in the Rice Country of Southwest Louisiana," by Steven W. Cardiff and Gwen B. Smalley (*Birding* 21:232-240).

The nearest accommodations are in Lafayette. Knights Inn, Lafayette (317-447-5611) and Red Roof Inn (317-448-4671) are the most affordable.

Florida

- ## THE DRY TORTUGAS

Dry Tortugas National Park encompasses seven small coral keys: "dry" because they have no fresh water, and "tortugas" from the Spanish word for sea turtles, which nest here. Dominating the scene is Fort Jefferson, a monstrous hexagonal brick structure built on Garden Key in the mid-nineteenth century; it was designed to protect shipping in the Gulf, but was never actually used for that purpose. It served as a maximum-security prison for a while, and was later abandoned. In 1935, Franklin Roosevelt designated the fort, the other six keys, and surrounding waters a national monument; the area became a national park in 1992. The Dry Tortugas are legendary among birders for the incredible concentration of birds occurring during spring migration, when the islands are a resting place for exhausted trans-Gulf fliers. At the same time, thousands of Brown Noddies and Sooty Terns are breeding. In all, it is quite spectacular.

Among *America's 100 Most Wanted Birds*, the Tortugas are especially good for the Masked, Brown, and Red-footed Boobies, White-tailed Tropicbird, Black Noddy, West Indian Cave Swallow, and Shiny Cowbird. Other birds from this book have also been seen here, such as the Bahama Mockingbird, La Sagra's Flycatcher, Fork-tailed Flycatcher, and Bahama Swallow. Mega-rarities that have shown up on the Tortugas include the Ruddy Quail-Dove, Variegated Flycatcher, Yellow-faced Grassquit, and Tawny-shouldered Blackbird.

The Dry Tortugas can be visited only by private boat or seaplane. For most birders not on tours, this limits your access to the 16-acre Garden Key, upon

Florida—The Dry Tortugas

Fort Jefferson — North Coaling Dock — Water For Birds — Bush Key — moat — Boat Dock — Camping Area — South Coaling Dock — Fort Jefferson/Garden Key — Loggerhead Key — Middle Key — East Key — Hospital Key — Garden Key & Fort Jefferson — Bush Key — Long Key — N — Miles

which Fort Jefferson rests. This is not a horrible thing, however. Garden Key is superb for migrants, and is an excellent spot for the Shiny Cowbird (peak is late April to early June), West Indian Cave Swallow (February to June), and White-tailed Tropicbird (March to July). The cowbird is common, the swallow uncommon, and the tropicbird nearly annual. From Garden Key, one can also usually see the Masked Boobies standing on distant Hospital Key, which lies to the northeast. If one of the boobies actually flies around, you should be able to make a firm ID through a telescope. Separated from Garden Key by only a narrow channel is Bush Key, where 100,000 Sooty Terns and Brown Noddies nest in a stunning assemblage each spring. The good news is that 80,000 of those terns are Sooties, which leaves only 20,000 look-alike Browns to sort through for a Black. Fortunately, Black Noddies (along with many Browns) land not too infrequently on the old coaling docks of Garden Key (peak is late April to mid-May). Brown Boobies (year-round) can sometimes be seen standing on the lane markers near the fort.

The standard seaplane day visit (check Key West Seaplane Service at 305-294-6978) provides only about two hours on Garden Key, which isn't much time to look around. Campers can fly out to Garden Key and spend one or more nights, but must bring everything they need, including fresh water. Nonetheless, there are clean bathrooms and few mosquitoes, making a one- or two-day stay reasonably comfortable.

To maximize your chances at Tortugas specialties, however, the best route is via an organized tour. These spend about three days at the Tortugas and allow you access to much more than Garden Key. Standard features include a small-boat trip around Bush Key (for the Black Noddy and, if very lucky, a Red-footed Booby), a tour of the channel markers and boundary buoys (for Brown Booby), a close-up of Hospital Key and its Masked Boobies, and an outing to Loggerhead Key (more migrants and chances at Shiny Cowbird and West Indian Cave Swallow).

Tours are offered by Florida Nature Tours (407-273-4400), WINGS (602-749-1967), and Field Guides (512-327-4953). For an updated listing of Tortugas tours, check each year's January issue of *Winging It*.

- **EVERGLADES NATIONAL PARK**

Everglades National Park is undoubtedly one of the most famous birding places in the United States and, perhaps, the world. Here swamps and marshes attract a tremendous number of waders, alligators, tourists, and mosquitoes. The Everglades is also a good spot for several of *America's 100 Most Wanted Birds* including Greater Flamingos, Short-tailed Hawks, White-cheeked Pintails, and Shiny Cowbirds.

From Florida City, take Palm Drive (344th SW) west. From there, follow the well-marked signs until you reach the entrance booth for the national park. Here

Everglades National Park

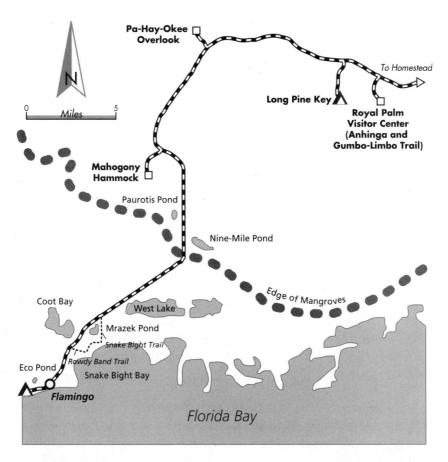

you will need to pay an entrance fee (good for one week), and you can pick up a park map.

If you are looking for White-cheeked Pintails, the first place to check is Paurotis Pond, roughly 24 miles past the entrance booth. After checking Paurotis Pond, drive 2 miles farther south and look at Nine Mile Pond. After scouring this water, continue approximately 4.5 miles farther to the much larger West Lake and look here. The next stop is Mrazek Pond about 1.5 miles later. After Mrazek Pond, take a peek at Coot Bay Pond yet another 0.5 mile toward Flamingo. Lastly, be sure to check the small but productive Eco Pond, which is just past Flamingo on the way to the campground. All of these stops are well marked by signs. Mid-December through late April is the best time to look for White-cheeked Pintails. Remember, there are only a few records of this species, and your chances are slim.

If you're looking for Shiny Cowbirds in the Everglades, try birding around Flamingo. The visitor center and the campground are the best spots. Shinies could be here any time of year, but from late April into early June is best.

For Short-tailed Hawks, try the hardwood woodland areas of the park. The area around Flamingo and between Flamingo and Nine Mile Pond are best. Short-tails occur year-round in the park but are most numerous from late October into February. The best time to look is when the Turkey Vultures first start to soar in the morning, but check the flocks of soaring vultures at any time of day. A good observation post is the platform at Eco Pond.

For those searching for Greater Flamingos, there are two main options. The cheaper but more strenuous choice is to walk the 1.6-mile (one-way) Snake Bight Trail, which begins on the main park road about 5 miles east of the Flamingo Visitor Center. The trail parallels a canal before arriving at a short boardwalk on the edge of the Snake Bight. Here, flamingos may be visible in the shallow water; get current reports from hotlines or park personnel. The trek out to Snake Bight is good for White-crowned Pigeons, and scanning at trail's end is good for shorebirds. This walk is also good for other winged creatures.

"Oh, you can walk to Snake Bight," a ranger at Flamingo once said to a group of visiting birders, "but you'll lose a quart of blood by the time you get back." Massive amounts of DEET proved him wrong—barely. Be forewarned: the mosquitoes in the Everglades can be ferocious. As a park brochure says, "Insect conditions are so severe during the summer months that visitation to the backcountry is minimal. . . ."

The second flamingo option is to go on a motorboat ride out of Flamingo. Several operators work out of the marina store there. They can take you to Snake Bight without fear of mosquitoes and go elsewhere in search of this exotic species as well. One knowledgeable guide we can recommend is Leon Howell. Call (941) 695-3101 for reservations and details. For experienced boater-birders, cruising among the scattered small keys in the bay might turn up some flamingos and would be a nice way to spend a day even if none were found. (Nautical charts are a must because of the bay's shallow water.) Canoes are available for rental at the Flamingo Visitor Center, whence it's a two-nautical-mile paddle to Snake Bight. Beware of sunburn, and check tide charts to make sure there's enough water for floating. Remember that a west wind will make the trip to Snake Bight easier, but the trip back harder. Yet another option is to bike to the end of Snake Bight Trail. Bikes can be rented at the visitor center.

The best time for Greater Flamingos in the Everglades is probably from July into February or March. Flamingos have been seen here, however, during other months as well.

The food and lodging at Flamingo is a bit limited, but there's not much else nearby. In Flamingo there is a hotel (941-695-3101) with nice but expensive accommodations. The cabins associated with the hotel are a bit more expensive but are even better, affording a good view of evening water bird roosts. For December and January be sure to make reservations well in advance. You can also camp in Flamingo, but in summer this is likely to be an itchy experience as the mosquito flocks are huge.

In Flamingo, food can be obtained between 6 A.M. and 9 P.M. at the marina store, which carries groceries, salads, sandwiches, and microwavable items. There is also a restaurant, but hours and season of operation have yet to be established after Hurricane Andrew.

If you want cheaper accommodations, try Homestead or Florida City, which are about an hour's drive from Flamingo. There are quite a few motels here; we recommend the Comfort Inn in Florida City. On the north side of Homestead, along US 1, there is a Denny's and a Dunkin' Donuts, both open all night.

- **HOMESTEAD AGRICULTURAL FIELDS**
A few miles south and west of Homestead, virtually on the way to Everglades National Park, lies one of the best spots for Shiny Cowbird.

To get there, take Palm Drive (344th Street SW) west from Florida City. Turn left at the "Robert is Here" fruit stand (worth a stop if you've got the time). Turn right at the next stop sign (you're still following signs for Everglades National Park). This road will take you past the well marked Benito Juarez Park (on your right) and C-111E Canal. Continue toward the Everglades until you reach the intersection with 212th (marked by a street sign). Turn around and head back the way you just came. The first road on your left is 209th Ave. (no street sign). Turn left (north) here. 209th Ave. goes one block and then ends at a "T" intersection. Within one block of this intersection, in all directions, is a great area for Shiny Cowbirds, which are year-round residents here. Bronzed Cowbirds have also been seen here and Brown-headeds are common (except in summer), so you'll have to use your identification skills. Then again, you may have a "three-cowbird" experience.

- **BRIGGS NATURE CENTER**
The Briggs Nature Center is along Rookery Bay south of Naples. Though good for many mangrove specialties, it is included in this book for its wintering flock of Shiny Cowbirds. To look for the cowbirds, try the feeders around the nature center building. The Briggs Nature Center is open Monday through Friday from 9 A.M. to 4:30 P.M. year-round. Additionally, from January through March, the nature center is open on Saturdays from 9 A.M. to 4:30 P.M. and on Sundays from 1 P.M. to 4:30 P.M. For further information call (813) 775-8569.

To get to the Briggs Nature Center, go south from Naples on US 41 to FL 951, and then go south on 951 about 3 miles to Shell Island Road and turn right. Take Shell Island Road to the nature center.

Florida's Atlantic Coastal Vagrant Traps

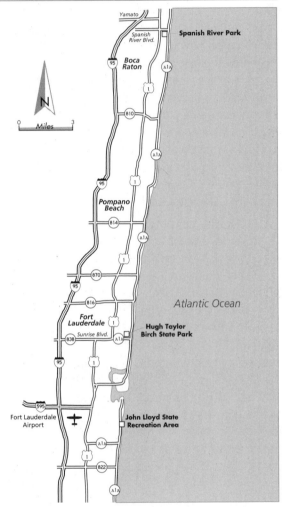

Most places to stay around the Briggs Nature Center are fairly expensive. Moderately priced rooms can be found, however, in Golden Gate, which is just a few miles up FL 951. Try the Best Western or the Comfort Inn. For food, Naples is just a few miles north on US 41.

- ### COASTAL PARKS: DANIA TO BOCA RATON

Parks along the heavily urbanized southern Florida Atlantic coast serve as oases to migrant birds. These parks are emerald islands amid a sea of gray concrete. On certain spring and fall days, the foliage is dripping with birds heading to or from their wintering grounds. During spring the occasional wanderer from the

Bahamas finds its way across the Straits of Florida to one of these parks. Formerly, the best park was probably Bill Baggs on Cape Florida. Since Hurricane Andrew, however, this is no longer so. Currently, the best spots are probably the three parks that lie between Dania and Boca Raton: John Lloyd State Recreation Area, Hugh Taylor Birch State Park, and Spanish River Park.

To get to John Lloyd take I-95 north from Miami or south from Fort Lauderdale to I-595. Take I-595 east to US 1, then go south to FL A1A. Follow A1A east to the entrance road for the park and turn left. There is an entrance fee. The best area to bird is the coppice-type habitat that surrounds a small lagoon. Trails through this area can be accessed from the first parking lots on your right.

To get to Birch State Park, take I-95 to Sunrise Boulevard (FL 838) and go east. When Sunrise splits into US 1 and FL A1A, continue on A1A east. Just before the ocean, you'll see the entrance to Birch State Park on your left. There is an entrance fee. After entering, you have the choice of parking in a lot to the right or following a one-way loop (approximately 2 miles) through the park. Native hardwood habitat in either area can be productive.

To get to Spanish River Park, take I-95 north from Fort Lauderdale past Boca Raton to Yamato. Go east on Yamato to US 1, then south on US 1 to Spanish River Boulevard. Go east on Spanish River Boulevard to FL A1A. Take A1A south to the park's entrance on your right. There is a rather steep (8 to 10 dollar) entrance fee. Bird the wooded parts of the park, focusing on the area south of the maintenance building and small campground.

Birds to look for in these parks include the La Sagra's Flycatcher, Bahama Mockingbird, Bananaquit, and Stripe-headed Tanager. Remember, finding any of these would require considerable luck. If you succeed, be sure to take detailed notes and call one of the local birders or hotlines. Mega-rarities that have occurred in these parks include the Thick-billed Vireo and Cuban (formerly Greater Antillean) Pewee.

There are a large number of places to stay along this stretch of coast. The neighborhoods are probably best around Spanish River and worst around John Lloyd. The Day's Inn in Boca Raton is a good choice, especially if you're birding Spanish River. Closer to Fort Lauderdale there are a great number of inexpensive selections along A1A, but many of these are of questionable cleanliness and/or quietness.

For food, there are also many options. One quick and inexpensive place we particularly like is the Sugar Shack Coffeehouse just over the bridge on Sunrise to the west of Birch State Park (2765 E. Sunrise Blvd., (954) 566-8605). The Sugar Shack opens at 7:30, giving you time to eat before Birch State Park opens at 8 A.M. It is also very convenient for lunch. Just west of the Sugar Shack is Studio One (2447 E. Sunrise Blvd., (954) 565-2502), which is a great place for a delicious, moderately priced dinner.

Florida: Short-tailed Hawk & Snail Kite (northern half)

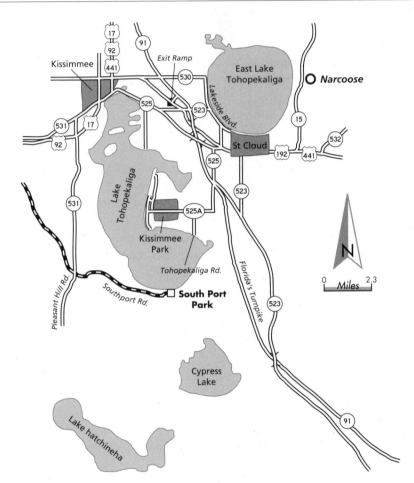

- CENTRAL FLORIDA: SHORT-TAILED HAWK AND SNAIL KITE

Polk and Osceola counties in central Florida hold some of the best areas for finding the Snail Kite and breeding Short-tailed Hawks. To bird these areas, a DeLorme *Florida Atlas and Gazeteer* is essential. Snail Kites are present year-round, but the Short-tailed Hawks are best looked for between March and September.

To look for Snail Kites, start on page 86 of the DeLorme atlas. East Lake Tohopekaliga and Lake Tohopekaliga are both excellent. At East Lake "Toho," try the south and east sides of the lake. Lakeside Boulevard offers several viewing opportunities as does the county park south of Narcoosee (the county park is not shown). At Lake "Toho" itself, try Red's Fish Camp in Kissimmee Park. Also look

Florida: Short-tailed Hawk & Snail Kite (southern half)

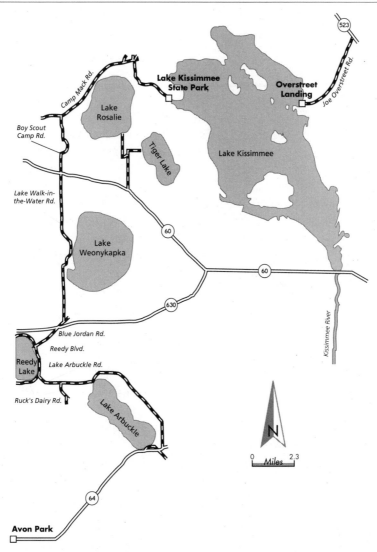

at the southern end of 525A (Tohopekaliga Road). Finally, at Lake Tohopekaliga check South Port Park at the lake's southern end. To get to this park take FL 531 to South Port Road (shown, but not labeled, on the DeLorme atlas) and follow this road east until it ends.

If you have no luck at the Toho lakes, or if you're coming from the south, try Lake Kissimmee for Snail Kite (see page 94 of the DeLorme atlas). One spot to search is labeled Camp Hammock on the DeLorme but is really called Overstreet

Landing. It lies at the end of Joe Overstreet Road. Another place to look is the south end of Lake Kissimmee where highway 60 crosses the Kissimmee River. If luck is still not with you, try the observation platform at Lake Kissimmee State Park. Any views from here will be distant. In general, give each spot 15 to 30 minutes. If you have not found a kite yet, they may well not be at that location at that time. You are probably best served by moving on to the next opportunity.

If Short-tailed Hawks are your heart's desire, the best place to check is near the southwest corner of Lake Walk-in-the-Water Road. Take this road north from Highway 630 until you reach Tiger Creek. Then, turn around and go back south 1 to 1.5 miles. Scan to the northeast between 8:30 and 10:00 A.M. Remember, the key is to be there when the first Turkey Vultures rise up on the morning thermals. Keep looking until no more vultures seem to be lifting off.

Another nearby Short-tailed Hawk spot lies between Reedy Lake and Lake Arbuckle. To get there, take Lake Arbuckle Road to Ruck's Dairy Road, which is a paved road that heads south (shown, but not labeled, on the Delorme atlas). Take Ruck's Dairy Road to the south until the public road ends near the dairy. Look to the north as the vultures head skyward.

Details on most of these areas will be included in the updated Lane/ABA.

Wisconsin

• MANITOWOC'S LITTLE GULLS

Manitowoc, Wisconsin, lies about one and one-half hours north of Milwaukee as the law-abiding citizen drives. For the past dozen or so years it has been summer home to a group of Little Gulls numbering between 2 and 18 birds. In a typical year they arrive during early to mid-May and are gone by early to mid-August. Seeing these birds does not require any long hikes, frigid temperatures, hordes of mosquitoes, or ridiculously early awakenings. Indeed, Manitowoc's Little Gulls can be seen any time of day, usually without too long a wait.

To get to the prime area, take I-43 north from Milwaukee to the most southerly Manitowoc exit. This exit is for WI 151, but is not clearly labeled as such. Go east on WI 151 until it ends at Washington and 8th, then go north on 8th until it crosses the bridge. At the first street past the bridge, Maritime Drive, go right. After about one-third mile, the dredge-spoil fill containment area will be visible. This marshy place is the best spot for the Little Gulls and is where they have nested. Just before reaching the containment area, you will have passed a marina, which is also worth checking for Little Gulls.

Local birders recommend staying at the Inn on Maritime Bay (414-682-7000), which is not very expensive and serves excellent meals.

Big Bend National Park

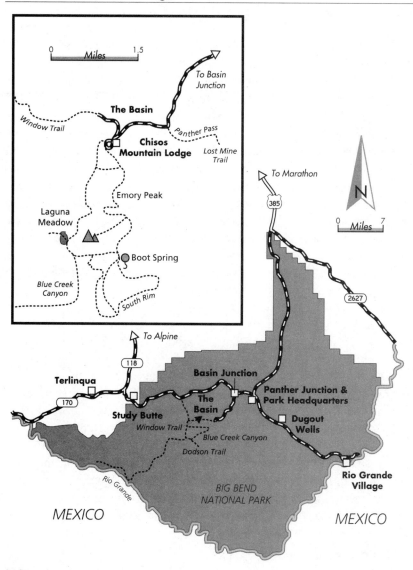

Texas

- ### BIG BEND NATIONAL PARK

    Big Bend National Park is a breathtaking and productive birding area located in West Texas. You may go there the first time for the Colima Warbler (peak is mid-April to mid-June) or Lucifer Hummingbird (peak is May to September), but you'll go back for the beauty and excellent all-around birding. You never know what you might see, for Big Bend has turned up such mega-rarities as the Black-vented Oriole, and Tufted Flycatcher.

Big Bend National Park harbors about 50 breeding female Lucifer Hummingbirds (Scott 1993). Some of the better sites during breeding season (April to June) include Blue Creek Canyon, on the southwest side of the Chisos Mountains, between Wilson Ranch and Laguna Meadow; and the lower end of Window Trail in Chisos Basin. From midsummer to mid-August, many Lucifers move higher into the mountains and can be found at such places as Boot Canyon. At all times, blooming century plants (*Agave havardiana*) are a most important food supply, and when in bloom these plants should be carefully scrutinized.

The Chisos Mountains also have great potential for the Aztec Thrush, even though there are only three records for here. Some of this is undoubtedly due to the poor coverage during the crucial July and August periods. Two of the Chisos' records are from Boot Canyon and the other is from the Lost Mine Trail. Try any moist wooded area above 5,000 feet.

For recent sightings of Lucifer Hummingbirds or other birds of interest, see the log at the visitor center at Panther Junction.

Lodging is to be had in Big Bend National Park or in the nearby towns. In the national park, there is a delightful lodge and a decent restaurant. Chisos Mountain Lodge is a bit more expensive than the average motel, but the location is magnificent and you are close to the trailheads. To make reservations call (915) 477-2291. Reservations for May should be made at least six months in advance; for June to August, call at least three months ahead. The restaurant in the basin opens at 7 A.M. Gas can be obtained nearby at Panther Junction between 7 A.M. and 7 P.M. For cheaper accommodations, try either the Big Bend Motor Inn/Mission Lodge (915-371-2218) in Study Butte or the Easter Egg Valley Motel (915-371-2254) in Terlingua. The drive to the basin from these spots is about 35 miles. For May reservations, call two months in advance. For the summer months, one month in advance should be fine. Unfortunately, there is no local restaurant that opens before 7 A.M. For gas, there is a Chevron in Study Butte that opens at 7 A.M.

- **LOWER RIO GRANDE VALLEY**

The lower Rio Grande valley contains a rather large group of prime birding spots located close to the Rio Grande from San Ygnacio to Brownsville. This stretch regularly turns up astonishing rarities from Mexico. Some of the better birds that have been seen here include Collared Forest Falcon, Masked Tityra, White-throated Robin, Crane Hawk, and Yellow-faced Grassquit. Several of *America's 100 Most Wanted Birds* are found solely or primarily in this area, hereafter called The Valley.

Birds found in both this book and The Valley include Masked Duck (year-round), Hook-billed Kite (year round), Northern Jacana (mostly November to April), Ferruginous Pygmy-Owl (year-round), Clay-colored Robin (year-round, peak is December to March), Tropical Parula (year-round, winter is best), Blue Bunting (late December to mid-February), and White-collared Seedeater (year-round, December to May is best). The kite, pygmy-owl, robin, parula, and seedeater are all regulars; the others tend to occur in less predictable spurts. There are several areas worth investigating. Good directions to each are covered in Holt (1992) and Kutac (1989) and will not be repeated here. For general navigation purposes we also recommend *The Roads of Texas,* published by Shearer Publishing (800-458-3808) and the Rand McNally maps for McAllen and Brownsville.

Near Brownsville the Sabal Palm Sanctuary is an excellent place for such rarities as the Gray-crowned Yellowthroat and Crimson-collared Grosbeak. The woodlands here would not be a bad spot to look for the Tropical Parula and Clay-colored Robin. There are also records from here of Ferruginous Pygmy-Owl and Hook-billed Kite.

Southeast of McAllen lies Santa Ana National Wildlife Refuge, one of the most famous birding spots in the United States. It has earned this fame by providing birders with their best chance at several southern Texas specialties. Santa Ana is one of the more regular places for the Clay-colored Robin, Tropical Parula, Hook-billed Kite, Masked Duck, and Northern Jacana. Stunning rarities such as Yellow-faced Grassquit, Golden-crowned Warbler, Gray-crowned Yellowthroat, and Crane Hawk have also turned up here. For the Masked Duck and the Jacana, the heavily vegetated Willow, Pintail, and Cattail Lakes are worth checking. Remember: these

Lower Rio Grande Valley

San Ygnacio

Zapata

Falcon Lake

83

Rio Grande

Falcon Dam

Salineño

Santa Margarita Ranch

Bentsen-Rio Grande Valley State Park

Anzalduas County Park

Santa Ana NWR

McAllen

Harlingen

South Padre Island

Brownsville

Sabal Palm Sanctuary

Gulf of Mexico

MEXICO

N

0   Miles   30

281

77

77

281

83

species are less than annual here. For the robin, the kite, and the parula, any of the wooded areas could be productive. Most records of woodland specialties come from near Willow Lake and Pintail Lake. An especially good spot is the site of the old manager's house. Check the log in the visitor center for any recent sightings.

Southwest of McAllen lies Bentsen-Rio Grande Valley State Park, hereafter known as Bentsen State Park. Bentsen is as good and as famous as Santa Ana. It is one of the more regular places for Clay-colored Robin, Tropical Parula, Hook-billed Kite, and Blue Bunting. The parula, robin, and kite are annual or nearly so; the bunting is somewhat rarer. More spectacular rarities that have been seen in Bentsen include the Collared Forest Falcon and Masked Tityra. There are several places to bird in Bentsen. The trailer loop is full of trailers and feeders during winter. It is at these feeders that many of North America's Blue Buntings have been found. The water dishes put out by the loop's denizens are also attractive to Clay-colored Robins. Finally, the trailer loop is a great place to get information (and rumors) about what's in the park and elsewhere in The Valley. Tropical Parulas might be found anywhere there are trees and are often with small bird parties. Check the trees around the trailer loop, the dump road, and along the trail to the Rio Grande. Hook-bills are best looked for by walking the Rio Grande trail. Another way to look for Hook-bills is to look over the woods from the dike road just outside Bentsen. To get to this road, leave the park and take the first left.

Between Bentsen State Park and the Santa Ana refuge is Anzalduas County Park. This park is not as good as Bentsen or Santa Ana, but has had Hook-billed Kites, Tropical Parulas, and Clay-colored Robins. For the parula and the robin, check the large picnic area. For the kites, scan over the woods in midmorning.

Heading farther upriver you'll come to Santa Margarita Ranch and Salineño. The Rio Grande here is currently the best bet for wild Muscovy Duck. The recommended strategy is to keep a careful eye along the river near dusk and dawn. At this time, Muscovies can be seen, with a little luck and vigilance, flying up or down river. These ducks are seen at other times as well but with a little less regularity. Keep in mind that not all Muscovies here are "wild." You need to be alert for plumage irregularities. Salineño and Santa Margarita Ranch are also decent places to see the Hook-billed Kite. Keep an eye for soaring birds, especially in midmorning. Finally, no discussion of this area would be complete without mentioning the feeders at Salineño. They have not been particularly productive for the birds in this book, but they are good for birding in general and are an excellent place during winter to see the Brown Jay and Audubon's Oriole. See Holt (1992) for details.

Heading downstream from Salineño and Santa Margarita Ranch, you will come to Falcon Dam. The woods downstream from the dam are the famed place for the Ferruginous Pygmy-Owl. To get to the best owl area, park at the spillway as described in Holt (1992). Then, on foot, follow the gravel road that parallels the river downstream. At the point where this road bends sharply to the left, a trail will head off into the mesquite woodland straight ahead. You will also notice an old clothesline pole at this spot. Start your search here and then follow the trail through the woods (still paralleling the river). After a short (0.25 to 0.5 mile) walk, you will come to an opening that was, rumor has it, a Girl Scout camp. This is about as far as you can go. The entire walk through the woods has good Ferruginous Pygmy-Owl potential, and the owls are probably always here. If you are frustrated in your first attempts, remember that many a fine birder has had to try 10 or 20 times before finding this elusive little predator.

The river below Falcon Dam is not a bad place to look for Muscovy Ducks. The same caveats mentioned for Salineño and Santa Margarita apply here. The Rio Grande immediately below the dam is heavily vegetated and has hosted Northern Jacanas in the past.

The usual end point for visits to The Valley is San Ygnacio, known among birders as the home of the seedeaters. For details, see the White-collared Seedeater account. Remember, early morning and late afternoon are best.

When birding the valley, we usually stay in McAllen, which has a wide range of amenities and is centrally located. The best hotel value in town is probably the Microtel (210-630-2727). There is also a Motel 6, which is unfortunately particularly noisy and grungy. Other offerings in town include a Best Western (210-630-3333) and a La Quinta (210-687-1101). An early breakfast can be obtained at the Taco Cabana (fast food, open 24 hours) on 10th Street or the Denny's, also on 10th. For dinner, we recommend the Bistro Cafe on 10th or the Lotus Inn, a good Chinese restaurant, also on 10th Street.

If you want to stay upriver, there is a Best Western in Zapata, not far from assorted White-collared Seedeater locations. If you wish to stay overnight downstream from McAllen, there are a number of hotels and restaurants in Brownsville and Harlingen, including Motel 6 and a couple of Best Westerns. There is a Denny's near the freeway in Harlingen (210-423-4117), and a Taco Cabana in Brownsville near US 77/83 and Boca Chica (210-541-9699).

Arizona

For many of these locations, excellent directions are already given in McMillon (1996) and the Tucson Audubon Society (1995) and Lane (1986) guides. For such locales, we will defer to their instructions.

Southeastern Arizona Overview

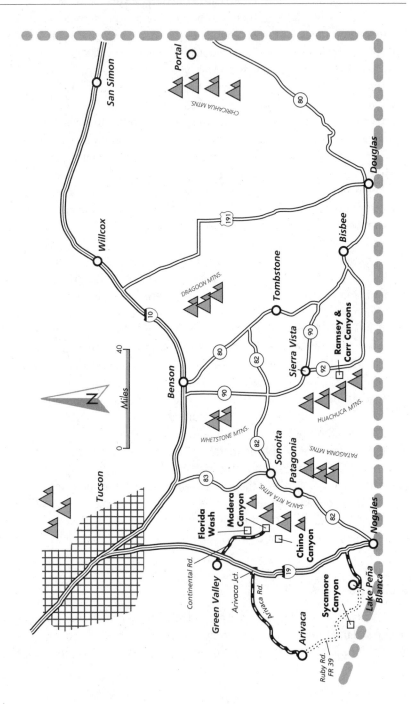

- ### SYCAMORE CANYON

Sycamore Canyon has been called the birder's Bataan. Indeed, it is one of the longest 5-mile hikes that a birder is likely to encounter in the Lower 48. There are frequent stream crossings (difficulty varies with current water level), oppressive heat, liberally strewn boulders, and no trail. In spite of these obstacles (or maybe because of them), Sycamore Canyon is one of the most exciting places to bird in the United States. A Fan-tailed Warbler was once found here, and who knows what other rarities have passed through. Sycamore Canyon is also one of the best places for Five-striped Sparrow, Elegant Trogon, and Montezuma Quail.

Among *America's 100 Most Wanted Birds*, this canyon is known for Rose-throated Becards and Black-capped Gnatcatchers. To find the becards, you need to find the sycamores. These are located in scattered patches along the first 3 miles or so of canyon floor. An especially good area is around and just below Sycamore Canyon's juncture with Peñasco Canyon. Peñasco Canyon is a sizable sycamore-lined canyon that comes in from your left about 2 miles down from the trailhead. During most years, becards are found in this area.

For Black-capped Gnatcatchers, you need to go farther. The target habitat has desert slopes with ocotillo and saguaro that descend almost all the way to canyon bottom. Here the intermittent stream is still nourishing enough to support the all important hackberry, mesquite, and sycamore habitat. Unfortunately, no Black-caps have been seen here since 1987, but the habitat apparently remains good. This is also the place to search for Five-striped Sparrows, and, during the spring of 1994, a Rufous-capped Warbler spent months singing in this part of the canyon.

The nearest lodging is in Nogales, which is approximately 40 minutes away. Because the drive is so long, many people camp at the parking area (for directions, see McMillon 1996 or Tucson Audubon Society 1995). The nearest food and water are at Lake Peña Blanca, about 20 minutes away. When birding Sycamore Canyon, your greatest enemy will be heat. Get as early a start as possible and bring water—lots of water. Two gallons per person would probably not be overkill on a day with a temperature over 100 degrees.

- ### MADERA CANYON

Madera Canyon is probably best known for its hummingbirds, owls, and Elegant Trogons. However, most of Arizona's specialties can be found here or in nearby Florida Wash. Among America's 100 Most Wanted Birds Madera has hosted the Berylline Hummingbird, Plain-capped Starthroat, Violet-crowned Hummingbird, White-eared Hummingbird, Lucifer Hummingbird, Eared Trogon, Buff-breasted Flycatcher, and Aztec Thrush. Furthermore, Florida Wash has been *the* place the Buff-collared Nightjar (though none were found in 1995).

If you are searching for hummingbirds, you should note that none of America's most wanted hummers are annual here, but during late summer and autumn there is often one or more of these species about. There are two groups of feeders to check. The first is at Santa Rita Lodge, the second is about a mile farther up at the Pallisport Gift Shop. Both can be good. White-eared Hummingbirds are also sometimes found in the coniferous woodlands above the upper parking lot.

Madera Canyon also has more records (nine) of Aztec Thrush (late May to late October) than any other locale. This is probably due in part to the intense coverage here. Likewise, most records at Madera come from the vicinity (within 0.5 mile) of the heavily birded upper parking lot, which is where most birders tread. Suitable habitat is also present elsewhere along the upper trails and could potentially yield this species.

Lodging is available at the Santa Rita Lodge, which has several fine cabins (with kitchens) for rent. If you wish to rent a cabin in April or May, call during the preceding October. For rentals between June and August, call by January or February (602-625-8746). There is also a bed-and-breakfast a short way up the canyon (602-625-2908). The nearest available food is in Green Valley, 13 miles away, where there is a variety of options, including the fast kind. The nearest gas station is also in Green Valley. Hotel rooms can be found at Green Valley's Quality Inn.

- ### CHINO CANYON

Chino Canyon lies on the northwest side of the Santa Rita Mountains. Its birding fame is due to the Five-striped Sparrows and Black-capped Gnatcatchers that have bred there. To access this area, carefully follow the directions in the Tucson Audubon Society guide (1995). Park and start birding at the oak tree near the base of Elephant Head. It was at this spot that Black-capped Gnatcatchers were last seen in 1991. After birding here, work your way up the canyon, checking areas with hackberries. These gnatcatchers often respond quite nicely to Ferruginous Pygmy-Owl imitations, so you might want to give this a try. A birder in 1992 tried this method and failed to lure in any Black-capped Gnatcatchers, but did have a Ferruginous Pygmy-Owl.

Recommended lodging is in Green Valley (see Madera Canyon). The nearest food also is in Green Valley or Nogales. Both places have several fast-food opportunities. Chino Canyon can heat up like a blast furnace during summer, so bird early and bring plenty of water.

- ### PATAGONIA

Birding around Patagonia focuses around Sonoita Creek, which winds through the town itself and then heads south past the famed Patagonia rest stop, through Circle Z Ranch, and into Lake Patagonia. The creek supports a wonderful riparian habitat replete with the usual southeastern Arizona riparian species. The Patagonia area is the best place in the Lower 48 for Violet-crowned Hummingbirds (late February to late October) and Rose-throated Becards (mid-May to early September). It has also entertained such rarities as the Rufous-backed Robin (mid-winter), Plain-capped Starthroat (summer), Ruddy Ground-Dove (winter), Crescent-chested Warbler, Cinnamon Hummingbird, Blue Mockingbird, and Yellow Grosbeak.

If you are searching for Violet-crowned and other hummingbirds, the premier location in Patagonia is the feeders of the Patons. Here, Violet-crowns can be found during almost any day from April through September and are often present from late February into early November. Other hummingbird greats that have visited these feeders include Plain-capped Starthroat and Cinnamon Hummingbird. Violet-crowns can also be found, not infrequently, along the Sonoita Creek Nature Conservancy Sanctuary's trails. To get to the Patons' house, follow Pennsylvania Avenue toward the Sonoita Creek Nature Conservancy Sanctuary. The house is just after a stream crossing and is the last residence on your left before the sanctuary itself. To get to the sanctuary, follow the directions in the McMillon 1996 or Lane or Tucson Audubon Society guides.

To bird the Patons' feeders, park outside the fence without blocking the gate or the road. After parking and entering through the gate, go to your right and walk around to the back of the house, where there are a number of hummingbird

Arizona—Patagonia area

To Sonoita

Patagonia 82

The Nature Conservancy Preserve

Patons' House

Harshaw Rd.

To San Rafael Valley

N

0 Miles 1

Circla Z Ranch

Sonoita Creek

Patagonia Rest Stop

Patagonia Lake State Park

82

To Nogales

Patons' House   Sonoita Creek

Pennsylvania Ave.

Sonoita Ave.

Naulge Ave.

McKeown Ave.

4th Ave.   3rd Ave.

Smelter Alley   Duquesne Ave.

Downtown Patagonia

feeders and chairs (the chairs are for human use). There is a small donation can as you enter the feeder area. Please be polite and quiet. Bad behavior has prevented access to other private feeders, and it would be very sad if that happened at this magnificent place. A donation wouldn't be a bad idea either—the Patons use POUNDS of sugar a day.

If you are searching for Rose-throated Becards, the place for you is the Patagonia Rest Stop of the famed "Patagonia rest stop effect." This term was coined to describe the cascade of rarities that often occurs when birders flood a previously little-known area to see a rare bird. In the case of the Patagonia rest stop, the instigating rarity was the nesting becards themselves. Finds since then have included Violet-crowned Hummingbirds (nesting), Five-striped Sparrow, Yellow Grosbeak, and Gray Silky-Flycatcher.

To get to the rest stop, head south from Patagonia on AZ 82 for about four miles. The rest stop will be on your left (east). Park at the northern end of the rest area and then, on foot, carefully cross the highway. The stream just across the fence is Sonoita Creek. To look for becards walk north, listen for their peculiar squeaky call, and look for their large hanging nests. Often an active nest is visible, allowing birders to easily watch the birds without disturbing them. Please do not tape these birds. Unlike some birds (such as the famous Florida Wash Buff-collared Nightjars), these becards are quite tape sensitive. In the past, taping has likely been a significant factor in nest abandonment by these birds.

Another spot for Rose-throated Becards near Patagonia is the Circle Z Ranch, which owns much of the tasty riparian and sycamore growth along Sonoita Creek. In fact, when you are birding at the rest stop, you are looking into Circle Z property. The ranch is open to birders but only if they stay there, and the accommodations are a bit expensive (but include meals). The most limiting factor is that the ranch is open only from October until mid-May. For details, call (602) 287-2091

There are several places to eat in Patagonia. A small grocery store at the corner of AZ 82 and First Street has many essentials. It's open from 7 A.M. to 8 P.M. The Ovens of Patagonia Bakery, a couple of doors down, has great croissants, bread, and sweets. It's open from 8 A.M. to 3 P.M., Saturdays and Sundays only, and the Ovens are closed during the entire month of September. Near the post office and family health center, the Home Plate provides an excellent traditional (i.e., bacon, eggs, and pancakes) breakfast as well as great burgers later in the day. It's open from 7 A.M. to 8 P.M., except on Sundays, when the closing time is 3 p.m. The gas station is next to the grocery store and is open until 6 p.m.

The Stage Stop Motel in town has adequate accommodations. Another option is to drive in from Tucson, just over an hour away. For a more relaxing approach try the bed-and-breakfast run by Regina Medley. Call (602) 394-2732.

- **RAMSEY AND CARR CANYONS**

Ramsey and Carr Canyons are two adjacent furrows in the eastern slope of the Huachuca Mountains. They offer a combination of great beauty and good birding. Some of the rarities seen in these canyons include the Flame-colored Tanager, Aztec Thrush, Eared Trogon, and Berylline Hummingbird. For the White-eared Hummingbird (peak is mid-May to mid-September), Eared Trogon (currently year-round), and Buff-breasted Flycatcher (early April to early September), these canyons are the best spot in the United States.

To look for hummingbirds, including the White-eared, you will want to go to the Ramsey Canyon Nature Conservancy visitor center and the nearby Ramsey Canyon Inn (which is a bed-and-breakfast). Both of these have clusters of excellent hummingbird feeders. White-eared Hummingbirds likely have nested in this area every year since 1989, and a Berylline sat on a nest just outside the visitor center door in 1991. Violet-crowned Hummingbirds are a nearly annual visitor, and there are at least five Lucifer records as well.

To get to the visitor center, just follow the directions in the Lane or Tucson

Arizona—Ramsey and Carr Canyons

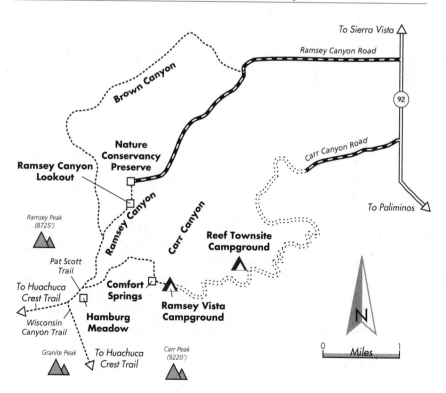

Audubon Society guides. The Nature Conservancy feeders are visible from the parking lot, and the Ramsey Canyon Inn is just a short walk back down the entrance road. Several rules apply to visiting this area: Parking is limited to the small lot at the visitor center (unless you are staying at the inn or renting one of the Conservancy cabins). This parking area is open only from 8 A.M. to 5 P.M. Reservations must be made on weekends and holidays and are recommended for weekdays too. Viewing the inn's feeders is not a problem as long as you stay on the road (fine views are easily had). Birding the trails on The Nature Conservancy property requires a pass, easily obtainable from the visitor center.

For Buff-breasted Flycatchers, you will want to go into Carr Canyon. The best strategy is to drive to the Ramsey Vista campground at the end of Carr Canyon Road and park. Look for Buff-breasts (early April to early September) around this campground first. If you have no luck here, bird your way down to the lower campground (Reef Townsite) about 1 mile downhill and look there as well. Several Buff-breasts are usually present at each campground, and sometimes they are in between as well.

To get to Carr Canyon from Sierra Vista, take AZ 90 to AZ 92 and go 6.9 miles south. Then turn right (west) on Carr Canyon Road and wind all the way up hill (about 30-minute drive) to the road's end, which is also the upper campground.

The famous Ramsey Canyon Eared Trogons spend much of their time in an area that can be reached from either the end of Carr Canyon Road or from the Nature Conservancy visitor center. This most interesting and lovely spot lies in Ramsey Canyon above the "Ramsey Lookout" and below the Huachuca Crest Trail. To get there from Carr Canyon, take the trail out of the uppermost campground. This trail will fork after a short distance. At this point, take the branch to Comfort Springs, not Miller Peak. The walk to Ramsey Canyon will go past the obscure Comfort Springs and is about 2.5 miles long. The birding along the way can be quite good. Indeed, the first seep you cross has had both Eared Trogon and Aztec Thrush, and the old burn you go through along the way has played host to Berylline and White-eared Hummingbirds. Once this trail descends into Ramsey Canyon and meets the trail there, you'll be near Hamburg Meadow, which is approximately halfway between the Ramsey Canyon Visitor Center and the Huachuca Crest Trail. Eared Trogons could be either uphill or downhill, but most sightings have been below this point. To reach this area from the visitor center, obtain the proper trail permit from The Nature Conservancy personnel and hike uphill. The Ramsey Canyon Lookout will be reached in only a mile or so, but the hike is steep. The distance from the parking lot to the juncture with the Comfort Springs Trail is about 2.5 miles. The hike to the crest, on the Huachuca Crest Trail, is about 5 miles one way. When looking for Eared Trogons, be circumspect since they are shy birds. Also, keep an eye out for Aztec Thrush because this is excellent habitat for this species (even though there is only one verified record from here).

For lodging when birding Carr and Ramsey canyons, there are several choices. One of the most relaxing and enjoyable options is to stay at the cabins on the Nature Conservancy sanctuary itself. These cabins have kitchens and are very popular. Reservations should be made six months to one year in advance by calling (602) 378-2785. The Ramsey Canyon Inn is another popular choice. Reservations here should be made one to two months in advance by calling (602) 378-3010. For those unable to get reservations here, a wide variety of motels, including a Motel 6, is available about 20 minutes away in Sierra Vista.

A fine restaurant nearby is the Mesquite Tree, at the corner of AZ 92 and

Arizona—Portal, NE Chiricahua Mountains

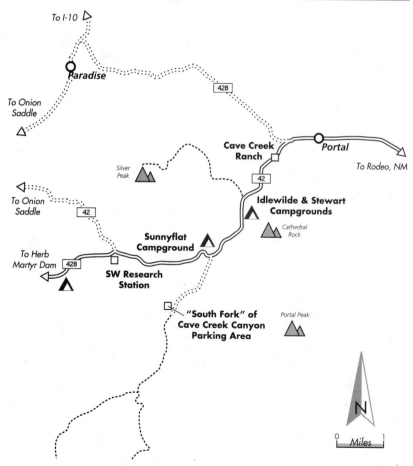

Carr Canyon Road (about a ten-minute drive). For cheaper but fun fare, there is a Po' Folks in town, and for those very early meals, there is a Denny's as well.

- **PORTAL**

The Portal area is where the riparian cottonwood woodland of Cave Creek fades into arid grassland and mesquite scrub. The feeders here are the best in Arizona for Lucifer Hummingbird (early April to mid-May and late July into early October) and have attracted the other rare Arizona hummers as well. There are three main feeder groups. The best is at the Spoffords', just out of town. From the Portal store in Portal, drive 1.1 miles west on FR 42 to Sierra Linda Ranch Road. Turn left onto this dirt road (on your right there will be a rectangular wooden arch over a drive). Go 0.3 mile to the Spoffords' yard, which will be on your left. Park outside the gate and walk through the yard as indicated by the signs. Anything larger than a van should *not* be driven down Sierra Linda Ranch Road. Visitors should not come before 7:30 A.M. and should not stay later than 5:30 P.M.

Nearby is Cave Creek Ranch, which is actually a collection of cabins for rent. It is also a place with many hummingbird feeders, and it once played host to a Blue Mockingbird. Sometimes birders who are not staying here are granted permission to bird the grounds. For permission or for information on lodging, call (602) 558-2334. At a higher elevation, in the oak woodland, is the Southwestern Research Station. The feeders here have had Berylline and White-eared Hummingbirds, and if you're lucky, you may be able to rent a room (comes with meals). Call (602) 558-2396.

In addition to the places above, lodging can be had in Portal itself at the Portal Store. The store, besides having some basic supplies, is also a restaurant and a bed-and-breakfast. Meals are served from 7:30 A.M. to 7 P.M. For more information call (602) 558-2223.

The nearest gas is in Rodeo, New Mexico (about 7 miles away), and is available from 9 A.M. to 6 P.M., New Mexico time.

California

- **LOWER KLAMATH NATIONAL WILDLIFE REFUGES**

The Lower Klamath National WIldlife Refuges are a string of ponds, lakes, and marshes along the Klamath River near the Oregon/California border. These refuges are famous for spectacular gatherings of waterfowl and tremendous concentrations of raptors. Among *America's 100 Most Wanted Birds*, the Lower Klamath National Wildlife Refuges are known for Emperor Geese. This species has been reported here during at least 9 of the last 18 falls.

Usually, the Emperor Geese occur with the swarms of "Cackling" Canada or

California—Tule Lake National Wildlife Refuges

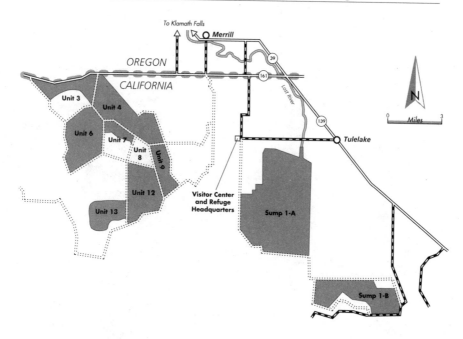

White-fronted Geese that migrate through the Klamath Basin. The best refuge of the group for Emperors is the Tule Lake National Wildlife Refuge (see map). The best time is the latter half of October and the first half of November. The helpful staff at the NWR headquarters should be able to tell you where the Cacklers and White-fronts are, and they may know of an Emperor if there is one around. For information about the refuges, call the headquarters at (916) 667-2231.

The Klamath Basin is a long way from any major city. The nearest airport is at Klamath Falls, Oregon, about 25 miles from Tule Lake. Klamath Falls has a Motel 6 and a Comfort Inn among other standard motel chains. Accommodations can also be found closer to the refuge at the town of Tulelake, itself. The two hotels there are the Park Motel (916-667-2913) and the Ellis Motel (phone 916-667-5242). The Ellis has several rooms with kitchens, but these need to be reserved about a year in advance. Their regular rooms should be reserved five to six months ahead of time. For the Park Motel, make reservations about three months in advance. Try the Bakery in Tulelake for breakfast (opens at 6 A.M.), and for all meals, try Captain Jack's Stronghold, which is about 7 miles south (916-664-5466). For more information on general birding in this area, see Westrich and Westrich (1991).

California—Point Reyes

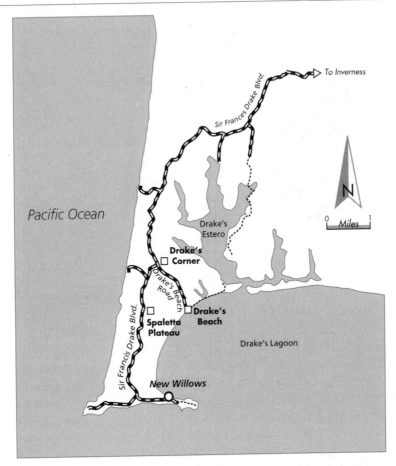

• POINT REYES

Point Reyes is one of the most awe-inspiring vagrant traps in North America. On the Point, birds from Asia meet birds from eastern North America. Some of the vagrant highlights include Eurasian Dotterel, Brown Shrike, Eurasian Skylark, Cerulean Warbler, and Gray-cheeked Thrush.

Though many of the species in *America's 100 Most Wanted Birds* have been seen at Point Reyes, the Point is in the "Site Guide" primarily for Pacific Golden-Plover. This species usually arrives at Point Reyes around late August and departs by the end of April. It can be found in any of the pastures and fields of outer Point Reyes, but the Spaletta Plateau and Drake's Corner seem to be best. These field areas can also harbor the occasional Red-throated Pipit, which should be looked for in late September and October.

To get to the outer Point, take CA 1 to Point Reyes Station and then go southwest on Sir Francis Drake Boulevard. Follow Sir Francis Drake Boulevard through Inverness until it intersects Drake's Beach Road (roughly 15 miles from Point Reyes Station). This intersection is known as Drake's Corner. Check the fields here and along Drake's Beach Road.

To reach the Spaletta Plateau, continue on Sir Francis Drake Boulevard past Drake's Corner. In a couple of miles you will see a dairy marked Spaletta Ranch. Go another 0.8 mile and you will see a pasture on your left with a track running through it. Park along the road here, but make sure you're well off the road and not blocking the track. Walk onto the field to look for golden-plovers. Please do not interfere with farm workers and the cows.

For a good discussion of how to bird Point Reyes in general, see Richmond (1985).

For food while on the Point, try the Drake's Beach Cafe (415-669-1297) at the end of Drake's Beach Road. Hours here are variable. The nearest gas is at Point Reyes Station and Inverness. San Francisco, which is about an hour away, has a huge variety of lodging choices. In Mill Valley, about 20 minutes closer, there is a Holiday Inn Express. If you wish to stay close to Point Reyes, most of the options are fairly expensive. For more details contact the West Marin Chamber of Commerce (415-663-9232) or the Inns of Marin (800-887-2880).

• SAN FRANCISCO'S TUFTED DUCKS

Over the past decade, no place has been as reliable for Tufted Ducks as the lakes and ponds around San Francisco. Some of the better locations include Lake Merced, Golden Gate Park, the Sutro Baths, and Lake Merritt. A diligent winter (late November to early March) search through the scaups at these ponds has a fair likelihood of revealing a Tufted Duck. Directions to each of these locations are given below, but obtaining a good San Francisco map would be a good idea. A call to the San Francisco area rare bird alerts may also prove helpful.

To get to Lake Merced, take I-280 or CA 1 to the southern end of San Francisco and exit at John Daly Boulevard. Take the boulevard west to Lake Merced Boulevard and go north about 0.5 mile to John Muir Drive. Make a left onto John Muir Drive. From this road, you will be able to scan the southwest portion of the lake. Then follow John Muir Drive until it ends at CA 35/Skyline Boulevard. From here go right (north) to Harding Road and make another right. Harding Road will take you into the park and allow you to scan much of the rest of the lake (with a short stroll). After checking here, take Harding Drive back to CA 35/Skyline Boulevard and turn right (north). Follow this road about 0.5 mile to Lake Merced Boulevard and turn right. By following Lake Merced Boulevard east and then south, you will have several more opportunities to scan the lake, and then you will be back at John Daly Boulevard.

California—Bay Area Tufted Ducks

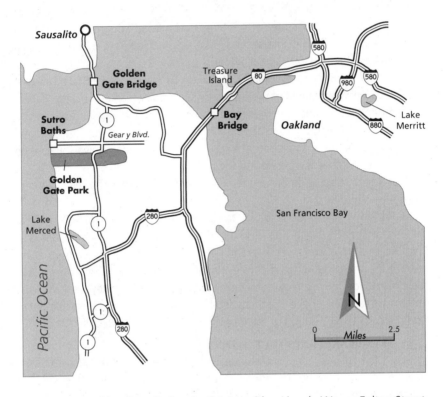

To get to Golden Gate Park, take CA 1 to either Lincoln Way or Fulton Street. By going either east or west, you will find several places at which to turn into the park. There are several ponds in the park (mostly west of CA 1) that have had Tufted Ducks in the past.

To get to the Sutro Baths, turn west onto Geary from CA 1 in northern San Francisco. Take Geary to Point Lobos Avenue, which splits off to the right (northwest). Take Point Lobos past 48th Avenue/El Camino del Mar to Merrie Way. Parking is available at the end of Merrie Way. A trail leads from the parking lot past the Sutro Baths and to the Cliff House.

Lake Merritt, unlike the bodies of water above, is not in San Francisco but is instead in nearby Oakland. To get to Lake Merritt, take the Bay Bridge/I-80 east from San Francisco. Once across San Francisco Bay, continue east on I-580 to Grand Avenue. Exit here and make a right at the light. Then go 0.6 mile to Bellevue Avenue and turn left into Lakeside Park. From here you can see much of the lake. To view the rest of the lake, turn left back onto Grand Avenue and keep left. You will be able to follow various roads most of the way around the lake.

For more details on birding around San Francisco, see Richmond (1985).

- ### McGrath Beach/Santa Clara River Estuary

This spot is one of the finest shorebirding areas in southern California. Its inclusion in this book, however, is based on the occurrence of Large-billed Sparrows here. During most winters, a couple are seen here in the dune grass and salicornia. To get to McGrath Beach, take US 101 north from Los Angeles to the Victoria Avenue exit and go south less than 1 mile to Olivas Park Drive. Here turn right and go west past the traffic light at Harbor Boulevard. Olivas Park Drive is now called Spinnaker Drive. Follow this around and park at the first beach lot you see on your left. Walk west onto the beach and then head south. You will see a lagoon with areas of *Salicornia* and dune grass nearby. Check these areas of short/sparse vegetation.

Be sure to look at the shorebirds here as well. In the past there has been Mongolian Plover, Red-necked Stint, and Sharp-tailed Sandpiper.

- ### Furnace Creek Ranch

Furnace Creek Ranch lies inside Death Valley National Park, approximately 130 miles from Las Vegas and approximately 300 miles from Los Angeles. The Furnace Creek Ranch area consists of a golf course, a series of cottages, date palm groves, and desert scrub. It is an oasis extraordinaire—an emerald in the bleakest of deserts. As such, it has been a popular spot for vagrant birds and California birders for many years. Such amazing rarities as Garganey, Red-throated Pipit, Streak-backed Oriole, Rufous-backed Robin, Sabine's Gull, and Red Phalarope have turned up here. Be forewarned, however: the temperatures can easily reach 120 during the "warm" months and can plunge below freezing during winter, plus there is usually a wind.

Furnace Creek Ranch is the most reliable spot in the United States for Ruddy Ground-Doves. This species has been present at Furnace Creek every fall and winter since the fall of 1987, except 1994. During three of the past seven years, birds have stayed all winter and to early April or beyond. Though far from common, Common Ground-Doves and Inca Doves are occasionally present, so scan carefully. Ruddy Ground-Doves have been found mostly around the golf course and the cottages. The golf course, unfortunately, is now posted "No Trespassing."

To get to Furnace Creek Ranch from Las Vegas, take US 95 approximately 86 miles to the town of Amargosa Valley. From Amargosa Valley, go south on NV 373 (which becomes CA 127) to Death Valley Junction. Here take CA 190 northwest 29 miles to Furnace Creek Ranch.

To get there from Los Angeles, take I-10 east to I-15. Take I-15 northeast to Baker. In Baker, go north on CA 127 to Death Valley Junction. Then go northwest on CA 190, 29 miles, to Furnace Creek Ranch.

Lodging can be found at Furnace Creek Ranch, the Furnace Creek Inn, or at Stovepipe Wells Village. Furnace Creek Ranch has a cafeteria that is open for

California—Death Valley/Furnace Creek Ranch

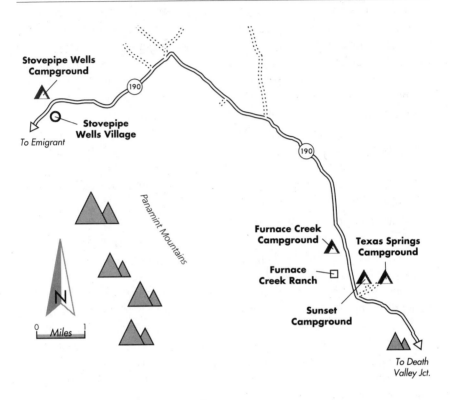

breakfast from 6 A.M. to 10 A.M., year-round. The coffee shop is open from 7 A.M. to 9 P.M. during the winter. There is also a steak house and a cocktail lounge. Stovepipe Wells Village has a dining room that is open from 7 A.M. to 10 A.M. for breakfast, 11:30 A.M. to 2 P.M. for lunch and 5:30 P.M. to 9 P.M. for dinner. For information on the ranch or the inn, call (619) 786-2345. For information on the Village, call (619) 786-2387.

Gas is available at Furnace Creek from 7 A.M. to 7 P.M., seven days a week. Stovepipe Wells has a gas station that is open from 7 A.M. to 9 P.M.

There are three campgrounds very close to the Furnace Creek Ranch: Furnace Creek, Sunset, and Texas Springs, but only Furnace Creek is open all year; the others are open from November to April only. Each costs about five dollars per night and has water and flush toilets. They are often crowded, so call ahead for availability. The Furnace Creek ranger's number is (619) 786-2331.

- **SALTON SEA**

The Salton Sea in summer is one of the most inhospitable birding places in North America. Temperatures regularly climb into the 110s and sometimes into the 120s. Furthermore, this is not the dry heat you might expect. Irrigation for local agriculture and evaporation from the sea often keep the relative humidity above 50 percent. Mitigating these hostile figures is the tremendous birding here. You will not be tallying hundreds of birds, but tens of thousands. No matter which specialty you come here for, plan to spend a couple days of general birding. For more information, see Holt (1990).

For Yellow-footed Gulls, the best time to come to the sea is from mid-July to mid-September, when Yellow-foots are widespread and numerous. A few can often be found anywhere that you can access the sea, especially along the western and southern shores. At other times of year, however, finding this species can be somewhat more challenging. In general, the Yellow-footed Gulls at the Salton Sea prefer sandy shores or rocky areas and shun mudflats. Some of the better areas include the shoreline at Salton City, Obsidian Butte, and Red Hill (see map).

To look for Blue-footed Boobies, the best time is late summer and early fall. The sea's north end has typically been best. The traditional favorite north-end birding spot is at the mouth of the Whitewater River. Sadly, this area is property of the Coachella Water District and has been officially off-limits (i.e., no trespassing) during the past few years. To reach this area, take CA 111 south from Indio or north from Brawley. Near Mecca, take CA 195 west, and then almost immediately take the left-hand fork (south) onto Lincoln Street. In about 3 miles you will come to two levees heading southeast along a waterway (this is the Whitewater River). Formerly, birders would drive south on the levee along the river's east side. However, this has been gated and is prominently marked "No Tresspassing." The walk to the sea's edge is about 2 miles and can be brutally hot. Contact local birders about access before going to this area.

Other spots at the north end include the end of Johnson Road and the end of the road opposite Oasis School (see map). Johnson Road intersects CA 111 at 1.3 miles south of CA 195. Go west on Johnson to the sea. To reach the Oasis School, follow CA 195 west from Mecca and then follow it as it turns south. About 0.5 mile before reaching CA 86, you will see the school on your right. Once here, turn left (west) on the southern of the two dirt roads and follow for 2 miles to the edge of the sea. If you have no luck with boobies at the above places, try birding the shoreline from Desert Shores through Salton City. Remember, Blue-footed Boobies occur sporadically at the Salton Sea (and U.S.) and are not to be expected.

For Large-billed Sparrows, you will want to go to the southern and eastern shores of the Salton Sea between July and February. There are several places to

California—Salton Sea

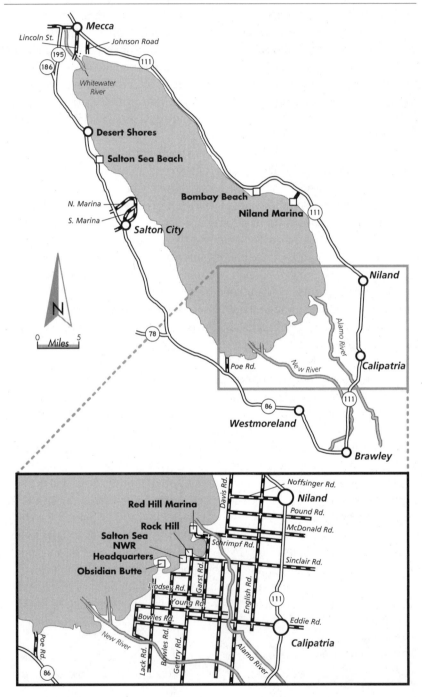

check for this species wannabe. The first is the the Niland boat ramp. This area is located approximately ten miles north of Niland and is reached by taking CA 111 north to Niland Marina Road and going southwest to the road's end. Bird around the shallow lagoon there. The south edge is usually best. Another spot to check for Large-bills is the New River mouth. This area is difficult to reach and requires four-wheel drive. It is probably best to access this area with birders familiar with the terrain. A third good place to look is along Davis Road, which is between Niland and the Salton Sea headquarters. To bird this area for Large-billed Sparrows, check the narrow roads that lead from Davis Road to Salton Sea. At times, some of these are posted "No Trespassing."

There are also a couple of less reliable spots around the sea to check for this sparrow. One is the Salton Sea headquarters/Rock Hill area. From the Salton Sea headquarters, take the nature trail (actually a gravel road) west for about 0.5 mile and then turn right onto the dike road, which heads toward Rock Hill. Carefully check the vegetation along this dike road. Another spot is around the intersection of Lack and Lindsey roads. Check the dike road that leads west from this intersection. You should be aware that there are occasional dike closures, and farmwork is sometimes active here.

Gasoline can be obtained at the following towns: El Centro, Brawley, Niland, Imperial, Calipatria, Mecca, Thermal, Indio, Coachella, and Salton City. Indio and El Centro both have a Motel 6. Near the Indio Motel 6 is a Denny's for early-morning getaways. A favorite breakfast spot of local birders is the Country Kitchen in Desert Shores, which opens at 7 A.M. Another favored place for edibles is the Date Oasis in Mecca. Here you can purchase a dazzling variety of delectable dates or better yet a smooth, cold date shake. Also, there is a McDonald's in Brawley, and Gastones in Niland is passable.

- **ANAHEIM BAY**

Anaheim Bay (in Seal Beach, Orange County, CA) is included only as a spot for Pacific Golden-Plover. A flock of about a dozen of these birds arrives here around early September and leaves around late April. They can be found on 50 to 75 percent of visits during this period.

To reach Anaheim Bay, take I-405 to the Seal Beach Blvd. exit and go south. After approximately 2.5 miles, you will come to the Pacific Coast Highway (PCH). Turn left. Shortly, you will cross a bridge over the inlet to Anaheim Bay. Go all the way across the bridge and find a safe place to turn around. You should now be on PCH heading back toward Seal Beach Blvd. From the point at which PCH starts uphill toward the Anaheim Bay Bridge, go 0.65 mile. Here you will see a narrow paved road heading off to the right across the marsh. There is a large sign reading "BreitBurns Lease." Turn here. Park before going through the gate. It's okay to park here as long as you do not block the gate, you remain within

California—Anaheim Bay

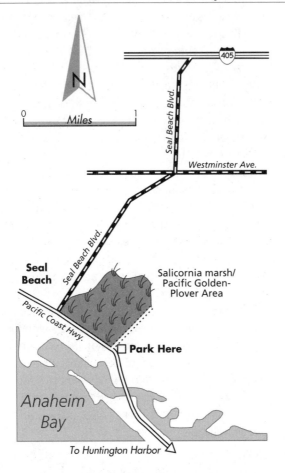

sight of your car, and you do not walk past the gate.

Between where you have parked and Seal Beach is a marsh with *Salicornia*, shallow pools, mudflat, and short green grass. The Pacific Golden-Plovers prefer the *Salicornia* and short grass but shun the mudflats where there are often hundreds of Black-bellied Plovers. Avoid midwinter high tides, which is when the marsh floods.

There are a multitude of places to stay and eat in the urban surroundings of Anaheim Bay. The nearest Motel 6 is in Garden Grove, about ten minutes away. A fine, moderately priced place to eat is the nearby Cafe Lafayette. This cafe is in Seal Beach less than 1 mile away. To get there, take PCH north into Seal Beach and turn left on Main Street. The Cafe Lafayette is less than one block on your left.

- **PELICAN POINT STATE PARK**

Pelican Point provides a beautiful venue with sweeping ocean vistas in which to look for California Gnatcatchers. To get to Pelican Point and Crystal Cove State Park, take I-405 south from Los Angeles or Long Beach to CA 73 in Costa Mesa. Then take CA 73 southeast and follow it as it becomes MacArthur Boulevard. When MacArthur Boulevard/CA 73 ends, you will be at Pacific Coast Highway (CA 1). Turn left here and follow the highway southeast. Between 1.5 and 2.0 miles south of MacArthur Boulevard, you will see an entrance for Pelican Point State Park/Crystal Cove State Park. Turn right into the park, pay the entrance fee, and park in any of the lots. Look and listen for California Gnatcatchers in the patches of sage scrub. Sometimes, you can even see them from your car.

If you head back northwest on the Pacific Coast Highway past MacArthur Boulevard, you will be in Newport Beach. North of MacArthur, there is a wide variety of eating establishments including McDonald's (north side of road) and Jack-in-the-Box (south side of road). The closest Motel 6 is not far away in Irvine (310-419-1234).

- **SAN PASQUAL BATTLEFIELD STATE HISTORIC PARK**

If you are searching for vagrants to North America, this is not your spot. However, if you are looking for species of the coastal sage scrub habitat such as California Gnatcatcher, this is where you want to be. To get to this park, take I-15 south from Riverside or north from San Diego to CA 78. Then, take CA 78 east through Escondido. About 7 miles east of Escondido, you will find the historic park on the north side of the road. Park in the lot, and then walk the nature trail, listening carefully as you go.

In Escondido there is a wide variety of fast-food joints as well as a Motel 6 and a Denny's. San Pasqual Park is approximately one hour from downtown San Diego and two to three hours from downtown Los Angeles.

- **TIJUANA RIVER VALLEY/SILVER STRAND**

The Tijuana River valley, known as "The Valley" to San Diego birders, lies about 12 miles south of San Diego and is just north of the Mexican border. The few remaining farms and trees here have attracted a wide variety of vagrants including Ruddy Ground-Dove, Golden-winged Warbler, Wood Stork, and Buff-breasted Sandpiper. Red-throated Pipits were seen here in 1964 for the first Lower 48 record. Since then, Red-throats have been found here almost annually.

During October, any field in the valley could have a Red-throated Pipit. A good way to look for this species is to drive the few roads looking carefully for flocks of American Pipits and listening for Red-throats. The sod farms, formerly so good for these pipits, are now abandoned. Instead, concentrate on fields with emergent vegetation.

California—Tijuana River Valley

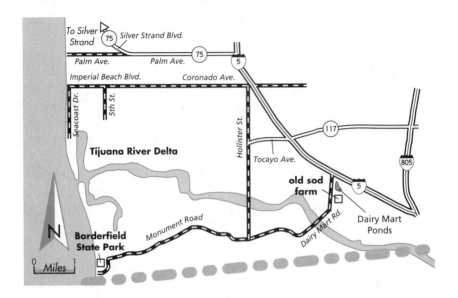

As a final and sad note, floods during the winter of 1992-93 washed away much of the valley's vegetation. This will undoubtedly have a big impact on Eastern vagrants, but no one knows what effect it will have on the Red-throats, as they prefer fields anyway.

If you want to find Large-billed Sparrows near here, try the Tijuana River estuary. Take I-5 south from San Diego to Coronado Avenue (not Coronado Island) and go west. Continue west as Coronado Avenue turns into Imperial Beach Boulevard. Turn left (south) on 5th Street and follow it to the end. Then walk south along the east edge of the marsh. Alternatively, take Imperial Beach Boulevard until its end and go left (south) on Seacoast Drive. Walk along the west edge of the marsh.

To look for Large-billed Sparrows along the Silver Strand, take I-5 south from San Diego to the Palm Avenue/Route 75 exit. Go west on Palm Avenue/Route 75 1 to 2 miles until route 75 veers to the north. Here follow Route 75 north. Soon you will see San Diego Bay on your right. You will also see several pull-offs and some dikes that you can walk on. Try looking along the water's edge for Large-bills.

Oregon and Washington Shorebirding

There are a number of excellent shorebirding spots in Washington and Oregon. It was hard to choose which to include, but we have chosen six of the best: Bandon, Nehalem, Clatsop Spit (a.k.a. south jetty of Columbia River), Leadbetter Point, Tokeland, and Ocean Shores. Which spots are best for which species is given in Table 1. For the Oregon sites (Bandon, Newhalem, and Clatsop Spit), we highly recommend using Evanich (1990) and for the Washington sites (Leadbetter Point, Tokeland, and Ocean Shores) use Wahl and Paulson (1991).

- ## LEADBETTER POINT

If Sycamore Canyon is birding's Bataan, then Leadbetter Point is birding's Waterloo. It's a land war in Asia. The excellent habitat lures you farther and farther out until your supply lines are thin, and you are at the mercy of the capricious weather. Still, if you are ready for miles of exposed dunes, willow thickets, *Salicornia* marshes, and tidal flats, then Leadbetter is your place.

To get to Leadbetter, take US 101 to Seaview, in the southwestern corner of Washington. Just east of Seaview, turn to the north on Sand Ridge Road (flashing light). Go about 16 miles north to Oysterville and follow the road when it turns left (west). Then, go a couple tenths of a mile and turn right on Stackpole Road. Take this until it ends in a parking lot. From here trails lead to the Willapa Bay and the Pacific Ocean sides of the peninsula. The walk to the northern tip varies in length from year to year as the peninsula grows and shrinks. As the Peregrine flies, the journey from parking lot to tip averages 2.5 miles each way. As the human walks, however, the round-trip could be almost 10 miles. Rubber boots often prove helpful. Another good alternative, however, is accepting wet, muddy feet and wearing an old pair of comfortable sneakers.

On the ocean side, high tide is often best for shorebirding because the birds flee the marsh to roost here. At most other times the bay side is usually better. Sharp-tailed Sandpipers and Pacific Golden-Plovers usually favor the *Salicornia* marshes of the bay side, even at high tide, but the plovers are also sometimes

Table 1

	Bar-tailed Godwit	Sharp-tailed Sandpiper	Ruff	Pacific Golden-Plover
Bandon	**	*	*	**
Clatsop	*	**	**	**
Nehalem	−	**	**	**
Leadbetter	−	**	*	**
Tokeland	**	−	−	−
Ocean Shores	**	**	**	**

** Relatively good chance
* fair chance
− poor chance

Oregon and Washington Shorebirding

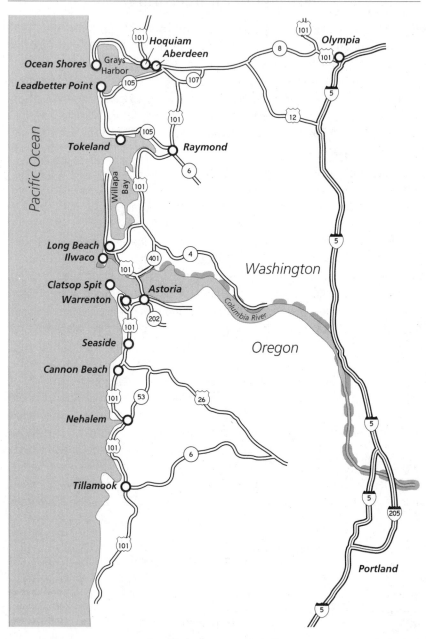

(continued on page 421)

(continued from page 420)

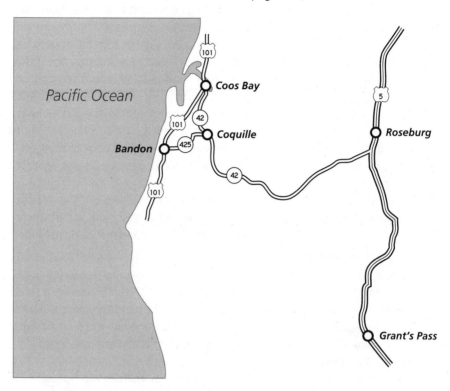

seen on the ocean side of the peninsula.

The nearest place to stay is Long Beach (just north of Seaview), which has a Super 8 Motel and several independents.

- **TOKELAND**

Tokeland and its associated birding areas lie in the northeastern corner of Willapa Bay. As the shorebird flies, it is a short distance from the tip of Leadbetter Point. As the car drives, however, it is well over an hour. The Tokeland area seems to have a particular affinity for Godwits and is perhaps the best place to find those with bars on their tails.

There are two strategies for finding Bar-tailed Godwits in this area. One approach is to look just before or after high tide, when tidal areas are limited and are easier to view. The best spots to check are between Raymond and Tokeland on WA 105. Use any of the many pulloffs where exposed mud is visible. In Tokeland, try the jetty for mudflat viewing. Other spots to check are south and west of Raymond along US 101. These include Bruceport Park (near Bruceport) and the Palix River mouth as seen from Bay Center Dike Road (near Bay Center).

A second approach is to check for roosting godwits at Tokeland at high tide. To get to Tokeland take WA 105 south from Westport or northwest from Raymond to Tokeland Road. Go southeast on this road to 7th. At 7th, turn right (west) for one-half block to a salt marsh channel. Pull off the road here and scan across the water to a sandy spit where flocks of shorebirds, gulls, and terns often roost at high tide. After you are done here, go back to the main road (i.e., Tokeland Road) and turn right. Go 0.6 mile and check the bayshore from the pullout here. After checking here, continue on the main road until it curves around and ends at the marina. At the north end of the marina, there is an old hook-shaped jetty where godwits often roost at high tide. This is probably the best single spot for the Bar-tailed Godwit in the Lower 48.

For lodging, Westport (about 20 minutes away) is your best bet. The McBee's Silver Sands Motel is particularly birder friendly and is reasonably priced. There are also two motels in Tokeland—Tradewinds on the Bay and the Tokeland Motel.

• OCEAN SHORES

Ocean Shores lies at the southern tip of a peninsula that separates Grays Harbor from the Pacific Ocean. At the southern tip of Ocean Shores lies a sand spit and a salicornia marsh that together make up one of Washington's finest birding areas. Such howling rarities as Yellow Wagtail and McKay's Bunting have been seen here. The golf course in the center of town is also good, especially for Pacific Golden-Plover.

To get to Ocean Shores, take US 101 north from Aberdeen to Hoquiam. In Hoquiam, turn left onto WA 109. After another 15 or 20 miles, WA 115 will go off to the left (south) toward Ocean Shores. Follow Route 115 to the arched entrance to the city. Here make a left and go a short distance to Ocean Shores Boulevard and turn right. This road goes west then turns south. Head south on the boulevard for several miles until it bends sharply to the left. At this point, you are at the southwestern corner of the peninsula. After following this curve to the left, a rocky seawall will appear to your right. Where the road once again starts to curve to the left, you will see a small fenced-off sewage treatment plant on your right.

Park off the road here. Walk past the sewage plant and then east along the seawall. In the recent past this walk would have put you onto the sand spit. The world of sand, however, is a shifty one. Access to the spit is now from Damon Point (see below). Nonetheless, the sewage pond access will allow you to scan a portion of the mudflat and you'll be able to walk some of the salicornia marsh as well. The marsh, here and elsewhere, is good for Ruffs and Sharp-tailed Sandpipers.

Access to the spit at Ocean Shores is now via Damon Point, which is worth birding in its own right. To get to Damon Point, go east on Marine View Drive

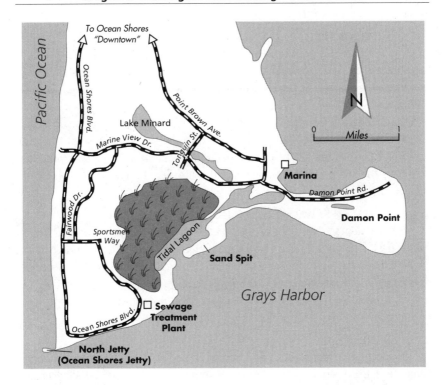

from Ocean Shores Boulevard. Take this to the gravel Damon Point Road and make a right turn. To access the sand spit, park near the outhouses near Marine View Drive. Walk south to the edge of Grays Harbor, and then west along the sand spit. Pacific Golden-Plovers are often along the spit. Also, Bar-tailed Godwits have been seen here with flocks of Marbled Godwits and Black-bellied Plovers, often at high tide.

To get to another good shorebird spot, continue east on Damon Point Road. About halfway to the tip of (0.6 mile from Marine View Drive) you will glimpse a shallow depression to your right. Park here and walk out to the depression, which is actually a small pond. This area can be excellent for shorebirds and should be checked for Ruff, Sharp-tailed Sandpiper, and Pacific Golden-Plover. For further details on birding Ocean Shores, see Morse (1994).

Because Ocean Shores is a resort town, there is a good choice of lodging. Some of the cheaper places in the Ocean Shores area include the Pacific Sands (206-289-3588), the Ocean Shores Motel (800-464-2526) and the North Beach Motel (800-289-4116). See Morse (1994) for more details on motels or call the Ocean Shores Chamber of Commerce at (800) 76-BEACH.

There are many dining choices. For fast food, there is a Dairy Queen along Ocean Shores Boulevard.

- **CLATSOP SPIT**

The Clatsop Spit is one of Oregon's premier birding spots. In years past, it has attracted the Spotted Redshank, Long-toed Stint, McKay's Bunting, and Black-throated Blue Warbler. It is truly worth birding in full. For details, seen Evanich (1990).

Clatsop Spit is reached by taking US 101 to Ridge Road and going north. Follow signs to the south jetty of the Columbia River. At the base of the jetty, park in lot C. The area just below the parking lot can be very good at high tide, especially for Sharp-tailed Sandpipers and Ruffs. For the Pacific Golden-Plover, try walking west to the beach and birding along the beach.

- **NEHALEM SEWAGE PONDS**

The Nehalem sewage ponds are just outside the town of Nehalem on Oregon's north coast. At high tide, it can be a superb place for shorebirds, including Ruffs, Pacific Golden-Plovers, and Sharp-tailed Sandpipers. To get to the sewage ponds, go south out of Nehalem on US 101. After crossing the Nehalem River, take the first right, which is Tideland Road. Go west a short distance to the sewage pond entrance and ask there for permission to bird.

- **BANDON**

Bandon is a prime West Coast shorebirding spot. It has had such rarities as Great Knot, Bristle-thighed Curlew, and Mongolian Plover. It is also the best place in Oregon for the Bar-tailed Godwit and one of the best places for Pacific Golden-Plovers.

For the godwit (remember, still a slim chance), try the flats near Bullards Beach State Park. To get here, take US 101 to the Coquille River bridge. Just north of the bridge is Bullards Beach State Park Road. Follow signs for the lighthouse for 1.3 miles and turn left at the first dunes. Then, go another 1.5 miles and turn left onto a small gravel road. This road will take you to some mudflats along the river. Midtide is best.

For Pacific Golden-Plover, Sharp-tailed Sandpiper, and Ruff, try the Bandon Marsh. To get here, take First Street west from US 101 in Bandon. Go a short distance to River Road and turn right. Follow River Road for 0.75 mile past the Bandon water treatment facility. Park on the left side of the road and follow the trail down into the marsh. Mid- to high tide is best.

Washington

- ### AMERICAN CAMP

American Camp is at the southern end of San Juan Island. It is an old army encampment from the 1800s when the island was claimed by both the United States and England. Oddly, the whole island is now American, but American Camp is inhabited by European Rabbits and Eurasian Skylarks. Both skylarks and rabbits are present year-round, and neither is usually difficult to find. The skylarks are easiest to locate from March through July when they perform their wonderful song and dance. When they are not in full song, the best way to find them is to

Washington—San Juan Island/American Camp

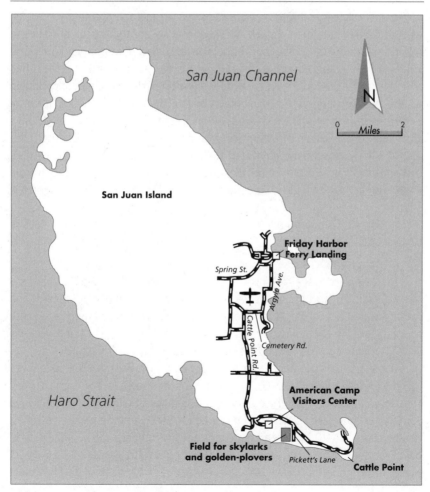

crisscross the field between Pickett's Lane and the redoubt. The Pacific Golden-Plover has been seen here with some frequency during September and October as well. This is also the site of Washington's only Red-throated Pipit.

San Juan Island is a popular tourist destination. This has good and bad points. The island is easy to get to, but transport is sometimes crowded and accommodations can fill early. To get to San Juan Island, take the ferry west from Anacortes, Washington, or east from Sidney, British Columbia. The sailing times vary from season to season. For up-to-date information, call (206) 464-6400. During the warm months, it is wise to arrive an hour early to ensure a place on board.

The ferry arrives at Friday Harbor. American Camp is about 5 miles to the south. To get to American Camp, take Spring Street southwest from the ferry landing. After a short distance, Argyle Road veers off to the left. Go south on Argyle and follow it as it turns west and then south again. At Cemetery Road, go west to Cattle Point Road. Follow Cattle Point Road south past the entrance to American Camp. At Pickett's Lane, a short distance past this entrance, turn right. The field full of rabbit burrows on your right is the skylark area. The rise a half mile away is the "redoubt." Friday Harbor has most of the food, gas, and lodging on the island. There are many lodging choices, but there are two that we've enjoyed. For a relatively inexpensive room plus continental breakfast, try Friday's (206-378-5848). For a bit more money you can stay at the Hillside House (800-232-4730) and get a hot breakfast in the deal. If desired, there are many other bed-and-breakfasts on the island. Next door to Friday's is the Bistro (open from 11:30 A.M. to 10 P.M.) which has some of the Pacific Coast's best Chicago-style pizza.

For details on birding the San Juan Islands, use Lewis and Sharpe (1987) or Wahl (1991).

• SKAGIT FLATS

The best place to search for your Gyrfalcon in the Lower 48 is in Washington's famed Skagit. The Skagit's secret lies in its tremendous number of shorebirds and waterfowl that are concentrated in a small area of farmland and mudflats. These factors keep the usually wide-ranging Gyrfalcons relatively confined, thereby increasing your chances for success (peak is November into March).

The Skagit lies about one hour north of Seattle just west of I-5 (see map for recommended areas to search). Certainly the best area is the Samish Flats, especially in the vicinity of the "West 90." The quickest way from Seattle to the Samish Flats is to take I-5 north from Seattle to WA 20 and then head west. Best Road crosses WA 20 at the rather conspicuous Farmhouse Inn. Continue west past Best Road to the next stoplight and turn right onto Bayview-Edison Road. Head north through the town of Bayview. About 2 miles north of Bayview State

Washington—Samish Flats & Skagit Flats

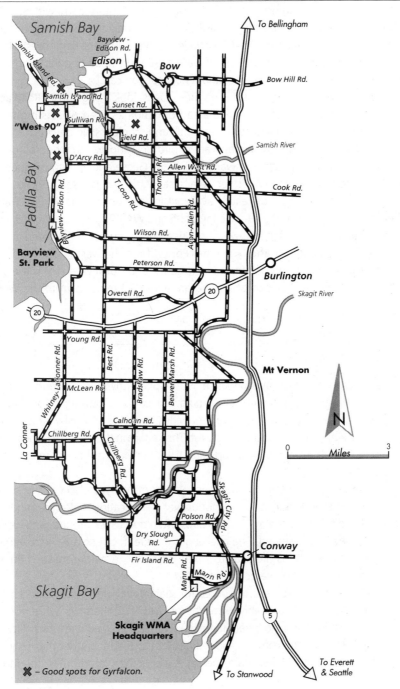

To Bellingham

Samish Bay

Bayview-Edison Rd.

Edison

Bow

Bow Hill Rd.

Samish Island Rd.

Samish Island Rd.

Sunset Rd.

"West 90"

Sullivan Rd.

field Rd.

Samish River

D'Arcy Rd.

Allen West Rd.

Padilla Bay

Bayview-Edison Rd.

Thomas Rd.

Cook Rd.

T Loop Rd.

Wilson Rd.

Avon-Allen Rd.

Bayview St. Park

Peterson Rd.

Burlington

Overell Rd.

20

Skagit River

20

Young Rd.

Whitney-LaConner Rd.

Best Rd.

Bradshaw Rd.

Beaver Marsh Rd.

Mt Vernon

McLean Rd.

N

Calhoun Rd.

La Conner

Chillberg Rd.

Chillberg Rd.

0   Miles   3

Skagit City Rd.

Polson Rd.

Conway

Dry Slough Rd.

Fir Island Rd.

Mann Rd.

Mann Rd.

Skagit Bay

5

Skagit WMA Headquarters

To Stanwood

To Everett & Seattle

✖ – Good spots for Gyrfalcon.

427

Park you will drop into the lowland farms of the Samish Flats. Carefully look for hawks while continuing north to the stop sign at the T intersection with Samish Island Road. Here turn left and go a little less than 1 mile to the 90-degree turn in the road that is called the West 90. While the West 90 is the single best place to scan from, the entire area west of Bayview-Edison Road is good, and you should check every telephone pole and fencepost you can.

If you have not had success driving these roads, look along Sunset Road and Field Road nearby. In fact, the entire area from Thomas Road west is probably worth a look. Don't forget to stop frequently and scan possible perches.

If you have more time, you may want to bird Fir Island, which is not far to the south. This area is fantastic for swans and Snow Geese and is not infrequently also home to Gyrfalcons. For further details, see Wahl and Paulson (1991).

Food for humans is not readily available in and around the Samish Flats. There is a McDonald's at the intersection of I-5 and WA 20, which opens at 6 A.M. Also, Edison has the Edison Inn, which serves a decent burger. It is located along Bayview-Edison Road just after you enter Edison from the west. Mount Vernon has the nearest chain motels with an Econo Lodge and a Best Western. These are both at the College Way exit of I-5 and are about 20 minutes from the West 90.

Pacific Pelagics

Seabirding is a mystical experience. From apparently uniform surroundings birds appear and disappear without warning, as if conjured by magic. Sometimes to blink is to miss your bird. The surface provides few clues as to why birds prefer one spot over another, yet patterns do exist. The key lies in the undersea landscape and currents that thrust nutrients upward in some places but are barren as the desert elsewhere.

Seabirding is sometimes like trying to identify flycatchers while on a trampoline. The world is in constant motion, yet identification is often dependent on obscure, difficult-to-see marks. The birds often don't stick around, and worst of all you may be nauseated. The challenges are great, but so are the rewards. Many of our rarest birds are seabirds, and their mobile nature makes finding them chancy at best. You've got to be lucky.

That said, there are keys to successful seabirding. Most important, know your field marks—you probably won't be able to look them up while you're watching the bird. Knowing where to go is also crucial and is the responsibility of trip leaders. Underwater canyons and seamounts can lead to nutrient upwellings that concentrate birds. For certain species, such as the pterodromas, the most

Pacific Pelagics

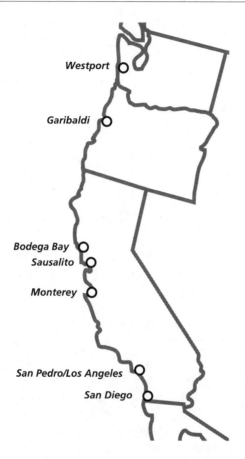

critical factor is getting near or beyond the edge of the continental shelf. Off the East Coast, day-to-day maps of water temperature are used to determine where to go. In ten years, we'll know much more. Now, we are merely at page one.

There are six major pelagic trips out of the West Coast. We will approach these from north to south. A complete listing of U.S. pelagics has been provided in recent years in the January issue of *Winging It* (published by the American Birding Association).

- **WESTPORT**

The Westport pelagic trips, run by Terry Wahl, are the northernmost in the Lower 48. They are especially good for the Flesh-footed Shearwater, Laysan Albatross, and South Polar Skua. Some of the rarities that have been recorded on these voyages include the Short-tailed Albatross, Red-legged Kittiwake, and

Selected Seabirds Off Westport 1971-1992

	JAN	FEB	MAR	APR	MAY	JUN	JUL	AUG	SEP	OCT	NOV	DEC
# of trips	3	1	1	8	28	4	29	52	54	26	2	1
Laysan Albatross												
# of occurrences	2	1	0	2	3	0	0	0	3	4	1	1
# of birds	3	1	0	4	6	0	0	0	3	4	3	1
% of occurrence	67%	100%	0%	25%	11%	0%	0%	0%	6%	15%	50%	100%
Flesh-footed Shearwater												
# of occurrences	0	0	0	0	17	2	14	32	20	11	1	0
# of birds	0	0	0	0	66	2	22	37	30	35	1	0
% of occurrence	0%	0%	0%	0%	61%	50%	48%	62%	37%	42%	50%	0%
South Polar Skua												
# of occurrences	0	0	0	0	2	2	15	28	36	18	0	0
# of birds	0	0	0	0	2	4	39	75	90	72	0	0
% of occurrence	0%	0%	0%	0%	7%	50%	52%	54%	67%	69%	0%	0%

Solander's Petrel. Trips have been run every month, but the majority are during May and from July to October. In recent years, deepwater pelagics have been scheduled during April to search for the Murphy's Petrel.

Many birders venturing out on a Westport pelagic stay at the McBee's Silver Sands Motel (360-268-9029) or the Albatross Motel (360-268-9233) in Westport. Both are inexpensive, clean, and quiet. The owners welcome birders and try to group their rooms together. The Albatross is only two blocks from the marina, and the Silver Sands is only a few minutes farther. In between the marina and the Silver Sands is the Red Apple Market, which is open 24 hours. A good place to eat near the marina and that opens very early is the New Hope Cafe.

To inquire about Westport pelagic trips, contact Terry Wahl at 3041 Eldridge, Bellingham, WA, 98225; 360-733-8255.

- **OREGON PELAGICS**

The Portland Audubon Society runs several trips per year, mostly during the fall. Trips go out of either Garibaldi, Oregon, or Ilwaco, Washington. They have much the same birds as Westport, but generally in smaller numbers.

To inquire about a Portland Audubon pelagic trip, contact the Portland Audubon Society at Audubon House, 5151 NW Cornell Road, Portland, OR 97210; (503) 292-6855.

- **SAUSALITO**

To birders Sausalito has become synonymous with deepwater pelagic birding. First started in 1990, the Sausalito pelagics have shed considerable light on the possibilties of pelagic birding in "blue water" off the Pacific Coast. These pelagic

Pterodromas from Sausalito

	APR 25 1993	MAY 2 1992	MAY 3 1991	MAY 3 1992	MAY 5 1991	MAY 10 1993	MAY 11 1991	MAY 17 1992	MAY 19 1990	JUL 28 1991	SEP 30 1990	OCT 17 1992	NOV 14 1992	NOV 16 1991	NOV 17 1990	DEC 14 1991
Murphy's Petrel	5	34	78	2	171	9	50	–	3	–	–	–	–	–	–	–
Cook's Petrel	1	1	–	–	5	–	2	–	1	–	5	10	2	12	–	–
Mottled Petrel	–	–	–	–	–	–	–	–	–	–	–	–	–	17	–	3
Dark-rumped Petrel	–	–	–	1	–	–	–	–	–	–	–	–	–	–	–	–
Stejneger's Petrel	–	–	–	–	–	–	–	–	–	–	–	–	–	–	2	–

Other selected seabirds from Sausalito

	APR 25 1993	MAY 2 1992	MAY 3 1991	MAY 3 1992	MAY 5 1991	MAY 10 1993	MAY 11 1991	MAY 17 1992	MAY 19 1990	JUL 28 1991	SEP 30 1990	OCT 17 1992	NOV 14 1992	NOV 16 1991	NOV 17 1990	DEC 14 1991
Laysan Albatross	5	34	78	2	171	9	50	–	3	–	–	–	–	–	–	–
Flesh-footed Shearwater	1	1	–	–	5	–	2	–	1	–	5	10	2	12	–	–
South Polar Skua	–	–	–	–	–	–	–	–	–	–	–	–	–	17	–	3
Parakeet Auklet	–	–	–	1	–	–	–	–	–	–	–	–	–	–	–	–
Craveri's Murrelet	–	–	–	–	–	–	–	–	–	–	–	–	–	–	2	–

voyages are your best bet for the Cook's Petrel, Murphy's Petrel, Mottled Petrel, Horned Puffin, and Laysan Albatross. Mega-rarities found on Sausalito pelagics include the Dark-rumped Petrel and Stejneger's Petrel (see table for more details). Trips have been run in April, May, July, September, October, November, and December. Most, however, are in spring.

The closest lodging is to be had at the Holiday Inn Express just off of US 101.

For further information call Bob Hirt at (408) 446-4478 or Ted Koundakjian at (510) 525-2069.

- **SHEARWATER JOURNEYS**

Shearwater Journeys are run by Debra Shearwater. She offers a variety of trips out Monterey including Monterey Bay itself (10 to 12 miles offshore), storm-petrel study trips (10 to 12 miles offshore), Monterey Seavalley (15 to 25 miles offshore), Albacore Fishing Grounds (30 to 50 miles offshore), and Davidson Seamount (80 to 100 miles offshore). For a full list of dates, contact Debra Shearwater at Shearwater Journeys, P.O. Box 1445, Soquel, CA 95073; (408) 688-1990.

For Flesh-footed Shearwaters, the standard Monterey Bay trip is a decent bet; the Monterey Seavalley and Albacore trips are not as good. For South Polar Skuas, your chances are fairly good on any trip, but the Albacore trips are best. Least Storm-Petrels are best sought on the storm-petrel study trips. Remember, they are not present every year, but when they are, they can be fairly numerous. Like Least Storm-Petrels, Craveri's Murrelets tend to occur sporadically. The Monterey Seavalley and Albacore trips are best when birds are present. Monterey trips have found such incredible rarities as the Wedge-rumped Storm-Petrel, Streaked Shearwater, Wedge-tailed Shearwater, and Red-tailed Tropicbird.

The Davidson Seamount trips have a tendency to be canceled because of inclement weather (about 50 percent stay in port). These trips go into deep water, and if the boat goes out they are good for many of the same birds as the Sausalito trips. Cook's Petrel has been seen on roughly 50 percent of outings and the Stejneger's Petrel and Wedge-rumped Petrel have been seen on one trip each. This is also the trip that found the Light-Mantled Sooty Albatross in 1994.

Also, Shearwater Journeys leads trips out of Bodega Bay. These voyages go primarily to the Cordell Banks, and if weather permits, farther out to sea. This is an excellent pelagic for the Flesh-footed Shearwater, Laysan Albatross, and South Polar Skua. The Cook's Petrel also has been seen.

Out of Monterey is a Motel 6 and a Denny's for traditional birder fare and lodging. After the trip, there are several convenient and good eateries on the wharf. Because Monterey is a major resort area the Motel 6 can fill months in advance, so make reservations accordingly. There is another Motel 6 not too far away in Salinas.

- ## LOS ANGELES AUDUBON SOCIETY

The Los Angeles Audubon trips usually go out of San Pedro to Santa Barbara Island. Winter trips are the exception. These stay closer to shore and search the Palos Verde Escarpment and Redondo Canyon. The San Pedro trips can be good, in season, for Least Storm-Petrels and Craveri's Murrelets. The ever-elusive Red-billed Tropicbird has been seen on several occasions, most recently in September 1993. There are no facilities particularly close by for eating or lodging. For information, call Audubon House at (213) 876-0202 (Tuesday to Saturday, 10 A.M. to 3 P.M.) or write Phil Sayre, Los Angeles Audubon Society, 7377 Santa Monica Boulevard, West Hollywood, CA 90046.

- ## SAN DIEGO

The Western Field Ornithologists have been running annual September pelagics out of San Diego's Mission Bay. These trips are probably the best for Craveri's Murrelet, Hypoleuca Xantu's Murrelet, and Least Storm-Petrel. Formerly, this was *the* trip for the Red-billed Tropicbird, but few have been seen in recent years.

Mission Valley (along I-8), which is about 10 to 15 minutes away from Mission Bay, has a number of places to stay, including a Super 8.

Atlantic Pelagics

Pelagic trip offerings vary considerably from year to year. For current listings see the January issue of *Winging It,* the ABA's monthly newsletter. Listed below are those ports where trips have run regularly over the past several years. Note that many of these trips fill up early, so advanced reservations are recommended.

- ## MAINE: THE BLUENOSE

The Bluenose Ferry is a monster of a pelagic birding boat that carries people (and cars) from Bar Harbor, Maine, to Yarmouth, Nova Scotia. Because of its size, people who often get seasick on other boats have a better chance for survival on this one, but remember, no boat is seasick-proof! Another advantage of the Bluenose is that it runs regularly. In summer it runs every day, and for most of the rest of the year it runs at least two or three times a week. For a schedule, call or write Marine Atlantic, P.O. Box 250, North Sydney, Nova Scotia B2A 3M3 (902-794-5700 or U.S. toll free 800-341-7981).

Great Skua is a possibility on the Bluenose in late August and September. Later fall or winter may also be good for Great Skua, and midsummer sightings are not unheard of. Note, however, that the identity of skuas in the Gulf of Maine is still somewhat contentious, and South Polar Skuas probably outnumber Greats there, at least in July and August. Dovekies are also a possibility on the

Atlantic Pelagics

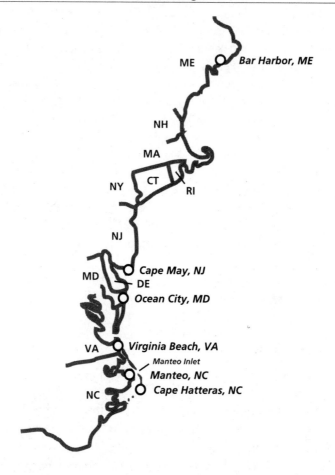

Bluenose, especially in November.

There are several motels in Bar Harbor that are open all year and are reasonably priced. These include the Atlantic Oaks Motel (207-288-5802), the Cadillac Motor Inn (207-288-3831), and the Golden Anchor Inn (207-288-5033). Food is available aboard the Bluenose.

- ### NEW JERSEY: CAPE MAY

Early August to mid-September trips off the New Jersey coast offer the possibility of the White-faced Storm-Petrel, and winter trips offer an excellent chance for Dovekies and a good chance for Great Skuas. Pelagic trips are run off New Jersey every year but the port, organizer, and dates vary. Recently there have been no late summer trips.

Site Guide

Some very successful winter trips have been run out of Cape May in recent years by Capt. Fred Ascoli. For more information, contact him at Miss Chris Boats, 3 Rabbit Run, Cape May, NJ 08204; (609) 884-3939.

Captain's Cove at the Miss Chris Marina opens early for breakfast. There are numerous motels in Cape May but only a handful that are open all year. The most reasonably priced ones are the Cape Motor Inn (609-884-4256) and the Queen Victoria Inn (609-884-8702).

- ### MARYLAND: OCEAN CITY

Early August to mid-September trips offer the possibility of White-faced and Band-rumped Storm-petrels. Winter trips offer an excellent chance for Dovekies (recorded nearly every trip) and a good chance for Great Skuas (recorded on about half the trips). In the 1970s there were two winter records of the Yellow-nosed Albatross off this port. Local birders anxiously await an encore.

Early breakfast can be had at the Kitchen at the intersection of Philadelphia Avenue and Wicomico Sreet. There are numerous dinner possibilities and many motels in and around Ocean City. Two popular motels in West Ocean City are Long Acres Motel and Cottages (410-213-1441) at the intersection of US 50 and MD 707, and the Francis Scott Key Motel (410-213-0088) on US 50 across from the White Marlin Mall. For winter trips, try the Talbot Inn (800-659-7703) on Talbot Street, Ocean City, on the bay side. For more information about Ocean City trips, contact Brian Patteson, Inc., P.O. Box 1135, Amherst, VA 24521; (804) 933-8687.

- ### VIRGINIA: VIRGINIA BEACH

Early August to mid-September trips off Virginia Beach offer the possibility of White-faced and Band-rumped Storm-Petrels. Band-rumps are probably more likely here than off ports to the north, but they are still much less likely than off North Carolina or in the Gulf of Mexico. Winter trips here offer an excellent chance for Dovekies (recorded on nearly every trip) and a good chance for Great Skua (recorded on about half the trips). In 1995, one trip here recorded six Great Skuas, the most found in one day off the mid-Atlantic coast in about 15 years.

Early breakfast can be had at Waffles and Things at Laskin Road and Pacific Avenue, open 24 hours. For lodging, try the Econo Lodge at 1211 Atlantic Avenue (804-428-1183). For more information about Virginia Beach trips, contact Brian Patteson, Inc., P.O. Box 1135, Amherst, VA 24521; (804) 933-8687.

- ### NORTH CAROLINA

Pelagic trips off North Carolina have long been among the most popular on the Atlantic Coast—and for good reason. They produce the largest numbers and widest variety of seabirds plus more rare and specialty species than any other Atlantic Coast outings. North Carolina's most famous seabird species is Black-capped Petrel, which is now known to be common year-round in the Gulf Stream. Since effort has increased here, a number of other species have proven to be rare but regular including the Herald Petrel (May to September), Soft-plumaged (Cape Verde Islands) Petrel (primarily late May and early June), White-faced Storm-Petrel (late July to early October), and Masked Booby (June to October). The Band-rumped Storm-Petrel has proven to be almost common at times (peak is from mid-June to mid-August), and South Polar Skua is regular in May and June and occasional in July and August. The White-tailed Tropicbird has become increasingly regular off North Carolina, especially from mid-June to mid-August, when the species was found on most summer trips off Hatteras in 1994 and 1995. The Red-billed Tropicbird has also shown up with increasing regularity (May to September) and may now be almost as likely off North Carolina as off any Pacific Coast port. If that's not enough, a number of super-rarities have been reported here including the Bermuda Petrel, Little Shearwater, Bulwer's Petrel, and others.

The birds off Hatteras and Oregon Inlets are similar. If you are seeking the White-faced Storm-Petrel, an Oregon Inlet trip might be a better bet because most records are from the cooler waters northeast of Oregon Inlet. The waters off Hatteras seem to be slightly better for tropicbirds. At this point there are more records of Herald and Soft-plumaged (Cape Verde Islands) Petrels off Oregon Inlet than off Hatteras, but the number of records may be too few to draw any conclusions.

For further details, contact any of the following tour companies.

Armas Hill, Focus on Nature Tours: P.O. Box 9021, Wilmington, DE 19809; (302) 529-1867; fax (302) 529-1085.

Brian Patteson, Inc.: P.O. Box 1135, Amherst, VA 24521; (804)933-8687

Michael Tove, Pterodroma Ptours: 303 Dunhagen Place, Carey, NC 27511; (919) 460-0338

A Hardee's at Oregon Inlet and a 7-Eleven in Manteo are usually the only places open for breakfast (beware of greasy food before a boat trip). Nags Head and Manteo are full of excellent dinner possibilities. There are plenty of places to stay, but be sure to book early! In Manteo, the Duke of Dare Motel (919-473-2175) and Dare Haven Motel (919-473-2322) are popular with birders.

At Hatteras Inlet, Sonny's Restaurant across from Oden's Dock is the most popular spot for breakfast. There is also a bakery in Hatteras that opens early. Eateries for dinner are numerous. For lodging, most birders stay at the Hatteras Marlin Motel (919-986-2141) or the Hatteras Harbor Motel (919-986-2565), both very close to the dock.

- **TEXAS: PORT O'CONNOR**

Recent spring, summer, and fall pelagic trips to deep waters off this port have produced numbers of Band-rumped Storm-Petrels. These Gulf of Mexico trips, though infrequent, are probably a good bet for finding Band-rumps, which appear to be the most common storm-petrel species in the Gulf. For more information about pelagic birds in the Gulf of Mexico, see "A New Frontier: Pelagic Birding in the Gulf of Mexico," by Dwight E. Peake and Mark Elwonger, *Winging It,* 1996, 8(1):1,4-9.

The nearest motel to Port O'Connor is the Express Inn in Port Lavaca (512-552-4511), about 30 miles away. The Kettle across the street from the motel opens early for breakfast. For more information about these trips, contact Mark Elwonger, 405 West Brazos, Victoria, TX 77901; (512) 578-5135; fax (512) 578-3041, or Dwight Peake, 30 LeBrun Court, Galveston, TX 77551; (409) 740-4621.

Bibliography

Abbott, J. M. 1972. Correcting the record on Barnacle Goose. *Atlantic Naturalist* 27:194.

Ainley, D. G. 1976. The occurrence of seabirds in the coastal region of California. *Western Birds* 7:33-68.

Ainley, D. G. and Bill Manolis. 1979. Occurrence and distribution of the Mottled Petrel. *Western Birds* 10:113-23.

Alcorn, J. R. 1988. *The Birds of Nevada*. Fallon, Nev.: Fairview West Publishing.

Allen, J. A. 1880. Langdon's ornithological field notes. *Bulletin of the Nuttall Ornithological Club* 5:232-3.

Allen, R. P. 1956. The flamingoes: their life history and survival, with special reference to the American or West Indian flamingo *(Phoenicopterus ruber). National Audubon Society Resource Report No. 5.*

Allen, R. P. 1952. The Whooping Crane. *National Audubon Society Resource Report 3.*

Allen, R. P. 1956. A report on the Whooping Cranes' northern breeding grounds. National Audubon Society Resour. Rept. 3.

American Ornithologists' Union. 1983. *The A.O.U. Check-list of North American Birds,* 6th ed. Lawrence, Kansas: The American Ornithologists' Union.

Anderson, W. L. and R. W. Storer. 1976. Factors influencing Kirtland's Warbler nesting success. *Jack-Pine Warbler* 54:105-15.

Andrews, R. and R. Righter. 1992. *Colorado Birds.* Denver, Colo: Denver Museum of Natural History.

Appleby, R. H., S. C. Madge, and K. Mullarney. 1986. Identification of divers in immature and winter plumages. *British Birds* 79: 365-91.

Armstrong, R. H. 1990. *Guide to the Birds of Alaska,* 3rd ed. Anchorage, Ala.: Alaska Northwest Books.

Arnold, K. A., ed. 1984. *The T.O.S. Checklist of the Birds of Texas,* second ed. Austin, Tex.: Texas Ornithological Society.

Arnold, K. A. 1980. Rufous-capped Warbler and White-collared Seedeater from Webb County, Texas. *Bulletin Texas Ornithological Society* 13:27.

Arvidson, D. R. 1991a. Wild Barnacles in quiet Osterville. *Bird Observer of Eastern Massachusetts* 19:2526.

Arvidson, D. R. 1991b. Another wild goose chase: addendum to Osterville Barnacles. *Bird Observer of Eastern Massachusetts* 19:147.

Atwood, J. L. 1980. Breeding biology of the Santa Cruz Island Scrub Jay. In *The California Islands: proceedings of a multidisciplinary symposium,* (D. M. Power, ed.), pp. 675-688. Santa Barbara, Calif.: Santa Barbara Museum of Natural History.

Atwood, J. L. 1980b. Body weights of the Santa Cruz Island Scrub Jay. *North American Bird-Bander* 4:148-53.

Atwood, J. L. 1992. A Closer Look: California Gnatcatcher. *Birding* 24:228-33.

Atwood, J. L. and J. S. Bolsinger. 1992. Elevational distribution of California Gnatcatchers in the United States. *Journal of Field Ornithology* 63:159-68.

Audubon, J. J. 1834. *Orn. Biogr* 2:387

Ayres, C. C. 1976. A rare Ivory Gull at Rathbun Lake. *Iowa Bird Life* 46:15-16.

Bailey, A. M. 1926. The Ivory Gull in Colorado. *Condor* 28:182-3.

Bailey, A. M. and R. J. Niedrach. 1965. *Birds of Colorado*. Denver, Colo.: Denver Museum of Natural History.

Bailey, S. F., Peter Pyle, and L. B. Spear. 1989. Dark Pterodroma petrels in the north Pacific: identification, status, and North American occurrence. *American Birds* 43:400-15.

Bailey, W. 1955. *Birds in Massachusetts*. Lancaster, Mass.: The College Press.

Balch, L. G. 1978. Redpoll identification. *Illinois Audubon Bulletin* 186:39-44.

Balch, L. G., H. D. Bohlen, and G. B. Rosenband. 1979. The Illinois Ross' Gull. *American Birds* 33:140-2.

Banks, R. C. 1970. Records of Brambling in North America. *Auk* 87:165-7.

Beedy, E. C. and S. L. Granholm. 1985. *Discovering Sierra Birds*. Yosemite Natural History Association and Sequoia Natural History Association.

Behle, W. H., E. D. Sorensen, and C. M. White. 1985. *Utah Birds: a Revised Checklist*. Salt Lake City, Utah: Utah Museum of Natural History.

Bellrose, F. C. 1976. *Ducks, Geese & Swans of North America*. Harrisburg, Pa.: Stackpole Books.

Bent, A. C. 1925. *Life Histories of North American Wildfowl*, part 2. New York, N.Y.: Dover Publications, Inc.

Bent, A. C. 1942. Life Histories of North American Flycatchers, Larks, Swallows and Their Allies. *U.S. National Museum Bulletin* 179:82.

Berg, E. O. 1974. Great Gray Owl in N.E. Iowa. *Iowa Bird Life* 44:75.

Berkey, G., D. Lambeth, and R. Martin. 1994. *Checklist of North Dakota Birds*.

Bevier, L. R. 1990. Eleventh report of the California Rare Birds Committee. *Western Birds* 21:145-76.

Blackwelder, E. 1899. A note of Kirtland's Warbler. *Auk* 16:359-60.

Bledsoe, A. H., R. Schwartz, and D. Varza. 1984. First Connecticut record of Ross' Gull (*Rhodostethia rosea*). *Connecticut Warbler* 4:19-22.

Bohlen, H. D. 1989. *The Birds of Illinois*. Bloomington, Ind.: Indiana University Press.

Bonaparte, C. L. 1825. *American Ornithology*.

Bond, James. 1940. Identity of United States specimens of Fork-tailed Flycatcher. *Auk* 57:418-19.

Bond, James. 1984. *Twenty-fifth Supplement to the Checklist of the Birds of the West Indies* (1956). Philadelphia, Pa.: Academy of Natural Sciences.

Bond, James. 1985. *Birds of the West Indies*, 5th ed. Boston, Mass.: Houghton Mifflin Co.

Bonney, Mrs. G. E. 1961. Stripe-headed Tanager (*Spindalis zena*) on the Florida Keys. *Florida Naturalist* 34:162-3.

Borrer, D. J. 1972. Yellow-green Vireo in Arizona. *Condor* 74:80-86.

Boulduan, B. 1994. Gyrfalcon in Kossuth County. *Iowa Bird Life* 64:21-2.

Brady, A. 1992. New Jersey's Pelagic Birding. *Winging It* 4(1):1-2, 4-5.

Bremser, W. J., Jr. and R. A. Duncan. 1992. Fork-tailed Flycatcher (*Tyrannus savana*) sighted on Dauphin Island, Ala. *Alabama Birdlife* 39:4-5.

Britten, M. W. 1984. A Fork-tailed Flycatcher in Florida. *Florida Field Naturalist* 12:10-11.

Brown, R. G. B. 1988. Oceanographic factors as determinants of the winter range of Dovekie (*Alle alle*) off Atlantic Canada. *Colonial Waterbirds* 11:176-80.

Bruun, B. 1980. The Greenland Wheatear (*Oenanthe oenanthe leucorrhoa*) in North America. *American Birds* 34:310-12.

Buckle, A. and F. Zino. 1989. Saving Europe's rarest bird. *Roundel* 67:112-16.

Bull, E. L. and J. R. Duncan. 1993. Great Gray Owl (*Strix nebulosa*). In *The Birds of North America,* No. 41 (A. Poole and F. Gill, eds.). Philadelphia, Pa.: The Academy of Natural Sciences.

Bull, J. L. 1964. Red-billed Tropicbird on Long Island, New York. *Auk* 81:433-4.

Bull, John. 1974. *Birds of New York State.* Ithaca, N.Y.: Cornell University Press.

Burleigh, T. D. 1958. *Georgia Birds.* Norman, Okla.: University of Oklahoma Press.

Butler, A. W. 1895. Additional notes on Indiana birds. *Proceedings Indiana Academy of Science* 1895:162-8.

Butler, A. W. 1929. Rare birds in Cincinnati collections. *Auk* 46:196-9.

Byers, C., J. Curson, and U. Olsson. 1995. *Sparrows and Buntings.* Boston, Mass.: Houghton Mifflin Co.

Campbell, L. 1968. *Birds of the Toledo Area.* Toledo, Ohio: The Blade.

Chapman, B. R., P. A. Buckley, and F. Buckley. 1979. First photographic record of Greater Flamingo in Texas. *Bull Texas Ornith Soc* 12:20-21.

Chartier, B. and F. Cooke. 1980. Ross' Gulls (*Rhodostethia rosea*) nesting at Churchill, Manitoba, Canada. *American Birds* 34:839-41.

Clapp, R. B. and W. B. Robertson, Jr. 1986. Nesting of the Masked Booby on the Dry Tortugas. *Colonial Waterbirds* 9:113-16.

Clark, W. S. and B. K. Wheeler. 1987. *A Field Guide to Hawks of North America.* Boston, Mass.: Houghton Mifflin Co.

Clary, B. L. 1930. Blue-footed Booby on Salton Sea. *Condor* 32:160-1.

Clement, P. 1987. Field identification of Western Palearctic Wheatears. *British Birds* 80:137-57 and 80:187-238.

Clench, M. H. 1973. The fall migration route of Kirtland's Warbler. *Wilson Bull* 85:417-28.

Coale, H. K. 1914. Richardson's Owl in northeastern Illinois. *Auk* 31:536

Conway, R. A. 1992. *Field-Checklist of Rhode Island Birds.* Smithfield, R.I.: Rhode Island Ornithological Club.

Cory, C. B. 1898. Kirtland's Warbler (*Dendroica kirtlandi*) in Florida. *Auk* 15:331.

Coues, E. 1880. Description of the female *Dendroica kirtlandi. Bulletin of the Nuttall Ornithological Club.* 5:49-50.

Covert, A. B. 1876. Birds of Lower Michigan. *Forest and Stream* 6:132.

Cox, J. 1992. Field observations. *Florida Field Naturalist* 20:24-8.

Cruickshank, A. 1942. *Birds around New York City.* New York, N.Y.: American Museum of Natural History.

Cruickshank, A. D. 1980. *The Birds of Brevard County*. Privately published.

Cruz, A., T. Manolis, and J. W. Wiley. 1985. The Shiny Cowbird: A brood parasite expanding its range in the Carribean region. *Ornithological Monogram* 36:607-20.

Curry, B. 1993. Birding Niagara. *Winging It* 5:1-4.

Danforth, D. W. 1979. An Aztec Thrush in Arizona. *Western Birds* 10:217-18.

Darnell, M. 1956. Kirtland's Warbler. *The Migrant* 37(1):15.

Davies, L. M. 1906. The Birds of Cleveland, Ohio, and Vicinity. *Wilson Bulletin* 13:110-20.

Davis, L. I. 1972. *A Field Guide to the Birds of Mexico and Central America*. Austin,Tex.: University of Texas Press.

Davis, W. A. and S. M. Russell. 1984. *Birds in Southeastern Arizona*, 2nd ed. Tucson, Ariz.: Tucson Audubon Society.

Davis, W. A. and S. M. Russell. 1990. *Birds in Southeastern Arizona*, 3rd ed. Tucson, Ariz.: Tucson Audubon Society.

Deane, R. 1903a. Richardson's Owl in Illinois. *Auk* 20:305

Deane, R. 1903b. Richardson's Owl in Illinois. *Auk* 20:433-4

Dennis, D. W. 1905. Capture of the Kirtland's Warbler near Richmond, Indiana. *Auk* 22:314.

Derrickson, S. R. 1980. *Whooping Crane Recovery Plan*. Washington, D.C.: U.S. Fish and Wildlife Service.

DeSante, David and Peter Pyle. 1986. *Distributional Checklist of North American Birds*, vol. 1. Lee Vining, Calif.: Artemisia Press.

Dinsmore, S. J. 1991. Ivory Gull at Red Rock Reservoir. *Iowa Bird Life* 61:110-11.

Dowling, H. P. 1989. FOS Records Committee report. *Florida Field Naturalist* 17:51-2.

Drennan, S. R. 1981. *Where to Find Birds in New York State*. Syracuse, N.Y.: Syracuse University Press.

Dunn, J. L. 1988. Tenth report of the California Rare Birds Committee. *Western Birds* 19:129-63.

Dunn, J. L. and K. L. Garrett. 1987. The identification of North American gnatcatchers. *Birding* 19:17-29.

Dunn, J. L. and K. L. Garrett. 1990. Identification of Ruddy and Common Ground-Doves. *Birding* 22:138-45.

Dunne, P., D. Sibley, and C. Sutton. 1988. *Hawks in Flight*. Boston, Mass.: Houghton Mifflin Co.

Dunning, J. S. 1987. *South American Birds: A Photographic Aid to Identification*. Newton Square, Pa.: Harrowood Books.

Easterla, D. A. 1972. Specimens of Black-throated Blue Warbler and Yellow-green Vireo from west Texas. *Condor* 74:489.

Eckert, K. R. 1982. Regional Report: Western Great Lakes Region. *American Birds* 36:298.

Eckert, K. R. and T. L. Savaloja. 1979. First documented nesting of the Boreal Owl south of Canada. *American Birds* 33:135-7.

Edge, E. R. 1934. Blue-footed Booby in San Bernardino County, California. *Condor* 36:88.

Elliott, B. G. 1976. Blue-footed Booby in northern California. *Western Birds* 7:155-7

Ely, C. A. and R. B. Clapp. 1973. The natural history of Laysan Island Northwestern Hawaiian Islands. *Atoll Research Bulletin* No. 171.

Emilio, S. G. and L. Griscom. 1930. The European Black-headed Gull (*Larus ridibundus*) in America. *Auk* 47:243.

Enticott, J. W. 1991. Identification of Soft-plumaged Petrel. *British Birds* 84:245-64.

Escott, C. J. 1995. Extralimital occurrence of Rufous-necked Stint, *Calidris ruficollis,* in North America. *Birder's Journal* 4:132-8.

Escott, N. 1992. Green Violet-ear: First for Canada. *Ontario Birds* 10:86-9.

Evanich, J. E., Jr. 1990. *The Birder's Guide to Oregon.* Portland, OR: Portland Audubon Society.

Farrand, J. Jr., ed. 1983. *The Audubon Society Master Guide to Birding.* New York Alfred A. Knopf, Inc.

Faver, A. R. 1949. Kirtland's Warbler seen at Eastover, Richland County, S.C. *Chat* 13:79-80.

Faver, A. R. 1951. Chats and other Warblers at Eastover, S.C. *Chat* 15:82-3.

Faver, A. R. 1967. Kirtland's Warbler at Eastover, S.C. *Chat* 31:98.

Finch, D. W. 1978. Black-headed Gull (*Larus ridibundus*) breeding in Newfoundland. *American Birds* 32:312.

Fintel, W. A. 1974 First Masked Duck sighting in Tennessee. *The Migrant* 45:47-8.

Fisher, H. I. 1948. Interbreeding of Laysan and Black-footed albatrosses. *Pac. Sci.* 2:132.

Fisher, H. I. 1972. Sympatry of Laysan and Black-footed Albatrosses. *Auk* 89:381-402.

Fisher, H. I. and J. R. Fisher. 1972. The oceanic distribution of the Laysan Albatross (*Diomeda immutabilis*). *Wilson Bulletin* 84:7-27.

Fleetwood, R. J. and C. E. Hudson, Jr. 1965. Probable Green Violet-ear Hummingbird in Cameron County, Texas. *Southwestern Naturalist* 10:312.

Forbush, E. H. 1925. *The Birds of Massachusetts.* vol 1. Massachusetts Dept. of Agriculture.

Ford, E. R. 1956. *Birds of the Chicago Region.* Chicago Academy of Sciences, Special Publication, No. 12.

Foster, F. A. 1917. *Muscivora tyrannus* (Linn.) in Massachusetts. *Auk* 34:337.

Gantlett, S. 1995. Identification Forum: field separation of Fea's, Zino's, and Soft-plumaged Petrels. *Birding World* 8:256-60.

Garber, C. S., R. L. Wallen, and K. E. Duffy. 1991. Distribution of Boreal Owl observation records in Wyoming. *Journal Raptor Research* 25:120-2.

Garrett, K. and J. Dunn. 1981. *Birds of Southern California.* Los Angeles, CA: Los Angeles Audubon Society.

Garrido, O. H. 1984. *Molothrus bonariensis (Aves: Icteridae), nuevo record para Cuba.* Miscelanea Zoologica, No. 19.

Gault, B. T. 1894. Kirtland's Warbler in northeastern Illinois. *Auk* 11:258.

Gilligan, Jeff, M. Smith, D. Rogers, and A. Contreras. 1994. *Birds of Oregon: Status and Distribution.* McMinnville, Ore.: Cinclus Publications.

Gochfeld, M. 1968. Notes on the status of the Tufted Duck (*Aythya fuligula*) in North America with a report of a new observation from Wyoming. *Condor* 70:186-7.

Goetz, R. E., W. . Rudden, and P. B. Snetzinger. 1986. Slaty-backed Gull winters on the Mississippi River. *American Birds* 40:207-16.

Golley, M. and A. Stoddart. 1991. Identification of American and Pacific Golden Plovers. *Birding World* 4:195-204.

Granlund, James. 1994. Field identification of Common and Hoary Redpolls. *Michigan Birds and Natural History* 1:21-7

Grant, P. J. 1986. *Gulls: A Guide to Identification,* 2nd ed. Vermillion, S.D.: Buteo Books.

Green, J. C. and R. B. Janssen. 1975. *Minnesota Birds*. St. Paul, Minn.: University of Minnesota.

Greene, E. R. 1943. Cuban nighthawk breeding in lower Florida Keys. *Auk* 61:302.

Greene, E. R., W. W. Griffin, E. P. Odum, H. L. Stoddard, and I. R. Tomkins. 1945. Birds of Georgia. Georgia Ornithological Society Occasional Publication No. 2. University of Georgia: Athens Press.

Greenman, D. 1972. Wisconsin's eighth Kirtland's Warbler. *Passenger Pigeon* 34:40.

Groschupf, Kathleen. 1992. A Closer Look: Black-capped Gnatcatcher. *Birding* 24:160-4.

Gross, M. E. 1938. Kirtland's Warber on migration. *Jack-Pine Warbler* 16:28-9.

Gruber, F. 1884. Die sievogel der Farallone-inseln. *Z. Gesamte Ornithol.* 1:167-72.

Gustafson, M. E. and B. G. Peterjohn. 1994. Adult Slaty-backed Gulls. *Birding* 26:243-9.

Halmi, N. S. 1974. Sight record of Sharp-tailed Sandpiper near Iowa City. *Iowa Bird Life* 44:106.

Hames, F. 1956. Masked Duck in Florida. *Auk* 73:291.

Haney, J. C. 1985. Band-rumped Storm-Petrel occurrences in relation to upwelling off the coast of the southeastern United States. *Wilson Bulletin* 97:543-7.

Haney, J. C. 1987. Aspects of the pelagic ecology and behavior of the Black-capped Petrel (*Pterodroma hasitata*). *Wilson Bulletin* 99:153-68.

Haney, J. C. 1993. A closer look: Ivory Gull. *Birding* 25:331-7.

Haney, J. C., P. Brisse, D. R. Jacobson, M. W. Oberle, and J. M. Paget. 1986. *Annotated Checklist of Georgia Birds.* Georgia Ornith. Soc. Occ. Pub. No. 10.

Harris, A., L. Tucker, and K. Vinicombe. 1989. *The MacMillan Field Guide to Bird Identification.* London, England: The MacMillan Press, Ltd.

Harris, E. 1844. [untitled note]. In Meeting for business, May 28, 1844, p. 65. *Proceedings Philadelphia Academy of Science* 1844-5.

Harris, S. W. and R. H. Gerstenberg. 1970. Common Teal and Tufted Duck in northwestern California. *Condor* 72:108.

Harrison, Peter. 1984. *Seabirds*. Boston, Mass.: Houghton Mifflin Company.

Harrison, Peter. 1987. *A Field Guide to Seabirds of the World*. Lexington, Mass.: The Stephen Greene Press.

Harrop, H. 1993. Identification of Sharp-tailed Sandpiper and Pectoral Sandpiper. *Birding World* 6:230-8.

Hatcher, J. B. 1960. Rare Kirtland's Warbler at Aiken, S.C. *Chat* 24:102-3.

Hayward, G. D. 1989. *Habitat use and population biology of Boreal Owls in the Northern Rocky Mountains, USA*. Ph.D. diss., University of Idaho, Moscow.

Hayward, G. D. and P. H. Hayward. 1993. Boreal Owl. In *The Birds of North America*, No. 63 (A. Poole and F. Gill, eds.). Philadelphia, Pa.: The Academy of Natural Sciences. Washington, D.C.: The American Ornithologists' Union.

Hayward, G .H., P. H. Hayward, E. O. Garton, and R. Escano. 1987. Revised breeding distribution of the Boreal Owl in the Northern Rocky Mountains. *Condor* 89:431-2.

Heard, C. D. W. and G. Walbridge. 1988. Field identification of Pechora Pipit. *British Birds* 81:452-63.

Helme, A. H. 1904. The Ipswich Sparrow, Kirtland's Warbler, and Sprague's Pipit in Georgia. *Auk* 21:291.

Henninger, W. F. 1906. A preliminary list of the birds of Seneca County, Ohio. *Wilson Bulletin* 18:47-60.

Henninger, W. F. 1908. Bird notes from middle western Ohio. *Wilson Bulletin* 20:208-0.

Henninger, W. F. 1910. Personals: Our members here and there. *Wilson Bulletin* 22:127-8.

Henshaw, H. W. 1886. Description of a new jay from California. *Auk* 3:452-3.

Hiemenz, N. 1980. A 1944 record for the Kirtland's Warbler. *Loon* 52:112.

Hill, N. P. 1965. *The Birds of Cape Cod, Massachusetts*. New York: William Morrow and Co.

Holder, M. 1996. Identification and status of the Yellow-green Vireo in North America. *Birder's Journal* 5:78.

Holt, D. W., J. P. Lortie, B. J. Nikula, and R. C. Humphrey. 1986. First record of Common Black-headed Gulls breeding in the United States. *American Birds* 40:204-6.

Holt, H. R. 1990. *A Birder's Guide to Southern California*. Colorado Springs, Colo.: American Birding Association.

Holt, H. R. 1992. *A Birder's Guide to the Rio Grande Valley*. Colorado Springs, Colo.: American Birding Association.

Howell, A. B. and A. J. van Rossem. 1911. Further notes from Santa Cruz Island. *Condor* 13:208-10.

Howell, A .H. 1932. *Florida Bird Life*. New York: Coward-McCann.

Howell, S. N. G. 1990. Identification of White and Black-backed Wagtails in alternate plumage. *Western Birds* 21:41-9.

Howell, S. N. G. and S. Webb. 1990. The seabirds of Las Islas Revillagigedo, Mexico. *Wilson Bulletin* 102:140-6.

Howell, S. N. G. and S. Webb. 1992. The Laysan Albatross in Mexico. *American Birds* 46:220-3.

Howell, S. N. G. and S. Webb. 1995. *A Guide to the Birds of Mexico and Northern Central America*. Oxford, England: Oxford University Press.

Hoxie, W. 1886. Kirtland's Warbler on St. Helena Island, South Carolina. *Auk* 3:412-3.

Humphrey, C. 1956. Bahama Swallow (*Callichelidon cyaneoviridis*) [at New Smyrna Beach]. *Florida Naturalist* 29:33.

Imhof, T. A. 1954. When do the birds occur at Birmingham? *Alabama Birdlife* 2:24-6.

Imhof, T. A. 1976. *Alabama Birds*. State of Alabama, Dept. of Conservation and Natural Resources, Game and Fish Division.

Jackson, Greg D. 1992. Field identification of teal in North America—Part II. *Birding* 24:214-23.

Jaeger, E. C. 1955. *A Sourcebook of Biological Names and Terms*, 3rd ed. Springfield, Ill.: Charles C Thomas.

James, D. A. and J. C. Neal. 1986. *Arkansas Birds*. Fayetteville, Ark.: The University of Arkansas Press.

James, P. 1963. Fork-tailed Flycatcher (*Muscivora tyrannus tyrannus*) taken in Texas. *Auk* 80:85.

Jehl, J. R., Jr. 1977. An annotated list of birds of Islas Los Coronados, Baja California, and adjacent waters. *Western Birds* 8:91-101.

Jehl, J. R. and S. I. Bond. 1975. Morphological variation and species limits of genus *Endomychura. Transactions San Diego Society of Natural History* 18(2):9-24.

Jennes, P. 1925. Kirtland's Warbler in North Carolina. *Bird-Lore* 27:252-3.

Johnsgard, P. A. 1983. *Cranes of the World*. Bloomington, Ind.: Indiana University Press.

Johnson, N. K. 1972. Origin and differentiation of the avifauna of the Channel Islands, California. *Condor* 74:295-315.

Johnston, D. W. 1962. The Whooping Crane in South Carolina— a résumé. *Chat* 26:39-40.

Jones, C. 1995. A review of North American Brambling records. *Birder's Journal* 4:75-9.

Jones, F. M. 1931. [Editorial notes] *Raven* 2(7):1

Jones, H. L. 1975. *Studies of avian turnover, dispersal and colonization of the California Channel Islands*. Ph.D. thesis, University of California, Los Angeles.

Jones, L. 1895. Record of the work of the Wilson Chapter for 1893 and 1894 on the *Mniotiltidae. Wilson Bulletin* 7:1-20.

Jones, L. 1903. *The Birds of Ohio*. Ohio State Academy of Science Papers, No. 6.

Jones, L. 1906. Some noteworthy Lorain County records for 1906. *Wilson Bulletin* 18:74-5.

Jonsson, Lars. 1992. *Birds of Europe*. Princeton, N.J.: Princeton University Press.

Kain, Teta, ed. 1987. *Virginia's Birdlife*. Virginia Society of Ornithology.

Kaufman, K. 1990. *Advanced Birding*. Boston, Mass.: Houghton Mifflin Co.

Kaufman, K. 1992. Lucifer Hummingbird identification. *Birding* 46:491-4.

Keller, C., S. Keller, and T. Keller. 1979. *Indiana Birds and Their Haunts*. Bloomington, Ind.: Indiana University Press.

Kelley, A. H. 1969. Michigan bird survey, spring, 1969. *Jack-Pine Warbler* 47:91-8.

Kemsies, E. 1930. Birds of the Yellowstone National Park, with some recent additions. *Wilson Bulletin*. 42:198-210.

Kenaga, E. E. 1959. Michigan bird survey, spring 1959. *Jack-Pine Warbler* 37:152-8.

Kenaga, E. E. 1960. Michigan bird survey, spring 1960. *Jack-Pine Warbler* 38:148-54.

King, Ben. 1981. The field identification of North American pipits. *American Birds* 35:778-88.

King, W. B. 1981. *Endangered Birds of the World*. Washington, D.C.: Smithsonian Institution Press.

Klett, E. V. 1982. A new bird for Oklahoma: Garganey. *Bulletin Oklahoma Ornithological Society* 15(2): 9-10.

Knight, O. W. 1910. Fork-tailed Flycatcher in Maine. *Auk* 27:80-1.

Knox, A. G. 1987. The taxonomy of redpolls. *Ardea* 76:1-26.

Koella, J. A. 1985. Sight record of Gyrfalcon in Jefferson County, Tennessee. *The Migrant* 56:14-15.

Koes, R. F. 1995. The Northern Wheatear in Canada. *Birder's Journal* 4:21-8.

Lack, P. 1986. *The Atlas of Wintering Birds in Britain and Ireland*. Town Head House, Calton, Great Britain: T & AD Poyser Ltd.

Lane, J. 1975. Kirtland's Warbler in Mexico. *American Birds* 29:144.

Lane, James A. 1986. *A Birder's Guide to Southeastern Arizona*. Denver, Colo.: L & P Press.

Lane, W. H. 1988. 1988 Boreal Owl survey in Cook County. *Loon* 60:99-104.

Langham, J. M. 1991. Twelfth report of the California Rare Birds Committee. *Western Birds* 22:97-130.

Langridge, H. P. 1985. First peninsular sighting of *Vireo olivaceus flavoviridis* in Florida. *Florida Field Naturalist* 13:37-8.

Lansdown, P., N. Riddiford, and A. Knox. Identification of Arctic Redpoll *Carduelis hornemanni exilipes*. *British Birds* 84:41-56.

Larrison, E. J. and K. G. Sonnenberg. 1968. *Washington Birds: their location and identification*. Seattle, Wash.: Seattle Audubon Society.

Lasley, G. W. and M. Krzywonski. 1991. First United States record of the White-throated Robin. *American Birds* 45:230-1.

Lawson, C. S. 1977. Non-passerine species new or unusual to Nevada. *Western Birds* 8:73-90.

Leck, C. F. 1984. *The Status and Distribution of New Jersey's Birds*. New Brunswick, N.J.: Rutgers University Press.

Lee, D. S. 1979. Second record of the South Trinidad Petrel (*Pterodroma arminjoniana*) for North America. *American Birds* 33:138-9.

Lee, D. S. 1984. Petrels and storm-petrels in North Carolina's offshore waters: including species previously unrecorded for North America. *American Birds* 38:151-63.

Lee, D. S. and J. C. Haney. 1984. The genus *Sula* in the Carolinas. *Chat* 48:29-45.

Lee, D. S. and W. Irvin. 1983. Tropicbirds in the Carolinas: status and periodic occurrence of two tropical pelagic species. *Chat* 47:1-13.

Lewington, I., P. Alstrom, and P. Colston. 1991. *A Field Guide to the Rare Birds of Britain and Europe*. St. Helier, Jersey, Great Britain: Domino Books.

Lewis, J. C. 1995. Whooping Crane (*Grus americana*). In *The Birds of North America* (A. Poole and F. Gill, eds). The Academy of Natural Sciences, Philadelphia. Washington, D.C.: The American Ornithologists' Union.

Lewis, J. C. and L. Finger. 1993. Endangered and threatened wildlife and plants; establishment of an experimental nonessential population of Whooping Cranes in Florida. *Fed. Regist.* 58:5647-58.

Lewis, M. G. and F. A. Sharpe. 1987. *Birding in the San Juan Islands*. Seattle, Wash.: The Mountaineers.

Lockwood, W. B., ed. 1984. *The Oxford Book of British Bird Names*. Oxford, England: Oxford University Press.

Loomis, L. M. 1889. A Rare Bird in Chester Co., South Carolina. *Auk* 6:74-5.

Lound, M. and R. Lound. 1956. 1956 in review. *Passenger Pigeon* 18:66-72.

Lowery, G. H., Jr. 1974. *Louisiana Birds*, 3rd ed. Louisiana State University Press.

MacDonald, S. 1978. First breeding record of Ross' Gull in Canada. *Proceedings Colonial Waterbird Group* 1:16.

Madge, S. and H. Burn. 1988. *Waterfowl*. Boston, Mass.: Houghton Mifflin Co.

Madge, S. and H. Burn. 1994. *Crows and Jays*. Boston, Mass.: Houghton Mifflin Co.

Mahan, T. A. and B. Simmers. 1992. Social preference of four cross-foster reared Sandhill Cranes. *Proc. N. Am. Crane Workshop* 6:114-19.

Mason, C. R. 1960. Heretofore unpublished records of the Kirtland's Warbler (*Dendroica kirtlandii*). *Florida Naturalist* 33:223.

Mayfield, H. F. 1960. *The Kirtland's Warbler*. Cranbrook Institute of Science. Bloomfield Hills, Michigan.

Mayfield, H. F. 1962. 1961 Decennial census of the Kirtland's Warbler. *Auk* 79:173-82.

Mayfield, H. F. 1972. Third decennial census of the Kirtland's Warbler. *Auk* 89:263-8.

Mayfield, H. F. 1972b. Winter habitat of Kirtland's Warbler. *Wilson Bulletin* 84:347-9.

Mayfield, H. F. 1988. Do Kirtland's Warblers migrate in one hop? *Auk* 105:204-5.

Mayfield, H. F. 1992. Kirtland's Warbler. In *The Birds of North America,* No. 19 (A. Poole, P. Stettenheim, and F. Gill, eds.). Philadephia, Pa.: The Academy of Natural Sciences. Washington, D.C.: The American Ornithologists' Union.

Mayfield, H. F. 1996. Kirtland's Warblers in winter. *Birding* 28:34-7.

McCaskie, Guy. 1970. The occurrence of four species of pelecaniformes in the southwestern United States. *Western Birds* 1:117-41.

McCaskie, Guy. 1983. Another look at the Western and Yellow-footed Gulls. *Western Birds* 14:85-107.

McCaskie, G., P. De Benedictis, R. Erickson, and J. Morlan. 1988. *Birds of Northern California*. Berkeley, Cali.: Golden Gate Audubon Society.

McCaskie, Guy and M. A. Patten. 1994. Status of the Fork-tailed Flycatcher (*Tyrannus savana*) in the United States and Canada. *Western Birds* 25:113-27.

McCaskie, R. G. (Guy). 1966. The occurrence of Red-throated Pipits in California. *Auk* 83:135-6.

McClanahan, R. C. 1935. Fifty years after. *Florida Naturalist* 8:53-9.

McKenzie, P. M. 1973. Kirtland's Warbler sighted in Somerset County. *Audubon Soc. Western Penna., Bull.,* 37(7):10.

McMillon, Bill. 1996. *Birding Arizona*. Helena, Mont.: Falcon Press.

McQuown, J. O. 1944. The Kirtland's Warbler in the Cleveland region. *Cleveland Bird Calendar* 40:8.

Merriam, C. H. 1883. On a bird new to northern North America. *Bulletin Nuttall Ornithological Club* 8:213.

Merriam, C. H. 1885. Kirtland's Warbler from the Straits of Mackinac. *Auk* 2:376.

Merrill, J. C. 1878. Notes on the ornithology of south Texas, being a list of birds observed in the vicinity of Fort Brown, Texas, from February 1876, to June 1878. *Proceedings United States National Museum* 1:113-73.

Miles, M. L. 1967. An addition to the avifauna of the United States: *Myiarchus stolidus sagrae*. *Auk* 84:279.

Miliotis, Paul and P. A. Buckley. 1975. The Massachusetts Ross' Gull. *American Birds* 29:643-6.

Miller, G. 1991. Birder's guide to Aransas National Wildlife Refuge. *Wild Bird* 1991:36-41.

Mirande, C., R. Lacy, and U. Seal. 1993. *Whooping Crane (Grus americana) conservation viability assessment workshop report*. Captive Breeding Specialist Group, International Union for Conservation of Nature, Apple Valley, Minnesota.

Mlodinow, S. 1984. *Chicago Area Birds*. Chicago, Ill.: Chicago Review Press.

Mlodinow, S. 1993. Finding the Pacific Golden-Plover (*Pluvialis fulva*) in North America. *Birding* 25:322-9.

Mlodinow, S. 1995. The Snohomish County Emperor Geese. *WOS News* 36:1-6.

Moldenhauer, R. K. 1974. First Clay-colored Robin collected in the United States. *Auk* 91:839-840.

Monroe, B. L., Jr. 1959. Occurrence of the Yellow-green Vireo in Florida. *Auk* 76:95-6.

Monroe, B. L., Jr. 1960. Yellow-green Vireo. *Florida Naturalist* 33:37-8.

Monroe, B. L., Jr., A. L. Stamm, and B. L. Palmer-Ball, Jr. 1988. *Annotated Checklist of the Birds of Kentucky*. Louisville, Ky.: Kentucky Ornithological Society.

Monson, G. 1986. Gray-collared Becard in Sonora. *American Birds* 40:562-3.

Monson, G. and A. R. Phillips. 1981. *Annotated Checklist of the Birds of Arizona*. Tucson, Ariz.: The Univerisity of Arizona Press.

Montevicchi, W. A., and J. Wells. 1984. Two new specimen records for insular Newfoundland: Barnacle Goose and Tricolored Heron. *American Birds* 38:257-8.

Montiero, L. R. and R. W. Furness. 1995. Fea's Petrel (*Pterodroma feae*) in the Azores. *Bull British Ornithological Club* 115:9-14.

Morlan, J. 1981. Status and identification of forms of White Wagtail in western North America. *Continental Birdlife* 2:37-50.

Morlan, J. and R. A. Erickson. 1983. A Eurasian Skylark at Point Reyes, California, with notes of skylark identification and systematics. *Western Birds* 14:113-26.

Morse, B. 1994. *A Birder's Guide to Ocean Shores*. Olympia, Wash.: R. W. Morse Co.

Moyer, L. B. 1908. Song of Kirtland's Warbler. *Bird-Lore* 10:264.

Mumford, R. E. and C. E. Keller. 1984. *The Birds of Indiana*. Bloomington, Ind.: Indiana University Press.

Murphy, ? 1939. Bahama Pintail in Virginia. *Auk* 56:471-2.

Naveen, R. 1981-1982. Storm-petrels of the world: an introductory guide to their identification. *Birding* 13:216-39; 14:10-15; 14:56-62; 14:140-7.

Nelson, J. B. 1978. *The Sulidae*. Oxford, England: Oxford University Press.

Nesbitt, S. A. 1982. The past, present, and future of the Whooping Crane in Florida. In *Proceedings 1981 international crane workshop* (J. C. Lewis, ed.). Tavernier, Fla.: National Audubon Society.

Nicholson, C. 1983. The Barnacle Goose in Humphreys County, Tennessee. *The Migrant* 54:39.

Oberholser, H. C. 1974. *The Bird Life of Texas*. Austin, Tex.: University of Texas Press.

Ogden, J. C. 1973. Field identification of difficult birds: Short-tailed Hawk. *Florida Field Naturalist* 1:30-3.

Ogden, J. C. 1974. The Short-tailed Hawk in Florida. *Auk* 91:95-110.

Ogden, J.C. 1978. Short-tailed Hawk In *Rare and Endangered Biota of Florida,* vol. 2. (H. W. Kale, II, ed.). Gainesville, Fla.: University Presses of Florida.

Ogden, J. C. 1968. Sharp-tailed Sandpiper collected in Florida. *Auk* 85:692.

Olsen, K. M. and H. Larsson. 1995. *Terns of Europe and North America*. Princeton, New Jersey: Princeton University Press.

Orr, R. T. 1950. A new North American record for the Tufted Duck. *Condor* 52:140.

Orr, R. T. 1962. The Tufted Duck in California. *Auk* 79:482-3.

Ortego, B. 1978. Blue-faced Boobies at an oil production platform. *Auk* 95:762-3.

Owen, Myrfyn. 1977. *Wildfowl of Europe*. London, England: The MacMillan Press Ltd.

Paget, J. M. 1983. Two recent Georgia sightings of the Kirtland's Warbler. *Oriole* 48:42.

Palmer, D. A. 1986. *Habitat selection, movements and activity of Boreal and Saw-whet owls*. M.Sc. thesis. Colorado State Univiversity, Fort Collins.

Palmer, R. S., ed. 1962. *Handbook of North American Birds*, vol. 1. New Haven, Conn.: Yale University Press.

Palmer, R. S., ed. 1976. *Handbook of North American Birds*, vol 2. New Haven, Conn.: Yale University Press.

Patten, M. A. and K. F. Campbell. 1994. Late nesting of the California Gnatcatcher. *Western Birds* 25:110-11.

Paul, R. T. and A. F. Schnapf. 1994. Seasonal report: Florida Region. *American Birds* 48:936-938.

Payne, R. B. 1983. *A Distributional Checklist of the Birds of Michigan*. Ann Arbor, Mich.: Museum of Zoology, University of Michigan.

Peake, D. E. and M. Elwonger. 1996. A new frontier: pelagic birding in the Gulf of Mexico. *Winging It* 8(1): 1, 4-9.

Pearson, T. G., ed. 1936. *Birds of America*. Garden City, N.Y.: Garden City Publishing Co, Inc.

Peterson, A. T. 1992. Phylogeny and rates of molecular evolution in the *Aphelocoma* jays (Corvidae). *Auk* 109:133-47.

Peterson, R. T. 1990. *A Field Guide to Western Birds*, 3rd ed. Boston, Mass.: Houghton Mifflin Co.

Peterson, R. T., and E. L. Chalif. 1973. *A Field Guide to Mexican Birds*. Boston, Mass.: Houghton Mifflin Co.

Philbrick, R. N. (ed.) 1967. Proceedings of the symposium on the biology of the California Islands, pp. 1-363. Santa Barbara Botanic Garden, Santa Barbara, California.

Phillips, A., J. Marshall, and G. Monson. 1964. *The Birds of Arizona*. Tucson, Ariz.: University of Arizona Press.

Pitman, R. L. and M. R. Graybill. 1985. Horned Puffin sightings in the eastern Pacific. *Western Birds* 16:99-102.

Post, W., A. Cruz, and D. B. McNair. 1993. The North American invasion pattern of the Shiny Cowbird. *J. Field Ornithology* 64:32-41.

Post, W. and S. A. Gauthreaux. 1989. *Status and Distribution of South Carolina Birds*. Charleston, S.C.: The Charleston Museum.

Post, W. and J. W. Wiley. 1977. The Shiny Cowbird in the West Indies. *Condor* 79:119-21.

Pratt, H. D., P. L. Bruner, and D. G. Berrett. 1987. *The Birds of Hawaii and the Tropical Pacific*. Princeton, N.J.: Princeton University Press.

Price, W. W. 1888. Occurrence of *Vireo flavoviridis* at Riverside, California. *Auk* 5:210.

Pulich, W. M., Sr. and W. M. Pulich, Jr. 1963. The nesting of the Lucifer Hummingbird in the United States. *Auk* 80:370-1.

Rappole, J. H. and G. W. Blacklock. 1985. *Birds of the Texas Coastal Bend*. College Station, Tex.: Texas A&M University Press.

Rappole, J. H. and G. W. Blacklock. 1994. *Birds of Texas: A Field Guide*. College Station, Tex.: Texas A & M University Press.

Raynard, G. B. and O. H. Garrido. 1988. *Birds Songs in Cuba* [33 rpm recording]. Ithaca, N.Y.: Cornell Laboratory of Ornithology.

Remsen, J. R. and L. Binford. 1975. Status of the Yellow-billed Loon (*G. adamsii*) in the western United States and Mexico. *Western Birds* 6:19.

Remsen, J. V. Jr., S. W. Cardiff, and D. L. Dittmann. 1996. Timing of migration and status of vireos (*Vireonidae*) in Louisiana. *Journal of Field Ornithology* 67:119-140.

Richmond, Jean. 1985. *Birding Northern California*. Walnut Creek, California: Mt. Diablo Audubon Society.

Ridgway, R. 1884. Another Kirtland's Warbler from Michigan. *Auk* 1:389.

Ringler, R. F. 1988. Barnacle Goose in Maryland. *Maryland Birdlife* 44:35-7.

Robbins, C. S., Bertel Bruun, and H. S. Zim. 1966. *Birds of North America*. New York: Golden Press.

Robbins, M. and D. Easterla. 1992. *Birds of Missouri*. Columbia, Mo.: University of Missouri Press.

Robbins, S. D. Jr. 1947. 1946 in review. *Passenger Pigeon* 9:48-52.

Roberson, D. 1980. *Rare Birds of the West Coast*. Pacific Grove, Calif.: Woodcock Publications.

Roberson, D. 1985. *Monterey Birds*. Monterey, Calif.: Monterey Peninsula Audubon Society.

Roberson, D. 1985b. *Barnacle Geese: which ones to count*. unpublished.

Roberson, Don and S. F. Bailey. 1991. Cookilaria petrels in the eastern Pacific Ocean. *American Birds* 45:1067-81.

Roberts, N. and H. Roberts. 1980. Field Notes: The summer season—June 1 to July 31, 1979. *Passenger Pigeon* 42:77-83.

Robertson, W. B., Jr, and J. A. Kushlan. 1974. The south Florida avifauna. Reprinted (1984) as pp. 219-57 in *Environments of South Florida: Present and Past,* Part II (P. J. Gleason, ed.). Coral Gables, Fla.: Miami Geological Society.

Robertson, W. B., Jr., D. R. Paulson, and C. R. Mason. 1961. A tern new to the United States. *Auk* 78:423-5.

Robertson, W. B., Jr, and G. E. Woolfenden. 1992. *Florida Bird Species: An Annotated List.* Gainesville, Fla.: Florida Ornithological Society.

Robinson, J. C. 1990. *An Annotated Checklist of the Birds of Tennessee*. Knoxville, Tenn.: University of Tennessee Press.

Rodgers, J. A., Jr., S. T. Schwikert, and A. S. Wenner. 1988. Status of the Snail Kite in Florida: 1981-1985. *American Birds* 42:30-5.

Rosche, L. 1988. *A Field Book of Birds of the Cleveland Region*. Cleveland, Ohio: Cleveland Natural History Museum.

Ross, R. 1982. Possible Garganey Teal in Roger Mills County, Oklahoma. *Bull Oklahoma Ornithological Society* 15(1):7-8.

Rundle, O. J. 1984. Bird-ringing report, 1981. Stavanger Museum. *Sterna* 17:129-55.

Rutledge, J. T. and R. E. Joseph. 1981. Competetive interactions between Lucifer and Black-chinned Hummingbirds in the Black Gap Wildlife Management Area of Texas. Austin, Texas: *Texas Academy of Sciences 84th Annual Meeting Program Supplement*.

Saunders, A. A. 1908. Some birds of central Alabama. *Auk* 25:413-24.

Schroeder, A. B. and T. B. DeBlaey. 1968. The birds of Ottawa County, Michigan. *Jack-Pine Warbler* 46:99-130.

Scott, P. E. 1993. A closer look: Lucifer Hummingbird. *Birding* 25:245-52.

Scott, S. L., ed. 1987. *National Geographic Society Field Guide to the Birds of North America, 2nd ed.* Washington, D.C.: National Geographic Society.

Scott, W. E. D. 1890a. Two species of swallows new to North America. *Auk* 7:264-5.

Scott, W. E. D. 1890b. On birds observed at the Dry Tortugas during parts of March and April. *Auk* 7:301-14.

Seutin, G., P. T. Boag, and L. M. Ratliffe. 1992. Plumage variability in redpolls from Churchill, Manitoba. *Auk* 109:771-85.

Shuntov, V. P. 1974. *Seabirds and the biological structure of the ocean.* Translation U.S. Dept. Commerce, Springfield, Virginia.

Sibley, D. 1993. *The Birds of Cape May.* Cape May, N.J.: Cape May Bird Observatory.

Skaar, P. D. 1992. *Montana Bird Distribution,* 4th ed. Self-published.

Small, A. 1994. *California Birds.* Vista, Calif.: Ibis Publishing Co.

Smith, H. M. and W. Palmer. 1888. Additions to the Avifauna of Washington and Vicinity. *Auk* 5:147-8.

Smith, H. R. and P. W. Parmalee. 1955. *A Distributional Checklist of the Birds of Illinois.* Illinois State Museum Popular Science Series, vol 4.

Smith, P. W. and D. S. Evered. 1992. Photo Note: La Sagra's Flycatcher. *Birding* 24:294-7.

Smith, P. W., W. B. Robertson, Jr., and H. M. Stevenson. 1988. West Indian Cave Swallow nesting in Florida, with comments on the taxonomy of *Hirundo fulva. Florida Field Naturalist* 16:86-90.

Smith, P. W. and S. A. Smith. 1990. The identification and status of the Bahama Swallow in Florida. *Birding* 22:264-71.

Smith, P. W. and A. Sprunt, IV. 1987. The Shiny Cowbird reaches the United States. *American Birds* 41:370-1.

Snyder, B. E. 1953. A great flight of Dovekies (*Plautus alle*). *Auk* 70:87-8.

Sowls, A. L., A. R. DeGrange, J. W. Nelson, and G. S. Lester. 1980. *Catalog of California Seabird Colonies.* U.S. Dept. of Interior, U.S. Fish and Wildlife Service, Project FWS/OBS37/80.

Spear, L. B., M. J. Lewis, M. T. Myres, and R. L. Pyle. 1988. The recent occurrence of Garganey in North America and the Hawaiian Islands. *American Birds* 42:385-92.

Sprunt, A., Jr. 1936. Some observations on the bird life of Cumberland Island, Camden Co., Georgia. *Oriole* 1:1-6.

Sprunt, A., Jr. 1945. The phantom of the marshes. *Audubon Magazine* 47:15-22.

Sprunt, A., Jr. 1954. *Florida Bird Life.* New York: Coward-McCann.

Sprunt, A., Jr. 1962. Birds of the Dry Tortugas 1857-1961 [part 4]. *Florida Naturalist* 35:129-32.

Sprunt, A., Jr. 1963. Addendum to *Florida Bird Life.* Privately published.

Stallcup, Rich. 1990. *Ocean Birds of the Nearshore Pacific.* Stinson Beach, Calif.: Point Reyes Bird Observatory.

Stevenson, H. M. and B. H. Anderson. 1994. *The Birdlife of Florida.* Gainesville, Fla.: University of Florida Press.

Stejskal, D. and J. Witzeman. 1985. The autumn migration: Southeast Region. *American Birds* 39:86-8.

Stewart, R. E. and C. Robbins. 1958. *Birds of Maryland and District of Columbia.* U.S.F.W.S., North America Fauna, no. 62.

Stieglitz, W. O. and R. Thompson. 1967. *Status and life history of the Everglade Kite in the United States*. U.S. Fish and Wildlife Serv. Spec. Sci. Rep., Wildl. No. 109.

Stiles, F. G. and A. F. Skutch. 1989. *A Guide to the Birds of Costa Rica*. Ithaca, N.Y.: Cornell University Press.

Stokie, A. 1994. Hoary Redpoll in DuPage County. *Meadowlark* 3:108-9.

Stone, A. E. 1986. *Migrating and wintering records of Kirtland's Warbler: an annotated bibliography*. U.S. Fish and Wildlife Service, Patuxent Wildlife Research Unit, Athens,Georgia.

Strangis, Jay Michael. 1996. *Birding Minnesota*. Helena, Mont.: Falcon Press.

Sutherland, C. A. 1963. Notes on the behavior of Common Nighthawk in Florida. *Living Bird* 2:31-9.

Sutton, G. M. 1967. *Oklahoma Birds*. Norman, Okla.: University of Oklahoma Press.

Sykes, P. W., Jr. 1979. Status of the Everglade Kite in Florida—1968-1978. *The Wilson Bulletin* 91:495-511.

Sykes, P. W., Jr. 1983. Recent population trend of the Snail Kite in Florida and its relationship to water levels. *Journal Field Ornithology* 54:237-46.

Sykes, P. W., Jr. 1984. The range of the Snail Kite and its history in Florida. *Bulletin Florida State Museum of Biological Sciences* 29:211-64.

Sykes, P. W., Jr. and H. W. Kale II. 1974. Everglade Kites feed on nonsnail prey. *Auk* 91:818-20.

Szantyr, M. S. 1985. A Barnacle Goose in Connecticut. *The Connecticut Warbler* 5:16-18.

Taylor, W. 1917. Kirtland's Warbler in Madison, Wisconsin. *Auk* 34:343

Tebeau, C. W. 1971. *A History of Florida*. Coral Gables, Fla.: University of Miami Press.

Terres, J. K. 1980. *The Audubon Society Encyclopedia of North American Birds*. New York: Alfred A Knopf, Inc.

Tessen, D. 1973. Field Notes: The autumn season, August 16-November 30, 1972. *Passenger Pigeon* 35:133-49.

Thomas, E. S. 1926. Notes on some central Ohio birds observed during 1925. *Wilson Bulletin* 38:118-19.

Thompson, M. C., W. Champeny, and J. Newton. 1983. Records of Garganey in Kansas. *Kansas Ornithological Society Bulletin* 34:29-30.

Tinker, A. D. 1908. Notes of Kirtland's Warbler at Ann Arbor, Michigan. *Bird-Lore* 10:81-2.

Townsend, C. W. 1905. *The Birds of Essex County, Massachusetts*. Memoirs of the Nuttall Ornithological Club No. III. Cambridge, Mass.: Nuttall Ornithological Club.

Trost, C. 1991. A Fork-tailed Flycatcher in Idaho! *Idaho Wildlife* 45:24.

Tucson Audubon Society. 1995. *Davis and Russell's Finding Birds in Southeast Arizona*. Tucson, Ariz.: Tucson Audubon Society.

Turner, A. and C. Rose. 1989. *Swallows and Martins: An Identification Guide and Handbook*. Boston, Mass.: Houghton Mifflin Co.

Ulrey, A. B. 1893. On the occurrence of Kirtland's Warbler (*Dendroica kirtlandi*) in Indiana. *Proceedings Indiana Academy of Science* 1893: 224-5.

Unitt, Philip. 1984. *The Birds of San Diego County*. San Diego, Calif.: San Diego Society of Natural History.

U.S. Fish and Wildlife Service. 1994. *Whooping Crane Recovery Plan*. Albuquerque, N.M.: U.S. Fish and Wildl. Serv.

Van Tyne, J. 1939. Kirtland's Warber at Kalamazoo, Michigan. *Auk* 56:480-1.

Veit, R. R. and L. Jonsson. 1984. Field identification of smaller sandpipers within the genus *Calidris*. *American Birds* 38:853-76 (and reprinted in *American Birds* 41:213-36).

Veit, R. R. and W. R. Peterson. 1993. *Birds of Massachusetts*. Boston, Mass.: Massachusetts Audubon Society.

Wallace, G. J. 1946. Seasonal records of Michigan birds... fall. *Jack-Pine Warbler* 24:23-37.

Wallace, G. J. 1965. Michigan bird survey, spring, 1964. *Jack-Pine Warbler* 43:26-38.

Wallace, R. 1971. Interesting sightings at St. Marks Wildlife Refuge and elsewhere. *Florida Naturalist* 44:63.

Walkinshaw, L. H. 1972. Kirtland's Warbler—endangered. *American Birds* 26:3-9.

Walkinshaw, L. R. 1976. A Kirtland's Warbler life history. *American Birds* 30:773-4.

Wamer, N. and B. Pranty. 1995. Regional Reports: Florida Region. *Field Notes* 49:37-40.

Washburn, F. L. 1889. Recent capture of Kirtland's Warbler in Michigan, and other notes. *Auk* 6:279-80.

Watson, G. E., D. S. Lee, and E. S. Backus. 1986. Status and subspecific identity of White-faced Storm-Petrel in the western North Atlantic Ocean. *American Birds* 40:401-8.

Wauer, R. H. 1985. *A Field Guide to Birds of the Big Bend*. Austin, Tex.: Texas Monthly Press, Inc.

Wauer, R. H., P. C. Palmer, and A. Windham. 1993. The Ferruginous Pygmy-Owl in South Texas. *American Birds* 47:1071-6.

Wayne, A. T. 1904. Kirtland's Warbler (*Dendroica kirtlandi*) on the coast of South Carolina. *Auk* 21:83-4.

Wayne, A. T. 1911. A third autumnal record of Kirtland's Warbler (*Dendroica kirtlandi*) for South Carolina. *Auk* 28:116.

Webb, B. E. and J. A. Conry. 1979. A Sharp-tailed Sandpiper in Colorado, with notes on plumage and behavior. *Western Birds* 10:86-91.

Wenner, A. M. and D. L. Johnson. 1980. Land vertebrates on the California Channel Islands: sweepstakes or bridges? In *The California Islands:* (D. M. Power, ed.), pp. 497-530. Proceedings of a multidisciplinary symposium. Santa Barbara, Calif.: Santa Barbara Museum of Natural History.

Weseloh, D. V. and P. Mineau. 1986. Apparent hybrid Common Black-headed Gull nesting in Lake Ontario. *American Birds* 40:18-20.

Westrich, L. L. and J. Westrich. 1991. *Birder's Guide to Northern California*. Houston, Tex.: Gulf Publishing Company.

Wheeler, B. K. and W. S. Clark. 1995. *A Photographic Guide to North American Raptors*. San Diego, Calif.: Academic Press.

Whelan, M. E. 1952. A fall Kirtland's Warbler observation. *Jack-Pine Warbler* 30:25.

Widmann, O. 1885. Note on the capture of *Coturniculus lecontei* and *Dendroica kirtlandi* within the city limits of St. Louis, Mo. *Auk* 2:381-2.

Williams, S. O. 1987. A Northern Jacana in Trans-Pecos Texas. *Western Birds* 18:123-4.

Winnett, K. A., K. G. Murray, and J .C. Wingfield. 1979. Southern race of Xantu's Murrelet breeding on Santa Barbara Island, California. *Western Birds* 10:81-2.

Wolf, D. E. 1978. First record of an Aztec Thrush in the United States. *American Birds* 32:156-7.

Wood, D. S. and G. D. Schnell. 1984. *Distributions of Oklahoma Birds*. Norman, Okla.: University of Oklahoma Press.

Wood, J. C. 1908. The Kirtland and Pine Warblers in Wayne Co., Michigan. *Auk* 25:480.

Wood, N. A. 1902. Capture of Kirtland's Warbler at Ann Arbor, Michigan. *Auk* 19:291.

Wood, N. A. 1906. Twenty-five years of bird migration at Ann Arbor, Michigan. *Mich. Acad. of Sci. Rep.* 8:151-6.

Wood, N. A. 1912. Notes on Michigan Birds. *Mich. Acad. of Sci. Rep.* 14:159-62.

Wood, N. A. 1951. *The Birds of Michigan*. Misc. Pub. no. 75, Mus. Zool. of Univ. of Michigan. Ann Arbor, Michigan: University of Michigan Press.

Woolfenden, G. E. 1965. A specimen of the Red-footed Booby from Florida. *Auk* 82:102-3.

Yee, D. G., S. F. Bailey, and B. E. Deuel. 1991. Seasonal report: Middle Pacific Coast Region. *American Birds* 45:491-4.

Zeranski, J. O. and T. R. Baptist. 1990. *Connecticut Birds*. University Press of New England.

Zimmer, K. J. 1992. Murphy's Petrels on Ducie Atoll: another piece of the puzzle. *American Birds* 46:1100-5.

Zimmerman, D. A. 1978. Eared Trogon—Immigrant or Visitor? *American Birds* 32:135-9.

Zimmerman, D. A. 1991. The Aztec Thrush in the United States. *Birding* 23:318-28.

Zino, P. A. and F. Zino. 1986. Contribution to the study of the petrels of the genus *Pterodroma* in the archipelago of Madeira. *Bol. Mus. Mun. Funchal Sup.* no. 2: 325-31.

© GREG W. LASLEY

Yellow-billed Loon
Gavia adamsii

Laysan Albatross
Diomedea immutabilis

© R.L. PITMAN/VIREO.

457

© R.L. PITMAN/VIREO.

Mottled Petrel
Pterodroma inexpectata

Herald Petrel
Pterodroma arminjoniana

© BRIAN PATTESON

© R.L. PITMAN/VIREO.

Cook's Petrel
Pterodroma cookii

© D. HADDEN/VIREO.

Flesh-footed Shearwater
Puffinus carneipes

© R.L. PITMAN/VIREO.

White-faced Storm-Petrel
Pelagodroma marina

© R.L. PITMAN/VIREO.

Band-rumped Storm-Petrel
Oceanodroma castro

© F.K. SCHLEICHER/VIREO.

White-tailed Tropicbird
Phaethon lepturus

© JASON DEWEY/VIREO.

Red-billed Tropicbird
Phaethon aethereus

© KEVIN T. KARLSON

Masked Booby
Sula dactylatra

© G. BEATON

Blue-footed Booby
Sula nebouxii

461

© KEVIN T. KARLSON

Brown Booby
Sula leucogaster

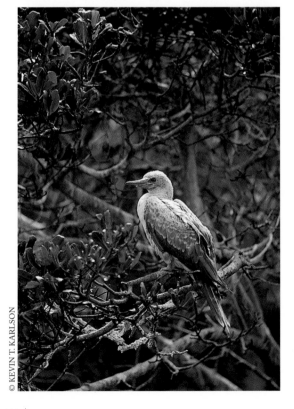

© KEVIN T. KARLSON

Red-footed Booby
Sula sula

Greater Flamingo
Phoenicopterus ruber

© T. J. ULRICH/VIREO.

Emperor Goose
Chen canagica

© T. J. ULRICH/VIREO.

Barnacle Goose
Branta leucopsis

© B. SMALL/VIREO.

Muscovy Duck
Cairina moschata

© W.S. CLARK/VIREO.

White-cheeked Pintail
Anas bahamensis

© R. TIPPER/VIREO.

Garganey
Anas querquedula

© STEVEN G. MLODINOW

Tufted Duck
Aythya fuligula

© KEVIN T. KARLSON

Masked Duck
Oxyura dominica

© KEVIN T. KARLSON

Hook-billed Kite
Chondrohierax uncinatus

© P.W. SYKES, JR./VIREO.

Snail Kite
Rostrhamus sociabilis

© B. K. WHEELER/VIREO.

Short-tailed Hawk
Buteo brachyurus

© MICHAEL O'BRIEN

Gyrfalcon
Falco rusticolus

© W. EDWARD HARPER

Pacific Golden-Plover
Pluvialis fulva

469

© W. EDWARD HARPER

Bar-tailed Godwit
Limosa lapponica

© GIFF BEATON

Red-necked Stint
Calidris ruficollis

470

© J.P. MYERS/VIREO.

Little Stint
Calidris minuta

© W. EDWARD HARPER

Sharp-tailed Sandpiper
Calidris acuminata

471

© B. CHUDLEIGH/VIREO.

Curlew Sandpiper
Calidris ferruginea

© R. J. CHANDLER/VIREO.

Ruff
Philomachus pugnax

© T.H. DAVIS/VIREO.

Little Gull
Larus minutus

© RICHARD CROSSLEY

Black-headed Gull (left)   **Bonaparte's Gull** (right)
Larus ridibundus   *Larus philadelphia*

© W.S. CLARK/VIREO.

Slaty-backed Gull
Larus schistisagus

© SGREG W. LASLEY

Yellow-footed Gull
Larus livens

© T. VEZO/VIREO.

Ross' Gull
Rhodostethia rosea

© H. DARROW/VIREO.

Ivory Gull
Pagophila eburnea

© KEVIN T. KARLSON

White-winged Tern
Chlidonias leucopterus

Black Noddy
Anous minutus

© KEVIN T. KARLSON

© D. ROBY/K. BRINK/VIREO.

Dovekie
Alle alle

Craveri's Murrelet
Synthliboramphus craveri

© D. ROBERSON/VIREO.

© W. EDWARD HARPER

Parakeet Auklet
Cyclorrhynchus psittacula

Horned Puffin
Fratercula corniculata

© D. ROBY/K. BRINK/VIREO.

© J. DUNNING/VIREO.

**Ruddy
Ground-Dove**
*Columbina
talpacoti*

© KEVIN T. KARLSON

**Northern
Hawk Owl**
Surnia ulula

479

Ferruginous Pygmy-Owl
Glaucidium brasilianum

© K. CASTELEIN

Great Gray Owl
Strix nebulosa

© R. & N. BOWERS/VIREO.

Buff-collared Nightjar
Caprimulgus ridgwayi

481

© GREG W. LASLEY

Green Violet-ear
Colibri thalassinus

© R. & N. BOWERS/VIREO

White-eared Hummingbird
Hylaocharis leucotis

482

© KEVIN T. KARLSON

**Violet-crowned
Hummingbird**
Amazilia violiceps

**Plain-capped
Starthroat**
Heliomaster constanti

© A. CLAY/VIREO.

© D. TRUE/VIREO.

Lucifer Hummingbird
Calothorax lucifer

© R. & N. BOWERS/VIREO.

**Buff-breasted
Flycatcher**
Empidonax fulvifrons

La Sagra's Flycatcher
Myiarchus sagrae

© G. BEATON

Fork-tailed Flycatcher
Tyrannus savana

© KEVIN T. KARLSON

485

© B. CHUDLEIGH/VIREO.

Eurasian Skylark
Alauda arvensis

© R. & N. BOWERS/VIREO.

West Indian Cave Swallow
Hirundo fulva fulva

© STEVEN G. MLODINOW

Island Scrub-Jay
Aphelocoma insularis

© H. CLARKE/VIREO.

California Gnatcatcher
Polioptila californica

© SHAWNEEN FINNEGAN

Northern Wheatear
Oenanthe oenanthe

© GREG W. LASLEY

Clay-colored Robin
Turdus grayi

© R. & N. BOWERS/VIREO.

Rufous-backed Robin
Turdus rufopalliatus

© D. & M. ZIMMERMAN/VIREO.

Aztec Thrush
Ridgwayia pinicola

© KEVIN T. KARLSON

Bahama Mockingbird
Mimus gundlachii

© T. SHIMBA/VIREO.

Black-backed Wagtail
Motacilla lugens

© S. FRIED/VIREO.

Red-throated Pipit
Anthus cervinus

© DOUG WECHSLER/VIREO.

Yellow-Green Vireo
Vireo flavoviridis

© J. DUNNING/VIREO.

Tropical Parula
Parula pitiayumi

© D. ROBY/K. BRINK/VIREO.

Kirtland's Warbler
Dendroica kirtlandii

Bananaquit
Coereba flaveola

© KEVIN T. KARLSON

Stripe-headed Tanager
Spindalis zena

© KEVIN T. KARLSON

493

© J. DUNNING/VIREO.

Blue Bunting
Cyanocompsa parellina

© SHAWNEEN FINNEGAN

Large-billed (Savannah) Sparrow
Passerculus (sandwichensis) rostratus

© KEVIN T. KARLSON

Shiny Cowbird
Molothrus bonariensis
(male)

Shiny Cowbird
Molothrus bonariensis
(female)

© KEVIN T. KARLSON

© SHAWNEEN FINNEGAN

Brambling
Fringilla montifringilla

© DAVE CZAPLAK

Hoary Redpoll
Carduelis hornemanni